Programming in Visual Basic

Version 5.0

Programming in Visual Basic

Version 5.0

Julia Case Bradley
Mt. San Antonio College

Anita C. Millspaugh
Mt. San Antonio College

Boston, Massachusetts   Burr Ridge, Illinois   Dubuque, Iowa
Madison, Wisconsin   New York, New York   San Francisco, California   St. Louis, Missouri

Irwin/McGraw-Hill

A Division of The McGraw·Hill Companies

PROGRAMMING IN VISUAL BASIC, VERSION 5.0

Copyright © 1998 by The McGraw-Hill Companies, Inc. All rights reserved. Printed in the United States of America. Except as permitted under the United States Copyright Act of 1976, no part of this publication may be reproduced or distributed in any form or by any means, or stored in a data base or retrieval system, without the prior written permission of the publisher.

This book is printed on acid-free paper.

5 6 7 8 9 0 VNH/VNH 9 0 9   (U.S. Edition)
5 6 7 8 9 0 VNH/VNH 9 0 9   (International Edition)

ISBN 0-256-25941-0

Vice president and editorial director: *Michael W. Junior*
Sponsoring editor: *Rhonda Sands*
Editorial coordinator: *Carrie Berkshire*
Marketing manager: *James Rogers*
Project manager: *Robert A. Preskill/Margaret Rathke*
Production supervisor: *Scott Hamilton*
Senior designer: *Crispin Prebys*
Designer: *Becky Lemma*
Cover illustration: *Peter Siv*
Compositor: *GTS Graphics, Inc.*
Typeface: *11/13 Bodoni Book*
Printers: *Von Hoffmann Press, Inc.*

Library of Congress Cataloging-in-Publication Data

Bradley, Julia Case.
    Programming in Visual Basic, version 5.0 / Julia Case Bradley,
Anita C. Millspaugh.
       p.   cm.
    Includes index.
    ISBN 0-256-25941-0
    1. BASIC (Computer program language)   2. Microsoft Visual BASIC.
I. Millspaugh, A. C. (Anita C.) II. Title.
QA76.73.B3B724   1998
005.26'8—dc21   97-21935

INTERNATIONAL EDITION
Copyright © 1998. Exclusive rights by The McGraw-Hill Companies, Inc. for manufacture and export.
This book cannot be re-exported from the country to which it is consigned by McGraw-Hill.
The International Edition is not available in North America.

When ordering this title, use ISBN 0-07-115432-9.

http://www.mhcollege.com

Preface

As the world turns to graphical user interfaces, computer programming languages are changing to accommodate the shift. Visual Basic 5 is designed to allow the programmer to develop applications that run under Windows without the complexity generally associated with Windows programming. With very little effort, the programmer can design a screen that holds standard Windows elements such as command buttons, check boxes, option buttons, text boxes, and list boxes. Each of these Windows objects operates as expected, producing a "standard" Windows user interface.

Visual Basic is easy to learn, which makes it an excellent tool for understanding elementary programming concepts. In addition, it has evolved into such a powerful and popular product that skilled Visual Basic programmers are in demand in the job market.

About This Text

This textbook is intended for use in an introductory programming course, which assumes no prior knowledge of computer programming. However, many of the later chapters are appropriate for an advanced-level course. The later chapters are also appropriate for professional programmers who are learning a new language to upgrade their skills.

This text assumes that the student is familiar with the Windows operating environment.

Approach

The authors have successfully taught Visual Basic to beginning and advanced programming students for several years. This text incorporates the basic concepts of programming, problem solving, programming logic, as well as the design techniques of an event-driven language.

Chapter topics are presented in a sequence that allows the programmer to learn how to deal with a visual interface while acquiring important programming skills such as creating projects with loops, decisions, and data management.

The later chapters may be used in various sequences to accommodate the needs of beginning and advanced-level courses, as well as a shorter quarter system or a semester-long course. For a shorter course, the professor may choose to skip the chapter on data files and cover only the first of the two database chapters.

New in Visual Basic 5

This latest version of Visual Basic is bound to be a success with students as well as professional application developers.

Visual Basic 5:

- Runs much faster than previous versions and incorporates more features required for professional application development. VB5 will be competitive with C++ for object-oriented program development.

- Incorporates many helpful new features in the editor, making it easier for beginners as well as advanced programmers to enter and edit code. For example:
  - Drag-and-drop editing for moving and copying lines.
  - Pop-up lists of available datatypes when declaring variables.
  - Pop-up lists of allowable properties and methods for controls.
  - Tips showing formats and arguments for functions and statements that appear automatically as you enter program code.

- Is easier to debug than previous versions. For example:
  - Data tips, similar to tool tips, display the current contents of variables, properties, and expressions, and pop up when you point to the expression during break time.
  - You can easily set breakpoints in code by clicking in the margin of a statement.
  - During break time, you can drag the highlighted line to set the next statement to execute.

- Includes many new controls. For example:
  - Many ActiveX controls for programming on the Web.
  - A new Web browser control that allows you to retrieve and display Web pages in an application.

New in This Edition of the Text

This edition is a major revision of the text. In addition to the update to Windows 95 and Visual Basic 5, many sections have been reorganized and expanded. This edition places more emphasis on the planning steps of project design to encourage students to develop good programming habits from the start.

In response to many helpful suggestions from students and reviewers, several topics have been rearranged. Control arrays now appear in the same chapter as variable arrays. The grid control is presented along with database handling. Do/Loops and For/Next loops now appear together in one chapter. The numeric functions have been moved to an appendix. Also, topics are now organized so that those teaching a short course can use only a few chapters.

Numerous new examples and tutorials are included in this revision. A new step-by-step tutorial demonstrates debugging techniques. Another tutorial illustrates how to create a new folder in Windows 95 and save projects into the new folder. Many new examples now appear in the chapters on calculations and decisions, and a new section covers string functions. The advanced techniques chapter (Chapter 14) now includes sections on creating a new class and Crystal Reports.

The screens for all projects have been modified to reflect the look and feel of Windows 95. New controls include the tabbed dialog control, the Web browser control, and ActiveX controls, including instructions on creating your own ActiveX controls.

Students and instructors will appreciate the new appendix, "Tips and Shortcuts for Mastering the VB Environment." This reference brings together many helpful tips that can save a programmer a significant amount of time.

The instructor materials are also updated and expanded. New materials include suggested coding standards and masters of forms for project planning that can be reproduced and distributed to students. The solutions to all exercises are available for download on the Web.

Chapter Organization

Each chapter begins with identifiable objectives and a brief overview. Numerous coding examples as well as hands-on projects with guidance for the coding appear throughout. Thought-provoking feedback questions give students time to reflect on the current topic and to evaluate their understanding of the details. The end-of-chapter items include a chapter review, questions, programming exercises, and two case studies. The case studies provide a continuing-theme exercise that may be used throughout the course.

Chapter 1 walks the student through the creation of a first Visual Basic project, incorporating command buttons and labels. The programming environment is introduced along with the concepts of objects and their related properties, methods, and events.

Chapter 2 continues coverage of controls, including text boxes, option buttons, check boxes, frames, images, lines, and shapes. It also covers some of the finer points of using the environment and working with keyboard access keys, multiple controls, and alignment. The color constants are used at this point to lead the novice programmer into Chapter 3, which introduces variables and constants. The text includes a naming convention to make the scope and data type of a variable or constant easier to determine from the coding syntax. Standards also provide for the use of Option Explicit to force the declaration of all variables and constants.

Chapter 4 introduces the relational and logical operators and their use with the If statement. Input validation and message boxes are also covered. In Chapter 5 students learn to set up custom menus and to write their own sub functions and sub procedures. Multiple forms, global variables, and standard code modules are presented in Chapter 6.

Chapter 7 incorporates list boxes and combo boxes into the projects, providing the opportunity to discuss looping procedures and printing lists of information. The list concept leads logically into the use of variable arrays and control arrays in Chapter 8 and to writing the information to disk in Chapter 9. Chapter 9 covers both sequential and random files, but the material may be covered in sections.

Chapters 10 and 11 deal with the use of Visual Basic as a front end for database programming. The projects display and update tables created by a database application such as Microsoft Access. Chapter 11 includes using a data-bound grid, error trapping, and writing queries in SQL.

The drag-and-drop feature of Windows programming is introduced in Chapter 12. This chapter normally brings great enthusiasm from students as they learn to deal with the source and target objects. The examples and assignments provide a blend of practical and just-for-fun applications. This approach is also true of Chapter 13, which introduces the graphics methods and graphics controls.

Chapter 14, the final chapter, covers various topics that build a bridge from Visual Basic to other applications. These include using and creating ActiveX controls, creating a new object class, the Windows API, DLLs, OLE, and Visual Basic for Applications.

Acknowledgments

We would like to express our appreciation to the many people who have contributed to the successful completion of this text. Most especially, we thank our students at Mt. San Antonio College who helped class-test the material and who greatly influenced the manuscript.

Many people have worked very hard to design and produce this text, including Carrie Berkshire, Robert A. Preskill, Crispin Prebys, Garrett Glanz, and June Waldman. A special thank you goes to Rhonda Sands, our editor, whose help has been invaluable.

We greatly appreciate Diane Murphey, Theresa Berry, and Dennis Fraser for their thorough technical reviews, constructive criticism, and many valuable suggestions. Thanks also to Theresa for writing the Instructors Manual and to Dennis for preparing the exercise solutions. And most importantly, we are grateful to Dennis, Andy, Eric, and Tricia for their support and understanding through the long days and busy phone lines.

We want to thank our reviewers, who have made many helpful suggestions:

Gary R. Armstrong
Shippensburg University

Ronald L. Burgher
Metropolitan Community College

Diane Murphey
Oklahoma Panhandle State University

Sheila J. Pearson
Southern Arkansas University

Thomas S. Pennington
Maple Woods Community College

Hwang Santai
Purdue University—Fort Wayne

Judy Yaeger
Western Michigan University

The Authors

We have had fun teaching and writing about Visual Basic. We hope that this feeling is evident as you read this book and that you will enjoy learning or teaching this outstanding programming language.

Julia Case Bradley
Anita C. Millspaugh

To the Student

The best way to learn to program in Visual Basic is to do it. If you enter and run the sample projects, you will be on your way to writing Windows applications. Reading the examples without trying to run them is like trying to learn a foreign language or mathematics just by reading about it. Enter the projects, look up your questions in Visual Basic's excellent Help files, and make those projects *run*.

Format Used for Visual Basic Statements

Visual Basic statements and functions are shown in `this font`. Any values you must supply are in *italics*. Optional items are in [square brackets]. Braces and a vertical bar indicate that you must choose one or the other value {one | other}.

Example:

```
Open "FileName" For {Input|Output|Append|Random} As #FileNumber [Len=RecLength]
```

As you work your way through this textbook, note that you may see a subset of the available options for a Visual Basic statement. Generally, the options that are included will reflect those covered in the chapter. If you want to see the complete format for any statement, refer to online Help.

J.C.B.
A.C.M.

Contents

1

Introduction to Visual Basic

At the completion of this chapter, you will be able to...

1. Describe the process of visual program design and development.

2. Explain the term *event-driven programming*.

3. Explain the concepts of objects, properties, and methods.

4. List and describe the three steps for writing a Visual Basic project.

5. Describe the various files that make up a Visual Basic project.

6. Identify the elements in the Visual Basic environment.

7. Explain the differences among design time, run time, and break time.

8. Write, run, save, print, and modify your first Visual Basic project.

9. Identify compile errors, run-time errors, and logic errors.

10. Look up Visual Basic topics in Help.

Writing Windows Applications with Visual Basic

Using this text, you will learn to write computer programs that run in the Microsoft Windows environment. Your projects will look and act like standard Windows programs. Visual Basic (VB) provides the tools you need to create windows with familiar elements like menus, text boxes, command buttons, option buttons, check boxes, list boxes, and scroll bars. Figure 1.1 shows some sample Windows user interfaces.

Figure 1.1

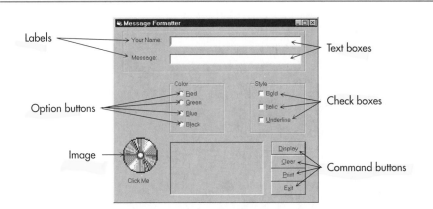

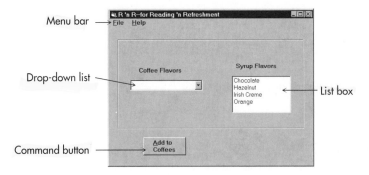

Graphical user interfaces for application programs designed with Visual Basic.

The Windows Graphical User Interface

Microsoft Windows uses a **graphical user interface**, or **GUI** (pronounced "gooey"). The Windows GUI defines how the various elements look and function. As a Visual Basic programmer, you have available a toolbox of these elements. You will create new windows, called **forms**. Then you will use the toolbox to add the various elements, called **controls**. The projects that you will write follow a relatively new type of programming, called ***event-driven programming***.

Programming Languages—Procedural, Object Oriented, and Event Driven

There are literally hundreds of programming languages. Each was developed to solve a particular type of problem. Most traditional languages, such as

BASIC, C, COBOL, FORTRAN, PL/I, and Pascal are considered *procedural* languages. That is, the program specifies the sequence of all operations step-by-step. Program logic determines the next instruction to execute in response to conditions and user requests.

The newer programming languages, such as C++ and Visual Basic, use a different approach: **object-oriented programming** (OOP) and event-driven programming. Microsoft refers to Visual Basic as an event-driven programming language, which has many (but not all) elements of an object-oriented language such as C++. Each release of Visual Basic moves it a little closer to a true object-oriented language.

In the event-driven model, programs are no longer procedural; they do not follow a sequential logic. You, as the programmer, do not take control and determine the sequence of execution. Instead, the user can press keys and click on various buttons and boxes in a window. Each user action can cause an *event* to occur, which triggers a Basic procedure that you have written. For example, the user clicks on a command button labeled Calculate. The clicking causes the button's Click event to occur, and the program automatically jumps to a procedure you have written to do the calculation.

The Object Model

In Visual Basic you will work with **objects**, which have **properties** and **methods**.

Objects

Think of an object as a thing, or a noun. Examples of objects are forms and controls. *Forms* are the windows and dialog boxes you place on the screen; *controls* are the elements you place inside a form, such as text boxes, command buttons, and list boxes.

Properties

Properties tell something about an object, such as its name, color, size, location, or how it will behave. You can think of properties as adjectives that describe objects.

When you refer to a property, you first name the object, add a period, and then name the property. For example, refer to the Caption property of a form called Form1 as Form1.Caption (say "form1 dot caption").

Methods

Actions associated with objects are called methods. Methods are the verbs of object-oriented programming. Some typical methods are Move, Print, Resize, and Clear.

You refer to methods as Object.Method ("object dot method"). For example, a Print method can apply to different objects. Printer.Print sends the output to the printer object; Form1.Print sends output to the form called Form1.

Versions of Visual Basic

Microsoft Visual Basic for Windows comes in a **Learning Edition**, a **Professional Edition**, and an **Enterprise Edition**. Anyone planning to do professional application development that includes the advanced features of database management should use the Professional Edition or Enterprise Edition. Another version runs under DOS, but it is considerably different from the Windows version and is not covered here.

In addition to the various editions of Visual Basic, you must also be aware of the release number. This text is based on release 5.0, the current release. Release 5.0 is significantly different from earlier releases. Although most of the projects in this text can be written with release 4.0, the menus and screens will not look the same as the text screen shots. Also, several new elements and statements were added in release 5.0. In short, you should use release 5.0 with this text.

Next to each new or changed feature you will see an icon (see margin).

New to VB 5!

Writing Visual Basic Projects

When you write a Visual Basic project, you follow a three-step process for planning the project and then repeat the process for creating the project. The three steps involve setting up the user interface, defining the properties, and then creating the code.

The Three-Step Process

Planning

1. *Design the user interface.* When you plan the **user interface**, you draw a sketch of the screens the user will see when running your project. On your sketch, show the forms and all the controls that you plan to use. Indicate the names that you plan to give the form and each of the objects on the form. Refer to Figure 1.1 for examples of user interfaces.

   Before you proceed with any more steps, consult with your user and make sure that you both agree on the look and feel of the project.
2. *Plan the properties.* For each object, write down the properties that you plan to set or change during the design of the form.
3. *Plan the Basic code.* This step is where you plan the procedures that will execute when your project runs. You will determine which events require action to be taken and then make a step-by-step plan for those actions.

   Later, when you actually write the Visual Basic **code**, you must follow the language syntax rules. But during the planning stage, you will write out the actions using **pseudocode**, which is an English expression or comment that describes the action. For example, you must plan for the event that occurs when the user clicks on the Exit command button. The pseudocode for the event could be *Terminate the project.*

Programming

After you have completed the planning steps and have agreement from your user, you are ready to begin the actual construction of the project. You will use the same three step process that you used for planning.

1. *Define the user interface.* When you define the user interface, you create the forms and controls that you designed in the planning stage.

Think of this step as *defining* all of the objects you will use in your project.

2. *Set the properties.* When you set the properties of the objects, you give each object a name and define such attributes as the contents of a label, the size of the text, and the words that appear on top of a command button and in the form's title bar.

You might think of this step as *describing* each object.

3. *Write the Basic code.* You will use Basic programming statements (called Basic code) to carry out the actions needed by your program. You will be surprised and pleased by how few statements you need to create a powerful Windows program.

You can think of this third step as defining the *actions* of your program.

Visual Basic Projects

Each Visual Basic project consists of at least two, and usually more, files.

1. The .VBP file, called the **project file**, is a small text file that holds the names of the other files in the project, as well as some information about the VB environment. *Note:* If you are using release 2.0 or 3.0 of Visual Basic, project files have a .MAK extension.

2. Each form in your project is saved in a file with a .FRM extension. To begin, your projects will have only one form (and therefore one **form file**). Later, you can expect your projects to have several forms, with one .FRM file for each form.

A form file holds a description of all objects and their properties for the form, as well as the Basic code you have written to respond to the events.

In Visual Basic each of these form files is referred to as a **form module**.

3. Optionally, your project can have .BAS extension files. These files hold Basic statements that can be accessed from any form. As soon as you begin writing multiform projects, you will need .BAS files.

.BAS files are called **standard code modules**.

4. Additional controls, called *custom controls*, are stored in files with an .OCX extension. If you include controls in your project that are not part of the standard control set, the .OCX file names will be included in the project.

5. After you save a project, Visual Basic automatically adds one more file to your project with an extension of .VBW. This file holds information about each of your project's forms.

Tip

Before creating any files for your project, first create a new folder on disk. Save your .VBP file, .FRM files, and .BAS files into the new folder. Then if you want to copy or move the project to another disk, you will get all the pieces. It is easy to miss parts of a project unless all files are together in one folder.

F. Ce J ric,
VB Project
. VBP — project file
. FRM — form module
. BAS — standard code module
. OCX

New to UB 5!

The Visual Basic Environment

The **Visual Basic environment** is where you create and test your projects. Figure 1.2 shows the various windows in the Visual Basic environment. Note that each window can be moved, resized, opened, and closed. Your screen may not look exactly like Figure 1.2; in all likelihood you will want to customize the placement of the various windows.

Main Visual Basic window   Toolbox   Form window   Menu Bar   Toolbar

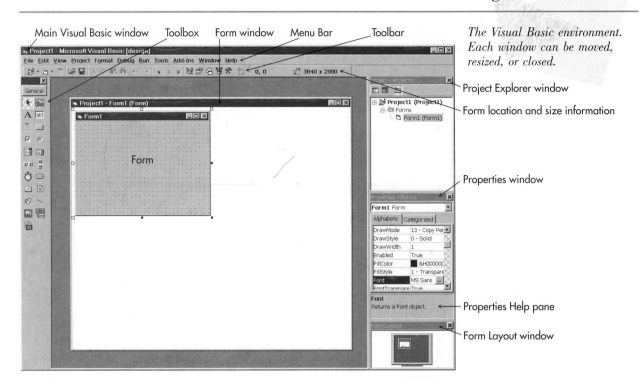

The Visual Basic environment. Each window can be moved, resized, or closed.

Project Explorer window

Form location and size information

Properties window

Properties Help pane

Form Layout window

The Form Window

The **Form window** is where you design the forms that make up your user interface. You can use standard Windows techniques to change the size and location of the form.

When you begin a new project, Visual Basic gives your new form the default name *Form1*. As soon as you save the file, you will give it a new (more meaningful) name.

The Project Explorer Window

The **Project Explorer window** holds the filenames for the files included in your project. The window's title bar holds the name of your project (.VBP) file, which is *Project1* by default until you save it with a new name.

The Properties Window

You use the **Properties window** to set the properties for the objects in your project. See "Set Properties" later in this chapter for instructions on changing properties.

The Form Layout Window

The position of the form in the form layout window determines the position of the form on the desktop when execution of the project begins.

The Toolbox

The **toolbox** holds the tools you use to place controls on a form. You may have more or different tools in your toolbox, depending on the edition and release of Visual Basic you are using. See Figure 1.3 for a labeled version of the toolbox.

Figure 1.3

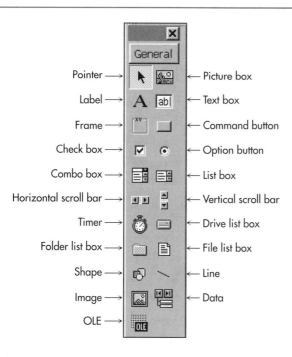

The toolbox for the Visual Basic Professional Edition. Your toolbox may have more or fewer tools, depending on the edition and release you are using.

The Main Visual Basic Window

The Main Visual Basic window holds the VB menu bar, the toolbar, and the form location and size information.

The Toolbar

You can use the buttons on the **toolbar** as shortcuts for frequently used operations. Each button represents a command that can also be selected from a menu. Figure 1.4 shows the toolbar buttons.

Figure 1.4

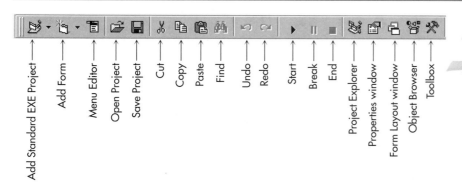

The Visual Basic toolbar. Each button represents a command that you can execute by clicking the button or by choosing a command from a menu.

The Form Location and Size Information

The two small diagrams at the right end of the Visual Basic toolbar (refer to Figure 1.2) show the position of the form on the screen along with the size of the form.

Help

Visual Basic has an extensive Help facility. It includes most of the reference manual, as well as many coding examples. In addition to the Help Index and Books Online, you will find Microsoft on the Web with a submenu containing various resources. Take some time to investigate the options on the Help menu.

Design Time, Run Time, and Break Time

Visual Basic has three distinct modes. While you are designing the user interface and writing code, you are in **design time**. When you are testing and running your project, you are in **run time**. If you get a run-time error or pause project execution, you are in **break time**. Notice the title bar notation in Figure 1.2, indicating that the project is currently in design time.

Writing Your First Visual Basic Project

For your first event-driven project, you will create a form with three controls (see Figure 1.5). This simple project will display the message "Hello World" when the user clicks the Push Me command button and will terminate when the user clicks the Exit button.

F i g u r e   1 . 5

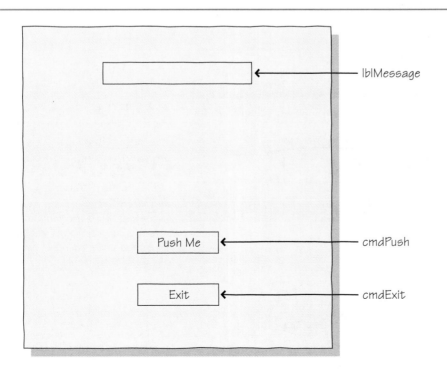

The Hello World form. The "Hello World" message will appear in the label when the user clicks on the Push Me command button.

Set Up Your Visual Basic Workspace

Before you can begin a project, you must run Visual Basic and set up your workspace the way you want it.

Run Visual Basic

STEP 1: Click on the Start button and move the mouse pointer to *Programs*.
STEP 2: Locate *Microsoft Visual Basic 5.0*.
STEP 3: Click on *Visual Basic 5.0* (Figure 1.6) in the submenu.

Note: If you see the dialog box pictured in Figure 1.7, check the box that says *Don't show this dialog in the future*. If you are using a shared computer lab, check with your instructor before checking this box.

The Visual Basic project will begin and display the VB environment on the screen (refer to Figure 1.2).

F i g u r e   1 . 6

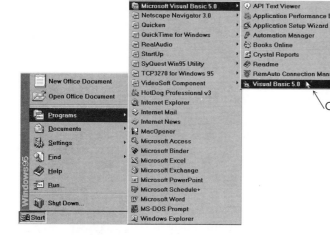

Locate the Visual Basic 5.0 command and click on it.

Click on the program name

F i g u r e   1 . 7

The New Project dialog box may appear when you start Visual Basic. Click on the check box to prevent the box from appearing for each project.

Click on this box

Set Up Your Workspace

STEP 1: Open the Visual Basic *Tools* menu and choose *Options.* Select the *Editor* tab if necessary. Then check each of these options, changing any that do not match (Figure 1.8).

Figure 1.8

Choose Options from the Tools menu and select the Editor tab; make sure the options are properly set.

Code Settings:	
Auto Syntax Check	Selected
Require Variable Declaration	Selected
Window Settings:	
Drag-and-Drop Text Editing	Selected
Default to Full Module View	Selected
Procedure Separator	Selected

STEP 2: Click on the *General* tab of the Options window and make sure the following options are selected (Figure 1.9). When you are finished, click OK.

New to UB 5!

Form Grid Settings:	
Show Grid	Selected
Align Controls to Grid	Selected
Show ToolTips	Selected

Figure 1.9

Set these options on the General tab of the Options window.

STEP 3: If the Project Explorer window is not displaying, open the *View* menu and select *Project Explorer*.

STEP 4: If the Properties window is not displaying, open the *View* menu and select *Properties Window*. (You may move or resize the Form window by dragging its title bar.)

STEP 5: If the toolbox is not displaying, open the *View* menu and select *Toolbox*.

STEP 6: Maximize the Form window by clicking on its Maximize button.

STEP 7: Adjust the size and location of the various windows if necessary. You can point to the divider between the Project Explorer window and the Properties window and drag to resize. Each window may be floating or docked, so your screen may not look like the examples. Try to make your screen layout similar to Figure 1.10.

Figure 1.10

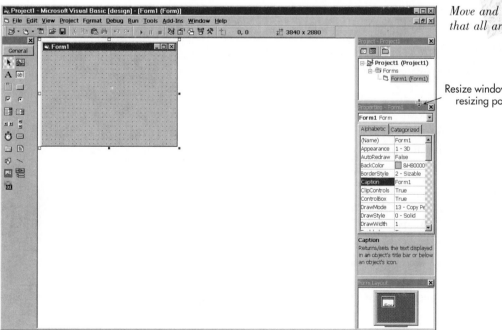

Move and resize the windows so that all are visible.

Resize windows with resizing pointer

Plan the Project

The first step in planning is to design the user interface. Figure 1.11 shows a sketch of the form that includes a label and two command buttons. You will refer to the sketch as you create the project.

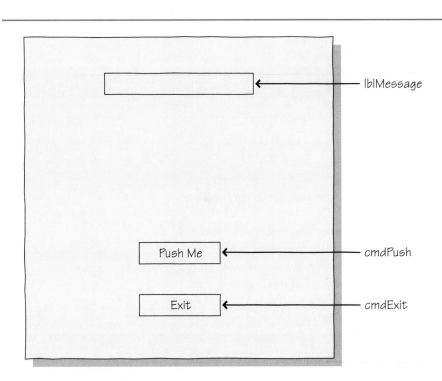

A sketch of the Hello World form for planning.

The next two steps, planning the properties and the code, have already been done for this first sample project. You will be given the values in the steps that follow.

Define the User Interface

Set Up the Form

Notice that the new form in the Form window has all the standard Windows features, such as a title bar, maximize and minimize buttons, and a close button.

STEP 1: Resize the form in the Form window: Drag the handle in the lower-right corner down and to the right (see Figure 1.12 on page 13).

STEP 2: Look at the Form Layout window in the lower-right corner of the screen (refer to Figure 1.12). The small picture of a form on the monitor shows the location where your form will appear when the project runs. You may drag the picture to a different location. (*Note:* Monitors have differing resolutions, and the location you choose when designing your project may not appear the same on a different monitor.)

Figure 1.12

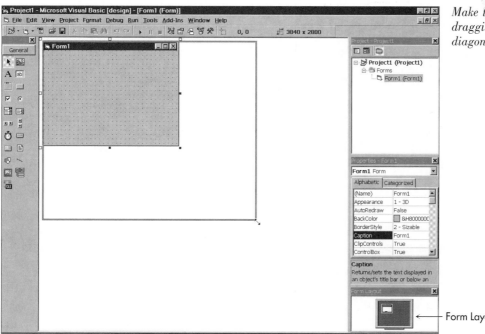

Make the form larger by dragging its lower-right handle diagonally.

Form Layout window

Place Controls on the Form

You are going to place three controls on the form: a **label** and two **command buttons**.

STEP 1: Point to the label tool in the toolbox and click. Then move the pointer over the form. Notice that the pointer becomes a crosshair, and the label tool looks like it has been pressed, indicating it is the active tool (Figure 1.13).

Figure 1.13

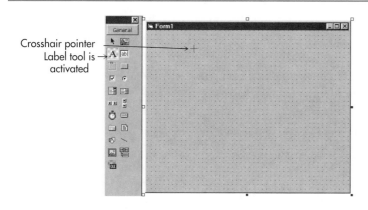

Crosshair pointer
Label tool is activated

When you click on the label tool in the toolbox, the tool's button is activated and the mouse pointer becomes a crosshair.

STEP 2: Point to the upper-left corner where you want the label to begin, press the mouse button, and drag the pointer to the opposite corner (Figure 1.14). When you release the mouse button, the label and its default contents (Label1) will appear (Figure 1.15).

Figure 1.14

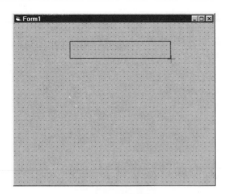

Drag the mouse pointer diagonally to draw the label on the form.

Figure 1.15

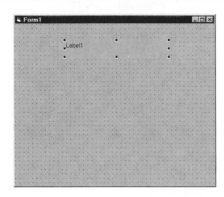

The newly created label has eight small handles, indicating that it is selected. Notice that the contents of the label are set to Label1 by default.

When you pause, Visual Basic's ToolTip pops up, indicating the size of the control in *twips*, which is a printer's measurement system. 1 twip = ¹⁄₁₄₄₀ inch.

The label has eight small square **handles**, indicating that the control is currently selected. While a control is selected, you can delete it, resize it, or move it. Refer to Table 1.1 for instructions for selecting, deleting, resizing, and moving controls. Click outside of a control to deselect it.

Table 1.1

Selecting, deleting, resizing, and moving controls on a form.

Select a control	Click on the control.
Delete a control	Select the control and then press the Delete key on the keyboard.
Move a control	Select the control, point inside the control (not on a handle), press the mouse button, and drag it to a new location.
Resize a control	Make sure the control is selected; then point to one of the handles, press the mouse button, and drag the handle. Drag a side handle to change the width, a bottom or top handle to change the height, or a corner handle to resize in two directions.

STEP 3: Draw a command button on the form: Click on the Command button tool in the toolbox, position the crosshair pointer for one corner of the button, and drag to the diagonally opposite corner (Figure 1.16).

The new command button should have selection handles.

Figure   1.16

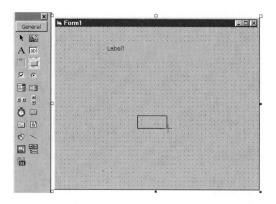

Select the Command button tool and drag diagonally to create a new command button control.

STEP 4: Create another command button using this alternative method: Point to the Command button tool in the toolbox and double-click. A new command button of the default size will appear in the center of the form (Figure 1.17).

Figure   1.17

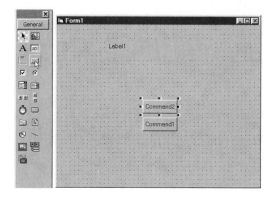

Place a new command button on the form by double-clicking the Command button tool in the toolbox. The new button appears in the center of the form.

STEP 5: Keep the new command button selected, point anywhere inside the button (not on a handle), and drag the button below your first button (Figure 1.18). As you drag the control, you see only its outline; when you release the mouse button, the control is actually moved to its new location.

Figure   1.18

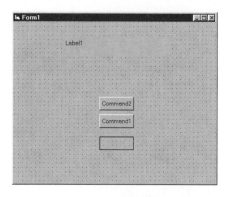

Drag the new command button (Command2) below Command1. An outline of the control shows the new location for the control.

STEP 6: Select each control and move and resize the controls as necessary. Make the two buttons the same size and line them up.

STEP 7: Point anywhere on the form except on a control and click the right mouse button. On the Shortcut menu, select *Lock Controls* (Figure 1.19). Locking prevents you from accidentally moving the controls. When your controls are locked, you see white handles, rather than the dark handles, around a selected control.

Note: You can unlock the controls at any time if you wish to redesign the form. Just click on *Lock Controls* on the Shortcut menu again to deselect it.

Figure 1.19

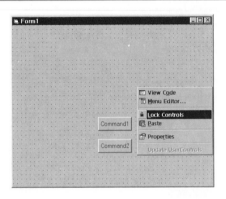

After the controls are placed into the desired location, lock them in place by selecting Lock Controls from the shortcut menu.

At this point you have designed the user interface and are ready to set the properties.

Set Properties

Set the Name and Caption Properties for the Label

STEP 1: Click on the label you placed on the form; selection handles will appear. Next click on the title bar of the Properties window to make it the active window (Figure 1.20).

Tip

If the Properties window is not visible, you can press the F4 key to show it.

Figure 1.20

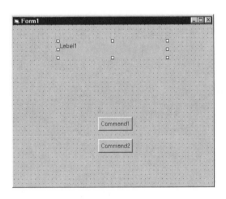

The currently selected control is shown in the Properties window.

— Properties window
— Name of selected object
— Class of selected object
— Object box
— Settings box

Notice that the Object box at the top of the Properties window is showing *Label1* (the name of the object) and *Label* (called the **class** of the object).

STEP 2: Select the Name property. Click on *(Name)* and notice that the Settings box shows *Label1*, the default name of the label (Figure 1.21).

The Properties window. Click on the Name property to change the value in the Settings box.

STEP 3: Type "lblMessage" (without the quotation marks). See Figure 1.22.

Type "lblMessage" into the Settings box for the Name property.

STEP 4: Click on the Caption property to select it. Scroll the list if necessary.
The **Caption** property of a label determines what will be displayed on the form. Since nothing should display when the project begins, you must delete the value of the Caption property (as described in the next two steps).

STEP 5: Double-click on *Label1* in the Settings box; the entry should appear selected (highlighted). See Figure 1.23.

STEP 6: Press the Delete key to delete the value of the Caption property.
Notice that the label on the form now appears empty (Figure 1.24).

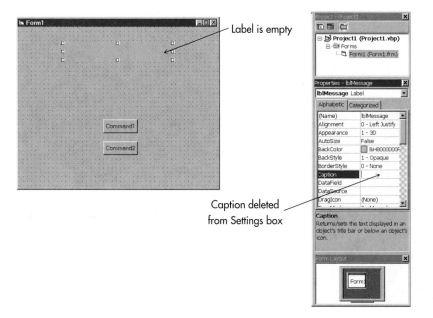

*Delete the value for the Caption
property from the Settings box;
the label on the form also
appears empty.*

Tip

Don't confuse the Name property
with the Caption property. You
will use the Name property to
refer to the control in your Basic code. The Caption property tells what the user will
see on the form. Visual
Basic sets both of these
properties   to   the
same value by default,   and   it   is
easy to confuse
them.

Set the Name and Caption Properties for the First Command Button

STEP 1: Click on the first command button (Command1) to select it and then
look at the Properties window. The Object box should show the name
(Command1) and class *(CommandButton)* of the command button. See
Figure 1.25.

Problem? If you should double-click and another window appears,
simply close the window by clicking on the new window's close button.

STEP 2: Change the Name property of the command button to "cmdPush"
(without the quotation marks).

Figure 1.25

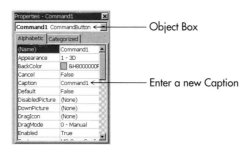

— Object Box

— Enter a new Caption

Change the Caption property for the first command button.

Tip

Always set the Name property of controls before writing code. If you change the name of an object after the code is typed, the code becomes separated from its object and the program does not run properly.

Although the project would work fine without this step, we prefer to give this button a meaningful name, rather than use Command1, its default name.

STEP 3: Change the Caption property to "Push Me" (without the quotation marks). This changes the words that appear on top of the button.

Set the Name and Caption Properties for the Second Command Button

STEP 1: Select Command2 and change its Name property to "cmdExit".

STEP 2: Change the Caption property to "Exit".

Change the Caption Property for the Form

STEP 1: Click anywhere on the form, except on a control. The Properties window Object box should now show the form as the selected object (*Form1* as the object's name and *Form* as its class).

STEP 2: Change the Caption property to "Hello World by *Your Name*" (again, no quotation marks).

The Caption property of a form determines the text to appear in the title bar. Your screen should now look like Figure 1.26.

Figure 1.26

The form's Caption appears in the title bar

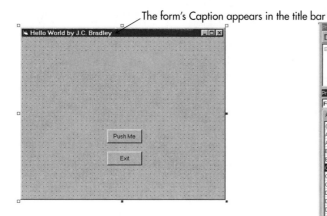

Change the form's Caption property to set the text that appears in the form's title bar.

Change the form's Caption property in the Settings box

Write Code

Visual Basic Events

While your project is running, the user can do many things, such as move the mouse around; click on either button; move, resize, or close your form's window; or jump to another application. Each action by the user causes an **event** to occur in your Visual Basic project. Some of the events you care about (like clicking on a command button), and some events you do not care about (like moving the mouse and resizing the window). If you write Basic code for a particular event, then Visual Basic will respond to the event and automatically execute your procedure. *VB ignores events for which no procedures are written.*

Visual Basic Event Procedures

You write code in Visual Basic in **procedures**. For now, each of your procedures will be a **sub procedure**, which begins with the words *Private Sub* and ends with *End Sub*. (Later you will also learn about function procedures.) *Note:* Many programmers refer to sub procedures as *subprograms* or *subroutines*. *Subprogram* is OK; *subroutine* is not, because Basic actually has a different statement for a subroutine, which is not the same as a sub procedure.

Visual Basic automatically names your **event procedures**. The name consists of the object name, an underscore (_), and the name of the event. For example, the Click event for your command button called cmdPush will be *cmdPush_Click*. For the sample project you are writing, you will need a cmdPush_Click procedure and a cmdExit_Click procedure.

Visual Basic Code Statements

This first project requires three Visual Basic statements: the **remark**, the **assignment statement**, and the **End statement**.

The Remark Statement

Remark statements, sometimes called *comments,* are used for project documentation only. They are not considered "executable" and have no effect when the project runs. The purpose of remarks is to make the project more readable and understandable by the people who read it.

Good programming practices dictate that programmers include remarks to clarify their projects. Every sub procedure should begin with a remark that describes the purpose of the sub. Every project module should have remarks that tell the purpose of the module, as well as provide identifying information such as the name of the programmer and the date the module was written and/or modified. In addition, it is a good idea to place remarks within the logic of a project, especially if the purpose of any statements might be unclear.

When you try to read someone else's project, or your own after a period of time, you will appreciate the generous use of remarks.

Visual Basic remarks begin with an apostrophe. Most of the time your remarks will be on a separate line that starts with an apostrophe. You can also add an apostrophe and a remark to the right end of a line of code.

The Remark Statement—Examples

```
'This project was written by Jonathon Edwards
'Exit the project
lblMessage.Caption = "Hello World" 'Assign the message to the Caption property
```

The Assignment Statement

The assignment statement assigns a value to a property or variable (you'll learn about variables in Chapter 3). Assignment statements operate from right to left; that is, the value appearing on the right side of the equal sign is assigned to the property named on the left of the equal sign. It is often helpful to read the equal sign as "is replaced by." For example, the assignment statement in the previous example box would read "lblMessage.Caption is replaced by Hello World."

The Assignment Statement—General Form

```
[Let] Object.Property = value
```

The value named on the right side of the equal sign is assigned to (or placed into) the property named on the left. The Let is optional and may be included if you wish. You may find that using Let improves the readability of your projects.

The Assignment Statement—Examples

```
lblTitle.Caption = "A Snazzy Program"
lblAddress.Caption = "1234 South North Street"
lblTitle.FontSize = 12
Let lblTitle.FontBold = True
```

Notice that when the value to assign is some actual text (called a *literal*), it is enclosed in quotation marks. This allows you to type any combination of alpha and numeric characters. If the value is numeric, do not enclose it in quotation marks. And do not place quotation marks around the terms *True* and *False*, which Visual Basic recognizes as special key terms.

The End Statement

The End statement stops execution of a project. In most cases, you will include an End statement in the sub procedure for an Exit button or an *Exit* menu choice.

The End Statement—Example

```
End
```

Code the Event Procedures for Hello World

Code the Click Event for the Push Me Button

STEP 1: Double-click on the Push Me command button. The Visual Basic **Code window** will open with the first and last lines of your sub procedure already in place (Figure 1.27).

Name of object   The event

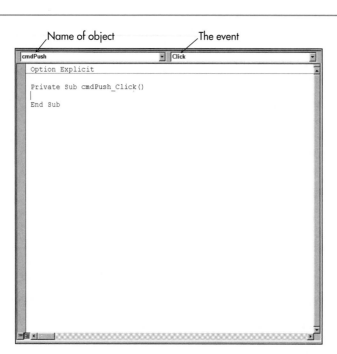

```
cmdPush                    ▼  Click                      ▼
Option Explicit

Private Sub cmdPush_Click()
|
End Sub
```

The Code window, showing the first and last lines of the sub procedure.

STEP 2: Press the Tab key once to indent and then type this remark statement:

`'Display the Hello World message`

STEP 3: Press Enter and notice that Visual Basic automatically changes remarks to green (unless you or someone else has changed the color with the Environment option).

Follow good coding conventions and indent all lines between Private Sub and End Sub. Also, always leave a blank line after the remarks at the top of a sub procedure.

STEP 4: Press Enter again and then type this assignment statement:

`lblMessage.Caption = "Hello World"`

Note: When you type the period after lblMessage, a list box appears showing the properties and methods available for a label control. Although you can type the entire word *Caption,* you can allow the Visual Basic editor to help you. As soon as you type the C, the list automatically scrolls to the word *Caption.* You can press the space bar to select the word and continue typing the rest of the statement.

New to **UB 5!**

This assignment statement assigns the literal "Hello World" to the Caption property of the control called lblMessage. Compare your screen to Figure 1.28.

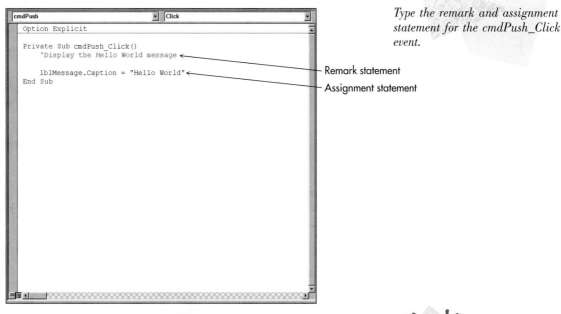

Type the remark and assignment statement for the cmdPush_Click event.

STEP 5: Return to the form by clicking on the View Object button on the Project Explorer window (Figure 1.29).

View Object button

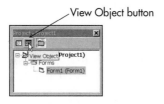

Click on the View Object button to return to the form.

Code the Click Event for the Exit Button

STEP 1: Double-click on the Exit command button to open the Code window for the cmdExit_Click event.

STEP 2: Press Tab once and type this remark:

    'Exit the project

STEP 3: Press Enter twice and type this Basic statement:

    End

STEP 4: Make sure your code looks like Figure 1.30 and then click on the
Code window's Close button.

Code window Close button

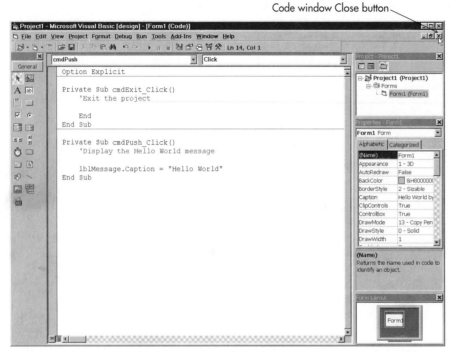

*Type the remark and End
statement for the cmdExit_Click
event and close the Code
window.*

Run the Project

After you have finished writing the code, you are ready to run the project.
Use one of these three methods:

1. Open the *Run* menu and choose *Start.*
2. Press the Start button on the toolbar.
3. Press F5, the shortcut key for the *Start* command.

Start the Project Running

STEP 1: Choose one of the three methods shown above to start your project
running.

Notice that the Visual Basic title bar now indicates that you are
in run time and that the grid dots have disappeared from your form
(Figure 1.31). (The grid dots help you align the controls; you may
turn them off if you prefer.)

Figure 1.31

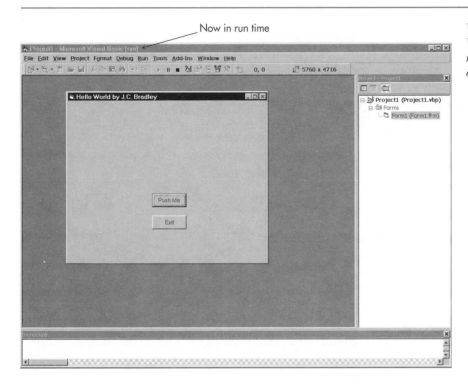

Now in run time

When you run the project, the Visual Basic title bar indicates run time and the form's grid dots disappear.

Click the Push Me Button

STEP 1: Click the Push Me button. Your "Hello World" message appears in the label (Figure 1.32).

Figure 1.32

Click on the Push Me button and "Hello World" appears in the label.

Click the Exit Button

STEP 1: Click the Exit button. Your project terminates, and you return to Visual Basic design time.

(Problems? See "Finding and Fixing Errors" later in this chapter.)

Save the Project

Of course, you must always save your work often. Except for a very small project like this one, you will usually save your work as you go along.

Create a Folder

It is very easy to lose parts of a Visual Basic project and neglect to include all of the files when you copy a project from disk to disk. Therefore, you should always create a new folder on disk before saving your first file.

Note: Because of the way Visual Basic stores its project files, it is sometimes difficult to make it recognize that you have changed the location of a file. Always create your folder *first* and save into the folder—do not save somewhere else first and plan to organize later.

Save the Form File

STEP 1: Open the Visual Basic *File* menu and choose *Save Form1 As*. This option allows you to save the current form.

STEP 2: Check the *Save in* box and change to the correct drive.

STEP 3: Click on the *Create New Folder* button (Figure 1.33).

Figure 1.33

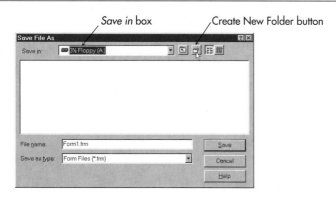

Save in box   Create New Folder button

The Save Form As dialog box. Click on the Create New Folder button and name the new folder.

STEP 4: Type the name of your new folder as "Hello" (without the quotation marks) and press Enter.

STEP 5: Open the new folder by double-clicking on it.

STEP 6: In the *File name* box, type "Hello" (without the quotation marks; see Figure 1.34). Visual Basic will add the correct .FRM extension to the filename.

Figure 1.34

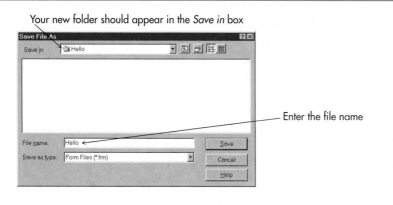

Your new folder should appear in the *Save in* box

Enter the file name

Double-click on your new folder so that it appears in the Save in box. Then enter the new file name.

STEP 7: Check the *Save in* list again to make sure the file will be saved in your new folder. Then press Enter or click *Save* to save the form file.

Save the Project File

STEP 1: Open the *File* menu and select *Save Project As*. This will allow you to save the project (.VBP) file.

STEP 2: Check the *Save in* box; your new folder should still be showing.

STEP 3: In the *File name* box, type "Hello" (without the quotation marks; see Figure 1.35). This file will be saved as *Hello.vbp*, since Visual Basic adds the correct file extension.

The Save Project As *dialog box. Make sure the correct folder is selected and type the name of the project file in the* File name *box.*

STEP 4: Press Enter or click *Save* to save the project file.

Open the Project

Now is the time to test your save operation by opening the project from disk.

Open the Project File

STEP 1: Either click on the Open Project button on the toolbar or choose *Open Project* from the *File* menu.

STEP 2: In the *Open Project* dialog box, check the *Look in* box. Your Hello folder should still be set correctly.

    When you begin a new session, you will need to change to your drive and directory before you can open a project.

STEP 3: You should see your project name, Hello.vbp, in the file list box (Figure 1.36). Click on the filename and then click on the *Open* button (or double-click on the filename).

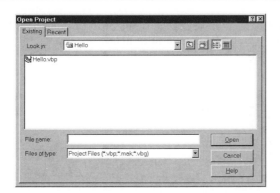

The Open Project dialog box. Select the correct folder and find your project name in the file list.

STEP 4: If you do not see your form on the screen, check the Project Explorer window—it should say *Hello.vbp* for the project. Click on the View Object button, and your form will appear.

Modify the Project

Now it's time to make some changes to the project. We'll change the size of the "Hello World" message, display the message in two different languages, and display the programmer name (that's you) on the form. We'll also provide a button that will print the form.

Change the Size and Alignment of the Message

STEP 1: Right-click somewhere on the form to display the *Shortcut* menu and select *Lock Controls* to unlock the controls so that you can make changes.

STEP 2: Click on the label on your form, which will make dark selection handles appear. (If your selection handles are white, you must unlock the controls, as described in Step 1.)

STEP 3: Widen the label on both ends by dragging the handles wider. (Drag the right end farther right and the left end farther left.)

STEP 4: With the label still selected, scroll to the Font property, and click to select it. The Settings box shows the currently selected font.

Notice the new button with an ellipses on top, which appears in the Settings box (Figure 1.37). The button is called the *Properties* button; the ellipses indicates that clicking on the button will display a dialog box with choices.

F i g u r e   1 . 3 7

Click on the Properties button to see the choices for the Font property.

Properties button

STEP 5: Click on the Properties button to display the *Font* dialog box (Figure 1.38). Select 12 point if it is available. (If it isn't available, choose another number larger than the current setting.) Close the *Font* dialog box.

Figure 1.38

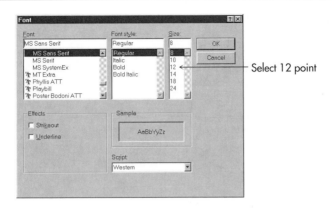

Choose 12 point from the Font dialog box.

— Select 12 point

STEP 6: Select the Alignment property. The Properties button that appears with the down-pointing arrow indicates a drop-down list of choices. Drop down the list and choose *2—Center*.

Add a New Label for Your Name

STEP 1: Click on the Label tool in the toolbox and create a new label along the bottom edge of your form (Figure 1.39). (You can resize the form if necessary.)

Figure 1.39

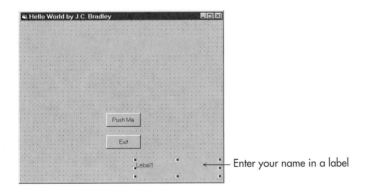

Add a new label for your name at the bottom of the form.

— Enter your name in a label

STEP 2: Change the label's Caption property to "by Your Name". (Use your name and omit the quotation marks.)

Change the Location and Caption of the Push Me Button

Since we plan to display the message in one of two languages, we'll change the caption on the Push Me button to English and move the button to allow for a second command button.

STEP 1: Select the Push Me button and change its Caption property to English.

STEP 2: Move the English button to the left to make room for a Spanish button (see Figure 1.40).

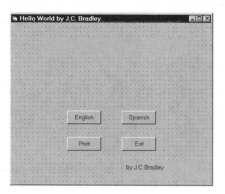

Add a Spanish Button

STEP 1: Add a new command button. Move and resize it as necessary, referring to Figure 1.40.

STEP 2: Change the Name property of the new button to cmdSpanish.

STEP 3: Change the Caption property of the new button to Spanish.

Add an Event Procedure for the Spanish Button

STEP 1: Double-click on the Spanish button to open the Code window for cmdSpanish_Click.

STEP 2: Press the Tab key once and add a remark:

```
'Display the Hello World message in Spanish
```

STEP 3: Press Enter twice and type the following Basic code line:

```
lblMessage.Caption = "Hola Mundo"
```

STEP 4: Close the Code window.

Add a Print Button

STEP 1: Move the Exit button to the right to make room for the Print button.

STEP 2: Add a new command button; move and resize it to match Figure 1.40.

STEP 3: Change the Name property of the new button to cmdPrint.

STEP 4: Change the Caption property of the new button to Print.

Lock the Controls

STEP 1: When you are satisfied with the placement of the controls on the form, display the Shortcut menu and select *Lock Controls* again.

Add an Event Procedure for the Print Button

To print the form, we will use the PrintForm method, which prints the current form without its title bar or borders.

STEP 1: Double-click on the Print button to open the Code window for the cmdPrint_Click event.

STEP 2: Indent and add a remark that tells what you plan to do in the subprogram.

STEP 3: Leave a blank line and indent the following code statement:

```
PrintForm
```

That's all there is to it. The actual format for a method is Object.Method (object dot method). However, we can leave off the object in this case, since it defaults to the current form.

Save and Run the Project

STEP 1: Save your project again. You can use the *Save File* and *Save Project* menu options or click on the Save button on the toolbar, which saves both.

STEP 2: Close the Code window and run your project again. Try clicking on the English button and the Spanish button. You can click on the Print button any time you wish. (Problems? See "Finding and Fixing Errors" later in this chapter.)

Add General Remarks

Good documentation guidelines require some more remarks in the project. Always begin each procedure with remarks that tell the purpose of the procedure. In addition, each project file needs identifying remarks at the top.

The **General Declarations section** is a good location for these remarks.

STEP 1: Click on the View Code button in the Project Explorer window; the Code window appears.

Your Code window may appear with or without an `Option Explicit` statement at the top. If you *do* see the `Option Explicit` statement, click at the left end of the line and press Enter; then skip to Step 3. (You will learn about the `Option Explicit` statement in Chapter 3. If it doesn't appear for this project, that's OK.)

STEP 2: Using the Code window's scroll bar, scroll to the top of the Code window. Then click in front of the first line and press Enter, creating a blank line.

STEP 3: Move the insertion point up to the blank line and type the following remarks, one per line (Figure 1.41):

```
'Hello World project
' by Your Name  (use your own name here)
'Today's date  (fill in today's date)
'This project will display a "Hello World" message in two different
' languages, and print the form on the printer.
```

Enter remarks in the General Declarations section of the form module.

Explore the Code Window

STEP 1: Notice the two drop-down lists at the top of the Code window.

   You can use these lists to move to any procedure in the Code window.

STEP 2: Click on the left down-pointing arrow to view the list of objects. Notice that every object in your form is listed there (Figure 1.42). At the top of the list, you see *(General)*.

Figure   1.42

View the list of objects in this form module by dropping down the object list. Select an object from the list to display the sub procedures for that object.

STEP 3: Click on *(General)* to select it. Then notice the Procedure list, on the right, which says *(Declarations)*. This is the quick way to jump to the General Declarations section of a module.

STEP 4: Drop down the Object list, (the left list) and select *cmdSpanish*. The insertion point jumps to the event procedure for cmdSpanish.

STEP 5: Look at the Procedure list box, (the right list box); it says *Click*. You are currently viewing the cmdSpanish_Click event procedure.

   To write code for more than one event for an object, use the Procedure drop-down list.

STEP 6: Drop down the Procedure list and view the list of events available for the selected object. You can jump to another procedure by selecting its name from the list.

Finish Up

STEP 1: Close the Code window.

STEP 2: Save the project again.

Print the Project Documentation

Select the Printing Options

STEP 1: Open the *File* menu and choose *Print*. The *Print* dialog box appears (Figure 1.43).

Figure   1.43

Select the options you want in the Print dialog box.

STEP 2: Click on the check boxes to select the printing options you want.

Range	
Selection	This option is available only when you have selected (highlighted) text in the Code window.
Current Module	This option will print all of the current module (form file).
Current Project	This option will print all modules in the project. Since this project has only one module, the two options give the same result.
Print What	
Form Image	Print a picture of the form as it appears at design time.
Code	Print all procedures and the General Declarations section.
Form as Text	Print a description of every object and its properties.

STEP 3: Select all three check boxes for *Print What* and click OK.

Sample Printout

This is the output produced when you choose to print the form image, the code, and the form as text.

The Form Image

When you select *Form Image*, the form prints without its title bar or borders. See Figure 1.44.

Figure 1.44

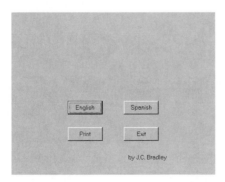

The form prints without its title bar or border.

The Code

The *Code* selection prints all module procedures, as well as the General Declarations section.

```
'Hello World project
' by Your Name
' July 4, 1997
' This project will display a "Hello World" message in two
' different languages, and print the form on the printer.
Option Explicit
```

```
Private Sub cmdExit_Click()
    'Exit the project

    End
End Sub
```

```
Private Sub cmdPrint_Click()
    'Print the form

    PrintForm
End Sub
```

```
Private Sub cmdPush_Click()
    'Display the Hello World message

    lblMessage.Caption = "Hello World"
End Sub
```

```
Private Sub cmdSpanish_Click()
    'Display the Hello World message in Spanish

    lblMessage.Caption = "Hola Mundo"
End Sub
```

The Form as Text

The output produced when you select *Form as Text* lists the objects and properties in the module.

```
VERSION 5.00
Begin VB.Form Form1
   Caption            =   "Hello World by J.C. Bradley"
   ClientHeight       =   4392
   ClientLeft         =   48
   ClientTop          =   276
   ClientWidth        =   5664
   LinkTopic          =   "Form1"
   LockControls       =   -1  'True
   ScaleHeight        =   4392
   ScaleWidth         =   5664
   StartUpPosition    =   3  'Windows Default
   Begin VB.CommandButton cmdPrint
      Caption         =   "Print"
      Height          =   372
      Left            =   1560
      TabIndex        =   5
      Top             =   3120
      Width           =   972
   End

   Begin VB.CommandButton cmdSpanish
      Caption         =   "Spanish"
      Height          =   372
      Left            =   3120
      TabIndex        =   4
      Top             =   2400
      Width           =   972
   End

   Begin VB.CommandButton cmdExit
      Caption         =   "Exit"
      Height          =   372
      Left            =   3120
      TabIndex        =   2
      Top             =   3120
      Width           =   972
   End

   Begin VB.CommandButton cmdPush
      Caption         =   "English"
      Height          =   372
      Left            =   1560
      TabIndex        =   1
      Top             =   2400
      Width           =   972
   End
```

```
Begin VB.Label Label1
   Caption           =  "by J.C. Bradley"
   Height            =  372
   Left              =  3240
   TabIndex          =  3
   Top               =  3840
   Width             =  2292
End
Begin VB.Label lblMessage
   BeginProperty Font
      Name           =  "MS Sans Serif"
      Size           =  12
      Charset        =  0
      Weight         =  400
      Underline      =  0  'False
      Italic         =  0  'False
      Strikethrough  =  0  'False
   EndProperty
   Height            =  372
   Left              =  840
   TabIndex          =  0
   Top               =  480
   Width             =  4092
   End
End
Attribute VB_Name = "Form1"
Attribute VB_GlobalNameSpace = False
Attribute VB_Creatable = False
Attribute VB_PredeclaredId = True
Attribute VB_Exposed = False
```

Finding and Fixing Errors

You may have already seen some errors as you entered the first sample project. Programming errors come in three varieties: **compile errors, run-time errors**, and **logic errors**.

Compile Errors

As Visual Basic attempts to convert your project code to machine language (called *compiling the code*), it finds any compile errors. You get compile errors when you break the syntax rules of Basic and sometimes when you use an illegal object or property.

For example, try spelling *End* as *ennd* or using the word *Quit* instead of *End.* The compiler can only translate the exact spelling of a word and cannot recognize either of these words; they would both cause a Compile Error message box.

You also receive a compile error if you accidentally use the wrong punctuation or place the punctuation in the wrong place. The compiler cannot understand `lblMessage,Caption` or `lblMessage.Caption;`.

Compile errors may be found by the editor as you move off the offending line. Or the compile error may not be found until you try to run the project. Before Visual Basic can actually run your code, it attempts to compile the code into machine language. If VB finds compile errors, it displays the Code window, highlights the offending line, and enters break time.

After you have corrected your compile errors, you can click the Run button to continue the compile and run, or click the Stop button to end.

One type of compile error that is all too common for beginning programmers is the inconsistent spelling of object names. For example, if you set a label control's Name property to `lblMessage`, you must always refer to it with that exact spelling. The following line of code will generate a compile error. Can you spot the problem?

```
lblMessages.Caption = "Hello World"
```

Run-Time Errors

If your project halts during execution, that's a run-time error. Visual Basic displays a dialog box, goes into break time, and highlights the statement causing the problem. Statements that cannot execute correctly cause run-time errors. The statements are correctly formed Basic statements that pass the syntax checking of the compiler; however, the statements fail to execute. Run-time errors can be caused by attempting to do impossible arithmetic operations such as calculate with nonnumeric data, divide by zero, or find the square root of a negative number.

Logic Errors

With logic errors, your project runs but produces incorrect results. Perhaps the results of a calculation are incorrect or the wrong text appears or the text is OK but appears in the wrong location.

Beginning programmers often overlook their logic errors. If the project runs, it must be right—right? All too often, that statement is not correct. You may need to use a calculator to check the output. Check all aspects of the project output: computations, text, and spacing.

For example, the Hello World project in this chapter has event procedures for printing "Hello World" in English and in Spanish. If the contents of the two procedures were switched, the program would work but the results would be incorrect.

The following code does not give the proper instructions to display the message in Spanish:

```
Private Sub cmdSpanish_Click
    'Display the Hello World Message in Spanish

    lblMessage.Caption = "Hello World"
End Sub
```

Project Debugging

If you talk to any computer programmer, you will learn that programs don't have errors, but that programs get "bugs" in them. Finding and fixing these bugs is called **debugging**.

For compile errors and run-time errors, your job is easier. Visual Basic displays the Code window with the offending line highlighted. However, you must identify and locate logic errors yourself.

If you are able to see the problem and fix it, you can continue project execution from that location by clicking on the Run button, pressing F5, or choosing *Start* from the *Run* menu. You can restart execution from the beginning by selecting *Restart* from the *Run* menu or by pressing Shift + F5.

Visual Basic has some very helpful tools to aid in debugging your projects. The debugging tools are covered in Chapter 4.

Naming Rules and Conventions for Objects

Using good, consistent, names for objects can help make a project easier to read and understand, as well as easier to debug. You *must* follow the Visual Basic rules for naming objects, procedures, and variables. In addition, conscientious programmers will also follow certain naming conventions.

The Naming Rules

When you select a name for an object, Visual Basic requires the name to begin with a letter. The name can be up to 40 characters in length and can contain letters, digits, and underscores. An object name cannot include a space or punctuation mark.

The Naming Conventions

This text follows the industrywide naming conventions, which help make projects more understandable: Always begin a name with a lowercase three-letter prefix, which identifies the object type (such as label, command button, or form) and capitalize the first character after the prefix (the "real" name of the object). For names with multiple words, capitalize each word in the name. All names must be meaningful and indicate the purpose of the object.

Examples

    lblMessage
    cmdExit
    frmDataEntry
    lblDiscountRate

Do not keep the default names assigned by Visual Basic, such as Command1 and Label3. Also, do not name your objects with numbers. The exception to this rule is for labels that never change during project execution. These labels usually hold items such as titles, instructions, and labels for other controls. Leaving these labels with their default names is perfectly acceptable and is practiced in this text.

Refer to Table 1.2 for the list of object prefixes.

Object Class	Prefix	Example
Form	frm	frmDataEntry
Command button	cmd	cmdExit
Text box	txt	txtPaymentAmount
Label	lbl	lblTotal
Option button	opt	optBold
Check box	chk	chkPrintSummary
Frame	fra	fraSelection
Horizontal scroll bar	hsb	hsbRate
Vertical scroll bar	vsb	vsbTemperature
Image	img	imgLogo
Picture box	pic	picLandscape
Combo box	cbo	cboBookList
List box	lst	lstIngredients
Shape	shp	shpBox

Recommended naming conventions for Visual Basic objects.

Visual Basic Help

The Visual Basic **Help** facility is great! With Help, you really don't need a printed manual. You can look up any Basic statement, object, property, method, or programming concept. Many coding examples are available, and you can copy and paste the examples into your own project, modifying them if you wish.

The *Search Master Index* option helps you access the online manuals. There is also an option to get additional information from the Internet, including a Web tutorial.

You can look up topics in Help by using the Help Contents list (like a table of contents) or Search (which resembles an index). Also, you can use **context-sensitive Help**, which automatically jumps to the Help topic relating to what you are working on at the moment. For context-sensitive Help, select any object on the screen and press F1; VB automatically displays the relevant Help page.

New to VB 5!

Feedback 1.1

Note: Answers for all Feedback questions are shown in Appendix A.

1. Use the *Help* menu's *Microsoft Visual Basic Help Topics.* Select the *Index* tab and type "label". Display and print the information for the Label control. Click on Properties and view the list of available properties for a

Label control. Repeat the procedure for the Command Button control—display the options for command button and then display the information for the Command Button control. Print out the information page; then view the list of properties for a Command Button control.

2. If you are connected to the Internet, check out the Help option *Microsoft on the Web*.

3. Display the code window of your Hello World project. Place the mouse pointer on the keyword `End` in your Exit procedure. Press the F1 key to view context-sensitive help.

S u m m a r y

---

1. Visual Basic is an event-driven language used to write application programs that run in the Windows operating environment.

2. The object model of programming has objects that have properties and methods.

3. The current release of Visual Basic is 5.0. There is a Learning Edition, a Professional Edition, and an Enterprise Edition.

4. To plan a project, first sketch the user interface and then list the objects and properties needed. Then plan the necessary event procedures.

5. The three steps to creating a Visual Basic project are (1) define the user interface, (2) set the properties, and (3) write the Basic code.

6. A Visual Basic project consists of at least a .VBP file and an .FRM file and may have multiple .FRM files, .BAS files, .OCX files, and a .VBW file.

7. The VB environment consists of the Form window, the Project Explorer window, the Properties window, the Form Layout window, the toolbox, the menu bar, and the toolbar.

8. VB has three modes: design time, run time, and break time.

9. Visual Basic code is written in procedures. Sub procedures begin with the words *Private Sub* and end with *End Sub*.

10. Project remarks are used for documentation. Good programming practices require remarks in every procedure and in the General Declarations section of a module.

11. Assignment statements assign a value to a property or a variable. Assignment statements work from right to left, assigning the value on the right side of the equal sign to the property named on the left side of the equal sign.

12. The `End` statement terminates project execution.

13. Each event to which you want to respond requires an event procedure.

14. You must save both the form file and the project file to properly save a Visual Basic project. The recommended practice is to first create a folder to hold the files.

15. The PrintForm method prints the current form on the printer.

16. You can print out an image of the form; the code, which is a listing of the Basic statements in the project; and the form text, which is a listing of all objects and their properties.

17. Three types of errors can occur in a Visual Basic project: compile errors (which violate the syntax rules of Basic statements), run-time errors

(which contain a statement that cannot execute properly), and logic errors (which produce erroneous results).

18. Finding and fixing programming errors is called *debugging*.
19. Following good naming conventions can help make a project easier to debug.
20. Visual Basic Help has very complete descriptions of all project elements and their uses. You can use the Contents list, Index, or context-sensitive Help. Additional help is available on the Web.

Key Terms

assignment statement   *20*
break time   *8*
Caption   *17*
class   *17*
code   *4*
Code window   *22*
command button   *13*
compile error   *36*
context-sensitive Help   *39*
control   *2*
debugging   *38*
design time   *8*
End statement   *20*
Enterprise Edition   *3*
event   *20*
event-driven programming   *2*
event procedure   *20*
form   *2*
form file   *5*
form module   *5*
Form window   *6*
General Declarations section   *31*
graphical user interface (GUI)   *2*
handle   *14*

Help   *39*
label   *13*
Learning Edition   *3*
logic error   *36*
method   *3*
object   *3*
object-oriented programming   *3*
procedure   *20*
Professional Edition   *3*
project file   *5*
Project Explorer window   *6*
Properties window   *6*
property   *3*
pseudocode   *4*
remark   *20*
run time   *8*
run-time error   *36*
standard code module   *5*
sub procedure   *20*
toolbar   *7*
toolbox   *7*
user interface   *4*
Visual Basic environment   *5*

Review Questions

1. What are objects and properties? How are they related to each other?
2. What are the three steps for planning and creating Visual Basic projects? Describe what happens in each step.
3. What is the purpose of these Visual Basic file types: .VBP, .FRM, .BAS, and .OCX?
4. When is Visual Basic in design time? run time? break time?
5. What is the purpose of the Name property of a control?
6. What property determines what appears on the form for a label control?

7. What is the purpose of the Caption property of a command button? the Caption property of a form?

8. What does *cmdPush_Click* mean? To what does cmdPush refer? To what does Click refer?

9. What is a Visual Basic event? Give some examples of events.

10. What property must be set to center text in a label? What should be the value of the property?

11. What is the General Declarations section of a form module? What belongs there?

12. What is a compile error, when does it occur, and what might cause it?

13. What is a run-time error, when does it occur, and what might cause it?

14. What is a logic error, when does it occur, and what might cause it?

15. Tell the class of control and the likely purpose of each of these object names:

> lblAddress
> cmdExit
> txtName
> optTextBlue

16. What does *context-sensitive Help* mean? How can you use it to see the Help page for a command button?

Programming Exercises

1.1 For your first Visual Basic exercise, you must first complete the Hello World project. Then add command buttons and event procedures to display the "Hello World" message in two more languages. You may substitute any other languages for those shown. Use Figure 1.44 as a guideline but feel free to modify the user interface to suit yourself (or your instructor).

Make sure to use meaningful names for your new command buttons, following the naming conventions in Table 1.2. (Begin the name with lowercase "cmd".) Include remarks at the top of every procedure and in the General Declarations section of the module.

"Hello World" in French: *Bonjour tout le monde*
"Hello World" in Italian: *Ciao Mondo*

1.2 Write a new Visual Basic project, which displays a different greeting, or make it display the name of your school or your company. Include at least three command buttons to display the greeting, print the form, and exit the project.

Include a label that holds your name at the bottom of the form and change the Caption property of the form to something meaningful.

Follow good naming conventions for object names; include remarks at the top of every procedure and in the General Declarations section of the module.

Select a different font name and font size for the greeting label. If you wish, you can also select a different color for the font. Select each font attribute from the *Font* dialog box, from the Properties window.

1.3   Write a project that displays four sayings, such as "The early bird gets the worm" or "A penny saved is a penny earned." (You will want to keep the sayings short, as each must be entered on one code statement. However, when the saying displays on your form, long lines will wrap within the label if the label is large enough.)

Make a command button for each saying with a descriptive Caption for each, as well as command buttons to print the form and to exit the project.

Include a label that holds your name at the bottom of the form. Also, make sure to change the Caption property of the form to something meaningful.

You may change the Font properties of the large label to the font and size of your choice.

Make sure the label is large enough to display your longest saying and that the command buttons are large enough to hold their entire Captions.

Follow good naming conventions for object names; include remarks at the top of every procedure and in the General Declarations section of the module.

1.4   Write a project to display company contact information. Include command buttons and labels for contact person, department, and phone. When the user clicks on one of the command buttons, display the contact information in the corresponding label. Include command buttons to print the form and to exit.

Include a label that holds your name at the bottom of the form and change the Caption property of the form to something meaningful.

You may change the Font properties of the labels to the font and size of your choice.

Follow good naming conventions for object names; include remarks at the top of every procedure and in the General Declarations section of the module.

CASE STUDIES

Very Busy (VB) Mail Order

If you don't have the time to look for all those hard-to-find items, tell us what you're looking for. We'll send you a catalog from the appropriate company or order for you.

We can place an order and ship it to you. We also help with shopping for gifts; your order can be gift wrapped and sent anywhere you wish.

The company title will be shortened to VB Mail Order. This name should appear as the Caption on the first form of every project that you create throughout the text for this case study.

Your first job is to create a project that will display the name and telephone number for the contact person for the customer relations, marketing, order processing, and shipping departments.

Include a command button for each department. When the user clicks on the button for a department, display the name and telephone number for the contact person in two labels. Also include identifying labels with Captions "Department Contact" and "Telephone Number".

Be sure to include a command button for Exit and another for Print Form.

Include a label at the bottom of the form that holds your name and give the form a meaningful Caption.

Test Data

Department	Department Contact	Telephone Number
Customer Relations	Tricia Mills	500-1111
Marketing	Michelle Rigner	500-2222
Order Processing	Kenna DeVoss	500-3333
Shipping	Eric Andrews	500-4444

Valley Boulevard (VB) Auto Center

Valley Boulevard Auto Center will meet all of your automobile needs. The center has facilities with everything for your vehicles including sales and leasing for new and used cars and RVs, auto service and repair, detail shop, car wash, and auto parts.

The company title will be shortened to VB Auto Center. This name should appear as the Caption on the first form of every project that you create throughout the text for this case study.

Your first job is to create a project that will display current notices.

Include four command buttons with the Captions: "Auto Sales", "Service Center", "Detail Shop", and "Employment Opportunities". One label will be used to display the information when the command buttons are clicked. Be sure to include command buttons for Exit and Print Form.

Include your name in a label at the bottom of the form.

Test Data

Command Button	Label Caption
Auto Sales	Family wagon, immaculate condition $12,995
Service Center	Lube, oil, filter $25.99
Detail Shop	Complete detail $79.95 for most cars
Employment Opportunities	Sales position contact Mr. Mann 551-2134 x475

2

More Controls

At the completion of this chapter, you will be able to...

1. Use text boxes, frames, check boxes, option buttons, images, shapes, and lines effectively.

2. Set the Appearance property to make controls appear flat or three-dimensional.

3. Select multiple controls and move them, align them, and set common properties.

4. Make your projects easy for the user to understand and operate by defining access keys, setting a default and a cancel button, controlling the tab sequence, and resetting the focus during program execution.

5. Clear the contents of text boxes and labels.

6. Change font attributes, such as bold, italic, underline, size, and color, during program execution.

7. Code multiple statements for one control using the `With` and `End With` statements.

8. Concatenate (join) strings of text.

9. Make a control visible or invisible by setting its Visible property.

Introducing More Controls

In Chapter 1 you learned to use labels and command buttons. In this chapter you will learn to use several more control types: text boxes, frames, check boxes, option buttons, image controls, shapes, and lines. Figure 2.1 shows the toolbox with the tools for these controls labeled. Figure 2.2 shows some of these controls on a form.

Each class of controls has its own set of properties. If you want to see a complete list of the properties for any class of control, you can (1) place a control on a form and examine the properties list or (2) click on a tool or a control and press F1 for context-sensitive Help. VB will display the Help page for that control, and you can view a list of the properties and an explanation of their use.

Figure 2.1

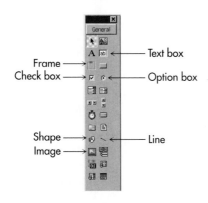

The toolbox showing the controls that will be covered in this chapter.

Figure 2.2

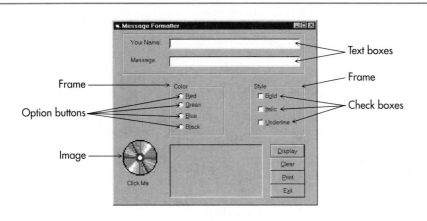

A form designed using text boxes, frames, check boxes, option buttons, and an image.

Text Boxes

Use a **text box** control when you want the user to type some input. The form in Figure 2.2 has two text boxes. The user can move from one box to the next, make corrections, cut and paste if desired, and click the Display button when finished. In your program code you can use the **Text property** of each text box.

Example

```
lblName.Caption = txtName.Text
```

In this example whatever the user enters into the text box is assigned to the Caption property of lblName. If you want to display some text in a text box during program execution, assign a literal to the Text property:

```
txtMessage.Text = "Watson, come here."
```

You can set the **Alignment property** of text boxes to change the alignment of text within the box. However, you must also set the **Multiline property** to True, or Visual Basic ignores the Alignment.

The values for the Alignment property, which can be set only at design time (not at run time), are

0 – Left Justify
1 – Right Justify
2 – Center

The three-letter prefix for naming a text box is "txt".

Examples

txtTitle
txtCompany

Frames

Frames are used as containers for other controls. Usually, groups of option buttons or check boxes are placed in frames. Using frames to group controls makes your forms easier to understand.

Set a frame's Caption property to the words you want to appear on the top edge of the frame. The three-letter prefix for naming a frame is "fra".

Examples

fraColor
fraStyle

Check Boxes

Check boxes allow the user to select (or deselect) an option. In any group of check boxes, any number may be selected. The **Value property** of a check box is set to 0 if unchecked, 1 if checked, or 2 if grayed (disabled). You can write an event procedure to execute when the user clicks in the box. In Chapter 4, when you learn about `If` statements, you can take one action when the box is checked and another action when it is unchecked.

Use the Caption property of a check box for the text you want to appear next to the box. The three-letter prefix for naming a check box is "chk".

Examples

chkBold
chkItalic

Option Buttons

Use **option buttons** when only one button of a group may be selected. Any option buttons placed directly on the form (not in a frame) function as a group. A group of option buttons inside a frame function together. The best method is to first create a frame and then to create each option button inside the frame. You must be careful to create the button inside the frame; don't create it on the form and drag it inside the frame—it still belongs to the form's group, not the frame's group. Therefore, you should not create an option button by double-clicking on its toolbox tool; instead, click to select the tool and use the crosshair pointer to draw the option button control.

The Value property of an option button is set to True if selected or to False if unselected.

You can write an event procedure to execute when the user selects an option button. In Chapter 4 you will learn to determine in your code whether or not a button is selected.

Set an option button's Caption property to the text you want to appear next to the button. The three-letter prefix for naming an option button is "opt".

Examples

optRed
optBlue

Images

An **image** control holds a picture. You can set an image's **Picture property** to a file with an extension of .BMP, .WMF, .ICO, .DIB, .GIF, .JPG, .EMF, or .CUR. First place the image control on a form and then select its Picture property in the Properties window. Click on the Properties button (Figure 2.3) to display the *Load Picture* dialog box where you can select a filename (Figure 2.4).

You can use any picture file (with the proper format) that you have available. You will find many icon files included with Visual Basic. Look in the Icons folder, under the Graphics folder, beneath the VB folder (Figure 2.5).

Default path for icon files:

```
Program Files
    DevStudio
        VB
            Graphics
                Icons
```

Figure 2.3

Click on the Picture property for an image control, and a Properties button appears. Click on the Properties button to view the Load Picture dialog box.

Figure 2.4

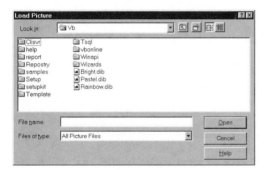

The Load Picture dialog box. Make your selection here for the picture file you want to appear in the image control.

Figure 2.5

Find the Visual Basic icon files in several folders beneath the VB\Graphics\Icons folder.

Image controls have several useful properties that you can set at design time or run time. For example, set the **Stretch property** to True to make the picture enlarge to fill the control. You can set the **Visible property** to False to make the image disappear.

For example, to make an image invisible at run time, use this code statement.

```
imgLogo.Visible = False
```

The three-letter prefix for naming an image is "img".

Setting a Border and Style

Most controls can appear to be three-dimensional (refer to Figure 2.2) or flat. Labels, text boxes, check boxes, option buttons, and images all have an **Appearance property**, with choices of 0 – Flat, or 1 – 3D. In order to make a label or an image appear three-dimensional, you must first give it a border. Set the BorderStyle to 1 – Fixed Single. The Appearance property defaults to 1 – 3D.

To remove a picture from a form or image, select the Picture property value in the Properties window and press the Delete key.

Feedback 2.1

Create an image control that displays an enlarged icon and appears in a "sunken" box. (Make up a name that conforms to this textbook's naming convention.)

Property	Setting
Name	
Stretch	
Appearance	
BorderStyle	
Visible	

The Shape Control

You can place rectangles, squares, ovals, and circles on a form using the **shape control** (Figure 2.6). Shapes can enhance the readability of a screen or add some fun. You may wish to use shapes to create a company logo or to separate a form into sections.

F i g u r e   2 . 6

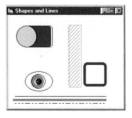

Shapes and lines created with the shape control and the line control.

Use the shape tool in the toolbox (refer to Figure 2.1) to draw a shape on the form. Then you can determine its shape by setting its Shape property. The property values are

0 – Rectangle
1 – Square
2 – Oval
3 – Circle
4 – Rounded Rectangle
5 – Rounded Square

You can draw, move, and resize shape controls in the same manner as the other controls. By changing properties, you can select the style and color of the shape's outline, the color of its fill, and whether it is transparent or solid.

The naming prefix for shape controls is "shp", such as *shpRectangle*.

The Line Control

You can draw a line on a form by using the **line control**. You may want to include lines when creating a logo, or you may simply want to divide the screen by drawing a line. Click on the line tool (refer to Figure 2.1) and use the crosshair pointer to drag a line; you may rotate the line in any direction and stretch it until releasing the mouse button.

Change other properties of line controls to set the color and style of the line. You can determine the thickness of a line by changing its Borderwidth property.

The naming prefix for a line control is "lin", for example, *linLogo*.

Working With Multiple Controls

You can select more than one control at a time, which means that you can move the controls as a group, set similar properties for the group, and align the controls.

Selecting Multiple Controls

There are two methods of selecting multiple controls. If the controls are near each other, the easiest method is to use the mouse to drag a selection box around the controls. Point to one corner of a box surrounding the controls, press the mouse button, and drag to the opposite corner (Figure 2.7). When you release the mouse button, each control will have light gray selection handles (Figure 2.8).

Figure 2.7

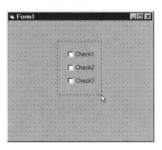

Using the pointer, drag a selection box around the controls you wish to select.

Figure 2.8

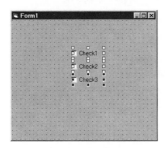

When multiple controls are selected, each has selection handles.

You can also select multiple controls, one at a time. Click on one control to select it, hold down the Ctrl key or the Shift key, and click on the next control. You can keep the Ctrl or Shift key down and continue clicking on controls you wish to select. Ctrl–click (or Shift–click) on a control a second time to deselect it without changing the rest of the group.

When you want to select most of the controls on the form, use a combination of the two methods. Drag a selection box around all of the controls to select them all and then Ctrl–click on the ones you want to deselect.

Deselecting a Group of Controls

When you are finished working with a group of controls, it's easy to deselect them. Just click anywhere on the form (not on a control) or select another (single) control.

Moving Controls as a Group

After selecting multiple controls, you can move them as a group. Point inside one of the selected controls, press the mouse button, and drag the entire group to a new location (Figure 2.9). As you drag the mouse pointer, an outline of the controls moves. When you release the mouse button, the controls move to their new location.

Figure 2.9

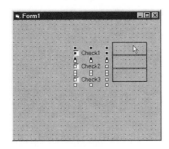

Drag a group of selected controls. An outline of the controls moves as you drag, and then the group moves when you release the mouse button.

Setting Properties for Multiple Controls

You can set some common properties for groups of controls. After selecting the group, check the Properties window. Any properties shown in the window are shared by all of the controls and can be changed all at once. For example, you may want to set the appearance for all your controls to three-dimensional or change the font used for a group of labels.

Aligning Controls

After you select a group of controls it is easy to resize and align them using the options on the *Format* menu. Figure 2.10 shows the *Align* submenu, and Figure 2.11 shows the *Make Same Size* submenu. Select your group of controls and first choose *Make Same Size*, then use the *Align* option. You may also find it necessary to move the entire group to a new location.

New to UB 5!

Figure 2.10

Choose the alignment for multiple selected controls from the Align submenu.

Figure 2.11

Resize multiple selected controls to make them all the same size using the Make Same Size submenu.

You can also set the spacing between controls using the *Horizontal Spacing* (Figure 2.12) and/or *Vertical Spacing* (Figure 2.13) options on the *Format* menu. Using these options you can create equal spacing between controls, or you can increase or decrease the space between controls.

Change the horizontal alignment of multiple selected controls using the Horizontal Spacing submenu.

Change the vertical alignment of multiple selected controls using the Vertical Spacing submenu.

Another way to align controls on a form is to select them and set their location using properties. For example, if you have a group of controls to align vertically, select them all and set their Left property to the same value. You can also set the Width property so the controls are all the same size. If you want to set the controls to align horizontally, set them to the same Top property. See Figure 2.14.

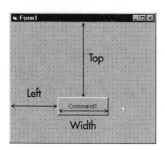

A control's Top property is its distance in twips from the top of the form; the Left property is its distance from left edge of the form, and the Width property is the width of the control.

The numbers you see in the Settings box for Left, Top, and Width may look strange. The measurements are shown in twips, which is a measuring system from the printing industry. One **twip** is $\frac{1}{20}$ of a printer's point or $\frac{1}{1440}$ of an inch. If you define a control to be 1440 twips wide, theoretically it is 1 inch wide. Actually, when it prints on the printer, it is 1 inch. However, on the screen it may be smaller or larger, depending on the resolution of monitors.

Designing Your Applications for User Convenience

One of the goals of good programming is to create programs that are easy to use. Your user interface should be clear and consistent. One school of thought says that if users misuse a program, it's the fault of the programmer, not the users. Since most of your users will already know how to operate Windows programs, you should strive to make your programs look and behave like other Windows programs. Some of the ways to accomplish this goal are to use controls in the standard way, define keyboard access keys, set a default command button, and make the Tab key work correctly.

Designing the User Interface

The design of the screen should be easy to understand and "comfortable" for the user. The best way that we can accomplish these goals is to follow industry standards in relation to color, size, and placement of controls. Once users become accustomed to a screen design, they will expect (and feel more familiar with) applications that follow the same design criteria. Design your applications to match other Windows applications. Take some time to examine the screens and dialog boxes in Microsoft Office as well as those in Visual Basic.

Microsoft has done extensive program testing with users of different ages, genders, nationalities, and disabilities. We should take advantage of this research and follow the guidelines.

One recommendation about interface design concerns color. You have probably noticed that Windows applications are predominantly gray. A reason is that many people are color blind. Also, gray is easiest and best for the majority of users. Although you may personally prefer brighter colors, if you want your applications to look professional, you will stick with gray.

Colors can indicate to the user what is expected. Use a white background for text boxes to indicate that the user is to input information. Use a gray background for labels, which the user cannot change. Labels that will display a message or result of a calculation should have a border around them; labels that provide a caption on the screen should have no border (the default).

Group your controls on the form to aid the user. A good practice is to create frames to hold related items, especially those controls that require user input. This visual aid helps the user understand the information that is being presented or requested.

Use a sans serif font on your forms, such as the default MS Sans Serif, and do not make them boldface. Limit large font sizes to a few items, such as the company name.

Defining Keyboard Access Keys

Many people prefer to use the keyboard, rather than use a mouse, for most operations. Windows is set up so that most everything can be done with either the keyboard or a mouse. You can make your projects respond to the keyboard by defining **access keys**. For example, in Figure 2.15 you can select the OK button with Alt + o and the Exit button with Alt + x.

Figure 2.15

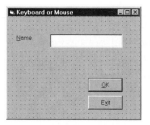

You can set access keys for command buttons, option buttons, and check boxes when you define their Caption properties. Type an ampersand (&) in front of the character you want for the access key; Visual Basic underlines the character.

For example, type the following Captions:

&OK	for OK
E&xit	for Exit

When you define access keys, you need to watch for several pitfalls. First, try to use the Windows-standard keys whenever possible. For example, use the x of Exit and the S of Save. Second, make sure you don't give two controls the same access key—it confuses the user. The first time he presses the access key, it selects the first button; the next time he presses the same key, it selects a different button.

Setting the Default and Cancel Properties of Command Buttons

Are you a keyboard user? If so, do you mind having to pick up the mouse and click a button after typing text into a text box? Once a person's fingers are on the keyboard, most people prefer to press the Enter key, rather than to click the mouse. If one of the command buttons on the form is the *default button,* pressing Enter is the same as clicking the button. You can always identify the default button on a form by its darker outline. Referring to Figure 2.15, the OK button is the default.

You can make one of your command buttons the default button by setting its **Default property** to True. When the user presses Enter, that button is automatically selected.

You can also select a *cancel button.* The cancel button is the button that is selected when the user presses the Esc key. You can make a command button the cancel button by setting its **Cancel property** to True. An example of a good time to set the Cancel property is on a form with OK and Cancel buttons. You may want to set the Default property to True for the OK button and the Cancel property to True for the Cancel button.

Setting the Tab Order for Controls

In Windows programs, one control on the form always has the **focus**. You can see the focus change as you Tab from control to control. For controls such as command buttons and option buttons, the focus appears as a light dotted line. For text boxes, the insertion point (also called the cursor) appears inside the box.

Some controls can receive the focus; others cannot. For example, text boxes and command buttons can receive the focus, but labels and images cannot.

The Tab Order

Two properties determine whether the focus stops on a control and the order in which the focus moves. Controls that are capable of receiving focus have a **TabStop property**, which you can set to True or False. If you do not want the focus to stop on a control when the user presses the Tab key, set the Tab-Stop property to False.

The **TabIndex property** determines the order the focus moves as the Tab key is pressed. As you create controls on your form, Visual Basic assigns the TabIndex property in sequence. Most of the time that order is correct, but if you want to Tab in some other sequence or if you add controls later, you will need to modify the TabIndex properties of your controls.

When your program begins running, the focus is on the control with the lowest TabIndex (usually 0). Since you want the insertion point to appear in the first text box on the form, its TabIndex should be set to 0. The next text box should be set to 1; the next to 2; and so forth.

You may be puzzled by the properties of labels, which have a TabIndex property, but not a TabStop. A label cannot receive focus, but it has a location in the tab sequence. This fact allows you to create keyboard access keys for text boxes. When the user types an access key, such as Alt + N, the focus jumps to the first TabIndex following the label. See Figure 2.16.

Figure 2.16

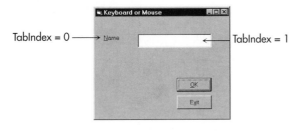

To use keyboard access keys for a text box, the TabIndex of the label must precede the TabIndex of the text box.

Setting the Form's Location on the Screen

When your project runs, the form will appear in the upper-left corner of the screen by default. The easiest way to choose a location for your form is to use the (new to VB 5) Form Layout window (Figure 2.17). Drag the image of the form to the screen location where you want the form to appear. Figure 2.18 shows the setting to make your form appear centered on the screen.

New to VB 5!

Figure 2.17

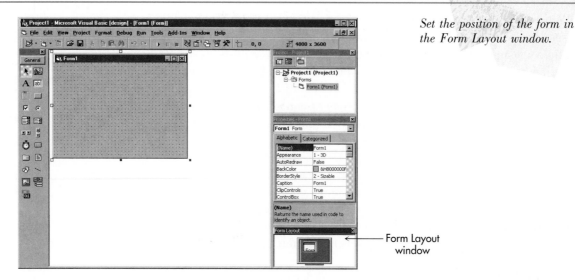

Set the position of the form in the Form Layout window.

Form Layout window

Figure 2.18

Drag the form to the center of the screen.

You can also set the form's screen position by setting the StartupPosition property of the form. Figure 2.19 shows your choices for the property setting. To center your form on the user's screen, set the StartupPosition property to *2-Center Screen*.

Figure 2.19

Set the StartupPosition property of the form to 2-Center Screen to make the form appear in the center of the screen.

Coding for the Controls

You already know how to set initial properties for controls at design time. You may also want to set some properties in code, as your project executes. You can clear out the contents of text boxes and labels; reset the focus; and change font attributes, such as bold, underline, italic, and the color of text.

Clearing Text Boxes and Labels

You can clear out the contents of a text box or label by setting the property to an **empty string**. Use "" (no space between the two quotation marks). This empty string is also called a *null string*.

Examples

```
txtName.Text = ""           'Clear the contents
lblMessage.Caption = ""     'Clear the contents
```

Resetting the Focus

As your program runs, you want the insertion point to appear in the text box where the user is expected to type. The focus should begin in the first text box. But what about later? If you clear the form's text boxes, you should reset the focus to the first text box. The **SetFocus method** handles this situation. Remember, the convention is Object.Method, so the statement to set the insertion point in the text box called txtName is

```
txtName.SetFocus    'Make the insertion point appear here
```

Setting the Value Property of Option Buttons and Check Boxes

Of course, the purpose of option buttons and check boxes is to allow the user to make selections. However, often you need to select or deselect an option in code. You can select or deselect option buttons and check boxes at design time (to set initial status) or at run time (to respond to an event).

To make an option button appear selected initially, set its Value property to True in the Properties window. In code, assign True to its Value property:

```
optRed.Value = True    'Make button selected
```

For check boxes, the procedure is slightly different, since the Value property has three settings: 0 – unchecked, 1 – checked, and 2 – grayed. You can set the initial state by making a selection in the Properties window. At run time, use these code statements:

```
chkBold.Value = 1      'Make box checked
chkItalic.Value = 0    'Make box unchecked
```

You can also use the Basic keywords `Checked` and `Unchecked` to set the Value property in code:

```
chkBold.Value = Checked        'Make box checked
chkItalic.Value = Unchecked    'Make box unchecked
```

Although a check box's Value property is set to 0, 1, or 2, sometimes you can treat its Value as True or False. For example, you can assign the Value of a check box to another property that must be True or False:

```
optDisplay.Value = chkScreen.Value    'Set option button Value _
                                       to check box Value
```

In the previous example, the Value of the option button will be set to True if the check box is checked and to False if the check box is unchecked.

Feedback 2.2

1. Write the Basic statements to clear the text box called txtCompany and reset the insertion point into the box.
2. Write the Basic statements to clear the label called lblCustomer and place the insertion point into a text box called txtOrder.
3. What will be the effect of each of these Basic statements?
   (a) `chkPrint.Value = 1`
   (b) `optColor.Value = False`
   (c) `imgDrawing.Visible = False`
   (d) `lblLocation.BorderStyle = 1`
       `lblLocation.Appearance = 1`
   (e) `lblCity.Caption = txtCity.Text`

Changing the Font Properties of Controls

It is easy to define initial properties of a text box or a label. You just select *Font* in the Properties window and display the *Font* dialog box. There you can change the name of the font, the size, the style (bold, italic, underline), and the color. But what if you want to change Font properties while the program is running? For that, you need to set Font properties in code.

Visual Basic has a special object called a **Font object**. A Font object has several properties, including Name, Size, Bold, Italic, Underline, and StrikeThrough. You can set each of the properties for the Font object and access it through the Font property of a control.

Examples

```
txtName.Font.Bold = True      'Set the font to bold
lblMessage.Font.Size = 12     'Change to 12-point font
lblTitle.Font.Italic = True   'Set the font to italic
```

Changing the Color of Text

You can change the color of text by changing the **ForeColor property** of a control. Actually, most controls have a ForeColor and a BackColor property. The ForeColor property changes the color of the text; the BackColor property controls the color around the text.

The Color Constants

Visual Basic provides an easy way to specify some of the most-used colors. These eight names are called **color constants**.

```
vbBlack
vbRed
vbGreen
vbYellow
vbBlue
vbMagenta
vbCyan
vbWhite
```

Examples

```
txtName.ForeColor = vbRed
lblMessage.ForeColor = vbWhite
```

Changing Multiple Properties of a Control

By now you can see that there are times when you want to change several properties of a single control. In versions of Visual Basic previous to version 4, you had to write out the entire name (Object.Property) for each statement.

Examples

```
txtTitle.Visible = True
txtTitle.ForeColor = vbWhite
txtTitle.Font.Bold = True
txtTitle.Font.Italic = True
txtTitle.SetFocus
```

Of course, you can still specify the statements this way, but now Visual Basic provides a statement to make this task easier—the With and End With.

The With and End With Statements—General Form

```
With ObjectName
     Statement(s)
End With
```

You specify an object name in the **With** statement. All subsequent statements until the **End With** relate to that object.

The With and End With Statements—Examples

```
With txtTitle
     .Visible = True
     .ForeColor = vbWhite
     .Font.Bold = True
     .Font.Italic = True
     .SetFocus
End With
```

The statements beginning with `With` and ending with `End With` are called a *With block*. The statements inside the block are indented for readability. Although indentation is not required by VB, it is required by good programming practices.

The real advantage of using the `With` statement, rather than spelling out the object for each statement, is that `With` is more efficient. Your Visual Basic projects will run a little faster if you use `With`. On a large, complicated project, the savings can be significant.

Concatenating Text

At times you need to join strings of text. For example, you may want to join a literal and a property. You can "tack" one string of characters to the end of another, in the process called **concatenation**. Use an ampersand (&), preceded and followed by a space, between the two strings.

Examples

```
lblMessage.Caption = "Your name is: " & txtName.Text
txtNameAndAddress.Text = txtName.Text & txtAddress.Text
lblFontSize.Caption = "The current fontsize is " & txtMessage.Font.Size & " points."
```

Continuing Long Program Lines

Basic interprets the code on one line as one statement. You can type *very* long lines in the Basic Code window; the window scrolls sideways and allows you to keep typing. However, this method is inconvenient. It isn't easy to see your program code, and printers can't handle the extra width. (Some printers wrap long lines to the next line; others just drop the extra characters.)

When a Basic statement becomes too long for one line, use a **line-continuation character**. You can type a space and an underscore, press Enter, and continue the statement on the next line. It is OK to indent the continued lines. The only restriction is that the line-continuation character must appear between elements; you cannot place a continuation in the middle of a literal or split the name of an object or property.

> # Tip
>
> **A**lthough Basic allows concatenation with the + operator, the practice is not advised. Depending on the contents of the text box, the compiler may interpret the + operator as an addition operator rather than a concatenation operator, giving unpredictable results.

Examples

```
lblGreetings.Caption = "Greetings " & txtName.Text & ": " & _
    "You have been selected to win a free prize. " & _
    "Just send us $100 for postage and handling."
```

Using the Default Property of a Control

Each class of control has one property that is the default property. When you use the default property of a control, you do not have name the property. For example, the Text property is the default property for a text box. Therefore, these two statements are equivalent:

```
txtCompany.Text = "R 'n R — for Reading 'n Refreshment"
txtCompany = "R 'n R — for Reading 'n Refreshment"
```

This text uses the complete form for consistency, readability, and understandability. You may choose to refer to the default property of controls in your projects, however. Table 2.1 shows controls and their default properties.

Table 2.1

Control	Default Property
Check box	Value
Combo box	Text
Command button	Value
Frame	Caption
Horizontal scroll bar	Value
Image	Picture
Label	Caption
Line	Visible
List box	Text
Menu	Enabled
Option button	Value
Picture box	Picture
Shape	Shape
Text box	Text
Timer	Enabled
Vertical scroll bar	Value

Controls and their default properties.

Your Hands-On Programming Example

For this example you will write a program that uses many of the new controls and topics introduced in this chapter. The program will input the user's name and a message, display the two items concatenated in a label, and change the format of the label. Using option buttons and check boxes for selection, the user can make the label bold, underlined, or italic, and change its color.

You will include command buttons to display the message in the label, clear the text boxes and label, print the form, and exit. Include keyboard access keys for the command buttons; make the Display button the default button and make the Clear button the cancel button.

Place a logo on the form. Actually, you will place two images with different sizes for the logo on the form. Each time the user clicks on the logo, it will toggle the large and small versions of the logo.

Planning the Project

Sketch a form (Figure 2.20), which your users sign off as meeting their needs. *Note:* Although this may seem unnecessary, it is standard programming practice and documents that your users have been involved and approve the design.

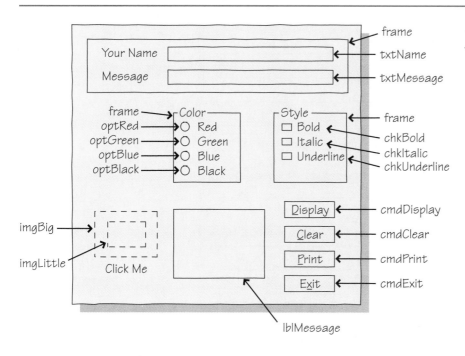

A planning sketch of the form for the hands-on programming example.

Plan the Objects and Properties

Plan the property settings for the form and for each control.

Object	Property	Setting	
Label1	Caption	Your Name:	
txtName	Name	txtName	
	Text	(blank)	
Label2	Caption	Message:	*Hint:* Do not change the name of this label.
txtMessage	Name	txtMessage	
	Text	(blank)	
			(continued)

Object	Property	Setting	
fraColor	Name	fraColor	
	Caption	Color	
optRed	Name	optRed	*Hint:* Don't forget to draw the option buttons *inside* the frame.
	Caption	&Red	
optGreen	Name	optGreen	
	Caption	&Green	
optBlue	Name	optBlue	
	Caption	&Blue	
optBlack	Name	optBlack	
	Caption	B&lack	
fraStyle	Name	fraStyle	
	Caption	Style	
chkBold	Name	chkBold	
	Caption	B&old	
chkItalic	Name	chkItalic	
	Caption	&Italic	
chkUnderline	Name	chkUnderline	*Hint:* If you can't see option button or checkbox captions, make your objects wider.
	Caption	&Underline	
imgBig	Name	imgBig	
	Stretch	True	
	Picture	VB\ICONS\COMPUTER\CDROM01.ICO	
	Visible	True	
imgLittle	Name	imgLittle (Note that the two images are in the same location, one on top of the other.)	
	Stretch	True	
	Picture	VB\ICONS\COMPUTER\CDROM02.ICO	
	Visible	False	
Label3 (or some other number)	Caption	Click Me	
lblMessage	Name	lblMessage	
	Caption	(blank)	
	Alignment	2 - Center	
	Appearance	1 - 3D	

(continued)

Object	Property	Setting
lblMessage	Name	lblMessage
	BorderStyle	1 - Fixed Single
cmdDisplay	Name	cmdDisplay
	Caption	&Display
	Default	True
cmdClear	Name	cmdClear
	Caption	&Clear
	Cancel	True
cmdPrint	Name	cmdPrint
	Caption	&Print
cmdExit	Name	cmdExit
	Caption	E&xit

Plan the Event Procedures

You will need event procedures for each command button, option button, check box, and image.

Procedure	Actions—Pseudocode
cmdDisplay_Click	Set lblMessage to both the name and message from the text boxes (concatenate them).
cmdClear_Click	Clear the two text boxes and label. Reset the focus in the first text box.
cmdPrint_Click	Print the form.
cmdExit_Click	End the project.
optRed_Click	Make the ForeColor of lblMessage red.
optGreen_Click	Make the ForeColor of lblMessage green.
optBlue_Click	Make the ForeColor of lblMessage blue.
optBlack_Click	Make the ForeColor of lblMessage black.
chkBold_Click	Set lblMessage's Font.Bold property to match the check box (selected or deselected).
chkItalic_Click	Set lblMessage's Font.Italic property to match the check box (selected or deselected).
chkUnderline_Click	Set lblMessage's Font.Underline property to match the check box (selected or deselected).
imgBig_Click	Make imgBig invisible (Visible = False). Make imgLittle visible (Visible = True).
imgLittle_Click	Make imgLittle invisible. Make imgBig visible.

Write the Project

Follow the sketch in Figure 2.20 to create the form. Figure 2.21 shows the completed form.

● Set the properties of each of the objects, as you have planned.

● Working from the pseudocode, write each event procedure.

● When you complete the code, thoroughly test the project.

Figure 2.21

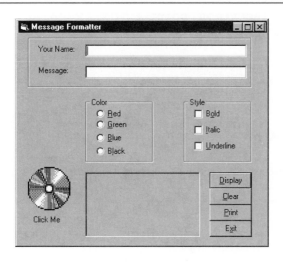

The form for the hands-on programming example.

The Project Coding Solution

```
'Project:      Chapter Example 2.1
'Date:         July 1997
'Programmer:   J.C. Bradley
'Description:   This project uses labels, text boxes, option buttons,
'              check boxes, images, and command buttons to change
'              the properties of text.
'Folder:       Ch0201
Option Explicit
```

```
Private Sub chkBold_Click()
    'Change the message text to/from bold

    lblMessage.Font.Bold = chkBold.Value
End Sub
```

```
Private Sub chkItalic_Click()
    'Change the message text to/from italic

    lblMessage.Font.Italic = chkItalic.Value
End Sub
```

```vb
Private Sub chkUnderline_Click()
    'Change the message text to/from underline

    lblMessage.Font.Underline = chkUnderline.Value
End Sub
```

```vb
Private Sub cmdClear_Click()
    'Clear the text controls

    With txtName
        .Text = ""      'Clear the text box
        .SetFocus       'Reset the insertion point
    End With
    lblMessage.Caption = ""
    txtMessage.Text = ""
End Sub
```

```vb
Private Sub cmdDisplay_Click()
    'Display the text in the message area

    lblMessage.Caption = txtName.Text & ": " & txtMessage.Text
End Sub
```

```vb
Private Sub cmdExit_Click()
    'Exit the project

    End
End Sub
```

```vb
Private Sub cmdPrint_Click()
    'Print the form

    PrintForm
End Sub
```

```vb
Private Sub imgBig_Click()
    'Switch the icon

    imgBig.Visible = False
    imgLittle.Visible = True
End Sub
```

```vb
Private Sub imgLittle_Click()
    'Switch the icon

    imgLittle.Visible = False
    imgBig.Visible = True
End Sub
```

```
Private Sub optBlack_Click()
    'Make label black

    lblMessage.ForeColor = vbBlack
End Sub
```

```
Private Sub optBlue_Click()
    'Make label blue

    lblMessage.ForeColor = vbBlue
End Sub
```

```
Private Sub optGreen_Click()
    'Make label green

    lblMessage.ForeColor = vbGreen
End Sub
```

```
Private Sub optRed_Click()
    'Make label red

    lblMessage.ForeColor = vbRed
End Sub
```

Programming Hints

1. To make the text in a text box right justified or centered, you must set the Multiline property to True, in addition to setting the Alignment property.
2. You can use the Value property of a check box to set other properties that must be True or False. For example:

```
txtMessage.Font.Bold = chkBold.Value   'Sets Bold property to True or _
                                        False to match check box
```

3. Always test the tab order on your forms. Fix it if necessary by changing the TabIndex properties.
4. You can create multiple controls of the same type without clicking on the tool in the toolbox every time. To create the first of a series, Ctrl—click on the tool; the tool will remain active and allow you to keep drawing more controls. Click on the pointer tool (the arrow) when you are finished.
5. Always remember to create an option button inside its frame. If you double-click to create an option button, it does not belong to the frame. You can make an option button belong to a frame by cutting and pasting it inside the frame.
6. Use text boxes when you want the user to enter or change the text. Use label controls when you do not want the user to change the data. You can set the BorderStyle and BackColor properties of a label so that it looks just like a text box, but cannot be changed.

S u m m a r y

1. Text boxes are used primarily for user input. The Text property holds the value input by the user. You can also assign a literal to the text property during run time.

2. Frames are used as containers for other controls and to group like items on a form.

3. Check boxes and option buttons allow the user to make choices. In a group of option buttons, only one can be selected; but in a group of check boxes, any number of the boxes may be selected.

4. Image controls hold a graphic, which is assigned to the Picture property.

5. The Appearance property of many controls can be set to 0 – Flat or 1 – 3D, which determines whether the control appears flat or three-dimensional.

6. You can select multiple controls and treat them as a group, including setting common properties at once, moving them, or aligning them.

7. Make your programs easier to use by following Windows standard guidelines for colors, control size and placement, access keys, default and cancel buttons, and tab order.

8. Define keyboard access keys by including an ampersand in the caption of command buttons, option buttons, and check boxes.

9. Set the Default property of one command button to True so that the user can press Enter to select the button. If you set the Cancel property to True, the button will be selected when the user presses the Esc key.

10. The focus moves from control to control as the user presses the Tab key. The sequence for tabbing is determined by the TabIndex properties of the controls.

11. Clear the Text property of a text box or the Caption property of a label by setting it to an empty string.

12. To place the insertion point into a text box as the program is running, use the SetFocus method.

13. To change font attributes of a text box or a label, use the Font property of the control. The Font property refers to a Font object with properties for bold, italic, underline, size, etc.

14. Change the color of text in a control by changing the ForeColor property.

15. You can use the Visual Basic color constants to change colors during run time.

16. The `With` and `End With` statements provide an easy way to refer to an object multiple times without repeating the object's name.

17. Joining two strings of text is called *concatenation* and is accomplished by placing an ampersand between the two elements. (A space must precede and follow the ampersand.)

18. Use a space and an underscore to continue a long statement on another line.

19. Using the default property of a control allows you to refer to an object without naming the property.

Key Terms

Review Questions

1. You can display program output in a text box or a label. When should you use a text box? When is a label appropriate?

2. How does the behavior of option buttons differ from the behavior of check boxes?

3. If you want two groups of option buttons on a form, how can you make the groups operate independently?

4. Explain how to make a graphic appear in an image control.

5. Describe how to select several labels and set them all to 12-point font size with one command.

6. What is the purpose of keyboard access keys? How can you define them in your project? How do they operate at run time?

7. Explain the purpose of the Default and Cancel properties of command buttons. Give an example of a good use for each.

8. What is the focus? How can you control which object has the focus?

9. Assume you are testing your project and don't like the initial position of the insertion point. Explain how to make the insertion point appear in a different text box when the program begins.

10. During program execution you want to return the insertion point to a text box called txtAddress. What Basic statement will make that happen?

11. What Basic statements will clear the current contents of a text box and a label?

12. Explain how to change a label's Caption to italic at design time and at run time.

13. How are the With and End With statements used? Give an example.

14. What is concatenation and when would it be useful?

15. Explain how to continue a very long Basic statement onto another line.

16. What is the default property of a control? Give an example.

P r o g r a m m i n g   E x e r c i s e s

2.1 Create a project that will switch a light bulb on and off, using the user interface shown below as a guide.

Form: Include a text box for the user to enter his/her name. Create two images, one on top of the other. Only one will be visible at a time. Use option buttons to select the color of the text in the label beneath the light bulb image.

Include keyboard access keys for the option buttons and the command buttons. Make the Print button the default button and the Exit button the cancel button.

Project operation: The user will enter a name and click an option button for the color (not necessarily in that order). When the light bulb is clicked, display the other image and change the message below it. Concatenate the user name to the end of the message.

The two icon files are

VB\ICONS\MISC\LIGHTOFF.ICO
VB\ICONS\MISC\LIGHTON.ICO

(You will need to find the location of the VB directory in order to find the icons.)

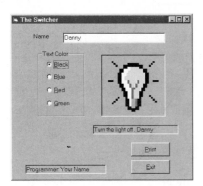 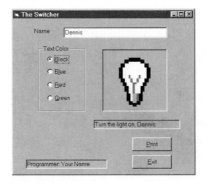

Coding: In the click event for each Color option button, change the color of the message below the light bulb. In the click event for the Print command button, print the form.

2.2 Write a project that will display the flags of four different countries, depending on the setting of the option buttons. In addition, display the name of the country in the large label under the flag image. The user can also choose to display or hide the form's title, the country name, and the name of the programmer. Use check boxes for the display/hide choices.

Include keyboard access keys for all option buttons, check boxes, and command buttons. Make the Print button the default button and the Exit button the cancel button.

You can choose the countries and flags. You will find more than 20 flag icons in VB\ICONS\FLAGS.

Hints: When a project begins running, the focus goes to the control with the lowest TabIndex. Since that is likely an option button, one button will appear selected. You must either display the first flag to match the option button or make the focus begin in a different control. You might consider beginning the focus on one of the command buttons.

Set the Visible property of a control to the Value property of the corresponding check box. That way when the check box is selected, the control becomes visible.

Since all three selectable controls will be visible when the project begins, set the Value property of the three check boxes to *1 - Selected* at design time. Set the images to *Visible = False* so they won't appear at startup. (If you plan to display one image at startup, its Visible property must be set to True.)

Rather than stack the images as was done in the chapter example, you might consider another method of setting up the four flag images. Try placing four small invisible flag icons near the bottom of the form. When the user selects a different country's flag, set the Picture property of the large flag image to the Picture property of one of the small, invisible images.

Example:

```
imgFlag.Picture = imgMexico.Picture
```

Make sure to set the Stretch property of the large image control to True.

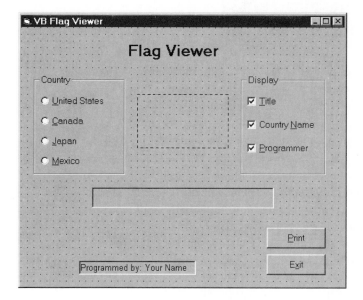

2.3   Write a project that will display a weather report. The user can choose one of the option buttons and display an icon and a message. The message should give the weather report in words and include the person's name (taken from the text box at the top of the form). For example, if the user chooses the Sunny button, you might display "It looks like sunny weather today, John" (assuming that the user entered "John" in the text box).

Include keyboard access keys for the option buttons and command buttons. Make the Exit button the cancel button.

You might consider the method of hiding and displaying images described in the hints for exercise 2. The four icons displayed are in the VB\ICONS\ELEMENTS subdirectory and are called CLOUD.ICO, RAIN.ICO, SNOW.ICO, and SUN.ICO.

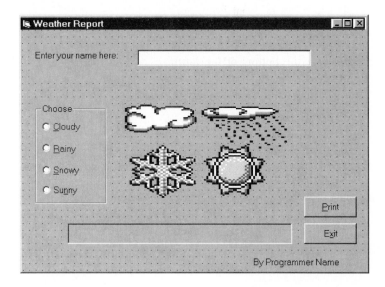

2.4   Write a project that will input the user name and display a message of the day in a label, along with the user's name. Include command buttons (with keyboard access keys) for Display, Clear, Print, and Exit. Make the Display button the default button and the Clear button the cancel button.

Include a group of option buttons for users to select the font size of the message. Give them a choice of three different sizes. *Hint:* Display the *Font* dialog box from the Properties window to determine the available sizes. Make sure your message label is large enough to display the longest message in the largest font size.

Make your form display a changeable image. You can use the happy face icon files or any other images you have available (VB\ICONS\MISC\FACE01.ICO, FACE02.ICO, and FACE03.ICO).

You may choose to have only one message of the day, or you can have several that the user can select from option buttons. You might want to choose messages that go with the different face icons.

Optional extra: Include check boxes to change the font attributes of the message. Include Bold, Underline, Italic, and StrikeThru. Make sure to include keyboard access keys.

2.5 Create a project that will allow the user to input information and then display the lines of output for a mailing label.

Remember that fields to be input by the user require text boxes while information to be displayed belongs in labels. Use text boxes for first name, last name, street address, city, state, and ZIP code; give meaningful names to the text boxes and set the Captions to blank. Add appropriate labels to each text box to indicate to the user what data will be entered into each box.

Use command buttons for Display Label Info, Clear, Print Form, and Exit. Make the Display button the default button and the Clear button the cancel button.

Use three labels for displaying the information for Line 1, Line 2, and Line 3.

A click event on the Display Label Info command button will display the following:

Line 1—The first name and last name concatenated together.
Line 2—The street address.
Line 3—The city, state, and ZIP code concatenated together. (Make sure to concatenate a comma and a space between the city and state using ", ", and 2 spaces between the state and ZIP code).

CASE STUDIES

Design and code a project that has shipping information.

VB Mail Order

Use an appropriate image in the upper-left corner of the form.

Use text boxes with labels attached for Catalog Code, Page Number, and Part Number.

Use two groups of option buttons on the form; enclose each group in a frame. The first frame should have a Caption of Shipping and contain buttons for Express and Ground. Use a Caption of Payment Type on the second frame and include buttons for Charge, COD, and Money Order.

Use a check box for New Customer.

Add command buttons for Print Form, Clear, and Exit. Make the Clear button the cancel button.

VB Auto Center

Modify the project from the Chapter 1 VB Auto Center case study, replacing the command buttons with images. Place a label above each image that indicates which department or command the image represents. A click on an image will produce the appropriate information in the special notices label.

Add an image that allows the form to be printed as well as an image that will clear the special notices label.

Add two option buttons that will allow the user to view the special notices label in 10-point font or 14-point font. Make sure that the label is large enough to hold the 14-point message.

Include a check box labeled Hours. When the check box is selected, a new label will display the message "Open 24 Hours--7 days a week".

Department/Command	Image
Auto Sales	vb\graphics\icons\industry\cars
Service Center	vb\graphics\icons\industry\wrench
Detail Shop	vb\graphics\icons\elements\water
Employment Opportunities	vb\graphics\icons\mail\mail12
Exit	vb\graphics\icons\computer\msgbox1
Print Form	vb\graphics\icons\dragdrop\drag1pg

3

Variables, Constants, and Calculations

At the completion of this chapter, you will be able to...

1. Distinguish between variables, constants, and controls.

2. Differentiate among the various data types.

3. Apply naming conventions incorporating standards and indicating scope and data type.

4. Declare variables using the `Dim` statement.

5. Select the appropriate scope for a variable.

6. Convert text input to numeric values using the `Val` function.

7. Perform calculations using variables and constants.

8. Accumulate sums and generate counts.

9. Format data for output.

10. Modify the environment to require `Option Explicit`.

In this chapter you will learn to do calculations in Visual Basic. You will start with text values input by the user, convert them to numeric values, and perform calculations on them. You will also learn to format the results of your calculations and display them for the user.

Although the calculations themselves are quite simple (adding, subtracting, multiplying, and dividing), there are some important issues to discuss first. You must learn about variables and constants, the various types of data used by Visual Basic, and how and where to declare variables and constants. Variables are declared differently, depending on where you want to use them and how long you need to retain their values.

The code below is a small preview that shows calculating the product of two text boxes. The first group of statements (the `Dims`) declares the variables and their data types. The second group of statements converts the text box contents to numeric and places the values into the variables. The last line performs the multiplication and places the result into a variable. The following sections of this chapter describe how to set up your code for calculations.

```
'Dimension the variables
Dim iQuantity          As Integer
Dim cPrice             As Currency

'Convert input text to numeric and assign values to variables
iQuantity = Val(txtQuantity.Text)
cPrice = Val(txtPrice.Text)

'Calculate the product
cExtendedPrice = iQuantity * cPrice
```

Data—Variables and Constants

So far, all data you have used in your projects have been properties of objects. You have worked with the Text property of Text Boxes and the Caption property of Labels. Now it is time to consider working with values that are not properties. Basic allows you to set up locations in memory and give each location a name. You can visualize each memory location as a scratch pad; the contents of the scratch pad can change as the need arises. In this example, the memory location is called *iMaximum*.

iMaximum = 100

iMaximum
100

After executing this statement, the value of iMaximum is 100. You can change the value of iMaximum, use it in calculations, or display it in a control.

In the preceding example, the memory location called iMaximum is a **variable**. Memory locations that hold data that can be changed during project execution are called *variables;* locations that hold data that cannot change during execution are called **constants**. For example, a customer's name will vary as the information for each individual is being processed. However, the name of the company and the sales tax rate will remain the same (at least for that day).

When you declare a variable or a named constant, Visual Basic reserves an area of memory and assigns it a name, called an **identifier.** You specify identifier names according to the rules of Basic as well as some recommended naming conventions.

The **declaration** statements establish your project's variables and constants, give them names, and specify the type of data they will hold. The statements are not considered executable; that is, they are not executed in the flow of instructions during program execution.

Here are some sample declaration statements:

```
Dim stName As String                 'Declare a string variable
Dim iCounter As Integer              'Declare an integer variable
Const cDISCOUNT_RATE As Currency = .15 'Declare a named constant
```

The next few paragraphs describe the data types, the rules for naming variables and constants, and the format of the declarations.

Data Types

The **data type** of a variable or constant indicates what type of information will be stored in the allocated memory space: perhaps a name, a dollar amount, a date, or a total. Note that the default data type is **variant**. If you do not specify a data type, your variables and constants will be variants. The advantage of using variant data type is that it's easy, and the variables and constants change their appearance as needed for each situation. The disadvantage is that variants are less efficient than the other data types; they require more memory and operate less quickly. The best practice is to always specify the data type.

Data Type	Use For
Boolean	True or False values.
Byte	A single ASCII character (code 0 to 255).
Currency	Decimal fractions, such as dollars and cents.
Date	An eight-character date.
Double	Double-precision floating-point numbers with 14 digits of accuracy.
Integer	Whole numbers in the range −32,768 to 32,767.
Long	Larger whole numbers.
Single	Single-precision floating point numbers with six digits of accuracy.
String	Alphanumeric data: letters, digits, and other characters.
Variant	Converts from one type to another, as needed.

The most common types of variables and constants we will use are string, integer, and currency. When deciding which data type to use, follow this guideline: If the data will be used in a calculation, then it must be numeric (usually integer or currency); if it is not used in a calculation, it will be string. Use currency as the data type for any decimal fractions in business applications; single and double data types are generally used in scientific applications.

Consider the following examples:

Contents	Data Type	Reason
Social Security number	String	Not used in a calculation.
Pay rate	Currency	Used in a calculation, contains a decimal point.
Hours worked	Currency	Used in a calculation, may contain a decimal point. (Currency can be used for any decimal fraction, not just dollars.)
Phone number	String	Not used in a calculation.
Quantity	Integer	Used in calculations, contains a whole number.

Naming Rules

Each programmer has to name (identify) the variables and named constants that will be used in a project. Basic requires identifiers for variables and named constants to follow these rules: names must be 1 to 255 characters in length; they may consist of letters, digits, and underscores; they cannot contain any spaces or periods; and they may not be reserved words. (Reserved words, also called *keywords*, are words to which Basic has assigned some meaning, such as *print, name,* and *value.*)

Naming Conventions

When naming variables and constants, you *must* follow the rules of Basic. In addition, you *should* follow some naming conventions. Conventions are the guidelines that separate good names from bad (or not so good) names. The meaning and use of all identifiers should always be clear.

Just as we established conventions for naming objects in Chapter 1, in this chapter we will adopt conventions for naming variables and constants. The following conventions are widely used in the programming industry:

1. Identifiers must be meaningful. Choose a name that clearly indicates its purpose. Do not abbreviate unless the meaning is obvious, and do not use very short identifiers, such as *X* or *Y.*
2. Precede each identifier with a lowercase prefix that specifies the data type. This convention is similar to the convention we already adopted for naming objects.
3. For variable names, capitalize each word of the name (following the prefix). Use mixed case for variable names, never all uppercase.

4. For named constants, use all uppercase following the prefix. Use underscore characters between the words to make names easier to read.

This text uses the following prefixes to specify data types:

b	Boolean
c	Currency
d	Double-precision floating point
i	Integer
l	Long integer
s	Single-precision floating point
st	string
v	Variant

Sample identifiers

Field of Data	Possible Identifier
Social Security number	stSocialSecurityNumber
Pay rate	cPayRate
Hours worked	cHoursWorked
Phone number	stPhoneNumber
Quantity	iQuantity
Tax rate (constant)	cTAX_RATE
Quota (constant)	iQUOTA
Population	lPopulation

Feedback 3.1

Indicate whether each of the following identifiers conforms to the rules of
Basic and to the naming conventions. If invalid, give the reason. Remember,
the answers to all Feedback questions are found in Appendix A.

1. omitted
2. i#Sold
3. i Number Sold
4. i.Number.Sold
5. s$Amount
6. Sub
7. stSub
8. Caption
9. conMaximum
10. MINIMUM_RATE
11. cMAXIMUM_CHECK
12. stCOMPANY_NAME

Constants—Named and Intrinsic

Constants provide a way to use words to describe a value that doesn't change. In Chapter 2 you used the Visual Basic constants vbBlue, vbRed, vbYellow, and so on. Those constants are built into Visual Basic—you don't need to define them anywhere. The constants that you define for yourself are called *named constants;* those that are built into VB are called *intrinsic constants.*

Named Constants

You declare named constants using the keyword `Const`. You give the constant a name, a data type, and a value. Once a value is declared as a constant, its value cannot be changed during the execution of the project. The data type that you declare and the data type of the value must match. For example, if you declare an integer constant, you must give it an integer value.

You will find two important advantages to using named constants rather than the actual values in code. The code is easier to read; for example, seeing the identifier cMAXIMUM_PAY is more meaningful than seeing a number, such as 1000. In addition, if you need to change the value at a later time, you need to change the constant declaration only once and not change every reference to it throughout the code.

Const Statement—General Form

```
Const Identifier [As Datatype] = Value
```

Naming conventions for constants require a prefix that identifies the data type and puts the name portion entirely in uppercase. The purpose of the uppercase is to make it obvious in other parts of the code that the identifer is a constant and therefore cannot have a new value assigned to it.

Although the data type is optional, the best practice is to always declare the data type. When you don't declare the data type, Visual Basic looks at the value given and chooses an appropriate data type.

This example sets the company name, address, and the sales tax rate as constants:

Const Statement—Examples

```
Const stCOMPANY_NAME As String = "R 'n R_for Reading 'n Refreshment"
Const stCOMPANY_ADDRESS As String = "101 S. Main Street"
Const cSALES_TAX_RATE As Currency = .08
```

Assigning Values to Constants

The values you assign to constants must follow certain rules. You have already seen that a text (string) value must be enclosed in quotation marks; numeric values are not so enclosed. However, you must be aware of some additional rules.

Numeric constants may contain only the digits (0–9), a decimal point, and a sign (+ or −) at the left side. You cannot include a comma, dollar sign, any other special characters, or a sign at the right side.

String literals (also called *string constants*) may contain letters, digits, and special characters, such as $ # @ % & *. The only problem comes when you want to include quotation marks inside a string literal, since quotation marks enclose the literal. The solution is to use two quotation marks together inside the literal; Visual Basic will interpret the pair as one symbol.

Example

`"He said, ""I like it."""` produces this string: `He said, "I like it."`

Although you can use numeric digits inside a string literal, remember that these numbers are text and cannot be used for calculations.

The string values are referred to as **string literal**s because they contain exactly (literally) whatever is inside the quotation marks.

Example constants

Data Type	Constant Value Example
Integer	5
	+25
	−170
	2000
Single or currency	101.25
	−5.0
String literals	`"Visual Basic"`
	`"ABC Incorporated"`
	`"1415 J Street"`
	`"102"`
	`"She said ""Hello."""`

Intrinsic Constants

Intrinsic constants are system-defined constants. Several sets of intrinsic constants are stored in library files and available for use in your Visual Basic programs. For example, the color constants you used in Chapter 2 are intrinsic constants.

Intrinsic constants use a two character prefix to indicate the source, such as *vb* for Visual Basic, *db* for Data Access Objects, and *xl* for Excel. In the next chapter we will use intrinsic constants for creating message boxes.

Declaring Variables

Although there are several ways to declare a variable, the most commonly used statement is the Dim statement.

Dim Statement—General Form

```
Dim Identifier [As Datatype]
```

If you omit the optional data type, the variable's type defaults to variant. It is best to always declare the type, even when you intend to use variants.

Dim Statement—Examples

```
Dim stCustomerName    As String
Dim iTotalSold        As Integer
Dim sTemperature      As Single
Dim cPrice            As Currency
Dim vChanging                      'Defaults to Variant type
```

The reserved word `Dim` is really short for *dimension*, which means "size." When you declare a variable, the amount of memory reserved depends on its data type. Table 3.1 shows the amount of memory allocated for each data type.

Data Type	Number of Bytes of Memory Allocated
Boolean	2
Byte	1
Currency	8
Date	8
Double	8
Integer	2
Long	4
Single	4
String (variable length)	10 bytes plus 1 byte for each character in the string.
Variant	Holding numbers—16 bytes. Holding characters—22 bytes plus 1 byte for each character in the string.

The amount of memory allocated for each data type.

Note: Visual Basic does not require you to declare a variable before using it—see "Programming Hints" at the end of this chapter for details.

Entering Dim Statements

Visual Basic's Auto Fill In feature helps you enter `Dim` statements. After you type the space that follows `Dim VariableName As`, a shortcut menu pops up (Figure 3.1). This list shows the possible entries for data type to complete the statement. The easiest way to complete the statement is to begin typing the correct entry; the list automatically scrolls to the correct section (Figure 3.2). When the correct entry is highlighted, press Enter, Tab, or the space bar to select the entry, or double-click if you prefer using the mouse.

New to UB 5!

Figure 3.1

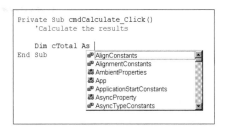

As soon as you type the space after **As**, *the Auto Fill In menu pops up. You can make a selection from the list with your mouse or the keyboard.*

Figure 3.2

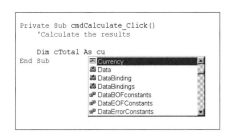

Type the first few characters of the data type and the Auto Fill In list will quickly scroll to the correct section. When the correct word is highlighted, press Enter, Tab, or the space bar to select the entry.

Note: Some people find the Auto Fill In feature annoying rather than helpful. You can turn off the feature by selecting *Tools/Options/Editor tab* and deselecting *Auto List Members*.

Feedback 3.2

Write a declaration for the following situations; make up an appropriate variable identifier.

1. You need variables for payroll processing to store the following:
   (a) Single-precision number of hours.
   (b) String employee's name.
   (c) Department number (not used in calculations).
2. You need variables for inventory control to store the following:
   (a) Integer quantity.
   (b) Description of the item.
   (c) Part number.
   (d) Cost.
   (e) Selling price.

Scope of Variables

A variable may exist and be visible for an entire project, for only one form, or for only one procedure. The visibility of a variable is referred to as its **scope**. *Visibility* really means "can this variable be used or 'seen' in this location." The scope is said to be global, module level, or local. A **global** variable may be used in all procedures of a project and will be discussed in

Chapter 6. **Module-level** variables are accessible from all procedures of a form. A **local** variable may be used only within the procedure in which it is declared.

The scope of a variable declared with a `Dim` statement is determined by where the declaration statement is made.

[handwritten margin note: life time of a variable is the period the variable exists.]

Variable Lifetime

When you create a variable, you must be aware of its **lifetime**. The *lifetime* of a variable is the period of time that the variable exists. The lifetime of a local variable is normally one execution of a procedure. For example, each time you execute a sub procedure, the local `Dim` statements are executed. Each variable is created as a "fresh" new one, with an initial value of 0 for numeric variables and an empty string for string variables. When the procedure finishes, its variables disappear; that is, their memory locations are released.

The lifetime of a module-level variable is the entire time the form is loaded, generally the lifetime of the entire project. If you want to maintain the value of a variable for multiple executions of a procedure, for example to calculate a running total, you must use a module-level variable (or a variable specified as Static, which is discussed in Chapter 6).

Local Declarations

Any variable that is declared inside a procedure is local in scope; it is known only to that procedure. A `Dim` statement may appear anywhere inside the procedure, as long as it appears prior to the first use of the variable in a statement. However, good programming practices dictate that all `Dim`s appear at the top of the procedure, prior to all other code statements (after the remarks).

```
Private Sub cmdCalculate_Click()
    'Calculate the price and discount

    Dim  iQuantity           As  Integer
    Dim  cPrice              As  Currency
    Dim  cExtendedPrice      As  Currency
    Dim  cDiscount           As  Currency
    Dim  cDiscountedPrice    As  Currency
    Const cDISCOUNT_RATE     As  Currency = 0.15

    'Convert input values to numeric variables
    iQuantity = Val(txtQuantity.Text)
    cPrice = Val(txtPrice.Text)

    'Calculate values
    cExtendedPrice = iQuantity * cPrice
    cDiscount = cExtendedPrice * cDISCOUNT_RATE
    cDiscountedPrice = cExtendedPrice - cDiscount
```

Notice the `Const` statement in the preceding example. You can declare named constants to be local, module-level, or global in scope, just as you can variables.

Module-Level Declarations

At times you need to be able to use a variable or constant in more than one procedure of a form. When you declare a variable or constant as module-level, it may be used anywhere in that form. Place the declarations (`Dim` or `Const`) for module-level variables and constants in the general declarations section of the form. (Recall that you have been using the general declarations section for remarks since Chapter 1.) If you wish to accumulate a sum or count items for multiple executions of a procedure, you should declare the variable at the module level.

Figure 3.3 illustrates the locations for coding local variables and module-level variables.

Figure 3.3

```
(General Declarations section)

Option Explicit
Dim ModuleLevelVariables
Const ModuleLevelConstants
_____

Private Sub cmdCalculate_Click
    Dim LocalVariables
    Const LocalConstants

    ...
End Sub
_____

Private Sub cmdSummarize_Click
    Dim LocalVariables
    Const LocalConstants

    ...
End Sub
_____

Private Sub cmdInitialize_Click
    Dim LocalVariables
    Const LocalConstants
    ...
End Sub
_____
```

The variables you dimension inside a procedure are local. Variables that you dimension in the General Declarations section of a form are module level.

```
'General Declarations section of a form

Option Explicit

'Dimension module-level variables
Dim miQuantitySum          As  Integer
Dim mcDiscountSum          As  Currency
Dim miSaleCount            As  Integer
```

Including the Scope in Identifiers

When you use variables and constants, it is important to know their scope. For that reason you should include scope information in your naming conventions. To indicate a module-level variable or constant, place a prefix of m before the identifier. Local variables and constants do not have an additional prefix, so any variable without an initial m can be assumed to be local.

M ar a prefix indicates variable as module level

Examples

```
Dim mcTotalPay As Currency
```

Note that the m stands for module level, and the c stands for currency data type.

```
Const miNUMBER_QUESTIONS As Integer = 50
```

The m stands for module level, and the i stands for integer data type.

Coding Module-Level Declarations

To enter module-level declarations, you must be in the Code window, in the General Declarations section (Figure 3.4). Recall how to display the General Declarations section:

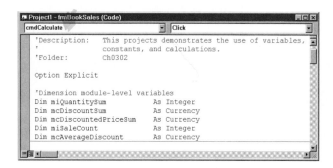

Code module-level declarations in the General Declaration section of a form module.

1. Select *Code* from the *View* menu or click on the *View Code* button in the *Project Explorer* window.
2. In the Object list, select *(General)*.
3. In the Procedure list, select *(Declarations)*.
4. Place the Dim (or Const) statements in this section of code, after the Option Explicit statement.

Feedback 3.3

Write the declarations (Dim or Const statements) for each of the following situations and indicate where each statement will appear.

1. The total of the payroll that will be needed in a Calculate event procedure and in a Summary event procedure.
2. The sales tax rate that cannot be changed during execution of the program but will be used by multiple procedures.
3. The number of participants that are being counted in the Calculate event procedure but not displayed until the Summary event procedure.

Calculations

In programming you can perform calculations with variables and with the properties of certain objects.

The properties you will use, such as the Text property of a text box and the Caption property of a label, are actually strings of text characters. These character strings, such as "Howdy" or "12345" should not be used directly in calculations. Visual Basic tries to make assumptions about the property values you use in calculations. Those assumptions are correct most of the time, but are incorrect often enough that we must take steps to convert all property values to numeric before using them in calculations.

Use the `Val` function to convert the property of a control to its numeric form before you use the value in a calculation:

```
'Convert input values to numeric variables
iQuantity = Val(txtQuantity.Text)
cPrice = Val(txtPrice.Text)

'Calculate the extended price
cExtendedPrice = iQuantity * cPrice
```

Function performs an action and returns a value

argument

Val

Val Function

Visual Basic supplies many functions that you can use in your programs. A **function** performs an action and returns a value. The expression to operate upon, called the **argument**, (or multiple arguments, in some cases), must be enclosed in parentheses.

The first Basic function we will use is `Val`. (Think of *val* as an abbreviation for *value*.) The `Val` function converts text data into a numeric value.

The Val Function—General Form

```
Val(ExpressionToConvert)
```

The expression you wish to convert can be the property of a control, a variable, or a constant.

A function cannot stand by itself. It returns (produces) a value that can be used as a part of a statement, such as the assignment statements in the following examples.

The Val Function—Examples

```
iQuantity = Val(txtQuantity.Text)
cPrice = Val(txtPrice.Text)
lCustomerNumber = Val(mstCUSTOMER_NUMBER)
```

When the `Val` function converts an argument to numeric, it begins at the argument's left-most character. If that character is a numeric digit, decimal point, or sign, `Val` converts the character to numeric and moves to the next character. As soon as a nonnumeric character is found, the operation stops. Here are some examples of the values returned by the `Val` function:

Contents of Argument	Numeric Value Returned by the Val function
(blank)	0
123.45	123.45
$100	0
1,000	1
A123	0
123A	123
4B5	4
−123	−123
+123	123
12.34.8	12.34

Arithmetic Operations

The arithmetic operations you can perform in Visual Basic include addition, subtraction, multiplication, division, and exponentiation.

Operator	Operation
+	Addition
−	Subtraction
*	Multiplication
/	Division
^	Exponentiation

Order of Operations

The order in which operations are performed determines the result. Consider the expression 3 + 4 * 2. What is the result? If the addition is done first, the result is 14. However, if the multiplication is done first, the result is 11.

The hierarchy of operations or **order of precedence** in arithmetic expressions from highest to lowest is

1. Exponentiation
2. Multiplication and division
3. Addition and subtraction

In the previous example, the multiplication is done before addition, and the result is 11. To change the order of evaluation, use parentheses: (3 + 4) * 2 will yield 14 as the result. One set of parentheses may be used inside another set. In that case, the parentheses are said to be nested.

Example

```
((iScore1 + iScore2 + iScore3)/3) * 1.2
```

Extra parentheses can always be used for clarity. The expressions

```
2 * cCost * cRate  and  (2 * cCost) * cRate
```

are equivalent, but the second is easier to understand.

Multiple operations at the same level (such as multiplication and division) are performed from left to right. The example 8 / 4 * 2 yields 4 as its result, not 1. The first operation is 8 / 4, and 2 * 2 is the second.

Evaluation of an expression occurs in this order:

1. All operations within parentheses. Multiple operations within the parentheses are performed according to the rules of precedence.
2. All exponentiation. Multiple exponentiation operations are performed from left to right.
3. All multiplication and division. Multiple operations are performed from left to right.
4. All addition and subtraction are performed from left to right.

Although the precedence of operations in Basic is the same as in algebra, take note of one important difference: There are no implied operations in Basic. The following expressions would be valid in mathematics, but they are not valid in Basic:

Mathematical Notation	Equivalent Basic Function
2A	2 * A
3(X + Y)	3 * (X + Y)
(X + Y)(X − Y)	(X + Y) * (X − Y)

Feedback 3.4

What will be the result of the following calculations using the order of precedence?

Assume that: X = 2, Y = 4, Z = 3

1. X + Y ^ 2
2. 8 / Y / X
3. X * (X + 1)

4. $X * X + 1$
5. $Y \wedge X + Z * 2$
6. $Y \wedge (X + Z) * 2$
7. $(Y \wedge X) + Z * 2$
8. $((Y \wedge X) + Z) * 2$

Using Calculations in Code

Calculations are performed in assignment statements. Recall that whatever appears on the right side of an = (assignment operator) is assigned to the item on the left. The left side may be the property of a control or a variable. It cannot be a constant.

Examples

```
cAverage = cSum / iCount
lblAmountDue.Caption = cPrice - (cPrice * cDiscountRate)
txtCommission.Text = cSalesTotal * cCOMMISION_RATE
```

In the preceding examples, the results of the calculations were assigned to a variable, the Caption property of a label, and the Text property of a text box. In most cases you will assign calculation results to variables or to the Caption properties of labels. Text boxes are usually used for input from the user, not for program output.

Formatting Data

When you want to **format** data for display, either on the printer or on the screen, use the Format function. To *format* means to control the way the output will look. For example, 12 is just a number, but $12.00 conveys more meaning for dollar amounts. The *currency* format is used to display dollar amounts.

The Format Function—General Form

```
Format[$](ExpressionToFormat [, "FormatDescription"])
```

The optional dollar sign in the function name specifies that the formatted value be a string. Without the dollar sign, the value returned is a variant data type. In most situations the results are the same, but using the dollar sign is more efficient.

The expression to be formatted may be numeric or string, a variable, a literal, or a property. In most cases you will use formats for numeric data to control the number of decimal positions. Formats are not generally needed for integer values.

The format description can take one of several forms. Visual Basic provides several predefined formats for the most common types of output. To select one of these formats, include the format name in quotation marks. You may also design your own format for the output, which will be covered shortly.

Predefined Format Names	Description
Currency	A dollar sign; two digits to the right of the decimal; a comma for thousands, if needed; negative numbers in parentheses.
Fixed	Two digits to the right of the decimal point; displays 0 to left of decimal if the value is less than one; no comma for thousands.
General Number	Displays the number as it appears.
Medium Time*	A 12-hour time format; uses hours and minutes and AM or PM.
On/Off	Displays the word Off if the value is 0; all other values will display as On.
Percent	Number multiplied by 100 with percent sign on right; two digits to the right of the decimal point.
Scientific	Standard scientific notation (E notation).
Short Date	Uses the system date format.
Short Time	A 24-hour time format, with hours and minutes, such as 15:30.
Standard	Two digits to the right of the decimal point and a comma for thousands if necessary.
True/False	Displays False if the value is 0; all other values display as True.
Yes/No	Displays No if the value is 0; all other values display as Yes.

*Time and Date may be Medium, Short, or Long.

The Format Function—Examples

```
lblTotal.Caption = Format$(cTotalAmount, "Currency")
lblDate.Caption = Format$(iBirthdate, "Short Date")
```

One extremely nice feature of the Format function is that it rounds fractional values to the requested number of decimal places. Note that the value is rounded for output; the stored value does not change. Any future calculations will be done with the nonrounded value.

These statements produce the following values displayed in the labels:

Statements	Displayed Output
sNumber = 1234.2766	
lblFormattedCurrency.Caption = Format$(sNumber, "Currency")	$1,234.28
lblFormattedStandard.Caption = Format$(sNumber, "Standard")	1,234.28
lblFormattedFixed.Caption = Format$(sNumber, "Fixed")	1234.28
lblFormattedScientific.Caption = Format$(sNumber, "Scientific")	123E+03
bFirstTime = True	
lblDisplay1.Caption = Format$(bFirstTime, "Yes/No")	Yes
lblDisplay2.Caption = Format$(bFirstTime, "True/False")	True
lblDisplay3.Caption = Format$(bFirstTime, "On/Off")	On
iScore = 45	
iPossible = 50	
sPercentCorrect = iScore / iPossible	
lblDisplay4.Caption = sPercentCorrect	0.9
lblDisplay1.Caption = Format$(sPercentCorrect, "Percent")	90.00%
dToday = Now 'Function to retrieve system clock	
Print Format$(dToday, "Short Date")	6/15/97
Print Format$(dToday, "Short Time")	21:12
Print Format$(dToday, "Medium Time")	09:12 PM

Feedback 3.5

Give the line of code that assigns the formatted output and tell how the output would be displayed for the specified value.

1. A calculated variable called mcAveragePay has a value of 123.456 and will be displayed in a label called lblAveragePay.
2. The variable sCorrect, which contains .76, must be displayed as a percentage in the label called lblPercentCorrect.
3. The total amount collected in a fund drive is being accumulated in a variable called mcTotalCollected. What statement will display the variable in a label called lblTotal with commas and two decimal positions but no dollar signs?

Creating Custom Numeric Formats

If the predefined numeric formats don't give the results you want, you can create your own formats. For example, you might want to display whole-dollar amounts without the pennies or to show leading zeros.

The following sections describe how to create custom numeric formats. You can also create custom formats for strings and date/time values; see the Help topics *User-Defined Date/Time Formats* and *User-Defined String Formats* for help creating these formats.

Symbol	Description	Purpose
0	Zero placeholder	Displays a digit in the position; if there is no digit, a zero will display.
#	Null placeholder	Displays a digit in the position; if there is no digit, nothing will display.
.	Decimal point	Displays the decimal point in the position.
,	Thousand separator	Inserts appropriate commas when the number is greater than or equal to 1,000.
%	Percentage	Multiplies the value by 100 and adds the percentage symbol.

Custom Numeric Format—Examples

Statements	Output
sAmount = 1542.788	
lblAmount1.Caption = Format$(sAmount, "####.#")	1542.8
lblAmount2.Caption = Format$(sAmount, "#,###")	1,543
lblAmount3.Caption = Format$(sAmount, "$##,###")	$1,543
sAmount = 542	
lblAmount4.Caption = Format$(sAmount, "###")	542
lblAmount5.Caption = Format$(sAmount, "###.##")	542.
lblAmount6.Caption = Format$(sAmount, "###.00")	542.00
lblAmount7.Caption = Format$(sAmount, "00000.00")	000542.00
sAmount = 0.5462	
lblAmount8.Caption = Format$(sAmount, "##.#%")	54.6%
lblAmount9.Caption = Format$(sAmount, "00.00%")	54.62%
lblAmount10.Caption = Format$(sAmount, "#%")	55%

Feedback 3.6

What will be displayed for each of the following?

```
Dim cAmount as Currency
cAmount = 1.345
```

1. lblAmount1.Caption = Format$(cAmount, "##.##")
2. lblAmount2.Caption = Format$(cAmount, "00.00")
3. lblAmount3.Caption = Format$(cAmount, "##.#")
4. lblAmount4.Caption = Format$(cAmount, "$#,###")
5. lblAmount5.Caption = Format$(cAmount, "$##.#")

A Calculation Programming Example

R 'n R—For Reading 'n Refreshment—needs to calculate prices and discounts for books sold. The company is currently having a big sale, offering a 15 percent discount on all books. In this project you will calculate the amount due for a quantity of books, determine the 15 percent discount, and deduct the discount, giving the new amount due—the discounted amount.

Planning the Project

Sketch a form (Figure 3.5) that meets the needs of your users.

Figure   3.5

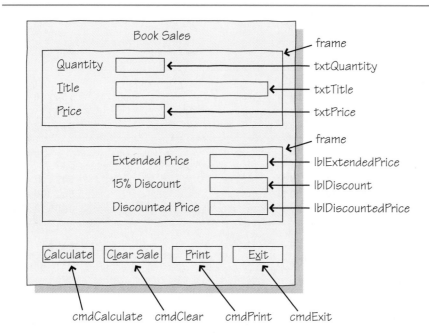

A planning sketch of the form for the calculation programming example.

Plan the Objects and Properties

Plan the property settings for the form and each of the controls.

Object	Property	Setting
Form	Name	frmBookSales
	Caption	R 'n R for Reading 'n Refreshment
Label1	Name	Label1
	Caption	Book Sales
	Font	Bold, 12 point
fraInput	Name	fraInput
	Caption	(blank)

(continued)

Object	Property	Setting
Label2	Name	Label2
	Caption	&Quantity
txtQuantity	Name	txtQuantity
	Text	(blank)
Label3	Name	Label3
	Caption	&Title
txtTitle	Name	txtTitle
	Text	(blank)
Label4	Name	Label4
	Caption	P&rice
txtPrice	Name	txtPrice
	Text	(blank)
fraOutput	Name	fraOutput
	Caption	(blank)
Label5	Name	Label5
	Caption	Extended Price
lblExtendedPrice	Name	lblExtendedPrice
	Caption	(blank)
	Alignment	Right Justify
	BorderStyle	Fixed Single
Label6	Name	Label6
	Caption	15% Discount
lblDiscount	Name	lblDiscount
	Caption	(blank)
	Alignment	Right Justify
	BorderStyle	Fixed Single
Label7	Name	Label7
	Caption	Discounted Price
lblDiscountedPrice	Name	lblDiscountedPrice
	Caption	(blank)
	Alignment	Right Justify
	BorderStyle	Fixed Single
cmdCalculate	Name	cmdCalculate
	Caption	&Calculate

(continued)

Object	Property	Setting
cmdClear	Name	cmdClear
	Caption	C&lear Sale
cmdPrint	Name	cmdPrint
	Caption	&Print
cmdExit	Name	cmdExit
	Caption	E&xit

Plan the Event Procedures

Since you have four command buttons, you need to plan the actions for four event procedures.

Event Procedure	Actions—Pseudocode
cmdCalculate_Click	Dimension the variables and constants. Convert the input Quantity and Price to numeric. Calculate Extended Price = Quantity * Price. Calculate Discount = Extended Price * Discount Rate. Calculate Discounted Price = Extended Price − Discount. Format and display output in labels.
cmdClear_Click	Set each text box and label to blanks. SetFocus in the first text box.
cmdPrint_Click cmdExit_Click	Print the form. Exit the project.

Figure 3.6

The form for the calculation programming example.

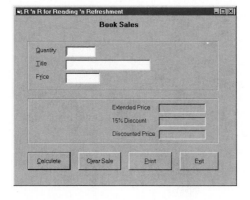

Write the Project

Follow the sketch in Figure 3.5 to create the form. Figure 3.6 shows the completed form.

- Set the properties of each object, as you have planned.

- Write the code. Working from the pseudocode, write each event procedure.

- When you complete the code, use a variety of test data to thoroughly test the project.

The Project Coding Solution

```
'Project:        Chapter Example 3.1
'Date:           February 1997
'Programmer:     J.C. Bradley
'Description:     This project demonstrates the use of variables,
'                constants, and calculations.
'Folder:         Ch0301

Option Explicit
```
```
Private Sub cmdCalculate_Click()
    'Calculate the price and discount

    Const cDISCOUNT_RATE      As Currency = 0.15
    Dim iQuantity             As Integer
    Dim cPrice                As Currency
    Dim cExtendedPrice        As Currency
    Dim cDiscount             As Currency
    Dim cDiscountedPrice      As Currency

    'Convert input values to numeric variables
    iQuantity = Val(txtQuantity.Text)
    cPrice = Val(txtPrice.Text)

    'Calculate values
    cExtendedPrice = iQuantity * cPrice
    cDiscount = cExtendedPrice * cDISCOUNT_RATE
    cDiscountedPrice = cExtendedPrice - cDiscount

    'Format and display answers
    lblExtendedPrice.Caption = Format$(cExtendedPrice, "currency")
    lblDiscount.Caption = Format$(cDiscount, "currency")
    lblDiscountedPrice.Caption = Format$(cDiscountedPrice, "currency")
End Sub
```
```
Private Sub cmdClear_Click()
    'Clear previous amounts from the form

    txtQuantity.Text = ""
    txtTitle.Text = ""
    txtPrice.Text = ""
    lblExtendedPrice.Caption = ""
    lblDiscount.Caption = ""
    lblDiscountedPrice.Caption = ""
    txtQuantity.SetFocus
End Sub
```
```
Private Sub cmdExit_Click()
    'Exit the project

    End
End Sub
```

```
Private Sub cmdPrint_Click()
    'Print the form

    PrintForm
End Sub
```

Counting and Accumulating Sums

Programs often need to sum numbers. For example, in the previous programming exercise each sale is displayed individually. If you want to accumulate a total of the sales amounts, of the discounts, or of the number of books sold, you need some new variables and new techniques.

As you know, the variables you declare inside a procedure are local to that procedure. They are re-created each time the procedure is called; that is, their lifetime is one time through the procedure. Each time the procedure is entered, you have a new fresh variable with an initial value of 0. If you want a variable to retain its value for multiple calls, in order to accumulate totals, you must declare the variable as module level. (Another approach, using Static variables, is discussed in Chapter 6.)

Summing Numbers

The technique for summing the sales amounts for multiple sales is to dimension a module-level variable for the total. Then, in the cmdCalculate_Click event for each sale, add the current amount to the total:

```
mcDiscountedPriceSum = mcDiscountedPriceSum + cDiscountedPrice
```

Reading this assignment statement from right to left, it says to add the cDiscountedPrice and the current contents of mcDiscountedPriceSum and place the result into mcDiscountedPriceSum. The effect of the statement is to add the current value for cDiscountedPrice into the sum held in mcDiscountedPriceSum.

Counting

If you want to count something, such as the number of sales in the previous example, you need another module-level variable. Dimension a counter variable as integer:

```
Dim miSaleCount as Integer
```

Then in the cmdCalculate_Click event procedure, add one to the counter variable:

```
miSaleCount = miSaleCount + 1
```

This statement, reading from right to left, adds one and the current contents of miSaleCount, placing the result in miSaleCount.

Calculating an Average

To calculate an average, divide the sum of the items by the count of the items. In the R 'n R book example, we can calculate the average sale by dividing the sum of the discounted prices by the count of the sales.

```
mcAverageDiscountedSale = mcDiscountedPriceSum / miSaleCount
```

Note: Error checking for division by zero is covered in Chapter 4.

Your Hands-On Programming Example

In this project, R 'n R—For Reading 'n Refreshment—needs to expand its book sale project done previously in this chapter. In addition to calculating individual sales and discounts, management wants to know the total number of books sold, the total number of discounts given, the total discounted amount, and the average discount per sale.

Planning the Project

Sketch a form (Figure 3.7) that your users sign off as meeting their needs.

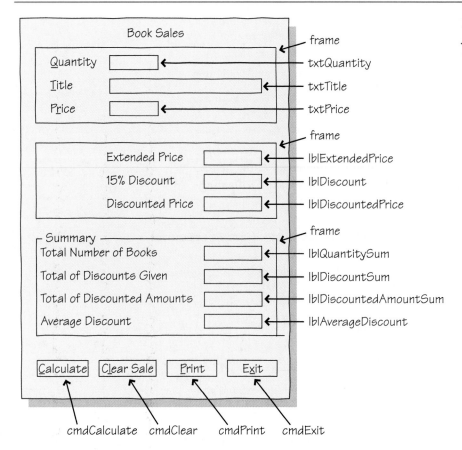

A planning sketch of the form for the hands-on programming example.

Plan the Objects and Properties

Plan the property settings for the form and each control. These objects and properties are the same as the previous example, with the addition of the summary information beginning with fraSummary.

Object	Property	Setting
Form	Name	frmBookSales
	Caption	R 'n R for Reading 'n Refreshment
Label1	Name	Label1
	Caption	Book Sales
	Font	Bold, 12 point
fraInput	Name	fraInput
	Caption	(blank)
Label2	Name	Label2
	Caption	&Quantity
		(continued)

Object	Property	Setting
txtQuantity	Name	txtQuantity
	Text	(blank)
Label3	Name	Label3
	Caption	&Title
txtTitle	Name	txtTitle
	Text	(blank)
Label4	Name	Label4
	Caption	P&rice
txtPrice	Name	txtPrice
	Text	(blank)
fraOutput	Name	fraOutput
	Caption	(blank)
Label5	Name	Label5
	Caption	Extended Price
lblExtendedPrice	Name	lblExtendedPrice
	Caption	(blank)
	Alignment	Right Justify
	BorderStyle	Fixed Single
Label6	Name	Label6
	Caption	15% Discount
lblDiscount	Name	lblDiscount
	Caption	(blank)
	Alignment	Right Justify
	BorderStyle	Fixed Single
Label7	Name	Label7
	Caption	Discounted Price
lblDiscountedPrice	Name	lblDiscountedPrice
	Caption	(blank)
	Alignment	Right Justify
	BorderStyle	Fixed Single
cmdCalculate	Name	cmdCalculate
	Caption	&Calculate
cmdClear	Name	cmdClear
	Caption	C&lear Sale

(continued)

Object	Property	Setting
cmdPrint	Name	cmdPrint
	Caption	&Print
cmdExit	Name	cmdExit
	Caption	E&xit
fraSummary	Name	fraSummary
	Caption	Summary
Label8	Name	Label8
	Caption	Total Number of Books
lblQuantitySum	Name	lblQuantitySum
	Caption	(blank)
	Alignment	Right Justify
	BorderStyle	Fixed Single
Label9	Name	Label9
	Caption	Total Discounts Given
lblDiscountSum	Name	lblDiscountSum
	Caption	(blank)
	Alignment	Right Justify
	BorderStyle	Fixed Single
Label10	Name	Label10
	Caption	Total of Discounted Amounts
lblDiscountedAmountSum	Name	lblDiscountedAmountSum
	Caption	(blank)
	Alignment	Right Justify
	BorderStyle	Fixed Single
Label11	Name	Label11
	Caption	Average Discount
lblAverageDiscount	Name	lblAverageDiscount
	Caption	(blank)
	Alignment	Right Justify
	BorderStyle	Fixed Single

Plan the Event Procedures

The planning that you did for the previous example will save you time now. The only procedure that requires more steps is the cmdCalculate_Click event.

Event Procedure	Actions—Pseudocode
cmdCalculate_Click	Dimension the variables and constants.
	Convert the input Quantity and Price to numeric.
	Calculate Extended Price = Quantity * Price.
	Calculate Discount = Extended Price * Discount Rate.
	Calculate Discounted Price = Extended Price − Discount.
	Calculate the summary values:
	Add Quantity to Quantity Sum.
	Add Discount to Discount Sum.
	Add Discounted Price to Discounted Price Sum.
	Add 1 to Sale Count.
	Calculate Average Discount = Discount Sum / Sale Count.
	Format and display sale output in labels.
	Format and display summary values in labels.
cmdClear_Click	Set each text box and label to blanks.
	SetFocus in the first text box.
cmdPrint_Click	Print the form.
cmdExit_Click	Exit the project.

Write the Project

Following the sketch in Figure 3.7 create the form. Figure 3.8 shows the completed form.

Figure 3.8

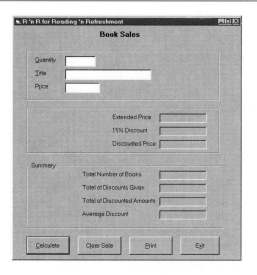

The form for the hands-on programming example.

- Set the properties of each of the objects, as you have planned.

- Write the code. Working from the pseudocode, write each event procedure.

- When you complete the code, use a variety of test data to thoroughly test the project.

The Project Coding Solution

```
'Project:          Chapter Example 3.2
'Date:             February 1997
'Programmer:       J.C. Bradley
'Description:       This project demonstrates the use of variables,
                   constants, and calculations.
'Folder:           Ch0302

Option Explicit

'Dimension module-level variables
Dim miQuantitySum          As Integer
Dim mcDiscountSum          As Currency
Dim mcDiscountedPriceSum   As Currency
Dim miSaleCount            As Integer
Dim mcAverageDiscount      As Currency
```
```
Private Sub cmdCalculate_Click()
    'Calculate the price and discount
    Const cDISCOUNT_RATE   As Currency = 0.15
    Dim iQuantity          As Integer
    Dim cPrice             As Currency
    Dim cExtendedPrice     As Currency
    Dim cDiscount          As Currency
    Dim cDiscountedPrice   As Currency
    Dim cAverageDiscount   As Currency

    'Convert input values to numeric variables
    iQuantity = Val(txtQuantity.Text)
    cPrice = Val(txtPrice.Text)

    'Calculate values for sale
    cExtendedPrice = iQuantity * cPrice
    cDiscount = cExtendedPrice * cDISCOUNT_RATE
    cDiscountedPrice = cExtendedPrice - cDiscount

    'Calculate summary values
    miQuantitySum = miQuantitySum + iQuantity
    mcDiscountSum = mcDiscountSum + cDiscount
    mcDiscountedPriceSum = mcDiscountedPriceSum + cDiscountedPrice
    miSaleCount = miSaleCount + 1
    mcAverageDiscount = mcDiscountSum / miSaleCount

    'Format and display answers for sale
    lblExtendedPrice.Caption = Format$(cExtendedPrice, "currency")
    lblDiscount.Caption = Format$(cDiscount, "currency")
    lblDiscountedPrice.Caption = Format$(cDiscountedPrice, "currency")
```

```
    'Format and display summary values
    lblQuantitySum.Caption = miQuantitySum
    lblDiscountSum.Caption = Format$(mcDiscountSum, "currency")
    lblDiscountedAmountSum.Caption = Format$(mcDiscountedPriceSum, "currency")
    lblAverageDiscount.Caption = Format$(mcAverageDiscount, "currency")
End Sub
```

```
Private Sub cmdClear_Click()
    'Clear previous amounts from the form

    txtQuantity.Text = ""
    txtTitle.Text = ""
    txtPrice.Text = ""
    lblExtendedPrice.Caption = ""
    lblDiscount.Caption = ""
    lblDiscountedPrice.Caption = ""
    txtQuantity.SetFocus
End Sub
```

```
Private Sub cmdExit_Click()
    'Exit the project

    End
End Sub
```

```
Private Sub cmdPrint_Click()
    'Print the form

    PrintForm
End Sub
```

Programming Hints

Use the Option Explicit statement to help avoid common coding errors.

Visual Basic does not require you to declare a variable before using it. When the variable is first used in the code, it will automatically become type Variant. However, good programming style suggests the declaration of all variables. The specification of a data type will save memory space. It is also to the programmer's advantage to declare all variables.

As an example of what might occur if the Option Explicit is not used, look at the following code:

```
Sub cmdCalcPay_Click()
    'Calculate Pay

    cHours = Val(txtHours.Text)
    cPayRate = Val(txtPayRate.Text)
    cPay = Hours * PayRate
    mcTotalPay = mcTotlPay + cPay
End Sub
```

Look carefully at this code, which does not generate any Visual Basic errors. What will be the values in cPay and mcTotalPay? This type of error is difficult to spot visually and, unfortunately, very easy to make. *Hint:* The code has three errors.

Are you ready for the answers? cPay and mcTotalPay will both be 0. Notice the different spellings of the variable names cHours/Hours, cPayRate/ PayRate, and mcTotalPay/mcTotlPay.

You can avoid this type of error completely by setting the option that requires all variables to be declared prior to use. This technique will help in debugging projects because the compiler will detect misspelled variable names when the project is run.

The steps to setting `Option Explicit` are

1. From the *Tools* menu select *Options.*
2. On the *Editor* tab, make sure that *Require Variable Declaration* is selected.
3. Click the OK button.

When you turn on the *Require Variable Declaration* option, Visual Basic automatically adds the `Option Explicit` statements to all new forms you create after that point. VB does not add an `Option Explicit` statement to a form that has already been created. You can add an `Option Explicit` statement yourself to any existing form.

S u m m a r y

1. Variables and constants are temporary memory locations that have a name (called an *identifier*), a data type, and a scope. The value stored in a variable can be changed during the execution of the project; the values stored in constants cannot change.
2. The data type determines what values may be stored in a variable or constant. The most common data types are string, integer, currency, single precision, and Boolean. Any variable not explicitly given a data type defaults to variant.
3. Identifiers for variables and constants must follow the Visual Basic naming rules and should follow good naming standards, called *conventions.* An identifier should be meaningful and have a lowercase prefix that indicates the data type and the scope. Variable names should be mixed upper- and lowercase. The name for a constant should be uppercase, following the lowercase prefix.
4. Instrinsic constants, such as vbRed and vbBlue, are predefined and built into Visual Basic. Named constants are programmer-defined constants and are declared using the `Const` statement. The location of the `Const` statement determines the scope of the constant.
5. Variables are declared using the `Dim` statement; the location of the statement determines the scope of the variable.

6. The scope of a variable may be global, module level, or local. Local variables are available only within the procedure in which they are declared; module-level variables are accessible in all procedures within a form; global variables are available in all procedures of all modules in a project with multiple modules.

7. A Visual Basic function performs an action and returns a value. The expressions named in parentheses are called *arguments*.

8. Use the `Val` function to convert text values to numeric before performing any calculations.

9. Calculations may be performed using the values of numeric variables, constants, and the properties of controls. The result of a calculation may be assigned to a numeric variable or to the property of a control.

10. A calculation operation with more than one operator follows the order of precedence in determining the result of the calculation. Parentheses alter the order of operations.

11. The `Format` and `Format$` functions indicate how information should appear when it is displayed or printed out. Formatting can be used to specify the number of decimal positions and request commas, dollar signs, and percent signs. There are predefined numeric formats for standard, fixed, or currency. You can also create custom formats.

12. You can calculate a sum by adding each transaction to a module-level variable. In a similar fashion, you can calculate a count by adding to a module-level variable.

13. A frequent cause of errors in Basic programming is the misspelling of variable names. You can avoid this error by including the `Option Explicit` statement in the General Declarations section of each module. VB will automatically add the `Option Explicit` statement to all new modules if you set the option to *Require Variable Declaration*.

Key Terms

argument *89*
constant *79*
data type *79*
declaration *79*
format *92*
function *89*
global *85*
identifier *79*
intrinsic constant *83*

lifetime *86*
local *86*
module-level *86*
order of precedence *90*
scope *85*
string literal *83*
variable *78*
variant *79*

R e v i e w   Q u e s t i o n s

1. Name and give the purpose of five types of data available in Visual Basic.
2. What does *declaring a variable* mean?
3. What effect does the location of a `Dim` statement have upon the variable it declares?
4. Explain the difference between a constant and a variable.
5. What is the purpose of the `Val` function?
6. Explain the order of precedence of operators for calculations.
7. What statement(s) can be used to declare a variable?
8. When would it be necessary to define a format string for numeric data?
9. Should the `Format` function be included for all captions and text display in a program? Justify your answer.

P r o g r a m m i n g   E x e r c i s e s

3.1 Create a project that calculates the total of fat, carbohydrate, and protein calories. Allow the user to enter (in text boxes) the grams of fat, the grams of carbohydrate, and the grams of protein. Each gram of fat is nine calories, while a gram of protein or carbohydrate is four calories.

Display the total calories for the current food item in a label. Use two other labels to display an accumulated sum of the calories and a count of the items entered.

Form: The form should have three text boxes for the user to enter the grams for each category. Include labels next to each text box indicating what the user is to enter.

Include command buttons to Calculate, to Clear the text boxes, to Print, and to Exit.

Make the form's caption "Calorie Counter".

Code: Write the code for each of the command buttons.

3.2 Lennie McPherson, proprietor of Lennie's Bail Bonds, needs to calculate the amount due for setting the bail. Lennie requires something of value as collateral, and his fee is 10 percent of the bail amount. He wants the screen to provide boxes to enter the bail amount and the item being used for collateral. The program must calculate the fee. He needs to print the screen form so that he can attach it to the legal documents.

Form: Include text boxes for entering in the amount of bail and the description of the collateral. Label each text box.

Include command buttons for Calculate, Clear, Print Form, and Exit.

The caption for the form should be "Lennie's Bail Bonds".

Code: Include event procedures for the click event of each command button. Calculate the amount due as 10 percent of the bail amount and display it in a label, formatted as Currency.

3.3 In retail sales, management needs to know the average inventory figure and the turnover of merchandise. Create a project that allows the user to enter the beginning inventory, the ending inventory, and the cost of goods sold.

Form: Include labeled text boxes for the beginning inventory, the ending inventory, and the cost of goods sold. After calculating the answers, display the average inventory and the turnover formatted in labels.

Include command buttons for Calculate, Clear, Print Form, and Exit. The formulas for the calculations are

$$\text{Average inventory} = \frac{\text{Beginning inventory } + \text{ Ending inventory}}{2}$$

$$\text{Turnover} = \frac{\text{Cost of goods sold}}{\text{Average inventory}}$$

Note: The average inventory is expressed in dollars; the turnover is the number of times the inventory turns over.

Code: Include procedures for the click event of each of the command buttons. Display the results in labels. Format the average inventory as Currency and the turnover as Standard.

Test Data

Beginning	Ending	Cost of Goods Sold
58500	47000	400000
75300	13600	515400
3000	19600	48000

Check Figures

Average Inventory	Turnover
$52,750.00	7.58
$44,450.00	11.60
$11,300.00	4.25

3.4   A local recording studio rents its facilities for $200 per hour. Management charges only for the number of minutes used. Create a project in which the input is the name of the group and the number of minutes it used the studio. Your program calculates the appropriate charges, accumulates the total charges for all groups, and computes the average charge and the number of groups that used the studio.

Form: Use labeled text boxes for the name of the group and the number of minutes used. The charges for the current group should be displayed formatted in a label. Create a frame for the summary information. Inside the frame, display the total charges for all groups, the number of groups, and the average charge per group.

Code: Use a constant for the rental rate per minute.

Test Data

Group	Minutes
Pooches	95
Hounds	5
Mutts	480

Check Figures

Total Charges for Group	Total Number of Groups	Average Charge	Total Charges for All Groups
$317.00	1	$317	$317.00
$17.00	2	$167	$334.00
$1,600.00	3	$645	$1,934.00

3.5 Create a project that determines the future value of an investment at a given interest rate for a given number of years. The formula for the calculation is

Future value = Investment amount * (1 + Interest rate) ^ Years

Form: Use labeled text boxes for the amount of investment, the interest rate (as a decimal fraction), and the number of years the investment will be held. Display the future value in a label.

Include command buttons for Calculate, Clear, Print Form, and Exit. Format all dollar amounts.

Test Data

Amount	Rate	Years
2000.00	.15	5
1234.56	.075	3

Check Figures

Future Value
$4,022.71
$1,533.69

3.6 Write a project that calculates the shipping charge for a package if the shipping rate is $0.12 per ounce.
Form: Use labeled text boxes for the package-identification code (a six-digit code) and the weight of the package—one box for pounds and another one for ounces. Use a label to display the shipping charge.

Include command buttons for Calculate, Clear, Print Form, and Exit.
Code: Include event procedures for each of the command buttons. Use a constant for the shipping rate, calculate the shipping charge, and display it formatted in a label.
Calculation hint: There are 16 ounces in a pound.

Test Data

ID	Weight
L5496P	0 lb. 5 oz.
J1955K	2 lb. 0 oz.
Z0000Z	1 lb. 1 oz.

Check Figures

Shipping Charge
$0.60
$3.84
$2.04

3.7 Create a project for the local car rental agency that calculates the rental charges. The agency charges $15 per day plus $0.12 per mile.
Form: Use text boxes for the customer name, address, city, state, ZIP code, beginning odometer reading, ending odometer reading, and the number of days the car was used. Use labels to display the miles driven and the total charge.

Include command buttons for Calculate, Clear, Print Form, and Exit.
Code: Include an event procedure for each command button. For the calculation, subtract the beginning odometer reading from the ending odometer reading to get the number of miles traveled. Use a constant for the $15 per day charge and the $0.12 mileage rate.

3.8   Create a project that will input an employee's sales and calculate the gross pay, deductions, and net pay. Each employee will receive a base pay of $900 plus a sales commission of 6 percent of sales.

After calculating the net pay, calculate the budget amount for each category based on the percentages given.

Pay

Base pay	$900; use a named constant
Commission	6% of sales
Gross pay	Sum of base pay and commission
Deductions	18% of gross pay
Net pay	Gross pay minus deductions

Budget

Housing	30% of net pay
Food and clothing	15% of net pay
Entertainment	50% of net pay
Miscellaneous	5% of net pay

Form: Use text boxes to input the employee's name and the dollar amount of the sales. Use labels to display the results of the calculations.

Provide command buttons for Calculate, Clear, Print Form, and Exit.

CASE STUDIES

VB Mail Order

The company has instituted a bonus program to give its employees an incentive to sell more. For every dollar the store makes in a four-week period, the employees receive 2 percent of sales. The amount of bonus each employee receives is based upon the percentage of hours he or she worked during the bonus period (a total of 160 hours).

The screen will allow the user to enter the employee's name, the total hours worked, and the amount of store's total sales. The amount of sales needs to be entered only for the first employee. (*Hint:* Don't clear it.)

The Calculate command button will determine the bonus earned by this employee, and the Clear button will clear only the name and hours worked fields. A Print Form button will be available only after the calculation has been made—it will be disabled until the Calculate button is pressed the first time. When the Clear button is pressed, the Print Form button will become disabled (Enabled = False).

Salespeople for used cars are compensated using a commission system. The commission is calculated based on the costs incurred for the vehicle.

VB Auto Center

Commission =
  Commission rate $\times$ (Sales price $-$ Cost value)

The screen will allow for the user to enter the salesperson's name, the selling price of the vehicle, and the cost value of the vehicle. Use a constant of 20 percent for the commission rate.

The Calculate command button will determine the commission earned by the salesperson; the Clear button will clear the text boxes. A Print Form button will be available only after the calculation has been made—it will be disabled until the Calculate button is pressed the first time. When the Clear button is pressed, the Print Form button will become disabled (Enabled = False).

4

Decisions and Conditions

At the completion of this chapter, you will be able to...

1. Use block Ifs to control the flow of logic.

2. Understand and use nested Ifs.

3. Read and create flowcharts indicating the logic in a selection process.

4. Evaluate conditions using the relational operators.

5. Combine conditions using And and Or.

6. Test the Value property of option buttons and check boxes.

7. Perform validation on numeric fields.

8. Call event procedures from other procedures.

9. Create message boxes to display error conditions.

10. Apply the message box constants.

11. Debug projects using breakpoints, stepping program execution, and displaying intermediate results.

In this section you will learn to write projects that can take one action or another, based on a condition. For example, you may need to keep track of sales separately for different classes of employees, different sections of the country, or different departments. You may want to check the value entered by the user to make sure it is valid and display an error message for inappropriate values.

If Statements

A powerful asset of the computer is its ability to make decisions and to take alternate courses of action based on the outcome.

A decision made by the computer is formed as a question: Is a given condition true or false? If it is true, do one thing; if it is false, do something else.

```
If the sun is shining Then        (condition)
    go to the beach               (action to take if condition is true)
Else
    go to class                   (action to take if condition is false)
End If                            (See Figure 4.1.)
```

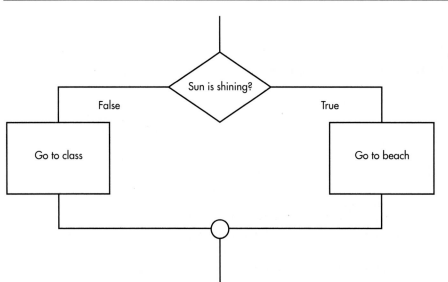

The logic of an `If...Then...Else` *statement in flowchart form.*

or

```
If you don't succeed Then         (condition)
    try, try again                (action)
End If                            (See Figure 4.2)
```

Figure 4.2

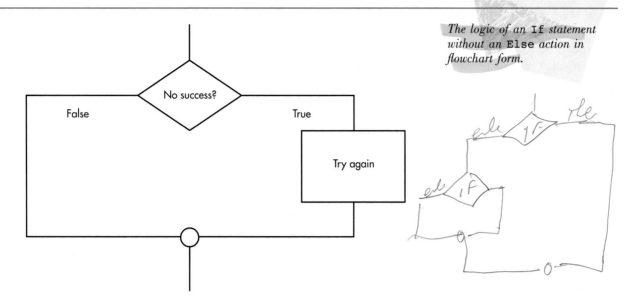

The logic of an If statement without an Else action in flowchart form.

Notice in the second example that no action is specified if the condition is not true.

In an `If` statement, when the condition is true, only the `Then` clause is executed. When the condition is false, only the `Else` clause, if present, is executed.

If...Then...Else Statement—General Form

```
If (condition) Then
    statement(s)
[ElseIf (condition) Then
    statement(s)]
[Else
    statements(s)]
End If
```

A block **If...Then...Else** must always conclude with **End If**. The word Then must appear on the same line as the `If` with nothing following Then (except a remark). End If and Else (if used) must appear alone on a line. The statements under the Then and Else clause are indented for readability and clarity.

Notice that the keyword ElseIf is all one word but that End If is two words.

If..Then..Else Statement—Examples

When the number of units in cUnits is less than 32, select the option button for *Freshman;* otherwise, make sure the button is unselected (Figure 4.3). Remember that when an option button is selected, the Value property has a Boolean value of True.

Figure 4.3

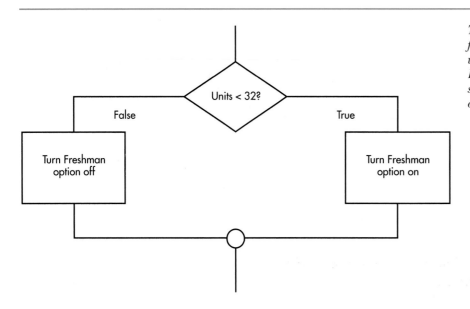

The If *statement logic in flowchart form. If the number of units is less than 32, the Freshman option button will be selected; otherwise, the Freshman option will be deselected.*

```
CUnits = Val(txtUnits.Text)

If cUnits < 32 Then
    optFreshman.Value = True
Else
    optFreshman.Value = False
End If
```

Tip

Always take the time to indent properly as you enter an If statement. You will save yourself debugging time; the indentation helps to visualize the intended logic.

Flowcharting If Statements

A flowchart is a useful tool for showing the logic of an If statement. It has been said that one picture is worth a thousand words. Many programmers find that a flowchart helps them organize their thoughts and design projects more quickly.

The symbols used in this text are a subset of the available flowcharting symbols. The diamond-shape symbol (called a *decision symbol*) represents a condition. The two branches from the symbol indicate which path to take when the condition evaluates True or False. (See Figure 4.4.)

The flowcharting symbols used for program decisions and processes.

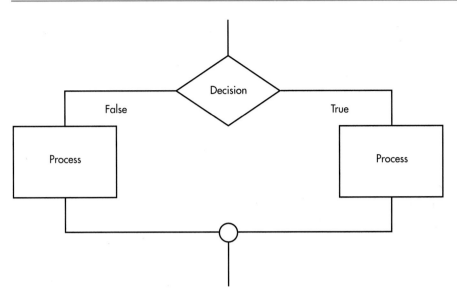

Conditions

The test in an `If` statement is based on a **condition**. To form conditions, six **relational operators** (Table 4.1) are used to compare values. The result of the comparison is either True or False.

T a b l e   4 . 1

The six relational operators.

Symbol	Relation Tested	Examples
>	greater than	`Val(txtAmount.Text) > mcLIMIT` `frmMain.Height > mcSize`
<	less than	`Val(txtSales.Text) < 10000` `txtName.Text < stName`
=	equal to	`txtPassword.Text = "101"` `optButton1.Value = True`
<>	not equal to	`optButton1.Value <> True` `txtPassword.Text <> "101"`
>=	greater than or equal to	`Val(lblCorrect.Caption) >= 1000` `frmMain.Height >= 500`
<=	less than or equal to	`txtName1.Text <= txtName2.Text`

The conditions to be tested can be formed with numeric variables and constants, string variables and constants, object properties, and arithmetic expressions. However, it is important to note that comparisons must be made on like types; that is, strings can be compared only to other strings, and numeric values can be compared only to other numeric values, whether a variable, constant, property, or arithmetic expression.

Comparing Numeric Variables and Constants

When numeric values are involved in a test, an algebraic comparison is made; that is, the sign of the number is taken into account. Therefore, negative 20 is less than 10, and negative 2 is less than negative 1.

Even though an equal sign (=) means replacement in an assignment statement, in a relation test the equal sign is used to test for equality. For example, the condition

```
If Val(txtPrice.Text) = cMAX Then
```

means "Is the current numeric value stored in txtPrice.Text equal to the value stored in cMAX?"

Sample Comparisons

iAlpha	iBravo	iCharlie
5	4	−5

Condition	Evaluates
iAlpha = iBravo	False
iCharlie < 0	True
iBravo > iAlpha	False
iCharlie <= iBravo	True
iAlpha >= 5	True
iAlpha <> iCharlie	True

Comparing Strings

String variables can be compared to other string variables or string literals enclosed in quotation marks. The comparison begins with the left-most character and proceeds one character at a time from left to right. As soon as a character in one string is not equal to the corresponding character in the second string, the comparison is terminated, and the string with the lower ranking character is judged less than the other.

The determination of which character is less than another is based on the code used to store characters internally in the computer. The code, called the **ASCII code** (pronounced "ask-key"), has an established order (called

Collating sequence

the *collating sequence*) for all letters, numbers, and special characters. (ASCII stands for American Standard Code for Information Interchange.) Note in Table 4.2, that *A* is less than *B*, *L* is greater than *K*, and all numeric digits are less than all letters. Some special symbols are lower than the numbers and some are higher, and the blank space is lower than the rest of the characters shown.

T a b l e   4 . 2

The ASCII collating sequence.

ASCII Code	Character
32	Space (blank)
33	!
34	"
35	#
36	$
37	%
38	&
39	' (apostrophe)
40	(
41	)
42	*
43	+
44	, (comma)
45	−
46	.
47	/
48	0
49	1
50	2
51	3
52	4
53	5
54	6
55	7
56	8
57	9
58	:
59	;

(continued)

ASCII Code	Character
60	<
61	=
62	>
63	?
64	@
65	A
66	B
67	C
68	D
69	E
70	F
71	G
72	H
73	I
74	J
75	K
76	L
77	M
78	N
79	O
80	P
81	Q
82	R
83	S
84	T
85	U
86	V
87	W
88	X
89	Y
90	Z
91	[
92	\
93	]

(continued)

ASCII Code	Character
94	^
95	_
96	'
97	a
98	b
99	c
100	d
101	e
102	f
103	g
104	h
105	I
106	j
107	k
108	l
109	m
110	n
111	o
112	p
113	q
114	r
115	s
116	t
117	u
118	v
119	w
120	x
121	y
122	z
123	{
124		
125	}
126	~
127	Del

txtPerson1.Text	txtPerson2.Text
JOHN	JOAN

The condition txtPerson1.Text < txtPerson2.Text evaluates False. The *A* in JOAN is lower ranking than the *H* in JOHN.

txtWord1.Text	txtWord2.Text
HOPE	HOPELESS

The condition txtWord1.Text < txtWord2.Text evaluates True. When one string is shorter than the other, it compares as if the shorter string is padded with blanks to the right of the string, and the blank space is compared to a character in the longer string.

lblCar1.Caption	lblCar2.Caption
300ZX	PORSCHE

The condition lblCar1.Caption < lblCar2.Caption evaluates True. When the number *3* is compared to the letter *P*, the *3* is lower, since all numbers are lower ranking than all letters.

Feedback 4.1

iCountOne	iCountTwo	iCountThree	txtFour.Text	txtFive.Text
5	5	−5	"Bit"	"Bite"

Determine which conditions will evaluate True and which ones will evaluate False.

1. iCountOne >= iCountTwo
2. iCountThree < 0
3. iCountThree < iCountTwo
4. iCountOne <> iCountTwo
5. iCountOne + 2 > iCountTwo + 2
6. txtFour.Text < txtFive.Text
7. txtFour.Text <> txtFive.Text
8. txtFour.Text > "D"
9. "2" <> "Two"
10. "$" <= "?"

Testing for True or False

You can use shortcuts when testing for True or False. Visual Basic evaluates the condition in an `If` statement. If the condition is a Boolean variable name, it holds the values True or False.

For example:

```
If bSuccessfulOperation = True Then ...
```

is equivalent to

```
If bSuccessfulOperation Then ...
```

Boolean variables hold the value 0 when False, and negative 1 when True. You can actually test *any* variable for True or False. Visual Basic considers any numeric variable with a value of 0 to be False; any other value will evaluate True. The variable or expression is referred to as an **implied condition**.

Examples

```
iCounter = 10
If iCounter Then ...       'Evaluates True

iTotal = 0
If iTotal Then ...         'Evaluates False
```

Comparing the Text Property of Text Boxes

When you compare the Text property of a text box with another value, you must be careful. The Text property behaves like a variant. That is, if you use it like a string, it acts like a string; but if you use it like a number, it acts like a number. However, sometimes your intentions are not clear, and sometimes you are using the Text property as numeric, but the user enters nonnumeric data or no data at all.

Visual Basic compares one text box to another as strings and compares a text box to a numeric variable or constant with a numeric compare. You can force a numeric comparison on a Text property by using the `Val` function. You should always use the `Val` function on a numeric Text property when you need to compare or calculate. Remember, the `Val` function converts blank values to zero.

Examples

txtFirst.Text	txtSecond.Text	txtFirst.Text > txtSecond.Text	Val(txtFirst.Text) > Val(txtSecond.Text)
1	+1	True	False
2	100	True	False
+100	−100	False	True
0	(blank)	True	False

Comparing Uppercase and Lowercase Characters

When comparing strings, the case of the characters is important. An uppercase *Y* is not equal to a lowercase *y*. Since the user may type a name or word in uppercase, lowercase, or as a combination of cases, we must check all possibilities. The easiest way is to use the string function `Ucase` or `Lcase`, which returns the uppercase or lowercase equivalent of a string, respectively.

Ucase and Lcase—General Form

```
Ucase(string)
Lcase(string)
```

Ucase and Lcase—Examples

txtOne.Text Value	Ucase(txtOne.Text)	Lcase(txtOne.Text)
Basic	BASIC	basic
PROGRAMMING	PROGRAMMING	programming
Robert Jones	ROBERT JONES	robert jones
hello	HELLO	hello

An example of a condition using the `Ucase` function follows.

```
If Ucase(txtOne.Text) = "BASIC" Then
    'Do something
End If
```

Note that when you convert txtOne.Text to uppercase, you must compare it to an uppercase literal ("BASIC") if you want it to evaluate as True.

Compound Conditions

You can use **compound conditions** to test more than one condition. Create compound conditions by joining conditions with **logical operators**. The logical operators are `Or`, `And`, and `Not`.

Logical Operator	Meaning	Example
`Or`	If one condition or both conditions are true, the entire condition is true.	`lblNumber.Caption = 1 Or _` `lblNumber.Caption = 2`
`And`	Both conditions must be true for the entire condition to be true.	`txtNumber.Text > 0 And _` `txtNumber.Text < 10`
`Not`	Reverses the condition so that a true condition will evaluate false and vice versa.	`Not lblNumber.Caption = 0`

```
If optMale.Value = True And Val(txtAge.Text) < 21 Then
      miMinorMaleCount = miMinorMaleCount + 1
End If
If optJunior.Value = True Or optSenior.Value = True Then
      miUpperClassmanCount = miUpperClassmanCount + 1
End If
```

The first example requires that both the option button test and the age test be true for the count to be incremented. In the second example, only one of the conditions must be true.

One caution when using compound conditions: Each side of the logical operator must be a complete condition. For example,

```
optJunior.Value Or optSenior.Value = True
```

is incorrect.

Combining `And` and `Or`

You can create compound conditions that combine multiple `And` and `Or` conditions. When you have both an `And` and an `Or`, the `And` is evaluated before the `Or`. However, you can change the order of evaluation by using parentheses; any condition inside parentheses will be evaluated first.

For example, will the following condition evaluate True or False? Try it with various values for cSale, optDiscount, and txtState.Text.

```
If cSale > 1000 Or optDiscount.Value = True And Ucase(txtState.Text) <> "CA" Then
      '(Calculate the discount)
End If
```

cSale	optDiscount.Value	Ucase(txtState.Text)	Condition Evaluates
1500	False	CA	True
1000	True	OH	True
1000	True	CA	False
1500	True	NY	True
1000	False	CA	False

Using If Statements with Option Buttons and Check Boxes

In Chapter 2 you used the Click event for option buttons and check boxes to carry out the desired action. Now that you can use `If` statements, you should not take action in the Click events for these controls. Instead, use `If` statements to determine which options are selected.

To conform to good programming practice and make your programs consistent with standard Windows applications, place your code in the Click event of command buttons. For example, refer to the Visual Basic *Print* dialog box (Figure 4.5); no action will occur when you click on an option button or check box. Instead, when you click on the OK button, VB checks to see which options are selected.

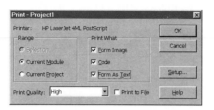

The Visual Basic Print *dialog box. When the user clicks OK, the program checks the state of all option buttons and check boxes.*

In an application such as the message formatter project in Chapter 2 (refer to Figure 2.18), you could add a Display command button and include code similar to the following:

```
If chkBlue.Value = True Then
    lblName.BackColor = vbBlue
End If
```

```
If optItalic.Value = True Then
    txtTitle.Font.Italic = True
Else
    txtTitle.Font.Italic = False
End If
```

A "Simple Sample"

Test your understanding of the use of the If statement by coding some short examples.

Test the Value of a Check Box

Create a small project that contains a check box, a label, and a command button. Name the command button cmdTest, the check box chkTest, and the label lblMessage. In the Click event for cmdTest, check the value of the check box. If the check box is currently checked, display "Check box is checked" in lblMessage.

```
Private Sub cmdTest_Click()
    'Test the value of the check box

    If chkTest.Value = Checked Then
        lblMessage.Caption = "Check box is checked"
    End If
```

Test your project. When it works, add an `Else` to the code that displays "Check box is not checked".

Test the Value of Option Buttons

Remove the check box from the previous project and replace it with two option buttons, named optFreshman and optSophomore and captioned "< 30 units" and ">= 30 units". Now change the `If` statement to display "Freshman" or "Sophomore" in the label.

```
If optFreshman.Value = True Then
    lblMessage.Caption = "Freshman"
Else
    lblMessage.Caption = "Sophomore"
End If
```

Can you modify the sample to work for Freshman, Sophomore, Junior, and Senior?

Nested If Statements

In many programs another `If` statement is one of the statements to be executed when a condition tests True or False. `If` statements that contain additional `If` statements are said to be *nested* `If` statements. The following example shows a nested `If` statement in which the second `If` occurs in the `Then` portion of the first `If` (Figure 4.6).

Flowcharting a nested `If` statement.

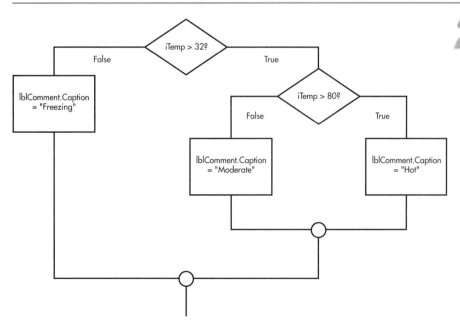

```
If iTemp > 32 Then
    If iTemp > 80 Then
        lblComment.Caption = "Hot"
    Else
        lblComment.Caption = "Moderate"
    End If
Else
    lblComment.Caption = "Freezing"
End If
```

To nest `If` statements in the `Else` portion, you may use either of the following approaches; however, your code is simpler if you use the second method (using `ElseIf...Then`).

```
If iTemp <= 32 Then
    lblComment.Caption = "Freezing"
Else
    If iTemp > 80 Then
        lblComment.Caption = "Hot"
    Else
     lblComment.Caption = "Moderate"
    End If
End If
```

```
If iTemp <= 32 Then
    lblComment.Caption = "Freezing"
ElseIf iTemp > 80 Then
    lblComment.Caption = "Hot"
Else
    lblComment.Caption = "Moderate"
End If
```

You may nest `Ifs` in both the `Then` and `Else`. In fact, you may continue to nest `Ifs` within `Ifs` as long as each `If` has an `End If`. However, projects become very difficult to follow (and may not perform as intended) when `Ifs` become too deeply nested (Figure 4.7.)

A flowchart of a nested If *statement with* Ifs *nested on both sides of the original* If.

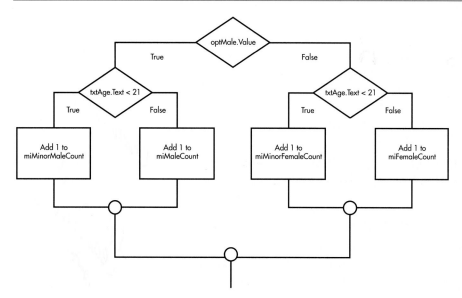

```
If optMale.Value = True Then
    If txtAge.Text < 21 Then
        miMinorMaleCount = miMinorMaleCount + 1
    Else
        miMaleCount = miMaleCount + 1
    End If
Else
    If txtAge.Text < 21 Then
        miMinorFemaleCount = miMinorFemaleCount + 1
    Else
        miFemaleCount = miFemaleCount + 1
    End If
End If
```

Tip

Indentation can help you catch errors. Visual Basic always matches an Else with the last unmatched If, regardless of the indentation.

Feedback 4.2

Assume that iFrogs = 10, and iToads = 5, and iPolliwogs = 6. What will be displayed for each of the following statements?

```
1. If iFrogs > iPolliwogs Then
        optFrogs.Value = True
        optToads.Value = False
    Else
        optFrogs.Value = False
        optToads.Value = True
    End If
```

2. If iFrogs > iToads + iPolliwogs Then
        lblResult.Caption = "It's the frogs"
   Else
        lblResult.Caption = "It's the toads and the polliwogs"
   End If
3. If iPolliwogs > iToads And iFrogs <> 0 Or iToads = 0 Then
        lblResult.Caption = "It's true"
   Else
        lblResult.Caption = "It's false"
   End If
4. Write the statements necessary to compare txtApples.Text and txtOranges.Text. Display in lblMost.Caption which has more, the apples or the oranges.
5. Write the Basic statements that will test the current value of cBalance. When cBalance is greater than 0, the check box for Funds Available called chkFunds should be selected, the cBalance set back to 0, and iCounter incremented by 1. When cBalance is 0 or less, chkFunds should not be selected (do not change the value of cBalance or increment the counter).

Input Validation

Careful programmers check the values entered into text boxes before beginning the calculations. Validation is a form of self-protection; it is better to reject bad data than to spend hours (and sometimes days) trying to find an error only to discover that the problem was caused by a "user error." Finding and correcting the error early can often keep the program from producing erroneous results or halting with a run-time error.

Checking to verify that appropriate values have been entered for a text box is called *validation*. The validation may include checking the type of data, checking for specific values, or checking a range of values.

Checking the Data Type

You can make sure that data entered is truly numeric with Visual Basic's IsNumeric function. The IsNumeric function returns True or False to indicate the result of the value checking.

The IsNumeric Function—General Form

```
IsNumeric(expression)
```

The IsNumeric function tests whether the value is numeric and therefore can be used in a calculation. If numeric, the result will be True; if not, the result is False. This function can help avoid problems in procedures that contain calculations. If the data cannot be converted to a number, the calculation cannot be performed and a run-time error will occur. The only way the programmer can prevent the user from making this type of error is to check the contents of the field after the data has been entered.

The IsNumeric Function—Example

```
If IsNumeric(txtQuantity.Text) Then
    iQuantity = Val(txtQuantity.Text)
    lblDue.Caption = cPrice * iQuantity
End If
```

Checking for a Range of Values

Data validation may also include checking the reasonableness of a value. Assume you are using a text box to input the number of hours worked in a day. Even with overtime, the company does not allow more than 10 work hours in a single day. You could check the input for reasonableness with this code:

```
If Val(txtHours.Text) > 10 Then
    '.......
End If
```

So what should we do if the value is out of range? One solution is to display a message box to the user.

Message Boxes

A **message box** is a special type of Visual Basic window in which you can display a message to the user. You can display a message, an optional icon, a title bar caption, and command button(s) in a message box (Figure 4.8).

Validating input data is an appropriate time to use a message box. If we reject bad data, we need to tell the user why the desired action was not achieved.

Figure 4.8

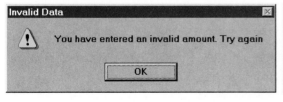
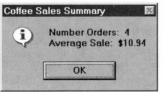

Two sample message boxes created with the MsgBox *statement.*

The MsgBox Statement—General Form

```
MsgBox "Message string" [, Buttons/icon][, "Caption of title bar"]
```

The *Message string* is the message you want to appear in the message box. The *Buttons* portion is optional; it determines the command buttons that will display and any icons that will appear. If you omit the *Caption of title bar*, the project name will appear in the message box title bar.

Usually you will display a message box in the `Else` clause of an `If` statement when checking the validity of data.

The MsgBox Statement—Example

```
If  IsNumeric(txtQuantity.Text)  Then
    iQuantity = Val(txtQuantity.Text)
    lblDue.Caption = cPrice * iQuantity
Else
    MsgBox "Please Enter a Numeric Value", vbOKOnly, "Error"
End If
```

Selecting the MsgBox Icon

For the button/icon entry, you can choose to use the numeric values in the following table, or to use the Visual Basic constant. For example, you can display the Warning Query icon with either of these statements:

```
MsgBox "Let this be a warning", vbQuestion, "Error"
```

or

```
MsgBox "Let this be a warning", 32, "Error"
```

Button/Icon	Value	Constant
OK button	0	vbOKOnly
Critical Message icon	16	vbCritical
Warning Query icon	32	vbQuestion
Warning Message icon	48	vbExclamation
Information Message icon	64	vbInformation

Note: MsgBox can be used as a statement, as explained here, which displays only an OK button. It can also be used as a function. When you use MsgBox as a function, you can choose the buttons to display (such as Yes, No, Cancel; or OK and Cancel). The function returns a value indicating which button was pressed. The MsgBox function is covered in Chapter 7.

Displaying a Message String

The message string you display may be a string literal enclosed in quotes or it may be a string variable. You may also want to concatenate several items, for example, combining a literal with a value from a variable. If the message you specify is too long for one line, Visual Basic will wrap it to the next line.

Combining Values into a Message String

You can concatenate a literal such as "Total Sales" with the value for the total sales:

```
Dim stMessageString As String

stMessageString = "Total Sales " & mcTotalSales
MsgBox stMessageString, vbOKOnly, "Sales Summary"
```

This example does not format the number. To remedy this condition, consider formatting the number before concatenating it to the string.

```
Dim stFormattedTotal  As String
Dim stMessageString   As String

stFormattedTotal = Format$(mcTotalSales, "Standard")
stMessageString = "Total Sales " & stFormattedTotal
MsgBox stMessageString, vbOKOnly, "Sales Summary"
```

Creating Multiple Lines of Output

If you want to display multiple lines of output, you can insert a line feed/carriage return code into the line. Use the Visual Basic intrinsic constant vbCRLF to determine line endings. You can concatenate this constant into a message string to set up multiple lines. This will allow you to determine the position of the line break, rather than rely on word wrap.

In this example, a second line is added to the MsgBox from the previous example.

```
Dim stFormattedTotal  As String
Dim stMessageString   As String

stFormattedTotal = Format$(mcTotalSales, "Standard")
stFormattedAvg = Format$(mcAverageSale, "Standard")
stMessageString = "Total Sales " & stFormattedTotal & vbCRLF & _
                "Average Sale " & stFormattedAvg
MsgBox stMessageString, vbOKOnly, "Sales Summary"
```

Calling Event Procedures

If you wish to perform a set of instructions in more than one location, you don't have to duplicate the code. Write the instructions once, in an event procedure, and "call" the procedure from another procedure. When you **call** an event procedure, the entire procedure is executed and then execution returns to the statement following the call.

The Call Statement (No Arguments)—General Form

```
[Call] ProcedureName
```

Notice that the keyword `Call` is optional and rarely used.

The Call Statement—Examples

```
Call cmdCalculate_Click
cmdCalculate_Click 'Equivalent to previous statement
```

In the programming example that follows, you will accumulate individual items for one customer. When that customer's order is complete, you need to clear the entire order and begin an order for the next customer. Refer to the interface in Figure 4.9; notice the two command buttons: *Clear for Next Item* and *New Order*. The command button for next item clears the text boxes on the screen. The command button for a new order must clear the screen text boxes *and* clear the subtotal fields. Rather than repeat the instructions to clear the individual screen text boxes, we can call the event procedure for cmdNewOrder from the cmdClear_Click procedure.

Figure 4.9

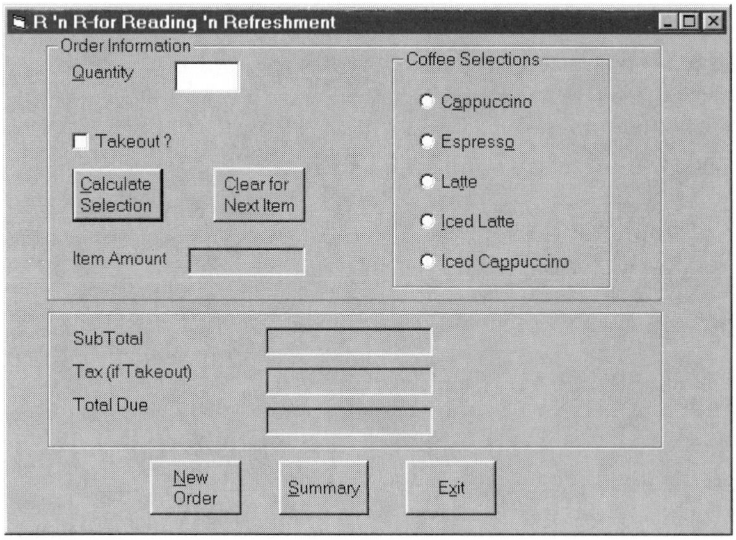

A form with command buttons that perform overlapping functions. The New Order button must do the same tasks as Clear for New Item.

```
Private Sub cmdNewOrder_Click()
     'Clear the current item and the current order

     cmdClear_Click 'call the procedure for the click event of cmdClear
     ... 'Continue with statements to clear subtotals
```

In the cmdNewOrder_Click procedure, all of the instructions in cmdClear_Click are executed. Then execution returns to the next statement following the call.

Your Hands-On Programming Example

Create a project for R 'n R—for Reading 'n Refreshment that calculates the amount due for individual orders and maintains accumulated totals for a summary. Have a check box for takeout items, which are taxable (8 percent); all other orders are nontaxable. Include option buttons for the five coffee selections—Cappuccino, Espresso, Latte, Iced Cappuccino, and Iced Latte. The prices for each will be assigned using these constants:

Cappuccino	2.00
Espresso	2.25
Latte	1.75
Iced (either)	2.50

Use a command button for Calculate This Item, which will calculate and display the amount due for each item. A button for Clear for Next Item will clear the selections and amount for the single item. Additional labels in a separate frame will maintain the summary information for the current order to include subtotal, tax, and total.

Buttons at the bottom of the form will be used for Next Order, Summary, and Exit. The Next Order button will clear the bill for the current customer and add to the totals for the summary. The button for Summary should display the average sale amount per customer and the number of customers.

Planning the Project

Sketch a form (Figure 4.10), which your users sign as meeting their needs.

The planning sketch of the form for the hands-on programming exercise.

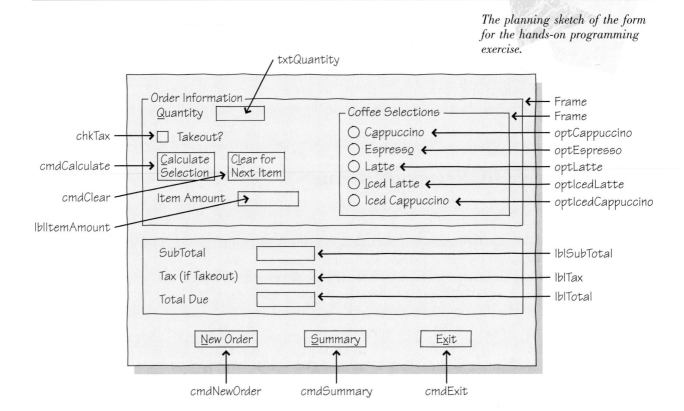

Plan the Objects and Properties

Plan the property settings for the form and each of the controls.

Object	Property	Setting
frmBilling	Name	frmBilling
	Caption	R 'n R—for Reading 'n Refreshment
Frame1	Caption	Order Information
Frame2	Caption	Coffee Selections
Frame3	Caption	(blank)
optCappuccino	Name	optCappuccino
	Caption	C&appuccino
optEspresso	Name	optEspresso
	Caption	Espress&o
optLatte	Name	optLatte
	Caption	La&tte
optIcedLatte	Name	optIcedLatte
	Caption	&Iced Latte

(continued)

Object	Property	Setting
optIcedCappuccino	Name	optIcedCappuccino
	Caption	Iced Ca&ppuccino
Label1	Caption	&Quantity
txtQuantity	Name	txtQuantity
	Text	(blank)
chkTax	Name	chkTax
	Caption	Takeout ?
Label2	Caption	Item Amount
Label3	Caption	SubTotal
Label4	Caption	Tax (if Takeout)
Label5	Caption	Total Due
lblItemAmount	Name	lblItemAmount
	Caption	(blank)
	BorderStyle	1 - FixedSingle
lblSubTotal	Name	lblSubTotal
	Caption	(blank)
	BorderStyle	1 - Fixed Single
lblTax	Name	lblTax
	Caption	(blank)
	BorderStyle	1 - Fixed Single
lblTotal	Name	lblTotal
	Caption	(blank)
	BorderStyle	1 - Fixed Single
cmdCalculate	Name	cmdCalculate
	Caption	&Calculate Selection
	Default	True
cmdClear	Name	cmdClear
	Caption	C&lear for Next Item
	Cancel	True
cmdNewOrder	Name	cmdNewOrder
	Caption	&New Order
cmdSummary	Name	cmdSummary
	Caption	&Summary
cmdExit	Name	cmdExit
	Caption	E&xit

Plan the Event Procedures

You need to plan the actions for five event procedures for the command.

Object	Procedure	Action
cmdCalculate	Click	Determine price per cup. Multiply price by quantity. Calculate tax if needed. Calculate total = subtotal + tax. Display the values.
cmdClear	Click	Clear the coffee selections. Clear the quantity and the item price. Disable the takeout check box. Set the focus to the quantity.
cmdSummary	Click	Display the average. Display the number of customers.
cmdNewOrder	Click	Clear the previous order. Accumulate total sales and count. Set subtotal and total due to 0. Enable takeout check box.
cmdExit	Click	Terminate the project.

Write the project

Follow the sketch in Figure 4.10 to create the form. Figure 4.11 shows the completed form.

Figure 4.11

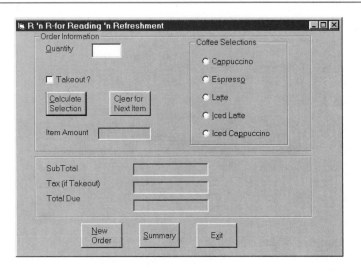

The form for the hands-on programming exercise.

- Set the properties of each object as you have planned.

- Write the code. Working from the pseudocode, write each event procedure.

- When you complete the code, use a variety of data to thoroughly test the project. Make sure the tab order is set correctly so that the insertion point begins in txtQuantity.

The Project Coding Solution

```
'Program Name:    Billing
'Programmer:      A. Millspaugh
'Date:            July 1997
'Description:     This project calculates the amount due
'                 based on the customer selection
'                 and accumulates summary data for the day.
'Folder:          Ch0401

Option Explicit
Dim mcSubtotal              As Currency
Dim mcTotal                 As Currency
Dim mcGrandTotal            As Currency
Dim miCustomerCount         As Integer
Const cCAPPUCCINO_PRICE     As Currency = 2
Const cESPRESSO_PRICE       As Currency = 2.25
Const cLATTE_PRICE          As Currency = 1.75
Const cICED_PRICE           As Currency = 2.5
```

```
Private Sub cmdCalculate_Click()
    'Calculate and display the current amounts, add to totals

    Dim cPrice              As Currency
    Dim iQuantity           As Integer
    Dim cTax                As Currency
    Dim cItemAmount         As Currency
    Const cTAX_RATE         As Currency = 0.08

    'Find the price
    If optCappuccino.Value = True Then
        cPrice = cCAPPUCCINO_PRICE
    ElseIf optEspresso.Value = True Then
        cPrice = cESPRESSO_PRICE
    ElseIf optLatte.Value = True Then
        cPrice = cLATTE_PRICE
    ElseIf optIcedCappuccino.Value = True Or _
            optIcedLatte.Value = True Then
        cPrice = cICED_PRICE
    Else
        MsgBox "Please Make Drink Selection", vbExclamation, "Oops"
    End If
```

```
        'Add the price times quantity to price so far
        If IsNumeric(txtQuantity.Text) Then
            iQuantity = Val(txtQuantity.Text)
            cItemAmount = cPrice * iQuantity
            mcSubtotal = mcSubtotal + cItemAmount
            If chkTax.Value = Checked Then
                cTax = mcSubtotal * cTAX_RATE
            End If
            mcTotal = mcSubtotal + cTax
            lblItemAmount.Caption = Format$(cItemAmount, "Currency")
            lblSubTotal.Caption = Format$(mcSubtotal, "Currency")
            lblTax.Caption = Format$(cTax, "Currency")
            lblTotal.Caption = Format$(mcTotal, "Currency")
        Else
            MsgBox "Quantity must be numeric", vbExclamation, "Oops"
            txtQuantity.SetFocus
        End If
End Sub
```

```
Private Sub cmdClear_Click()
    'Clear appropriate controls

    optCappuccino.Value = True    'Make first button selected to begin
    optEspresso.Value = False
    optLatte.Value = False
    optIcedLatte.Value = False
    optIcedCappuccino.Value = False
    lblItemAmount.Caption = ""
    chkTax.Enabled = False    'Allow change for new order only
    With txtQuantity
        .Text = ""
        .SetFocus  — Sets focus back to txt Quantity for tab function
    End With
End Sub
```

```
Private Sub cmdExit_Click()
    'Terminate the project

    End
End Sub
```

```
Private Sub cmdNewOrder_Click()
    'Clear the current order and add to totals

    cmdClear_Click
    lblSubTotal.Caption = ""
    lblTax.Caption = ""
    lblTotal.Caption = ""

    'Add to Totals
    mcGrandTotal = mcGrandTotal + mcTotal
    mcSubtotal = 0
    mcTotal = 0    'reset for next customer
    miCustomerCount = miCustomerCount + 1
```

```
    'Clear appropriate display items and enable check box
    With chkTax
         .Enabled = True
         .Value = False
    End With
End Sub
```

```
Private Sub cmdSummary_Click()
    'Calculate the average and Display the totals

    Dim cAverage As Currency
    Dim stMessageString As String
    Dim stFormattedAvg As String

    If miCustomerCount > 0 Then
        If mcTotal <> 0 Then
            cmdNewOrder_Click   'Make sure last order is counted
        End If
        cAverage = mcGrandTotal / miCustomerCount

        'Format the numbers
        stFormattedAvg = Format$(cAverage, "Currency")
        'Concatenate the message string
        stMessageString = "Number Orders: " & miCustomerCount & vbCrLf & _
            "Average Sale: " & stFormattedAvg
        MsgBox stMessageString, vbInformation, "Coffee Sales Summary"
    Else
        MsgBox "No data to summarize", vbExclamation, "Coffee Sales Summary"
    End If
End Sub
```

Debugging Visual Basic Projects

One of the advantages of programming in the Visual Basic environment is the availability of debugging tools. You can use these tools to help find and eliminate logic and run-time errors. The debugging tools can also help you to follow the logic of existing projects to better understand how they work.

You can use the buttons in the toolbar or the *Debug* menu to access Visual Basic's debugging tools. (See Figure 4.12.) The debugging tools include the Debug window, single-stepping through a project, and watching the contents of variables and expressions.

F i g u r e   4 . 1 2

The debugging options on the Run *menu.*

Pausing Execution with the Break Button

You can click on the Break toolbar button to pause execution. This places the project into break time at the current line. The disadvantage of this method is that usually you prefer to break in the middle of a procedure. To choose the location of the break, you can force a break.

Forcing a Break

During the debugging process, often you want to stop at a particular location in code and watch what happens (which branch of an `If...Then...Else`; which procedures were executed; the value of a variable just before or just after a calculation). You can force the project to break by inserting a **break-point** in code.

```
If IsNumeric(txtQuantity.Text) Then
    lblDue.Caption = cPrice * txtQuantity.Text
Else
    MsgBox "Please Enter a Numeric Value", vbOKOnly, "Error"
End If
```

To set a breakpoint, place the cursor in the gray margin indicator area at the left edge of the Code window and click; the line will be highlighted in red and a large red dot will display in the margin indicator (Figure 4.13). You can also set a breakpoint by placing the cursor on the line before which you want to break and clicking on the Set Breakpoint button, by choosing *Toggle Breakpoint* from the *Run* menu, or by pressing F9, the keyboard short-cut. The breakpoint line will change to red (unless colors have been altered on your system).

F i g u r e   4 . 1 3

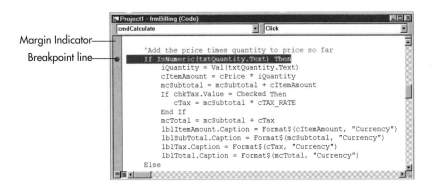

Margin Indicator
Breakpoint line

The highlighted line is set as a breakpoint. Note the dot in the gray margin indicator area.

After setting a breakpoint, start (or restart) program execution. When the project reaches the breakpoint, it will halt, display the line, and go into break time.

You can use *Toggle Breakpoint* again to turn off an individual breakpoint or clear all breakpoints from the *Run* menu.

Using the Immediate Window

The **Immediate window** is available at design time, run time, and break time. You can display the values of data or messages in the Immediate window while the project is executing. In break time you can use the Immediate window to view or change the current contents of variables or to execute lines of code. At design time you can view the window to see values from the previous run, but you cannot execute any code. You can display the window by selecting it from the *View* menu or use the shortcut Ctrl + G. You may want to move and resize the window to make it more visible. Figure 4.14 shows the Immediate window.

Figure 4.14

You can execute program statements in the Immediate window.

Checking the Current Values of Expressions

You can quickly check the current value of an expression, such as a variable, a control, a condition, or an arithmetic expression. During break time, display the Code window and point to the name of the expression that you want to view; a small label will pop up, similar to a ToolTip, which displays the current contents of the expression. If you want to view the contents of an expression of more than one word, such as a condition or arithmetic expression, highlight the entire expression and then point to the highlighted area; the current value will display. *Note:* For True/False values, Visual Basic displays 0 for False and −1 for True.

The steps for viewing the contents of a variable during run time are

1. Break the execution (using the *Run* menu, the toolbar button, or a breakpoint).
2. Click on the View Code button in the Project Explorer window or select *Code* from the *View* menu.
3. Point to the variable or expression you wish to view.

The current contents of the expression will pop up in a label (Figure 4.15).

Figure 4.15

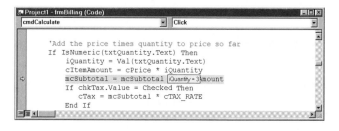

Point to a variable name, control name, condition, or arithmetic expression during break time to display the current value.

Stepping through Code

The best way to debug a project is to thoroughly understand what the project is doing every step of the way. Previously, this task was performed by following each line of code manually to understand its effect. You can now use the Visual Basic stepping tools to trace program execution line by line and see the progression of the program as it executes through your code.

You step through code at break time. You can use one of the techniques already mentioned to break execution or choose one of the stepping commands at design time; the program will begin running and immediately transfer to break time.

Two stepping commands on the *Debug* menu are *Step Into* and *Step Over*. You can also use the toolbar buttons for Step Into and Step Over or the keyboard shortcuts shown on the menu (refer to Figure 4.12).

These commands force the project to execute a single line at a time and to display the Code window with the current statement highlighted. As you execute the project, by pressing a command button, for example, the Click event occurs. Execution transfers to the click procedure, the Code window for that procedure appears on the screen, and you can follow line-by-line execution.

Step Into

Most likely you will use the **Step Into** command more than Step Over. When you choose Step Into (from the menu, the toolbar button, or F8), the next line of code is executed and the program pauses again in break time. If the line of code is a call to another procedure, the first line of code of the other procedure will be displayed.

To continue stepping through your program execution, continue choosing the Step Into command. When a procedure is completed, your form will display again, awaiting an event. You can click on one of your command buttons to continue stepping through code in an event procedure. If you want to continue execution without stepping, choose the Start command (from the menu, the toolbar button, or F5).

Step Over

The **Step Over** command also executes one line of code at a time. The difference between Step Over and Step Into occurs when your code has calls to other procedures. Step Over displays only the lines of code in the current procedure being analyzed; it does not display lines of code in the called procedures.

You can choose *Step Over* from the menu, from the toolbar button, or press Shift + F8. Each time you choose the command, one more program statement executes.

Debugging Step-by-Step Tutorial

In this exercise you will learn to set a breakpoint; pause program execution; single step through program instructions; display the current values in properties, variables, and conditions; and debug a Visual Basic project.

Test the Project

STEP 1: Open the debugging project on your student diskette. The project is found in the Ch04Debug folder.

STEP 2: Run the project.

STEP 3: Enter color Blue, quantity 100, and press Enter or click on the Calculate button.

STEP 4: Enter another color Blue, quantity 50, and press Enter. Are the totals correct?

STEP 5: Enter color Red, quantity 30, and press Enter.

STEP 6: Enter color Red, quantity 10, and press Enter. Are the totals correct?

STEP 7: Enter color White, quantity 50, and press Enter.

STEP 8: Enter color White, quantity 100, and press Enter. Are the totals correct?

STEP 9: Exit the project. You are going to locate and correct the errors in the red and white totals.

Break and Step Program Execution

STEP 1: Display the program code and click in the gray margin indicator area for the first calculation line in the cmdCalculate_Click event procedure:

```
cQuantity = Val(txtQuantity.Text)
```

A breakpoint will be set on the selected line. You screen should look like Figure 4.16.

Figure 4.16

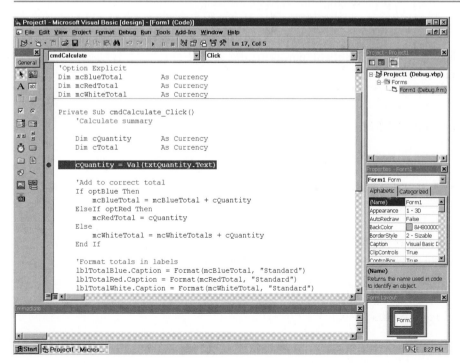

A program statement with a breakpoint set appears highlighted, and a dot appears in the gray margin indicator area.

STEP 2: Close the Code window.

STEP 3: Run the project, enter Red, quantity 30, and press Enter.

       The project will transfer control to the cmdCalculate_Click procedure, stop when the breakpoint is reached, highlight the current line, and enter break time (Figure 4.17).

       Note: The highlighted line has not yet executed.

Figure 4.17

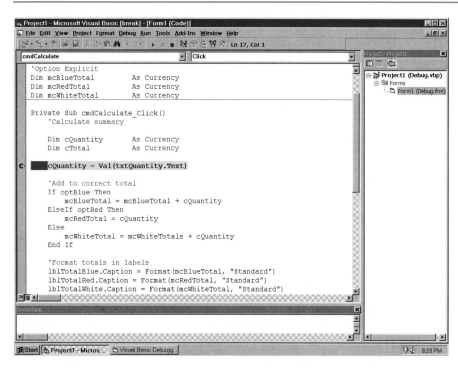

When a breakpoint is reached during project execution, Visual Basic enters break time, displays the Code window, and highlights the breakpoint line.

STEP 4: Press the F8 key, which causes VB to execute the current program statement (the assignment statement). F8 is the keyboard shortcut for *Debug/Step Into*.

       The statement is executed and the highlight moves to the next statement (the `If` statement).

STEP 5: Press F8 again; the condition (`optBlue`) is tested and found to be False.

STEP 6: Continue pressing F8 and watch the order in which program statements execute.

View the Contents of Properties, Variables, and Conditions

STEP 1: Scroll up if necessary and point to `txtQuantity.Text` in the breakpoint line. The current contents of the Text property pops up (Figure 4.18).

Figure 4.18

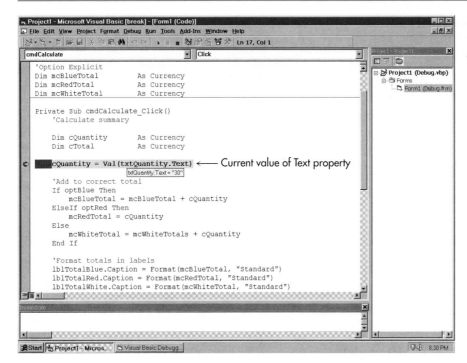

Point to a property reference in code, and the current content pops up.

STEP 2: Point to `cQuantity` and view the contents of that variable. Notice that the Text property is enclosed in quotes and the numeric variable is not.

STEP 3: Point to `optBlue` in the `If` statement; then point to `optRed`. The value that pops up is the current state of the Value property (the default property of an option button).

STEP 4: Point to `mcRedTotal` to see the current value of that total variable. This value looks correct, since you just entered 30, which was added to the total.

Continue Project Execution

STEP 1: Press F5, the keyboard shortcut for the Start command. The Start command continues execution.

If the current line is any line other than `Exit Sub`, execution continues and your form reappears. If the current line is `Exit Sub`, you must click on your project's Taskbar button (Figure 4.19) to make the form reappear.

Figure   4.19

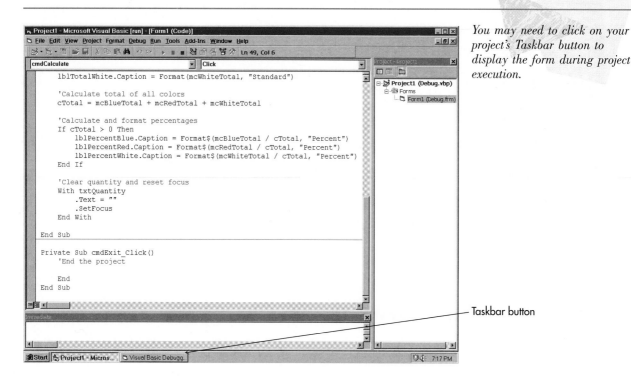

You may need to click on your project's Taskbar button to display the form during project execution.

Taskbar button

STEP 2: Enter color Red and quantity 10. When you press Enter, program execution will again break at the breakpoint.

   The 10 you just entered should be added to the 30 previously entered for Red, producing 40 in the Red total.

STEP 3: Use F8 to step through execution. Keep pressing F8 until the 10 is added to mcRedTotal. Display the current contents of the total. Can you see what the problem is?

   Hint: mcRedTotal has only the current amount, not the sum of the two amounts. The answer will appear a little later; try to find it yourself first.

   You will fix this error soon, after testing the White total.

Test the White Total

STEP 1: Press F5 to continue execution. If the form does not reappear, click the project's Taskbar button.

STEP 2: Enter color White, quantity 100, and press Enter.

STEP 3: When execution halts at the breakpoint, press F5 to continue.

STEP 4: Enter color White, quantity 50, and press Enter.

STEP 5: Press F8 several times when execution halts at the breakpoint until you execute the line that adds the 50 to the White total. Remember that the highlighted line has not yet executed; press F8 one more time, if necessary, to execute the addition statement.

STEP 6: Point to each variable name to see the current values (Figure 4.20). Can you see the problem?

Figure 4.20

Point to a variable name in code, and its current value displays.

— Current value of variable

STEP 7: Identify all the errors. When you are ready to make the corrections, continue.

Correct the Red Total Error

STEP 1: Stop program execution by clicking on the End toolbar button (Figure 4.21).

Figure 4.21

Click on the End toolbar button to halt project execution.

— End toolbar button

STEP 2: Locate this line:

```
mcRedTotal  =  cQuantity
```

This statement *replaces* the value of mcRedTotal with cQuantity rather than *adding* to the total.

STEP 3: Change the line to read

```
mcRedTotal  =  mcRedTotal  +  cQuantity
```

Correct the White Total Error

STEP 1: Locate this line:

```
mcWhiteTotal  =  mcWhiteTotals  +  cQuantity
```

Have you found the problem with this line? Look carefully at the spelling of the variable names. The compiler would find this error if the project included an `Option  Explicit` statement.

STEP 2: First scroll up to the General Declarations section and remove the apostrophe from the `Option  Explicit` statement.

STEP 3: Run the project again.

STEP 4: Enter color White and quantity 100; then press Enter.

The compiler displays a compile error message; click OK, and the Code window redisplays with the offending variable name highlighted (Figure 4.22).

```
'Add to correct total
If optBlue Then
    mcBlueTotal = mcBlueTotal + cQuantity
ElseIf optRed Then
    mcRedTotal = mcRedTotal + cQuantity
Else
    mcWhiteTotal = mcWhiteTotals + cQuantity
End If

'Format totals in labels
lblTotalBlue.Caption = Format(mcBlueTotal, "Standard")
lblTotalRed.Caption = Format(mcRedTotal, "Standard")
lblTotalWhite.Caption = Format(mcWhiteTotal, "Standard")
```

— Problem area highlighted

After a compile error, the Code window displays with the problem area highlighted.

STEP 5: Remove the s from `mcWhiteTotals`. The line should read:

```
mcWhiteTotal = mcWhiteTotal + cQuantity
```

STEP 6: Press F5 to continue project and execution. Remember that you already entered White and 100.

STEP 7: Press F5 to continue when the project halts at the breakpoint.

STEP 8: Enter White, 50, and Enter.

STEP 9: At the breakpoint, click on the breakpoint line, and select *Toggle Breakpoint* from the *Debug* menu to clear the breakpoint.

STEP 10: Press F5 to continue and check the total on the form. It should be correct now.

STEP 11: Test the totals for all three colors carefully and then click Exit.

Force a Run-Time Error

STEP 1: Display the code window and locate this line:

```
If cTotal > 0 Then
```

STEP 2: Type an apostrophe at the beginning of the line; then place another apostrophe on the End If line (Figure 4.23). This practice, called *commenting out* a statement, is a useful way to test program code.

Figure 4.23

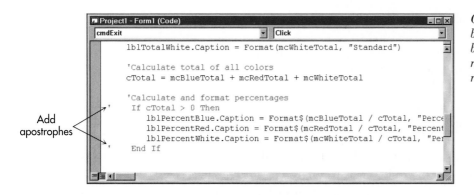

Add apostrophes

Convert statements to comments by typing an apostrophe at the beginning of the line. You can remove the apostrophes later to restore the lines.

STEP 3: Run the project. This time click the Calculate button without entering an Amount.

A run-time error will occur.

STEP 4: Click *Debug* on the error dialog box, and the Code window will display with the offending line highlighted.

STEP 5: Point to each variable name to see its value. Of course this error occurred because it is illegal to divide by zero.

STEP 6: Notice that the program is in break time. Click the End toolbar button to return to design time.

STEP 7: Remove the apostrophes from the If and End If lines.

STEP 8: Test the project carefully and thoroughly. If you have corrected all the errors, it should run correctly now.

Summary

1. Visual Basic uses the `If...Then...Else` statement to make decisions. An `Else` clause is optional and specifies the action to be taken if the condition is false. An `If...Then...Else` statement must conclude with an `End If`.

2. Flowcharts can help visualize the logic of an `If...Then...Else` statement.

3. The conditions for an `If` statement can be composed of the relational operators, which compare items for equality, greater than, or less than. The comparison of numeric values is based on the quantity of the number, while string comparisons are based on the ASCII code table.

4. The `Ucase` and `Lcase` functions can convert a text value to upper- or lowercase.

5. The `And` and `Or` logical operators may be used to combine multiple conditions. With the `And` operator, both conditions must be true for the entire condition to evaluate True. For the `Or` operator, if either or both conditions are true, the entire condition evaluates as True. When both `And` and `Or` are used in a condition, the `And` condition is evaluated before the `Or` condition.

6. The state of option buttons and check boxes should be tested with `If` statements in the event procedure for a command button, rather than coding event procedures for the option button or check box.

7. A nested `If` statement contains an `If` statement within either the true or false actions of a previous `If` statement. Nesting an `If` statement inside of another requires the use of the `End If` clause. An `Else` clause always applies to the last unmatched `If` regardless of indentation.

8. Data validation checks the reasonableness or appropriateness of the value in a variable or property. Since an error will occur if the data placed in a text box are not numeric, a popular validation tool is the `IsNumeric` function.

9. The `MsgBox` statement can be used to display a message to the person running the program. The programmer must supply the message and can optionally select an icon to display and enter a caption for the message box title bar.

10. One procedure can call another procedure.

11. A variety of debugging tools are available in Visual Basic. These include breaking program execution, displaying the current contents of variables, and stepping through code.

Key Terms

Review Questions

1. What is the general format of the statement used to code decisions in an application?
2. What is a condition?
3. Explain the purpose of relational operators and logical operators.
4. Differentiate between a comparison performed on numeric data and a comparison performed on string data.
5. How does Visual Basic compare the Text property of a text box?
6. Why would it be useful to include the Ucase function in a comparison?
7. Name the types of items that can be used in a comparison.
8. Explain a Boolean variable test for True and False. Give an example.
9. Give an example of a situation where nested Ifs would be appropriate.
10. When would you use a message box?
11. Give an example of three message box constants.
12. Define the term *validation*. When is it appropriate to do validation?
13. Define the term *checking a range*.
14. Explain the difference between Step Into and Step Over.
15. What steps are necessary to view the current contents of a variable during program execution?

Programming Exercises

4.1 Lynette Rifle owns an image consulting shop. Her clients can select from the following services at the specified regular prices: Makeover $125, Hair Styling $60, Manicure $35, and Permanent Makeup $200. She has distributed discount coupons that advertise discounts of 10 percent and 20 percent off the regular price. Create a project that will allow the receptionist to select a discount rate of 10 percent, 20 percent, or none, and then select a service. Display the price for the individual service in a label and have another label to display the total due after each visit is entered. Include command buttons for *Calculate, Clear, Print Form*, and *Exit.*

4.2   Modify project 4.1 to allow for sales to additional patrons. Include command buttons for *Next Patron* and *Summary*. When the receptionist clicks the *Summary* button, display the number of clients and the total dollar value for all services rendered in a summary message box.

4.3   Create a project to compute your checking account balance.
Form: Include option buttons to indicate the type of transaction—deposit, check, or service charge. A text box will allow the user to enter the amount of the transaction. Display the new balance in a label. Calculate the balance by adding deposits and subtracting service charges and checks. Include command buttons for *Calculate*, *Clear*, and *Exit*.

4.4   Add validation to project 4.3 by displaying a message box if the new balance would be a negative number. If there is not enough money to cover a check, do not deduct the check amount. Instead, display a message box with the message "Insufficient Funds" and deduct a service charge of $10.

4.5   Modify project 4.3 or 4.4 by adding a *Summary* command button that will display the total number of deposits, the total dollar amount of deposits, the number of checks, and the dollar amount of the checks. Do not include checks that were returned for insufficient funds, but do include the service charges.

4.6   Piecework workers are paid by the piece. Workers who produce a greater quantity of output are often paid at a higher rate.
Form: Use text boxes to obtain the person's name and the number of pieces completed. Include a *Calculate* command button to display the dollar amount earned. You will need a *Summary* button to display the total number of pieces, the total pay, and the average pay per person. A *Clear* button should clear the name and the number of pieces for the current employee.

    Include validation to check for missing data. If the user clicks on the *Calculate* button without first entering a name and number of pieces, display a message box. Also, you need to make sure to not display a summary before any data are entered; you cannot calculate an average when no items have been calculated. You can check the number of employees in the Summary event procedure or disable the *Summary* command button until the first order has been calculated.

Pieces Completed	Price Paid per Piece for All Pieces
1–199	.50
200–399	.55
400–599	.60
600 or more	.65

4.7   Modify project 2.3 (the weather report) to treat option buttons the proper way. Do not have an event procedure for each option button; instead use a *Display* command button to display the correct image and message.

4.8 Modify project 2.2 (the flag viewer) to treat option buttons and check boxes in the proper way. Include a *Display* command button and check the settings of the option buttons and check boxes in the button's event procedure, rather than code event procedures for each option button and check box.

··

CASE STUDIES

Calculate the amount due for an order. For an order, the user should enter the following information into text boxes: customer name, address, city, state (two-letter abbreviation), and ZIP code. An order may consist of multiple items. For each item, the user will enter the product description, quantity, weight, and price into text boxes.

You will need command buttons for *Next Item, Update Summary, Print*, and *Exit*.

For the *Next Item* button, validate the quantity, weight, and price. Each must be present and numeric. For any bad data, display a message box. Calculate the charge for the current item and add the charge and weight into the appropriate totals. Do not calculate shipping and handling on individual items; rather, calculate shipping and handling on the entire order.

When the *Update Summary* button is clicked, calculate the sales tax, shipping and handling, and the total amount due for the order. Sales tax is 8 percent of the total charge and is charged only for shipments to a California address. Do not charge sales tax on the shipping and handling charges.

The shipping and handling charges depend on the weight of the products. Calculate the shipping charge as $.25 per pound and add that amount to the handling charge (taken from the following table).

VB Mail Order

Display the entire amount of the bill in labels titled *Dollar amount due, Sales tax, Shipping and handling*, and *Total amount due*.

Test Data

Description	Quantity	Weight	Price
Planter	2	3	19.95
Mailbox	1	2	24.95
Planter	2	3	19.95

Test Data Output

	Nontaxable	Taxable
Dollar Amount Due	$110.80	$110.80
Sales Tax	0.00	8.86
Shipping and Handling	5.75	5.75
Total Amount Due	116.55	125.41

Weight	Handling
Less than 10 pounds	$1.00
10 to 100 pounds	$3.00
Over 100 pounds	$5.00

Create a project that will be used to determine the total amount due for the purchase of a vehicle. You will need text boxes for the base price and the trade-in allowance. Check boxes will indicate if the buyer wants additional accessories: stereo system, leather interior, and/or computer navigation. A frame for the exterior finish will contain option buttons for Standard, Pearlized, or Customized Detailing.

VB Auto Center

Have the trade-in allowance default to 0; that is, if the user does not enter a trade-in value, use 0 in your calculation. Validate the values from the text boxes, displaying a message box if necessary.

To calculate, add the price of selected accessories and finish to the base price and display the result in a label called *Subtotal*. Calculate the sales tax on the subtotal and display the result in a *Total* label. Then subtract any trade-in value from the total and display the result in an *Amount Due* label.

Include command buttons for *Calculate*, *Clear*, *Exit*, and *Print Form*. The Calculate button must display the total amount due after trade-in.

Item	Price
Stereo System	425.76
Leather Interior	987.41
Computer Navigation	1,741.23
Standard	No additional charge
Pearlized	345.72
Customized Detailing	599.99
Tax Rate	8%

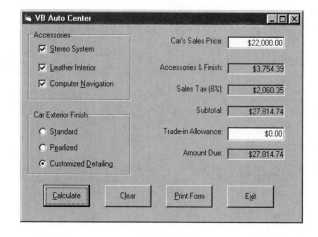

5

Menus, Sub Procedures, and Sub Functions

At the completion of this chapter, you will be able to...

1. Create menus and submenus for program control.

2. Display and use the Windows common dialog boxes.

3. Write reusable code in sub procedures and function procedures, and call the procedures from other locations.

4. Create an executable file that can be run from the Windows environment.

Menus

Undoubtedly you have used menus quite extensively while working with the computer. **Menus** consist of a menu bar with menu names, each of which drops down to display a list of menu commands. You can use menu commands in place of or in addition to command buttons to activate a procedure.

Menu commands are actually controls; they have properties and events. Each menu command has a Name property and a Click event, similar to a command button.

It is easy to create a menu for your form, using the Visual Basic menu editor. Your menu will appear across the top of the window and look like a standard Windows menu.

To use the menu editor, select *Menu Editor* from the *Tools* menu or click on the Menu Editor toolbar button (Figure 5.1).

Figure 5.1

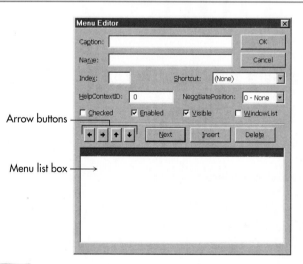

The Menu Editor toolbar button.

Defining Menus

You will use the Menu Editor window to set up your menus. Figure 5.2 shows the Menu Editor window with the various parts labeled.

Figure 5.2

Define menus with the Menu Editor window.

The Caption

The Caption property holds the words you want to appear on the screen (just like the Caption property of a label or command button). Start creating a new menu by entering the Caption of the item you want for your first menu.

To conform to Windows standards, your first menu Caption should be File, with a keyboard access key. Use the ampersand (&) in the Caption to specify the key to use for keyboard access, as you learned in Chapter 2. For example, for File, the Caption should be &File.

The Name

The Name box indicates the name of the menu control, similar to other controls. The Name is required.

menu = "mnu"

Naming Standards

The three-character prefix for a menu name is "mnu". Therefore, the name for the *File* menu should be mnuFile. For the commands on a menu use the prefix plus the name of the menu plus the name of the command. (You can abbreviate long names, if you do so consistently and clearly.) The name for the *Print* command on the *File* menu should be mnuFilePrint. The *Exit* command should be called mnuFileExit, which will trigger the mnuFileExit_Click event when the user selects it.

SubMenus

The drop-down list of commands below a menu name is called a *menu*. When a command on the menu has another list of commands that pops up, the new list is called a *submenu*. A filled triangle to the right of the command indicates that a menu command has a submenu (Figure 5.3).

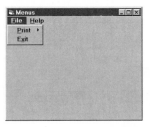

Figure 5.3

A filled triangle on a menu command indicates that a submenu will appear.

    You specify menu names, menu commands, and submenu commands by their indentation levels. Menu names appear at the left of the list box; for a menu command, click on the Right arrow button to indent one level. For submenus, click on the Right arrow button again to indent two levels. The indentations show as dots (....) in the list box.

The Menu List Box

The menu list box contains a list of the menu items you have created and shows their indentation levels. You can move an item up or down, left or right by clicking on its name in the list box and clicking on one of the arrow buttons (refer to Figure 5.2).

```
&File
....E&xit
&Help
....&About
```

Separator Bars

When you have many commands in a menu, you should group the commands according to their purpose. You can create a **separator bar** in a menu, which draws a bar across the entire menu. To define a separator bar, type a single hyphen (-) for the Caption and give it a name. Even though you can never refer to the separator bar in code, and it does not have a Click event, you must still give it a unique name. Call your first separator bar mnuSep1, your second separator bar mnuSep2, and so on.

Creating a Menu—Step-by-Step

You are going to create a project with one form and a menu bar that contains these menu items:

<u>F</u>ile   <u>H</u>elp
   E<u>x</u>it   About

STEP 1: Display the Menu Editor window (refer to Figure 5.2) by selecting *Menu Editor* from the *Tools* menu or clicking on the Menu Editor tool-bar button (refer to Figure 5.1).

STEP 2: Type the Caption (&File) and Name (mnuFile) for the first menu (Figure 5.4).

F i g u r e   5 . 4

Type the Caption and Name for the first menu name.

STEP 3: Click on the *Next* button or press Enter; the text boxes will clear, and the name of your first menu appears in the menu list box (Figure 5.5).

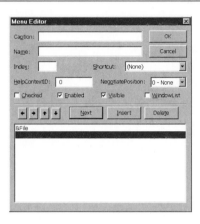

After entering the first menu name, the text boxes clear and the Caption of the first menu appears in the menu list box.

STEP 4: Click on the Right arrow button, which sets the indentation level for a menu command.

STEP 5: Click in the Caption text box to set the focus and then type the Caption and the Name for the Exit menu command (Figure 5.6).

Type the Caption and Name for the Exit menu command.

STEP 6: Click on the Left arrow (outdent) button to return to the previous level.

STEP 7: Repeat the steps to create the *Help* menu and the *About* command indented below it (Figure 5.7).

Figure   5.7

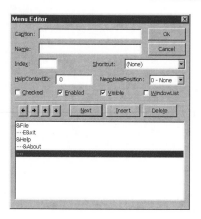

The completed menu appears in the menu list box.

STEP 8: Click OK when you are finished. The new menu will appear on your form.

Coding for Menu Commands

After you create your form's menu bar, it will appear on the form in design time. Just select any menu command, and the control's Click event procedure will appear in the Code window where you can write the code. For example, in design time, open your form's *File* menu and choose *Exit*. The Code window will open with the mnuFileExit_Click procedure displayed (assuming you have followed the suggested naming conventions and named the Exit command mnuFileExit).

STEP 9: Code the procedure for the Exit by pulling down the menu and clicking on the word *Exit*. Type in the remark and the *End* statement.

STEP 10: Use a MsgBox statement in the procedure for the Click event of the *About* on the *Help* menu. The Message string should say "Programmed by " followed by your name (Figure 5.8).

Tip

You can rearrange the order of the menus and menu commands. Click on a name in the text box and click on the up and down arrows. Add or remove items using the Insert and Delete buttons.

Figure   5.8

Display a message box for an About box.

Modifying a Menu

You can easily make changes to a menu bar you have created. With the form displaying in design time, display the Menu Editor window. Your complete menu will appear in the window.

   You can click to select any menu item in the list box, and its information will appear in the top of the window where you can make modifications if desired. You can click on the Delete button to delete the selected item, or click Insert to insert a new blank line before the selection. To change the indentation level of any item, first select it and then click on the Left or Right arrow button. You can move an item up or down in the list by first selecting it and then clicking on the Up or Down arrow button.

Adding to your Sample Menu

To add a new menu and commands to the previous sample project, display the Menu Editor. Click on &Help in the list box and click the *Insert* button, which inserts a blank line in the list box above &Help (Figure 5.9). Add the following items to your menu, one at a time. (You must insert a new line for each item, including the separator bar.) Make sure to click the right arrow to indent each menu item, including the separator bar. Separator bars must also be indented.

Tip

If you receive the message "Cannot use separator bar as menu name for this control," check your separator bar. It must be indented.

Figure 5.9

Click on the Insert *button to insert a blank line above &Help.*

```
&Edit
....&Color
....-
....&Font
```

Checked and Enabled

A menu command may contain a check mark beside it (**checked**), or it may be grayed (**disabled**). (See Figure 5.10.) An **enabled** menu item appears in black text and is available for selection, while the grayed out or disabled items are not available. A check mark placed next to a menu command usually indicates that the option is currently selected.

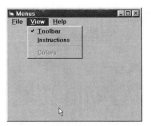

Menu commands can be disabled (grayed) or checked. A check mark usually indicates that the option is currently selected.

Check marks are often used on menu commands for options that can be toggled on and off. For example, for the option *Bold*, the check mark would indicate that Bold is currently selected. Choosing the *Bold* command a second time should remove the check mark and turn off the Bold option.

The check boxes in the Menu Editor for *Checked* and *Enabled* determine the beginning state for these options. By default, menu commands are enabled. If you wish the item to be grayed, the check box must be empty.

Toggling Check Marks On and Off

If you create a menu option that can be turned on and off, you should include a check mark to indicate the current state. You can set the initial state of the check mark in the Menu Editor (refer to Figure 5.2). In code you can change its state by setting the menu item's Checked property.

```
Private Sub mnuFormatBold_Click()
    If mnuFormatBold.Checked = True Then
        mnuFormatBold.Checked = False
        txtChangeable.Font.Bold = False
    Else
        mnuFormatBold.Checked = True
        txtChangeable.Font.Bold = True
    End If
End Sub
```

Standards for Windows Menus

When you write applications that run under Windows, you should make sure your programs follow the Windows standards. You should always include keyboard access keys; if you include keyboard shortcuts (Ctrl + key), stick with the standard keys, such as Ctrl + P for printing. Also follow the Windows standards for placing the *File* menu on the left end of the menu bar and ending the menu with an *Exit* command; if you have a *Help* menu, it belongs at the right end of the menu bar.

Plan your menus so that they look like other Windows programs unless your goal is to confuse people.

Common Dialog Boxes

You can use a set of predefined standard dialog boxes in your projects for such tasks as specifying colors and fonts, printing, opening, and saving. The **common dialog** control, which is a custom control, allows your project to use the dialog boxes that are provided as part of the Windows environment.

To use the common dialog control, you first place a control on your form (Figure 5.11). You cannot change the size of the control, and its location doesn't matter, since it will be invisible when your program runs. In code when you wish to display one of the standard dialog boxes, you will refer to properties and methods of the control. You don't need more than one common dialog control on your form, even if you plan to use several different dialog boxes; each time you refer to the control, you specify which dialog box you want. *Note:* Windows determines the size of the dialog boxes; you cannot modify their size.

Figure   5.11

Use the common dialog tool in the toolbox to place a control on the form.

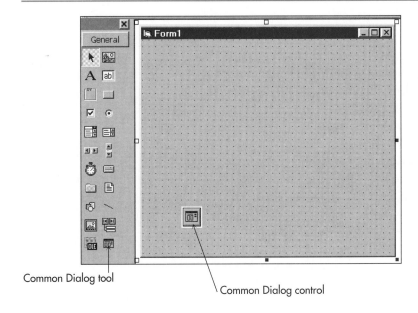

Common Dialog tool

Common Dialog control

The common dialog control may not appear in your toolbox. It is a custom control, and you must add it to Visual Basic before you can use it. Custom controls are stored in files with an extension of .OCX. To use the common dialog, you must have Comdlg32.ocx in your Windows\System folder. Open the *Project* menu and choose *Components*; you should see *Microsoft Common Dialog Control 5.0* in the list (Figure 5.12). Make sure that a check appears next to the item, and its tool should appear in your toolbox.

Figure 5.12

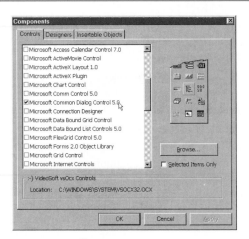

Select the common dialog control in the **Components** *dialog box to make the Common Dialog tool appear in the toolbox.*

When you name a common dialog control, use "dlg" as its three-character prefix.

Using a Common Dialog Box

Once you have placed a common dialog control on your form, you can display any of its dialog boxes at run time. In code you specify which box you want with the Show method.

Show Method—General Form

```
Object.ShowMethod
```

The method can be one of the following:

Dialog Box	Method
Open	ShowOpen
Save As	ShowSave
Color	ShowColor
Font	ShowFont
Print	ShowPrint

For example, assume you have a common dialog control called dlgCommon and a menu item named mnuEditColor. You could display the *Color* dialog box in the Click event for the menu command:

```
Private Sub mnuEditColor_Click()
    'Display the Color Dialog Box

    dlgCommon.ShowColor    'Display the Color dialog box
End Sub
```

The Windows dialog box for choosing colors (Figure 5.13) will appear when the user clicks on the *Color* menu option.

Figure 5.13

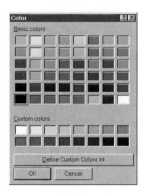

The Color common dialog box.

Using the Information from the Dialog Box

Just because you displayed the *Color* dialog box doesn't make the color of anything change. You must take care of that in your program code. What *does* happen is that the user's choices are stored in properties that you can access. You can assign these values to the properties of controls in your project.

Color Dialog Box

The color selected by the user is stored in the Color property. You can assign this property to another object, such as a control or the form.

```
frmMain.BackColor = dlgCommon.Color
```

Since Basic executes the statements in sequence, you would first display the dialog box with the ShowColor method. (Execution then halts until the user responds to the dialog box.) Then you can use the Color property:

```
Private Sub mnuEditColor_Click()
    'Display the Color dialog box

    dlgCommon.ShowColor
    'Assign dialog box color to the form
    frmMain.BackColor = dlgCommon.Color
End Sub
```

When the *Color* dialog box displays, it shows black as the default color. If you want to initialize the box to show the form's currently selected color when it appears, you must set the control's Flags property to cdlCCRGBInit and set its Color property before showing the dialog box.

```
Private Sub mnuEditColor_Click()
    'Select the color and set initial color
    With dlgCommon
        .Flags = cdlCCRGBInit        'Initialize the dialog box
        .Color = frmMain.BackColor   'Set initial color
        .ShowColor                   'Display dialog box
    End With

    'Assign dialog box color to the form
    frmMain.BackColor = dlgCommon.Color   'Set color of form
End Sub
```

Font Dialog Box

Before you can use the ShowFont method, you must set the Flags property of the control. This coding step installs the fonts to appear in the list box. The value of the Flags property may be cdlCFScreenFonts, cdlCFPrinter-Fonts, or cdlCFBoth. If you should forget to set the flags, an error will occur at run time that says "There are no fonts installed."

The Font properties for the common dialog control are different from those used for other controls. Instead of a group of properties for a Font object, each Font property is listed separately.

Font Object of Other Controls	Font Property of Common Dialog Control	Values
Font.Bold	FontBold	True or False (Boolean)
Font.Italic	FontItalic	True or False (Boolean)
Font.Name	FontName	System dependent
Font.Size	FontSize	Font dependent
Font.StrikeThrough	FontStrikeThru	True or False (Boolean)
Font.Underline	FontUnderline	True or False (Boolean)

Assign the FontName property before assigning the size and other attributes. The following code allows the user to change the font of a label.

```
Private Sub mnuEditFont_Click()
    'Display the Font dialog box

    With dlgCommon
        .Flags = cdlCFScreenFonts
        .ShowFont
    End With

    'Assign dialog box font to the label
    With lblEmployee.Font
        .Name = dlgCommon.FontName
        .Bold = dlgCommon.FontBold
    End With
End Sub
```

When the user clicks on the *Font* menu command, the *Font* dialog box appears on the screen (Figure 5.14).

Figure 5.14

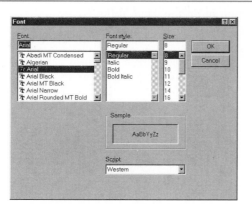

The Font common dialog box.

Setting Current Values

Before calling the common dialog box for colors or fonts, you should assign the existing values of the object properties that will be altered. This step will provide for the display of the current values in the dialog box. It also ensures that if the user selects the Cancel button, the property settings for the objects will remain unchanged.

```
Private Sub mnuEditFont_Click()
    'Display the Font common dialog box
'   and make the changes in the label settings

'Assign the current settings to the dialog box
With dlgCommon
    .FontName = lblEmployee.Font.Name
    .FontBold = lblEmployee.Font.Bold
    .FontItalic = lblEmployee.Font.Italic
    .FontSize = lblEmployee.Font.Size
End With
```

```
'Set the method for Font dialog box
With dlgCommon
     .Flags = cdlCFScreenFonts 'Specify screen fonts
     .ShowFont
End With

'Assign dialog box font to the label
With lblEmployee.Font
     .Bold = dlgCommon.FontBold
     .Italic = dlgCommon.FontItalic
     .Name = dlgCommon.FontName
     .Size = dlgCommon.FontSize
   End With
End Sub
```

Writing General Procedures

Often you will encounter programming situations in which multiple procedures perform the same operation. This condition can occur when the user
can select either a command button or a menu option to do the same thing.
Rather than retyping the code, you can write reusable code in a **general
procedure** and call it from both event procedures.

Creating a New Sub Procedure

To add a new general procedure to a form:

STEP 1: Display the Code window for the form.
STEP 2: Select *Add Procedure* from the *Tools* menu.
STEP 3: Enter a name in the *Add Procedure* dialog box (Figure 5.15).

Figure 5.15

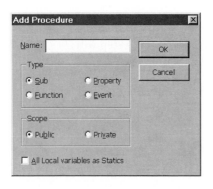

Use the Add Procedure *dialog
box to add a new general
procedure to your form module.*

STEP 4: Select *Private* for *Scope*. Choosing *Public* makes a procedure available from other project modules. *Note:* Leave the *Type* set to *Sub* for
now.
STEP 5: Click OK.

In this example of a new general sub procedure, notice that the Select-
Color sub procedure is not attached to any event.

```
Private Sub SelectColor()
    'Allow user to select a color

    dlgColor.ShowColor
End Sub
```

The coding of the new procedure is similar to the other procedures we have been coding, but is not yet attached to any event. Therefore, this code cannot be executed unless we specifically **call** the procedure from another procedure. To call a sub procedure, just give the procedure name, which in this case is SelectColor.

```
Private Sub cmdChangeMessage_Click()
    'Change the color of the message

    SelectColor
    lblMessage.ForeColor = dlgColor.Color
End Sub
```

```
Private Sub cmdChangeTitle_Click()
    'Change the color of the title

    SelectColor
    lblTitle.ForeColor = dlgColor.Color
End Sub
```

Passing Variables to Procedures

At times you may need to use the value of a variable in one procedure and also in a second procedure that is called from the first. In this situation you could declare the variable as module level, but that makes it visible to all other procedures. In order to keep the scope of a variable as narrow as possible, consider declaring the variable as local and passing it to any called procedures.

As an example, we will expand the capabilities of the previous Show-Color sub procedure to display the original color when the dialog box appears. Since the ShowColor procedure can be called from various locations, the original color must be passed to the procedure. Note that Visual Basic stores colors in Long Integer variables.

```
Private Sub SelectColor(lIncomingColor As Long)
    'Allow user to select a color

    With dlgColor
        .Flags = cdlCCRGBInit      'Initialize the Color dialog box
        .Color = lIncomingColor    'Set the initial color
        .ShowColor
    End With
End Sub
```

```
Private Sub cmdChangeMessage_Click()
    'Change the color of the message
    Dim lOriginalColor As Long

    lOriginalColor = lblMessage.ForeColor
    SelectColor lOriginalColor
    lblMessage.ForeColor = dlgColor.Color
End Sub
```

```
Private Sub cmdChangeTitle_Click()
    'Change the color of the title
    Dim lOriginalColor As Long

    lOriginalColor = lblTitle.ForeColor
    SelectColor lOriginalColor
    lblTitle.ForeColor = dlgColor.Color
End Sub
```

Notice that in this example the SelectColor procedure now has an argument inside the parenthesis. This specifies that when called, an argument must be supplied.

When a sub procedure definition names an argument, any call to that procedure must supply the argument. In addition, the argument value must be the same data type in both locations. Notice that in the two calling procedures (cmdChangeMessage_Click and cmdChangeTitle_Click), the variable lOriginalColor is declared as a Long Integer.

Another important point is that the *name* of the argument does not have to be the same in both locations. The ShowColor sub procedure will take whatever Long Integer value it is passed and refer to it as lIncomingColor inside the procedure.

You may specify multiple arguments in both the sub procedure header and the call to the procedure. The number of arguments, their sequence, and their data types must match in both locations! You will see some examples of multiple arguments in the sections that follow.

Function Procedures versus Sub Procedures

When you insert a new procedure, recall that you can choose to create a sub procedure or a function procedure (refer to Figure 5.15). Let's consider the difference between these two types of procedures. A **sub procedure** is a procedure that performs actions. A **function procedure** may perform an action, but it also returns a value (the **return value**) to the point from which it was called.

In the past we have used predefined functions, such as the `Format` function and the `Val` function. The `Format` function returns the formatted characters; the `Val` function returns the numeric value of the named argument.

As a programmer, you may need to calculate a value that will be needed in several different procedures or programs. You can write your own function that will calculate a value and call the function from the locations where it is needed. As an example we will create a function procedure called Commission, which calculates a salesperson's commission.

To create the new Commission function, follow the same steps as for creating a sub procedure. In the *Add Procedure* dialog box (refer to Figure 5.15), select the *Function* option button prior to selecting the OK command button.

When you insert a function procedure named Commission, your new Code window contains these statements:

```
Private Function Commission()
End Function
```

Notice that this procedure looks just like a sub procedure except that the word `Function` replaces the word `Sub` on both the first line and the last line.

Remember that functions also have arguments. You supply arguments to a function when you call the function by placing a value or values inside the parentheses.

When you write a function, you declare the argument(s) that the function needs. You give each argument an identifier and a data type. The name that you give an argument in the Function procedure header is the identifier that you will use inside the function to refer to the value of the argument.

Examples

```
Private Function Commission(cSalesAmount As Currency)
Private Function Payment(cRate As Currency, cTime As Currency, cAmount As Currency)
```

In the function procedure the argument list you enter establishes the number of arguments, their type, and their sequence. When using multiple arguments, the sequence of the arguments is critical, just as when you use the predefined Visual Basic functions.

The main difference between coding a function procedure and coding a sub procedure is that in a function you must set up the return value. This return value is placed in a variable that Visual Basic names with the same name as the function name. In the previous example the variable name is Commission. *Note:* Somewhere in the function, you *must* set the function name to a value.

You can also specify the data type of the return value by adding the As clause after the function name. Because the data type of the return value in this example is Currency, the function name has been changed to `cCommission`.

```
Private Function cCommission(cSalesAmount As Currency) As Currency
    'Calculate the sales commission

    If cSalesAmount < 1000 Then
        cCommission = 0
    ElseIf cSalesAmount <= 2000 Then
        cCommission = 0.15 * cSalesAmount
    Else
        cCommission = 0.2 * cSalesAmount
    End If
End Function
```

In another procedure in the project, you can call your function by using it in an expression.

Example

```
Dim cSales as Currency
If IsNumeric(txtSales.Text) Then
    cSales = Val(txtSales.Text)
    lblCommission.Caption = cCommission(cSales)
End If
```

Notice in the preceding example that the argument named in the function call does not have the same name as the argument named in the function definition. When the function is called, cSales is passed to the function and is assigned to the named argument, in this case cSalesAmount. As the calculations are done (inside the function), for every reference to cSales-Amount, the value of cSales is actually used.

In creating a function with multiple arguments such as a Payment function, the list of arguments is enclosed within the parentheses. The following example indicates that three arguments are needed in the call: The first argument is the interest rate, the second is the time, and the third is the loan amount. All three argument values will have a data type of currency, and the return value will be currency. Look carefully at the following formula and notice how the identifiers in the parentheses are used.

```
Private Function cPayment(cRate As Currency, cTime As Currency, _
        cAmt As Currency) As Currency
        'Calculate the monthly payment on an amortized loan

        cPayment = cAmt * (1 + cRate/12) ^ (cTime * 12) 'Set the _
                return value of the function
End Function
```

To call this function from another procedure, use this statement:

```
cRate = Val(txtRate.Text)
cTime = Val(txtTime.Text)
cAmount = Val(txtAmount.Text)
lblPayment.Caption = cPayment(cRate, cTime, cAmount)
```

You can format the result, as well as pass the Val of the text boxes, by nesting functions:

```
lblPayment.Caption = Format$(cPayment(Val(txtRate.Text), _
        Val(txtTime.Text), Val(txtAmount.Text)), "Currency")
```

Feedback 5.1

You need to write a procedure to calculate and return the average of three integer values.

1. Should you write a sub procedure or a function procedure?
2. Write the first line of the procedure.
3. Write the calculation.
4. How is the calculated average passed back to the calling procedure?

Your Hands-On Programming Example

Modify the hands-on programming example from Chapter 4 by replacing some of the command buttons with menus. Use a function procedure to calculate the sales tax. You will need to move the constant for tax rate to the module level.

The project for R 'n R—for Reading 'n Refreshment calculates the amount due for individual orders and maintains accumulated totals for a summary. Have a check box for takeout items, which are taxable (8 percent); all other orders are nontaxable. Include option buttons for the five coffee selections—Cappuccino, Espresso, Latte, Iced Latte, and Iced Cappuccino. The prices for each will be assigned using these constants:

Cappuccino	2.00
Espresso	2.25
Latte	1.75
Iced (either)	2.50

Use a command button for Calculate Selection, which will calculate and display the amount due for each item. A button for Clear for Next Item will clear the selections and amount for the single item. Additional labels in a separate frame will maintain the summary information for the current order to include subtotal, tax, and total.

The Next Order menu will clear the bill for the current customer and add to the totals for the summary. The menu for Summary should display the total of all orders, the average sale amount per customer, and the number of customers.

The Edit menu contains options that duplicate the Calculate and Clear button. The Font and Color options change the contents of the subtotal, tax, and total labels.

The *About* selection on the *Help* menu will display a message box with information about the programmer.

<pre>
<u>F</u>ile   <u>E</u>dit   <u>H</u>elp
   <u>N</u>ew Order   <u>C</u>alculate <u>S</u>election   <u>A</u>bout
   <u>S</u>ummary   C<u>l</u>ear Item
   E<u>x</u>it   _____
                     <u>F</u>ont
                     <u>C</u>olor
</pre>

Planning the Project

Sketch a form (Figure 5.16), which your users sign as meeting their needs.

Figure 5.16

A sketch of the form for the hands-on programming example.

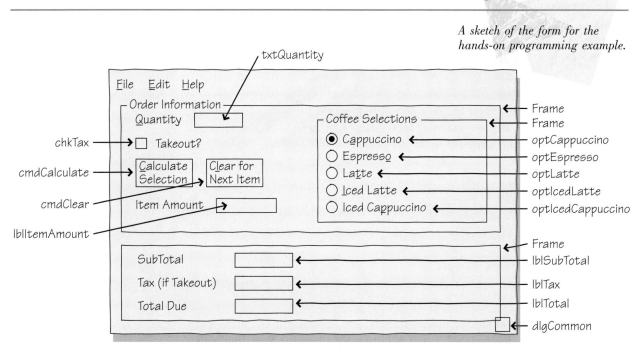

Plan the Objects and Properties

Plan the property settings for the form and each of the controls.

Object	Property	Setting
frmBilling	Name	frmBilling
	Caption	R 'n R—for Reading 'n Refreshment
Frame1	Caption	Order Information
Frame2	Caption	Coffee Selections
Frame3	Caption	(blank)
optCappuccino	Name	optCappuccino
	Caption	C&appuccino
	Value	True
optEspresso	Name	optEspresso
	Caption	Espress&o
optLatte	Name	optLatte
	Caption	La&tte
optIcedLatte	Name	optIcedLatte
	Caption	&Iced Latte
optIcedCappuccino	Name	optIcedCappuccino
	Caption	Iced Ca&ppuccino
Label1	Caption	Quantity
txtQuantity	Name	txtQuantity
	Text	(blank)
chkTax	Name	chkTax
	Caption	Takeout ?
Label2	Caption	Item Amount
Label3	Caption	SubTotal
Label4	Caption	Tax (if Takeout)
Label5	Caption	Total Due
lblItemAmount	Name	lblItemAmount
	Caption	(blank)
	BorderStyle	1 - FixedSingle
lblSubTotal	Name	lblSubTotal
	Caption	(blank)
	BorderStyle	1 - Fixed Single
lblTax	Name	lblTax
	Caption	(blank)
	BorderStyle	1 - Fixed Single

(continued)

Object	Property	Setting
lblTotal	Name	lblTotal
	Caption	(blank)
	BorderStyle	1 - Fixed Single
cmdCalculate	Name	cmdCalculate
	Caption	&Calculate Selection
	Default	True
cmdClear	Name	cmdClear
	Caption	C&lear for Next Item
	Cancel	True
mnuFile	Name	mnuFile
	Caption	&File
mnuFileNew	Name	mnuFileNew
	Caption	&New Order
mnuFileSummary	Name	mnuFileSummary
	Caption	&Summary
mnuFileExit	Name	mnuFileExit
	Caption	E&xit
mnuEdit	Name	mnuEdit
	Caption	&Edit
mnuEditCalc	Name	mnuEditCalc
	Caption	Calculate &Selection
mnuEditClear	Name	mnuEditClear
	Caption	C&lear Item
mnuSep1	Name	mnuSep1
	Caption	-
mnuEditFont	Name	mnuEditFont
	Caption	&Font
mnuEditColor	Name	mnuEditColor
	Caption	&Color
mnuHelp	Name	mnuHelp
	Caption	&Help
mnuHelpAbout	Name	mnuHelpAbout
	Caption	&About
dlgCommon	Name	dlgCommon

Plan the Event Procedures

You need to plan the actions for the command buttons, and the actions of the menu commands.

Object	Procedure	Action
cmdCalculate	Click	Determine price per cup. Multiply price by quantity. Call tax procedure if needed. Add quantity to item total. Display the values.
cmdClear	Click	Clear the coffee selections. Clear the quantity and the item price. Disable the takeout check box. Set the focus to the quantity.
mnuFileNew	Click	Clear the previous order. Accumulate total and count. Set subtotal and total to 0.
mnuFileSummary	Click	Display the Average. Display Total Sales. Display the number of customers.
mnuFileExit	Click	Terminate the project.
mnuEditCalc	Click	Call calculate command event.
mnuEditClear	Click	Call clear command event.
cFindTax	(call)	Calculate the sales tax.

Write the Project

Follow the sketch in Figure 5.16 to create the form. Figure 5.17 shows the completed form.

Figure 5.17

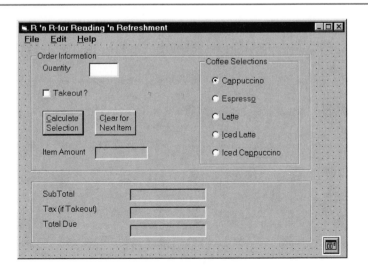

The form for the hands-on programming example.

- Set the properties of each object according to your plan.

- Write the code. Working from the pseudocode, write each event procedure.

- When you complete the code, use a variety of data to thoroughly test the project.

The Project Coding Solution

```
'Project Name:   Billing
'Programmer:     A. Millspaugh
'Date:           July 1997
'Description:     This project calculates the
'   amount due based on the customer selection
'   and accumulates summary data for the day.
'   The project incorporates menus and common dialog boxes.
'   The common dialog box allows the user to change
'   the color and font.
'Folder:         Ch0501

Option Explicit
Dim mcSubtotal              As Currency
Dim mcTotal                 As Currency
Dim mcGrandTotal            As Currency
Dim miCustomerCount         As Integer
Const cCAPPUCCINO_PRICE     As Currency = 2
Const cESPRESSO_PRICE       As Currency = 2.25
Const cLATTE_PRICE          As Currency = 1.75
Const cICED_PRICE           As Currency = 2.5
Const mcTAX_RATE            As Currency = 0.08
```

```
Private Sub cmdCalculate_Click()
    'Calculate and display the current amounts; add to totals

    Dim cPrice              As Currency
    Dim iQuantity           As Integer
    Dim cTax                As Currency
    Dim cItemAmount         As Currency


    'Find the price
    If optCappuccino.Value = True Then
        cPrice = cCAPPUCCINO_PRICE
    ElseIf optEspresso.Value = True Then
        cPrice = cESPRESSO_PRICE
    ElseIf optLatte.Value = True Then
        cPrice = cLATTE_PRICE
    ElseIf optIcedCappuccino.Value = True Or _
            optIcedLatte.Value = True Then
        cPrice = cICED_PRICE
    Else
        MsgBox "Please Make Drink Selection", vbOKOnly, "Oops"
    End If


    'Add the price times quantity to price so far
    If IsNumeric(txtQuantity.Text) Then
        iQuantity = Val(txtQuantity.Text)
        cItemAmount = cPrice * iQuantity
        mcSubtotal = mcSubtotal + cItemAmount
        If chkTax.Value = Checked Then
            cTax = cFindTax(mcSubtotal) 'call a function procedure
        End If
        mcTotal = mcSubtotal + cTax
        lblItemAmount.Caption = Format$(cItemAmount, "Currency")
        lblSubTotal.Caption = Format$(mcSubtotal, "Currency")
        lblTax.Caption = Format$(cTax, "Currency")
        lblTotal.Caption = Format$(mcTotal, "Currency")
    Else
        MsgBox "Quantity must be numeric", vbExclamation, "Oops"
        txtQuantity.SetFocus
    End If
End Sub
```

```
Private Sub cmdClear_Click()
    'Clear appropriate controls

    optCappuccino.Value = True 'Make first button selected to begin
    optEspresso.Value = False
    optLatte.Value = False
    optIcedLatte.Value = False
    optIcedCappuccino.Value = False
    lblItemAmount.Caption = ""
    chkTax.Enabled = False 'Allow change for new order only
    With txtQuantity
        .Text = ""
        .SetFocus
    End With
End Sub
```

```
Private Sub mnuEditCalc_Click()
    'Call the Calculate event

    cmdCalculate_Click
End Sub
```

```
Private Sub mnuEditClear_Click()
    'Call the Clear command event

    cmdClear_Click
End Sub
```

```
Private Sub mnuEditColor_Click()
    'Change the color of the total labels

    dlgCommon.ShowColor
    lblSubTotal.ForeColor = dlgCommon.Color
    lblTax.ForeColor = dlgCommon.Color
    lblTotal.ForeColor = dlgCommon.Color
End Sub
```

```
Private Sub mnuEditFont_Click()
    'Change the font name for the subtotal labels

    dlgCommon.Flags = cdlCFScreenFonts 'Set up Font dialog box fonts
    dlgCommon.ShowFont
    lblSubTotal.Font.Name = dlgCommon.FontName
    lblTax.Font.Name = dlgCommon.FontName
    lblTotal.Font.Name = dlgCommon.FontName
End Sub
```

```
Private Sub mnuFileExit_Click()
    'Terminate the project

    End
End Sub
```

```
Private Sub mnuFileNew_Click()
    'Clear the current order and add to totals

    cmdClear_Click
    lblSubTotal.Caption = ""
    lblTax.Caption = ""
    lblTotal.Caption = ""

    'Add to Totals
    mcGrandTotal = mcGrandTotal + mcTotal
    mcSubtotal = 0
    mcTotal = 0 'reset for next customer
    miCustomerCount = miCustomerCount + 1

    'Clear appropriate display items and enable check box
    With chkTax
        .Enabled = True
        .Value = False
    End With
End Sub
```

```
Private Sub mnuFileSummary_Click()
    'Calculate the average and display the totals

    Dim cAverage As Currency
    Dim stMessageString As String
    Dim stFormattedAvg As String

    If miCustomerCount > 0 Then
        If mcTotal <> 0 Then
            mnuFileNew_Click 'Make sure last order is counted
        End If
        cAverage = mcGrandTotal / miCustomerCount

        'Format the numbers
        stFormattedAvg = Format$(cAverage, "Currency")
        'Concatenate the message string
        stMessageString = "Number of Orders: " & miCustomerCount & vbCr & _
            "Average Sale: " & stFormattedAvg
        MsgBox stMessageString, vbInformation, "Coffee Sales Summary"
    Else
        MsgBox "No data to summarize", vbExclamation, "Coffee Sales Summary"
    End If
End Sub
```

```
Private Sub mnuHelpAbout_Click()
    'Display a message box about the program

    MsgBox "R "n R Billing" & vbCrLf & vbCrLf _
        & "Programmed by A Millspaugh", vbOKOnly, "About R 'n R Billing"
End Sub
```

```
Public Function cFindTax(cAmount As Currency) As Currency
    'Calculate the sales tax

    cFindTax = cAmount * mcTAX_RATE
End Function
```

Programming Hints

Creating Executable Files

You can convert your project into an **executable file** that can be run from the Windows desktop. The resulting .EXE file contains the information from all your project's files, including the form files and the modules. The .EXE file will run much faster than the project runs in the VB environment.

After you create an .EXE file, the original project files are still intact and can be used to make any modifications. Any time you make changes in the original project files, you must re-create the .EXE file to incorporate the changes.

To create the .EXE file, select the *Make ...* command from the *File* menu. The *Make ...* menu choice displays the name of the current project. For example, Figure 5.18 show the menu for the chapter hands-on project, called Chap5Billing. Choose *Make Chap5Billing* from the *File* menu and the *Make Project* dialog box appears (Figure 5.18).

F i g u r e   5 . 1 8

Use the Make Project dialog box to create an executable version of your project.

You will choose the location and name for your .EXE file. You can also set properties for your project by clicking on the *Options* button. In the *Project Properties* dialog box (Figure 5.19), you can specify the version number, company name, and an icon for your file.

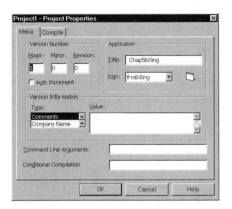

The Project Properties *dialog box allows you to specify version information, a company name, and an icon for your .EXE file.*

S u m m a r y

1. Menus are created in Visual Basic using the Menu Editor. The editor enables you to create menus, menu commands, and submenus, each with keyboard access keys.

2. The Caption and Name properties are required for each menu item.

3. In the Menu Editor, the order and level of menu items can be set and modified, as well as the initial settings of the Enabled and Checked properties.

4. Each menu command has a Click event. The code to handle selection of a menu command belongs in the command's Click event procedure.

5. Common dialog boxes allow Visual Basic programs to display the predefined Windows dialog boxes for *Print*, *Open*, *Save*, *Fonts*, and *Colors*. Since these dialog boxes are already a part of the operating environment, it is an unnecessary duplication of effort to have each programmer re-create them.

6. The programmer can write reusable code in general procedures. These procedures may be sub procedures or sub functions and may be called from any other procedure in the form module.

7. Sub procedures and sub functions can both perform an action. However, sub functions return a value and sub procedures do not. The value returned by a sub function will have a data type.

8. It is easy to convert a project to an .EXE file that can be run from the Windows environment. Use the *Make Project* command on the *File* menu.

Key Terms

call (procedure call) *173*

checked *165*

common dialog *167*

disabled *165*

enabled *165*

executable file *186*

function procedure *174*

general procedure *172*

menu *160*

return value *174*

separator bar *162*

sub procedure *174*

submenu *161*

Review Questions

1. Explain the difference between a menu and a submenu.
2. How can the user know if a menu command contains a submenu?
3. What is a separator bar and how is it created?
4. Explain the purpose of the Name and Caption properties of menu items.
5. What does the term *common dialog box* mean?
6. Name at least three types of common dialog boxes.
7. Why would you need procedures that are not attached to an event?
8. Code the necessary statements to produce a color dialog box and use it to change the background color of a form.
9. Explain the difference between a sub procedure and a function procedure.
10. What is a *return value*? How can it be used?
11. Give the steps required to convert a project into an .EXE file.

Programming Exercises

5.1 Modify project 4.6 (Piecework Pay) to replace command buttons with menus and add a function procedure.

This project will input the number of pieces and calculate the pay for multiple employees. It also must display a summary of the total number of pieces, the total pay, and the average pay for all employees. *Menu*: The menu bar must have these commands:

File	Edit	Help
Calc Pay	Clear	About
Summary	————	
Exit	Font	
	Color	

Piecework workers are paid by the piece. Workers who produce a greater quantity of output may be paid at a higher rate.

Use text boxes to obtain the name and the number of pieces completed. The *Calc Pay* menu command calculates and displays the dollar amount earned. The *Summary* menu command displays the total number of pieces, the total pay, and the average pay per person in a message box. The *Clear* menu choice clears the name and the number of pieces for the current employee and resets the focus.

The *Color* and *Font* commands should change the color and font of the information displayed in the amount earned label.

Use a message box to display your name for the *About* option on the *Help* menu.

Use a function procedure to find the pay rate and return a value to the proper event procedure.

Pieces Completed	Price Paid per Piece for All Pieces
1 to 199	.50
200 to 399	.55
400 to 599	.60
600 or more	.65

5.2   Redo the checking account programming exercises from Chapter 4 (4.3, 4.4, and 4.5), using menus and sub procedures.

Menu:

```
File                 Edit            Help
   Transaction          Clear           About
   Summary              _____
   Exit                 Font
                        Color
```

Form: Use option buttons to indicate the type of transaction—deposit, check, or service charge. A text box will allow the user to enter the amount of the transaction. Display the balance in a label.

Include validation that displays a message box if the amount of the transaction is a negative number. If there is not enough money to cover a check, display a message box with the message "Insufficient Funds." Do not pay the check, but deduct a service charge of $10.

Use function procedures for deposits, checks, and service charges. The deposit function adds the deposit to the balance; the check function subtracts the transaction amount from the balance; the service charge function subtracts $10 from the balance.

The *Summary* menu command displays the total number of deposits and the dollar amount of deposits, the number of checks, and the dollar amount of the checks in a message box.

The *Clear* menu command clears the option buttons and the amount and resets the focus.

The *Color* and *Font* menu commands change the color and font of the information displayed in the balance label.

Use a message box to display your name as the programmer for the *About* option on the *Help* menu.

5.3 A salesperson earns a weekly base salary plus a commission when sales are at or above quota. Create a project that allows the user to input the weekly sales and the salesperson name, calculates the commission, and displays summary information.

Form: The form will have text boxes for the salesperson name and his or her weekly sales.

Menu:

```
File                Edit        Help
   Pay                 Clear       About
   Summary             _____
   Exit                Font
                       Color
```

Use constants to establish the base pay, the quota, and the commission rate.

The *Pay* menu command calculates and displays in labels the commission and the total pay for that person. However, if there is no commission, do not display the commission amount (do not display a zero-commission amount).

Use a function procedure to calculate the commission. The function must compare sales to the quota. When the sales are equal to or greater than the quota, calculate the commission by multiplying sales by the commission rate.

Each salesperson receives the base pay plus the commission (if one has been earned). Format the dollar amounts to two decimal places; do not display a dollar sign.

The *Summary* menu command displays a message box containing total sales, total commissions, and total pay for all salespersons. Display the numbers with two decimal places and dollar signs.

The *Clear* menu command clears the name, sales, and pay for the current employee and then resets the focus.

The *Color* and *Font* menu commands should change the color and font of the information displayed in the amount earned label.

Use a message box to display your name as programmer for the *About* option on the *Help* menu.

Test Data: Quota = 1000; Commission rate = .15; and Base pay = 250.

Name	Sales
Sandy Smug	1,000.00
Sam Sadness	999.99
Joe Whiz	2,000.00

Totals should be:

Sales	$3,999.99
Commissions	450.00
Pay	1,200.00

5.4   The local library has a summer reading program to encourage reading.
       The staff keeps a chart with readers' names and bonus points earned.
       Create a project using a menu and a function procedure that will deter-
       mine the bonus points.
       Menu:

```
File                  Edit          Help
   Points                Clear      About
   Summary               _____
   Exit                  Font
                         Color
```

Form: Use text boxes to obtain the reader's name and the number of
books read. Use a label to display the number of bonus points.

The *Points* menu command should call a function procedure to calculate the points using this schedule: the first three books are worth 10
points each. The next three books are worth 15 points each. All books
over six are worth 20 points each.

The *Summary* menu command displays the average number of books
read for all readers that session.

The *Clear* menu command clears the name, the number of books read,
and the bonus points and then resets the focus.

The *Color* and *Font* menu commands change the color and font of the
information displayed in the bonus points label.

Use a message box to display your name as programmer for the *About*
option on the *Help* menu.

5.5   Modify project 2.2 (the flag viewer) to use a menu instead of option but-
       tons, check boxes, and command buttons. Include check marks next to
       the name of the currently selected country and next to the selected dis-
       play options.
       Menu:

```
File          Country               Display
   Print         United States         Title
   Exit          Canada                Country Name
                 Japan                 Programmer
                 Mexico
```

CASE STUDIES

VB Mail Order

Modify the case study from Chapter 4 using menus and a function procedure. Refer to Chapter 4 for project specifications.

Use a function procedure to calculate the shipping and handling, based on the weight for an entire order. (Do not calculate shipping and handling on individual items—wait until the order is complete.)

Menu:

File	Edit	Help
Print Form	Next Item	About
Summary	Next Order	
Exit	———	
	Font	
	Color	

VB Auto Center

Modify the case study project from Chapter 4 using menus and a function procedure. Refer to Chapter 4 for project specifications.

Use a function procedure to calculate the sales tax.

Menu:

File	Edit	Help
Print Form	Calculate	About
Exit	Clear	
	———	
	Font	
	Color	

6

Multiple Forms

At the completion of this chapter, you will be able to...

1. Create a project with multiple forms.

2. Use the Show and Hide methods to display and hide forms.

3. Create procedures that are accessible from multiple form modules.

4. Differentiate between variables that are global to a project and those visible only to a form.

5. Create an *About box* using a form.

6. Add a splash screen to your project.

7. Set the startup form or Sub Main to start project execution.

Multiple Forms

All the projects that you have created up to now have operated from a single form. It has probably occurred to you that the project could appear more professional if you could use different windows for different types of information. Consider the example in Chapter 5 in which summary information is displayed in a message box when the user presses the Summary button. You have very little control over the appearance of the message box. The summary information could be displayed in a much nicer format in a new window with identifying labels. Another window in Visual Basic is actually another form.

The first form a project displays is called the ***startup form***. You can add more forms to the project and display them as needed.

Creating New Forms

To add a new form to a project, select *Add Form* from the *Project* menu or click on the Form button on the toolbar (Figure 6.1). In the *Add Form* dialog box (Figure 6.2), you can select from a new form or an existing form. Notice in Figure 6.2 that VB provides several types of new forms that you can use; you will learn about some of these later in the chapter. For now, choose *Form* to add a regular new form.

Figure 6.1

Add a new form to a project by clicking on the Add Form toolbar button.

Figure 6.2

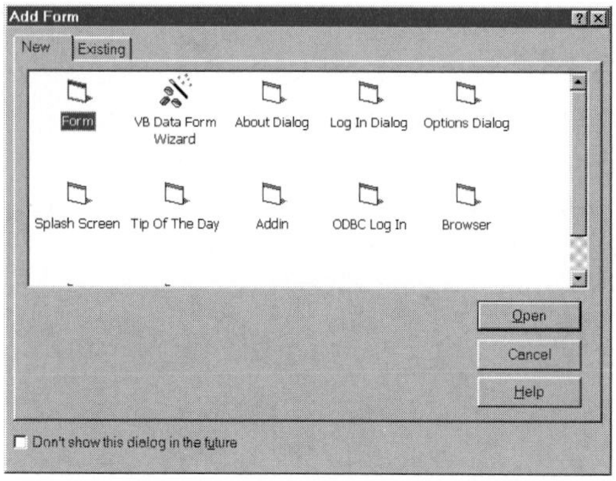

Select the type of new form you want in the Add Form dialog box.

Steps for adding a new form to a project:

STEP 1: Select *Add Form* from the *Project* menu.

STEP 2: In the dialog box select the *New* tab and indicate the type of form
you want (Form, About, Splash).

STEP 3: Click on *Open*.

The new form will display on the screen and be added to the Project
Explorer window (Figure 6.3).

Figure 6.3

After adding a new form, the Project Explorer window shows the name of the new form.

If you want your newly created form to be the startup form (the one that
appears when the project starts running), you will need to follow the steps
for setting a startup form, which are found later in this chapter.

While in design time, you can switch between forms two ways. If you can
see any part of the other form on the screen, just click on the form to make
it active. You can also use the Project Explorer window. The Project Explorer
window's View Form button and View Code button switch to the form or code
of the module that is selected (highlighted). You can switch between forms
by clicking on the form name in the Project Explorer window and clicking
the View Form button, or by double-clicking on a form name.

Each form module is a separate file and a separate entity. The code that
exists in one form module is not visible to any other form module. Note one
exception: Any procedure declared with the `Public` keyword is callable from
other modules in the project.

Adding and Removing Forms

The Project Explorer window shows the files that are included in a project.
You can add new files and remove files from a project.

Adding Existing Form Files to a Project

Forms may be used in more than one project. You might want to use a form
that you created for one project in a new project.

Each form is a separate module, which is saved as a separate file with
an .FRM extension. All of the information for the form resides in the file,
which includes the code procedures and the visual interface as well as all
property settings for the controls.

To add an existing form to a project, use the *Add Form* command on the
Project menu and select the *Existing* tab (Figure 6.4). You will need to supply the name of the form and the folder where it can be found.

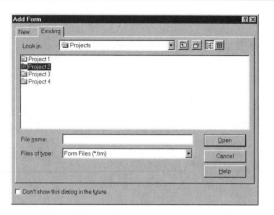

Steps for adding an existing form to a project:

STEP 1: Select *Add Form* from the *Project* menu.

STEP 2: In the *Add Form* dialog box, select the *Existing* tab and locate the folder and file desired.

STEP 3: Click on *Open*.

Removing Forms From a Project

If you want to remove a file from a project, select its name in the Project Explorer window. You can then either choose *Remove File* from the *Project* menu or right-click on the filename to display the Shortcut menu and choose *Remove Filename*.

The Hide and Show Methods

In code, you can display a form with the **Show method** and conceal a form with the **Hide method**. If both forms are the same size, the process of showing the second form will cover the first form on the screen. Use the Hide method when you want to make sure a form disappears.

The Show Method—General Form

```
FormName.Show [Style]
```

The FormName is the name of the form you wish to display. The optional *Style* determines whether the form will display modeless or modal. The values for Style can be 0 (for modeless) or 1 (for modal); the default is 0. You can also use the VB intrinsic constants: vbModal and vbModeless.

When you display a form as **modal**, the user must respond to the form in some way, usually by clicking a command button. No other program code can execute until the modal form has been responded to and hidden or unloaded. However, if you display a **modeless** form, the user may switch to another form in the project without responding to the form. *Note:* Even with a modal form, the user can switch to another application within Windows.

The Show Method—Examples

```
frmSummary.Show 1            'Display the summary form, modal style
frmSummary.Show vbModal      'Display the summary form, modal style
frmSummary.Show vbModeless   'Display the summary form, modeless style
frmSummary.Show              'Display the summary form, modeless style
```

When you choose whether to display a form as modal or modeless, you must be aware of an important difference in the way VB executes the statements. As you already know, code statements within a procedure execute one after another, in sequence. When you have a modal `Show` method in code, VB executes the `Show` and pauses; it does not execute any further statements until the user responds to the modal form. Conversely, when VB encounters a modeless `Show` method, it displays the form and continues execution; if additional statements follow the `Show`, they will be executed immediately, without waiting for response from the user. In most cases, you will want to display forms modally.

Recall the sample programs in Chapters 4 and 5, which display summary information in a message box. A nicer solution would be to display the summary data in a second form, called frmSummary. Replace the `MsgBox` statement in the cmdSummary_Click event procedure with this statement:

```
frmSummary.Show vbModal 'Display the summary form
```

The Form Load and Form Activate Events

The first time a form is displayed in a project, Visual Basic generates two events—a Form_Load and a Form_Activate. The Load event calls the form module into memory; the Activate event occurs after the Load event, just as control is passed to the form. Each subsequent time the form is shown, the Activate event occurs, but not the Load event. Therefore, if a form may be displayed multiple times, you may want to place initializing steps into the Form_Activate event procedure rather than into the Form_Load. Also, if you wish to set the focus in a particular place on the new form, place the Set-Focus method in the Form_Activate procedure.

When you use a `Show` method, the size and location of the form depend upon the Left, Top, Height, and Width properties of the form being displayed. You can calculate these properties when the form is shown by placing the calculations in the Form_Activate event. If you would like to make your form fill the screen, see the hints for working with maximized forms in the "Programming Hints" at the end of this chapter.

Tip

To write code for the Form_Activate event, display the code window and choose *Form* in the *Object* box and *Activate* in the *Procedure* box.

Hiding a Form

The `Hide` method is very similar to the `Show` method but is used to remove a form from the screen.

The Hide Method—General Form

```
FormName.Hide
```

The Hide Method—Example

```
frmSummary.Hide
```

The Load and Unload Statements

When you work with multiple forms, you may also want to use the **Load** and **Unload** statements. Although you can explicitly load a form, in most cases the `Load` isn't necessary. When you `Show` a form, the `Load` is done automatically. The only time you will code a `Load` statement is when you want to load a form but not display it until later.

To remove a form from the screen, you can hide it or unload it. Hiding a form removes it from the screen, but the form still remains in memory and uses system resources. If you have many forms and you are sure you will not need a form again, it's best to unload it rather than to hide it.

The Load and Unload Statements—General Form

```
Load FormName
Unload FormName
```

The Load and Unload Statements—Examples

```
Load frmSummary
Unload frmSummary
```

> **Tip**
>
> **Y**ou can quickly jump to another location in a project and then jump back to the same spot. Click on the name of a procedure or form where you want to jump and press Shift + F2. To jump back to the earlier spot, press Ctrl + Shift + F2.

The Me Keyword

You can refer to the current form by using the special keyword `Me`. `Me` acts like a variable and refers to the currently active form. You can use `Me` in place of the form name when coding form statements and methods.

The Me Keyword—Examples

```
Unload Me    'Unload the form that is currently executing code
Me.Hide      'Hide the form that is currently executing code
```

Referring to Objects on a Different Form

Each form is a separate module, with its own variables, objects, properties, and code. When your project has only one form, you can refer to any object and its properties in any procedure. But when you use multiple forms, the code in one module cannot "see" the objects in another module without some help. One way to reference an object in another form module is to expand the reference to include the name of the form:

```
FormName!ObjectName.Property
```

Using this technique, you can set the properties of objects in a form before displaying it.

Example
```
frmSummary!lblTotalAmount.Caption = mcTotal
frmSummary.Show vbModal
```

Consequently, you can use the same name for objects in two different forms. Although it may be confusing to have similarly named objects in multiple forms it is perfectly acceptable. An example is having an OK button in two forms, both named cmdOK. The two buttons would be referred to as frmStartup!cmdOK and frmSummary!cmdOK.

Note: Programmers have a language of their own. Just as you learned to say "dot" for the period ("Object dot Property"), if you want to speak like a programmer, you must call the exclamation point "bang." Therefore, to refer to a form's objects and properties, it's "FormName bang Object dot Property."

Standard Code Modules

When using multiple forms in a project, it is important for you to consider each sub procedure or function procedure that you create. If the procedure will be used in only one form, then it should be included in the code for that form module. If, in fact, you will need to use the procedure in multiple forms, write the procedure in a **standard code module.** A *standard code module* is a Basic file with the extension **.BAS**, which is added to the project. Standard code modules do not contain a form, only code.

Create a new standard code module by selecting the *Add Module* command on the *Project* menu. A new Code window titled *Module1* opens on the screen (Figure 6.5). Also note that Module1 is added to your Project Explorer window (Figure 6.6). Make sure that Module1 is highlighted in the Project Explorer window and choose *Save Module1* from the *File* menu to give the new file a name. It is a good idea to name this file the same as your project file unless you plan to use it for multiple projects. The file extension is .BAS by default.

Figure 6.5

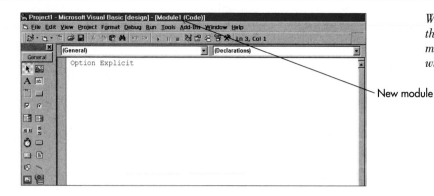

New module

Figure 6.6

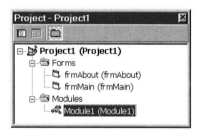

The new module, Module1, is added to the project in the Project Explorer window.

A standard code module has a General Declarations section and procedures, just like a form module. You can declare variables with the `Dim` statement in procedures or in the General Declarations section. Any `Dim`med variables or constants in the General Declarations section of a standard code module are visible to all the procedures in that module, but not to the procedures in the form module(s).

Variables and Constants in Multiple-Form Projects

When you have multiple modules in a project, the scope of the variables and constants becomes a little more complicated. The variables and constants can be local to a procedure; module level, which are available to all procedures in the module; or **global**, which are available to all procedures in all modules in the project.

Global Variables and Constants

If you want variables and constants to be accessible to more than one form in the project, they must be global variables. To declare global variables, use the **Public** statement in place of the `Dim` statement.

The Public Statement—General Form

```
Public Identifier [As DataType]
Public Const Identifier [As DataType] = Value
```

The format of the `Public` statement is similar to the `Dim` and `Const` statements. If the data type is omitted for a variable, the type defaults to variant. For a constant, if you omit the data type, Visual Basic selects the type most appropriate for the value.

It is important to know the scope of a variable when programming. A module-level variable or constant has a prefix of "m", and a public variable or constant has a prefix of "g" (for global; "p" refers to private). Any variable or constant without a scope prefix is assumed to be local to a procedure.

The Public Statement—Examples

```
Public  gcGrandTotal As Currency
Public  gPersonName 'Defaults to Variant data type
Public  Const gsTAX_RATE As Single = .0825
Public  Const gstCOMPANY = "R 'n R — for Reading and Refreshment" _
                          'Defaults to String data type
```

Note: Visual Basic also has a `Private` statement with the same syntax as the `Public` statement. Since all variables and constants are private by default, the `Private` statement is rarely used.

Static Variables

Another statement you can use to declare variables at the procedure level is the **Static** statement. Static variables retain their value for the life of the project, rather than being reinitialized for each call to the procedure. If you need to retain the value in a variable for multiple calls to a procedure, such as a running total, declare it as Static. (In the past we used module-level variables for this task. Using a static local variable is better than using a module-level variable because it is always best to keep the scope of a variable as narrow as possible.)

The Static Statement—General Form

```
Static Identifier [As DataType]
```

The format of the `Static` statement is the same as the format of the `Dim` statement. However, `Static` statements can appear only in procedures; `Static` statements never appear in the General Declarations section of a module.

The Static Statement—Examples

```
Static iPersonCount As Integer
Static cReportTotal As Currency
```

Static variables do not require a scope prefix, since all static variables are local.

Guidelines for Declaring Variables and Constants

When you declare variables and constants, select the location of the declaration carefully. These general guidelines will help you decide where to place declarations:

1. Place all local declarations (`Dim`, `Const`, `Static`) at the *top* of a procedure. Although Basic will accept declarations placed further down in the code, such placement is considered a poor practice. Your code will be easier to read, debug, modify, and maintain if you follow this guideline.

2. Use named constants for any value that doesn't change during program execution. It is far more clear to use named constants such as cMAXIMUM_RATE and stCOMPANY_NAME than to place the values into your code; and if in the future the values must be modified, having a constant name (at the top of your project) makes the task *much* easier.

3. Keep the scope of variables and constants as narrow as possible. Don't declare them all to be global or module level for convenience. There are books full of horror stories about strange program bugs popping up because the value of a variable was changed in an unknown location.

4. Consider making variables and constants local if possible.

5. If you need to keep the value of a variable for multiple executions of a procedure, but don't need the variable in any other procedure, make it Static.

6. If you need to use a variable both in a procedure and also in a second procedure called by the first procedure, declare the variable as local and pass it as an argument. (Refer to "Passing Variables to Procedures" in Chapter 5.)

7. If you need to use a variable in multiple procedures, such as to add to the variable in one procedure and to display it in another, use module-level variables. (Use a `Dim` statement in the General Declarations section of the module.)

8. If you need to use the value of a variable in multiple forms, you may still have two choices. Do you actually need to use the variable in the second form, or are you just displaying it in a control? Remember, you can assign a variable to a property in another form by specifying FormName!Object.Property.

9. Finally, if you really need the value of a variable in more than one form, make it global. Declare the variable with the `Public` statement in the General Declarations section of a standard code module. *Note:* Visual Basic allows you to use the `Public` statement in the General Declara-

tions section of *any* module, which means that you can declare global variables in any form module. Don't do it! Keep your `Public` declarations in a standard code module.

Feedback 6.1

For each of these situations, write the declaration statement and tell where it should appear. Assume the project will have multiple form modules and a standard code module. Be sure to give the proper prefixes to your identifiers.

1. The number of calories in a gram of fat (nine), to use in the calculations of a procedure.
2. The name of the person with the highest score, which will be determined in one procedure and displayed in a label on a different form. (The value must be retained for multiple executions of the procedure.)
3. The name of the company ("Bab's Bowling Service"), which will appear in several forms.
4. A total dollar amount to be calculated in one procedure of a form, added to a grand total in a procedure of a second form, and formatted and displayed in a third form.
5. A count of the number of persons entered using a single form. The count will be used to help calculate an average in a second form.
6. The formatted version of a dollar total, which will be displayed in a label in the next statement.
7. For each of these identifiers, tell the scope, data type, and whether it represents a variable or constant.
   (a) miLocations
   (b) gcPayment
   (c) cPayment
   (d) cPAYMENT
   (e) gstTEAM_NAME
   (f) stTeamName
   (g) mstTeamName
   (h) gstTeamName

An About Box

One type of additional form in a project is an **About box**, such as the one you find in most Windows programs in *Help/About*. Usually an About box gives the name and version of the project as well as information about the programmer or company. The About box may be displayed initially when the application begins or displayed when a specific event occurs (such as pressing a command button or selecting a menu command).

You can create your own About box by creating a new form and entering the information in labels. Of course, you may use any of the normal controls on this new form, but About boxes typically hold labels, an OK command button, and perhaps an image or shape controls for a logo. Figure 6.7 shows a typical About box.

Figure 6.7

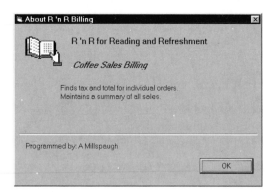

A typical About box containing labels, a line control, an image, and an OK command button.

You can also use VB's About Dialog template to create a new About box. Choose *Add Form* from the *Project* menu and on the *New* tab select *About Dialog* (Figure 6.8). A new form is added to your project with controls you can modify (Figure 6.9). You can change the captions and image by setting the properties as you would on any other form. Once you create the form in your project, it is yours and may be modified as you please.

New to
UB 5!

Figure 6.8

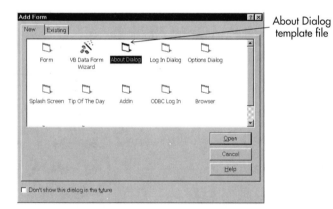

About Dialog template file

*Select *About Dialog* from the New tab of the Add Form dialog box.*

Figure 6.9

A new form created with the About Dialog template.

A Splash Screen

Perhaps you have noticed the logo or window that often appears while a program is loading, such as the one in Figure 6.10. This initial form is called a **splash screen**. Professional applications use splash screens to tell the user that the program is loading and starting. It can make a large application appear to load and run faster, since something appears on the screen while the rest of the application loads.

Figure 6.10

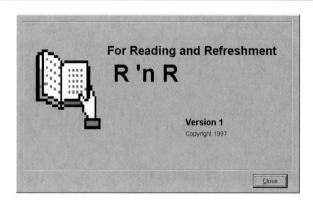

A splash screen.

You can create your own splash screen or use the splash screen template included with VB5 (Figure 6.11). In the *Add Form* dialog box (refer to Figure 6.8), choose *Splash Screen* to add the new form; then modify the form to fit your needs. In the case of this splash screen, you will need to make major modifications to all the labels and to the code.

New to VB 5!

Figure 6.11

A new form created with the Splash Screen form template.

When you use this style of splash screen, your project does not display the main form as a startup form. Instead, when you run the project, execution begins with a sub procedure named Main, which is located in your .BAS file.

Tip

To switch from one form to another in design time, use the Project Explorer window. Double-click on a form name to display the form. Or click on a form name and then click either the View Object or the View Code button.

Using Sub Main for Startup

A project may begin execution by displaying a startup form or by executing a procedure called Main, which you will code in your standard code module. You will use a Main sub procedure when you have tasks that should be done before the first form loads, such as when you want to display a splash screen while the main form loads.

When you begin execution with a Main sub procedure, you must explicitly load and/or show each form. In the following example, the splash screen is displayed as modeless, so that the Load statement in the next statement will execute. In the Load statement, the project's main form is loaded but not shown. The last actions performed by the form module will be to unload the splash screen and show the main form.

You have some choices about when to unload the splash screen and show the main form. In a large application, where it may take several seconds to load the main form, the logic is usually set up to exit the splash screen as soon as the main form finishes loading. In a small application, such as the ones we are writing in this text, the main form loads so quickly that the splash screen disappears before you can see it. We will place a Close button on the splash screen rather than have the form disappear automatically. You might also consider using a Timer control to close the form after an interval of time. See Chapter 13 or Visual Basic Help for information on the Timer control.

Coding the Standard Code Module

This code goes in the standard code module (.BAS file):

```
Sub Main()
    'Display the splash screen while the main form loads

    frmSplash.Show vbModeless 'Display the splash form
    Load frmMain              'Load the main form
End Sub
```

Coding the Splash Screen Event Procedure

The following code goes in the cmdClose_Click event procedure of the splash screen form. *Note:* If you started with the VB Splash Screen template, first remove all code that appeared automatically, add a cmdClose command button, and add this procedure:

```
Private Sub cmdClose_Click()
    'Unload splash screen and show the main form

    Unload Me              'Unload the splash screen form
    frmMain.Show vbModal   'Show the main form
End Sub
```

Setting the Startup Form or Procedure

The startup form by default is the first form created in a project. However, you can select a different form to be the startup form, or you can specify that your Main sub procedure should begin when the project is run. In the *Project Properties* dialog box (Figure 6.12), you can choose one of the project's forms or *Sub Main*.

F i g u r e   6 . 1 2

Set the startup form or procedure in the Project Properties *dialog box.*

To change the startup option:

STEP 1: Select *Project Properties* from the *Project* menu (or right-click on project name in the Project Explorer window and choose *Project Properties*).

STEP 2: In the *Project Properties* dialog box, click on the *General* tab.

STEP 3: Drop down the list for *Startup Object* (Figure 6.13) and select the desired form or the *Sub Main* procedure.

F i g u r e   6 . 1 3

Drop down the Startup Object *list to select a startup form or* Sub Main.

STEP 4: Click OK.

Your Hands-On Programming Example

Modify the hands-on project from Chapter 5 to include multiple forms. This version of the project requires four forms: frmBillling, frmAbout, frmSplash, and frmSummary.

frmBilling: Add the frmBilling form from Chapter 5 to a new project. Do a *Save As*, create a new folder, and save the form into the new folder. This step will create a copy of the Chapter 5 form which you can modify for this project.

frmAbout: Replace the MsgBox About Box from Chapter 5 with a new form using the About Dialog template. Delete all of the code attached to the new form file. Delete the command button for system information from the form. (You may want to test this command on your own.)

frmSplash: Create a splash screen using the Splash Screen template. Customize the label captions and the image and delete all of the code attached to the new form file.

frmSummary: Replace the summary labels from the main form (frmBilling) with a separate form for the summary.

Startup Object: Create a standard code module with a Main sub procedure. Set the form properties Startup Object to Sub Main.

Reviewing the project requirements:

frmBilling: The user enters the number of items, selects the coffee type from option buttons, and selects the check box for taxable items. The price for each coffee is calculated according to these prices:

Cappuccino	2.00
Espresso	2.25
Latte	1.75
Iced (either)	2.50

The Calculate Selection command button calculates and displays the amount due for each item, adds the current item to the order, and calculates and displays the order information in labels. The Clear for Next Item button clears the selections and amount for the single item.

The *Next Order* menu command clears the bill for the current customer and add to the totals for the summary. The *Summary* menu command shows the summary form that displays the total of all orders, the average sale amount per customer, and the number of customers.

The *Edit* menu contains options that duplicate the Calculate and Clear buttons. The *Font* and *Color* options change the contents of the subtotal, tax, and total labels.

The *About* selection on the *Help* menu displays the About form, which contains information about the program and the programmer.

<u>F</u>ile   <u>E</u>dit   <u>H</u>elp
    <u>N</u>ew Order   <u>C</u>alculate Amount   <u>A</u>bout
    <u>S</u>ummary   Cl<u>e</u>ar Item
    E<u>x</u>it   _____
                               <u>F</u>ont
                               <u>C</u>olor

Planning the Project

Sketch the four forms (Figure 6.14). Your user checks the sketches and signs
off the design.

Figure 6.14

*Sketches of the four forms for the
hands-on programming example.*

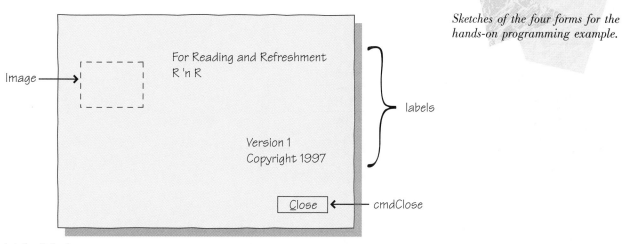

(a) frmSplash

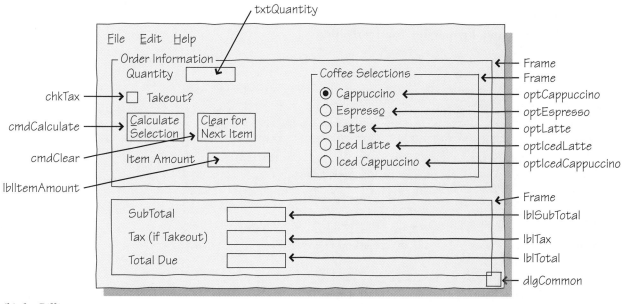

(b) frmBilling

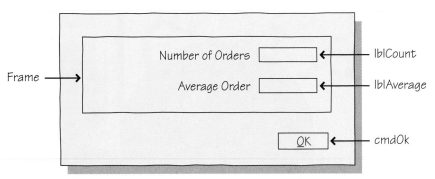

(c) frmSummary

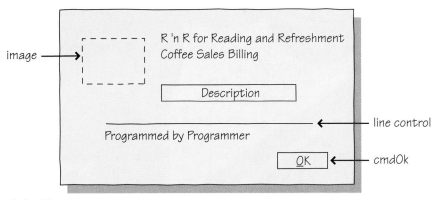

(d) frmAbout

The next step is to plan the property settings for each of the forms and the controls. *Note:* The frmBilling user interface is unchanged from Chapter 5.

frmBilling

Plan the Objects and Properties for frmBilling

Object	Property	Setting
frmBilling	Name	frmBilling
	Caption	R 'n R—for Reading 'n Refreshment
	WindowState	Maximized
Frame1	Caption	Order Information
Frame2	Caption	Coffee Selections
Frame3	Caption	(blank)
optCappuccino	Name	optCappuccino
	Caption	C&appuccino
optEspresso	Name	optEspresso
	Caption	Espress&o

(continued)

Object	Property	Setting
optLatte	Name	optLatte
	Caption	La&tte
optIcedLatte	Name	optIcedLatte
	Caption	&Iced Latte
optIcedCappuccino	Name	optIcedCappuccino
	Caption	Iced Ca&ppuccino
Label1	Caption	Quantity
txtQuantity	Name	txtQuantity
	Text	(blank)
chkTax	Name	chkTax
	Caption	Takeout ?
Label2	Caption	Item Amount
Label3	Caption	SubTotal
Label4	Caption	Tax (if Takeout)
Label5	Caption	Total Due
lblItemAmount	Name	lblItemAmount
	Caption	(blank)
	BorderStyle	1 - FixedSingle
lblSubTotal	Name	lblSubTotal
	Caption	(blank)
	BorderStyle	1 - Fixed Single
lblTax	Name	lblTax
	Caption	(blank)
	BorderStyle	1 - Fixed Single
lblTotal	Name	lblTotal
	Caption	(blank)
	BorderStyle	1 - Fixed Single
cmdCalculate	Name	cmdCalculate
	Caption	&Calculate Selection
	Default	True
cmdClear	Name	cmdClear
	Caption	C&lear for Next Item
	Cancel	True
mnuFileNew	Name	mnuFileNew

(continued)

Object	Property	Setting
	Caption	&New Order
mnuFileSummary	Name	mnuFileSummary
	Caption	&Summary
mnuFileExit	Name	mnuFileExit
	Caption	E&xit
mnuEditCalc	Name	mnuEditCalc
	Caption	&Calculate Selection
mnuEditClear	Name	mnuEditClear
	Caption	C&lear Item
mnuEditFont	Name	mnuEditFont
	Caption	&Font
mnuEditColor	Name	mnuEditColor
	Caption	&Color
mnuHelpAbout	Name	mnuHelpAbout
	Caption	&About

Plan the Event Procedures for frmBilling

Plan the actions for the event procedures for the menu commands and command buttons.

Object	Procedure	Action
cmdCalculate	Click	Determine price per cup. Multiply price by quantity. Call tax procedure if needed. Add quantity to item total. Display the values.
cmdClear	Click	Clear the coffee selections. Clear the quantity and the item price. Disable the takeout check box. Set the focus to the quantity.
mnuFileNew	Click	Clear the previous order. Accumulate total and count. Set subtotal and total to 0.
mnuFileSummary	Click	Display the Average. Display Total Sales. Display the number of customers.
mnuFileExit	Click	Terminate the project.
mnuEditCalc	Click	Call calculate command event.
mnuEditClear	Click	Call clear command event.
cFindTax	(call)	Calculate the sales tax.

frmSplash

Plan the Objects and Properties for frmSplash

Object	Property	Setting
frmSplash	Name	frmSplash
	Caption	(blank)
	ControlBox	False (Already set by the form template)
	MaxButton	False (Already set by the form template)
	MinButton	False (Already set by the form template)
All labels	Caption	Program information (*Note:* Student information goes here.)
cmdClose	Name	cmdClose
	Caption	&Close

Plan the Event Procedures for frmSplash

Object	Procedure	Action
cmdClose	Click	Unload the splash form. Show the main form.

frmAbout

Plan the Objects and Properties for frmAbout

Object	Property	Setting
frmAbout	Name	frmAbout
	Caption	About R 'n R Billing
	MaxButton	False (Already set by the form template)
	MinButton	False (Already set by the form template)
All labels	Caption	Program and programmer information
cmdOK	Name	cmdOK
	Caption	&OK

Plan the Event Procedures for frmAbout

Object	Procedure	Action
cmdOK	Click	Hide the About form.

frmSummary

Plan the Objects and Properties for frmSummary

Object	Property	Setting
frmSummary	Name	frmSummary
	Caption	Coffee Sales Summary
Frame1	Caption	Program and programmer information (*Note:* Student information goes here.)
Label1	Name	Label1
	Caption	Number of Orders
Label2	Name	Label2
	Caption	Average Order
lblCount	Name	lblCount
	Caption	(blank)
	Alignment	Right Justify
lblAverage	Name	lblAverage
	Caption	(blank)
	Alignment	Right Justify
cmdOK	Name	cmdOK
	Caption	&OK

Plan the Event Procedures for frmSummary

Object	Procedure	Action
cmdOK	Click	Hide the Summary form.

Form	Activate	If Count > 0 then
		    Calculate Average = Total / Count
		Else
		    Average = 0
		End If
		Format and display Count and Average.

Standard Code Module

Plan the Procedures for the Standard Code Module

Procedure	Action
Main	Show the Splash screen. Load frmBilling.

Write the Project

After completing the planning steps, create the forms following the sketches in Figure 6.14. Figure 6.15 shows the completed forms.

Figure 6.15

The four forms for the hands-on programming example are frmSplash, frmBilling, frmSummary, and frmAbout.

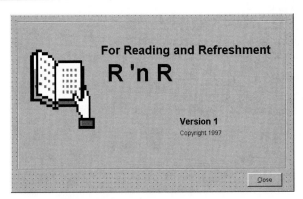

(a) frmSplash

(b) frmBilling

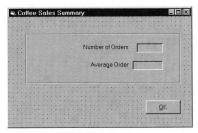

(c) frmSummary

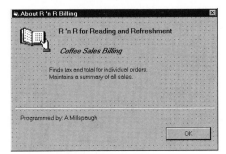

(d) frmAbout

frmBilling:

STEP 1: Begin a new project.

STEP 2: Point to *Form1* in the Project Explorer window, right-click to display the shortcut menu, and select *Remove Form1*.

STEP 3: Select *Add Form* from the *Project* menu and click on the *Existing* tab.

STEP 4: Locate frmBilling in the Ch0501 folder (or wherever you placed the hands-on project from Chapter 5). Click on *Open.*

STEP 5: Click on *frmBilling* in the Project Explorer window and select *Save frmBilling.frm As* from the *File* menu. Open the *Save In* list and select the location you want for a new folder and then click on the *Create New Folder* button. Name your new folder *Ch0601.*

STEP 6: Double-click on your new folder so that it appears in the *Save In* box, check the filename, and click *Save.* Your Project Explorer window should resemble Figure 6.16.

F i g u r e 6 . 1 6

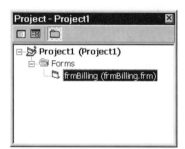

The Project Explorer window shows the newly added form in the project.

STEP 7: Make the planned changes to the mnuFileSummary_Click and mnuHelpAbout_Click event procedures, as well as changes to global variables used for the summary.

    Note: If you wish you can continue adding forms to your project and return later to the steps that modify the forms and code.

frmAbout:

STEP 1: Select *Add Form* from the *Project* menu and click on the *New* tab.

STEP 2: Double-click on *About Dialog.*

STEP 3: Set the form's properties to match the plans detailed earlier.

STEP 4: Choose *Save frmAbout As* from the *File* menu, check the folder and filename, and save the new form.

STEP 5: Modify the label captions on the form to match your planning sketch.

STEP 6: Add the OK command button.

STEP 7: Switch to the code window and delete all code there except `Option Explicit`.

STEP 8: Write the code for frmAbout.

frmSplash:

STEP 1: Select *Add Form* from the *Project* menu and click on the *New* tab.

STEP 2: Double-click on *Splash Screen.*

STEP 3: Set the form's properties to match the plans detailed earlier.

STEP 4: Choose *Save frmSplash As* from the *File* menu, check the folder and filename, and save the new form.

STEP 5: Modify the label captions on the form to match your planning sketch.

STEP 6: Add the Close command button.

STEP 7: Switch to the code window and delete all code there except `Option Explicit`.

STEP 8: Write the code for frmSplash.

frmSummary:

STEP 1: Select *Add Form* from the *Project* menu and click on the *New* tab.

STEP 2: Double-click on *Form*.

STEP 3: Set the form's properties to match the plans detailed above.

STEP 4: Choose *Save Form1 As* from the *File* menu, check the folder, change the filename to *frmSummary*, and save the new form.

STEP 5: Create the controls on the form to match your planning sketch.

STEP 6: Set the properties for the controls.

STEP 7: Write the code for frmSummary.

Standard Code Module:

STEP 1: Select *Add Module* from the *Project* menu and click on the *New* tab.

STEP 2: Double-click on *Module*.

STEP 3: Choose *Save Module1 As* from the *File* menu, check the folder, change the filename to *Ch0601*, and save the new code module. Your Project Explorer window should look like Figure 6.17.

F i g u r e   6 . 1 7

The completed project should show all four forms and the standard code module.

STEP 4: Write the code for the standard code module, which includes declarations for the global variables and the Main sub procedure.

Set the Startup Object:

STEP 1: Select *Project Properties* from the *Project* menu (or right-click on project name in the Project Explorer window and choose *Project Properties*).

STEP 2: In the *Project Properties* dialog box, click on the *General* tab.

STEP 3: Drop down the list for *Startup Object* and select *Sub Main*. The Main sub procedure displays frmSplash and loads frmBilling.

STEP 4: Click on OK.

Write the Code

frmBilling

```
'Program Name:    Billing
'Programmer:      A. Millspaugh
'Date:            July 1997
'Description:     This project calculates the
'                 amount due based upon the customer selection
'                 and accumulates summary data for the day.
'                 The project incorporates menus, common dialog
'                 boxes, and multiple forms.
'Folder:          Ch0601

Option Explicit
Dim mcSubtotal               As Currency
Dim mcTotal                  As Currency
Const cCAPPUCCINO_PRICE      As Currency = 2
Const cESPRESSO_PRICE        As Currency = 2.25
Const cLATTE_PRICE           As Currency = 1.75
Const cICED_PRICE            As Currency = 2.5
Const mcTAX_RATE             As Currency = 0.08
```

```
Private Sub cmdCalculate_Click()
    'Calculate and display the current amounts, add to totals

    Dim cPrice       As Currency
    Dim iQuantity    As Integer
    Dim cTax         As Currency
    Dim cItemAmount  As Currency

    'Find the price
    If optCappuccino.Value = True Then
        cPrice = cCAPPUCCINO_PRICE
    ElseIf optEspresso.Value = True Then
        cPrice = cESPRESSO_PRICE
    ElseIf optLatte.Value = True Then
        cPrice = cLATTE_PRICE
    ElseIf optIcedCappuccino.Value = True Or _
        optIcedLatte.Value = True Then
    cPrice = cICED_PRICE
    Else
        MsgBox "Please Make Drink Selection", vbOKOnly, "Oops"
    End If

    'Add the price times quantity to running total
    If IsNumeric(txtQuantity.Text) Then
        iQuantity = Val(txtQuantity.Text)
        cItemAmount = cPrice * iQuantity
        mcSubtotal = mcSubtotal + cItemAmount
        If chkTax.Value = Checked Then
            cTax = cFindTax(mcSubtotal) 'Call a function procedure
```

```
        End If
        mcTotal = mcSubtotal + cTax
        lblItemAmount.Caption = Format$(cItemAmount, "Currency")
        lblSubTotal.Caption = Format$(mcSubtotal, "Currency")
        lblTax.Caption = Format$(cTax, "Currency")
        lblTotal.Caption = Format$(mcTotal, "Currency")
    Else
        MsgBox "Quantity must contain a number", vbExclamation, "Oops"
        txtQuantity.SetFocus
    End If
End Sub
```

```
Private Sub cmdClear_Click()
    'Clear appropriate controls

    optCappuccino.Value = True      'Make first button selected to begin
    optEspresso.Value = False
    optLatte.Value = False
    optIcedLatte.Value = False
    optIcedCappuccino.Value = False
    lblItemAmount.Caption = ""
    chkTax.Enabled = False          'Allow change for new order only
    With txtQuantity
        .Text = ""
        .SetFocus
    End With
End Sub
```

```
Private Sub mnuEditCalc_Click()
    'Call the Calculate event

    cmdCalculate_Click
End Sub
```

```
Private Sub mnuEditClear_Click()
    'Call the Clear command event

    cmdClear_Click
End Sub
```

```
Private Sub mnuEditColor_Click()
    'Change the color of the total labels

    dlgCommon.ShowColor
    lblSubTotal.ForeColor = dlgCommon.Color
    lblTax.ForeColor = dlgCommon.Color
    lblTotal.ForeColor = dlgCommon.Color
End Sub
```

```vb
Private Sub mnuEditFont_Click()
    'Change the font name for the subtotal labels
    dlgCommon.Flags = cdlCFScreenFonts 'Set up Font dialog box fonts
    dlgCommon.ShowFont
    lblSubTotal.Font.Name = dlgCommon.FontName
    lblTax.Font.Name = dlgCommon.FontName
    lblTotal.Font.Name = dlgCommon.FontName
End Sub


Private Sub mnuFileExit_Click()
    'Terminate the project

    End
End Sub


Private Sub mnuFileNew_Click()
    'Clear the current order and add to totals

    cmdClear_Click
    lblSubTotal.Caption = ""
    lblTax.Caption = ""
    lblTotal.Caption = ""

    'Add to Totals
    gcGrandTotal = gcGrandTotal + mcTotal
    mcSubtotal = 0     'Reset totals for next order
    mcTotal = 0
    giCustomerCount = giCustomerCount + 1

    'Clear and enable tax check box
    With chkTax
        .Enabled = True
        .Value = False
    End With
End Sub


Private Sub mnuFileSummary_Click()
    'Load and display the summary information

    If mcTotal <> 0 Then
        mnuFileNew_Click 'Make sure last order is counted
    End If
    frmSummary.Show vbModal
End Sub


Private Sub mnuHelpAbout_Click()
    'Display a message box about the program

    frmAbout.Show vbModal
End Sub
```

```
Public Function cFindTax(cAmount As Currency) As Currency
    'Calculate the sales tax

    cFindTax = cAmount * mcTAX_RATE
End Function
```

frmAbout

```
'Module:        frmAbout
'Description:   Display information about the program and the
'               programmer.
'Folder:        Ch0601

Option Explicit

Private Sub cmdOK_Click()
    'Hide the form

    Me.Hide
End Sub
```

frmSplash

```
'Module:        frmSplash
'Description:   Splash screen to display while main form loads.
'Folder:        Ch0601

Option Explicit

Private Sub cmdClose_Click()
    'Unload the form and display the main form

    Unload Me               'Close the Splash form
    frmBilling.Show vbModal 'Display the Billing form
End Sub
```

frmSummary

```
'Module:        frmSummary
'Description:   Display summary information on a separate form
'Folder:        Ch0601

Option Explicit

Private Sub cmdOK_Click()
    'Return to the main form

    Me.Hide
End Sub
```

```
Private Sub Form_Activate()
    'Calculate the average and display the totals
    Dim cAverage As Currency

    If giCustomerCount > 0 Then
        cAverage = gcGrandTotal / giCustomerCount
    Else
        cAverage = 0
    End If
    lblCount.Caption = giCustomerCount
    lblAverage.Caption = Format$(cAverage, "Currency")
End Sub
```

Standard Code Module

```
'Module:        ch0601.BAS
'Programmer:    A Millspaugh
'Date:          March 1997
'Description:   Code module to declare the global variables
'               and the Main procedure, which displays the
'               splash screen.
'Folder:        CH0601

Public gcGrandTotal       As Currency
Public giCustomerCount    As Integer

Sub Main()
    'Display a splash screen while the main form is being loaded

    frmSplash.Show vbModeless       'Show the splash screen
    Load frmBilling                 'Load the main form
End Sub
```

Programming Hints

Here are some useful tips for working with maximized forms.

Working with Maximized Forms

Until this point all of our forms have been smaller than the full screen. If you want your application's form to fill the entire screen, these techniques can help you in designing and running your project.

Design-Time Tips

Make your form run maximized by setting its WindowState property to *2–Maximized*. To work on the form in design time, click on the form's Maximize button, which will make it larger. You can use the Form window's scroll bars to view the entire area of the form.

You can close the extra windows on the screen or undock them so that they float on top of your form. The borders of each window are resizable, and you can hide the toolbar. Figure 6.18 shows one possible screen setup for working on a maximized form.

The keyboard shortcut for the Code window is F7. Of course, you can always double-click on a control to display the Code window, if you prefer.

Figure   6.18

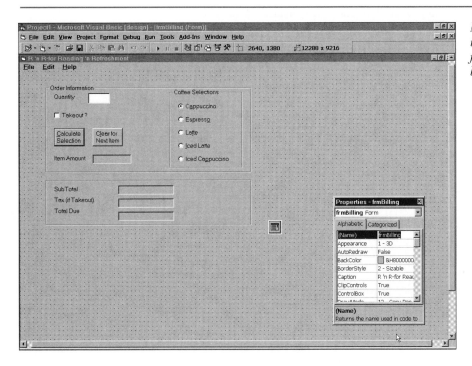

Modify the screen layout to make it easier to work on maximized forms. Here is one possible layout.

Stopping Execution with a Maximized Form

To stop program execution, it is best to have a working Exit command button, but even if you don't, you can still stop your program. Click on your form's Close box, which exits the program, or click on the form's Restore button, which will make it smaller so you have access to the Visual Basic toolbar buttons and menu bar.

S u m m a r y

1. Projects may need more than one form—there is virtually no limit to the number of forms that can be used within a single project. Add forms by clicking the Form toolbar button or the *Add Form* command on the *Project* menu.
2. The first form displayed when a project runs is called the startup form.
3. Forms used for one project can be added to another project. Forms can also be removed from a project.
4. The Show and Hide methods are used to display a form or remove one from the screen.
5. A form displayed as modal requires the user to respond to the form; it must be closed or unloaded before any execution continues. When a form is displayed as modeless, the user can switch to another form without closing the modeless form.

6. The `Load` statement loads a form but does not show it. The `Unload` statement hides a form, removes it from memory, and releases any system resources used by the form.

7. The `Me` keyword refers to the current active form. `Me` can be used to hide or unload the active form.

8. To refer to an object in a different form, use the form name, an exclamation point, and the object name.

9. A standard code module contains global declarations and procedures that may be used by multiple forms. To add a standard code module use the *Add Module* command on the *Project* menu; the file will have a .BAS extension.

10. Global variables, which are visible to all forms within a project, are declared using the keyword `Public`. The `Public` statement can appear only in the General Declarations section of a module and *should* be placed in a standard code module.

11. Variables declared with the keyword `Static` retain their values for multiple calls to the procedure in which they are defined.

12. An About box, which typically contains information about the version of an application and the programmer and copyrights, may be created by adding a new form. VB5 has an About Dialog template form that can be used to create an About box.

13. A splash screen may be displayed while a program loads. VB5 provides a splash screen template that may be used to create a new splash screen form.

14. Program execution can start with a startup form or from a sub procedure called *Main*. Use a Sub Main to display a splash screen.

Key Terms

About box *203*

.BAS file extension *199*

global *200*

`Hide` method *196*

`Load` statement *198*

`Me` *198*

modal *196*

modeless *196*

`Public` *200*

`Show` method *196*

splash screen *205*

standard code module *199*

startup form *194*

`Static` *201*

`Unload` statement *198*

Review Questions

1. What does the phrase *standard code module* mean?

2. Discuss the difference between declaring a variable in the General Declarations section of a standard code module and declaring a variable in the General Declarations section of a form code module.

3. List some of the items generally found in an About box.

4. What is the purpose of a splash screen?

5. What is the term used for the first form to display in a project?
6. How can you choose a different form as the startup form after the project has been created?
7. Explain how to include an existing form in a new project.

Programming Exercises

6.1 Modify project 5.5 (the flag viewer) to include a splash screen and an About form.
   Menus:

File	Country		Display	Help
Print	United States		Title	About
Exit	Canada		Country Name	
	Japan		Programmer	
	Mexico			

6.2 Create a project that will produce a summary of the amounts due for Pat's Auto Repair Shop. Display a splash screen first; then display the main form.

   The main form menus:

File	Process	Help
Exit	Job Information	About

   Job Information command:
   The Job Information menu command will display the Job Information form.
   The Job Information form:
   The Job Information form must have text boxes for the user to enter the job number, customer name, amount charged for parts, and the hours of labor. Include labels for Parts, Labor, SubTotal, Sales Tax, and Total.
   Include command buttons for Calculate, Print, Clear, and OK.
   The Calculate button finds the charges and displays them in labels. The tax rate and the hourly labor charge should be set up as named constants so that they can be easily modified if either changes. Current charges are $30 per hour for labor and 8 percent (.08) for the sales tax rate. Sales tax is charged only on parts, not on labor.
   The Print button prints the current contents of the form.
   The Clear button clears the text boxes and resets the focus in the first text box.
   The OK button hides the Job Information form and displays the main form.

6.3 Modify project 6.2 so that summary information is maintained for the total dollar amount for parts, labor, sales tax, and total for all customers.
   Add a *Summary* command under the *Process* menu with a separator bar between the two menu commands. When the user selects the *Summary* command, display the summary information in a Summary form. The Summary form should have an OK button that hides the Summary form and returns the user to the main form.

6.4 A battle is raging over the comparative taste of Prune Punch and Apple Ade. Each taste tester rates the two drinks on a scale of 1 to 10 (10 being best). The proof of the superiority of one over the other will be the average score for the two drinks.

Display a splash screen and then the main form.

The main form menus:

```
File              Help
    New Tester        About
    Summary
    Exit
```

New Tester command:

The *New Tester* command displays a form that inputs the test results for each drink. The form contains an OK button and a Cancel button.

When the user clicks the OK button, add the score for each type of drink to the drink's total, clear the text boxes, and reset the focus. Leave the form on the screen in case the next tester is ready to enter scores. If either score is blank when the OK button is pressed, display a message in a message box and reset the focus to the box for the missing data.

The Cancel button returns to the startup form without performing any calculation.

Summary command:

The *Summary* command displays a form that contains the current results of the taste test. It should display the winner, the total number of taste testers, and the average rating for each drink. The form contains an OK button that returns to the startup form. (The user will be able to display the summary at any time and as often as desired.)

The About form:

The About form should display information about the program and the programmer. Include an OK button that returns the user to the main form.

CASE STUDIES

Modify the VB Mail Order project from Chapter 5 to include a splash screen, an About form, and a summary form. Include

VB Mail Order

an image on both the splash form and the About form.

Create a project that uses three forms. Add the form from the Chapter 5 case study and create a splash screen and an About form.

The splash screen:

Display a splash screen and then the main form.

The About form:

Include an image and identifying information about the program and programmer.

The main form:

The main form should display "Valley Boulevard Auto Center—Meeting all your vehicle's needs" and appropriate image(s).

VB Auto Center

The main form menus:

File		Edit	Help
Input Sale		Color	About
Exit		Font	

The Color and Font commands should allow the user to change the large label on the form.

The Input Sale command should display the form from Chapter 5. You will need to modify the Chapter 5 form to hide itself rather than to terminate execution.

7

Lists, Loops, and Printing

At the completion of this chapter, you will be able to...

1. Create and use list boxes and combo boxes.

2. Enter items into list boxes using the Properties window and the AddItem method.

3. Determine which item in a list is selected.

4. Use the ListCount property to determine the number of items in a list.

5. Display a selected item from a list.

6. Differentiate among the available types of combo boxes.

7. Use `Do/Loops` and `For/Next` statements to iterate through a loop.

8. Use the `MsgBox` function to determine the button pressed by the user.

9. Use the string functions `Left`, `Right`, and `Mid` to refer to part of a string and use the `Len` function to count the number of characters in a string.

10. Send information to the printer using the `Print` method.

11. Control the format of printing using commas, semicolons, the `Tab` function, and the `Spc` function.

To offer list of items to choose from
- list box
- combo box

You may want to offer the user a list of items from which to choose. You can use the Windows list box and combo box controls to display lists on a form. You may choose to add items to a list during design time, during run time, or perhaps during a combination of both. Several styles of list boxes are available; the style you use is determined by design and space considerations, as well as whether or not you will allow the user to add items to the list.

List Boxes and Combo Boxes

Both **list box controls** and **combo box controls** allow you to have a list of items from which the user can make a selection. Figure 7.1 shows the toolbox tools for creating the controls; Figure 7.2 shows several types of list boxes and combo boxes, including simple list boxes, **simple combo boxes**, **dropdown combo boxes**, and **dropdown lists**. The list boxes on the left of the form in Figure 7.2 are all created with the List box tool; the boxes on the right of the form are created with the Combo box tool. Notice the three distinct styles of combo boxes.

Figure 7.1

Combo Box → ← List box

Use the list box tool and the combo box tool to create list boxes and combo boxes on your forms.

Figure 7.2

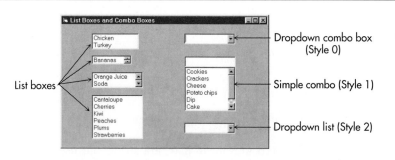

List boxes →

Dropdown combo box (Style 0)

Simple combo (Style 1)

Dropdown list (Style 2)

Various styles of list box controls and combo box controls.

List boxes and combo boxes have most of the same properties and operate in a similar fashion. One exception is that a combo box control has a Style property, which determines whether or not the list box also has a text box for user entry and whether or not the list will drop down (refer to figure 7.2). The second exception is that combo boxes have a Text property and list boxes do not.

Both list boxes and combo boxes have a great feature. If the list has more items than can be seen at one time, given the size of the box, VB automatically adds a scroll bar. You do not have to be concerned with the location of the scroll box in the scroll bar; the scrolling is handled automatically.

When you add a list box to a form, choose the style according to the space you have available and how you want the box to operate. Do you want the user to select from an existing list? If so, use a simple list box or a dropdown list (combo box Style 2). Do you want the user to be able to type a new entry if necessary? In this case, use one of the two styles with an added text box: the dropdown combo box (Style 0) or the simple combo box (Style 1).

When you create a list box or combo box at design time, you determine the size of the control. There is no Caption property, so for list boxes Visual Basic displays the Name property in the control during design time. For combo boxes, the Text property displays. Don't spend any time trying to make a list box or dropdown list (combo box style 2) appear empty during design time; the box will appear empty at run time. Dropdown combo boxes and simple combos (styles 0 and 1) have a Text property, which you can set or remove at design time.

When you name list boxes and combo boxes, use "lst" as the list box prefix and "cbo" as the prefix for combo boxes.

Filling the List

You can use several methods to fill a list box and combo box. If you know the list contents at design time and the list never changes, you can define the list items in the Properties window. If you must add items to the list during program execution, you will use the AddItem method in an event procedure. In Chapter 9 you will learn to fill a list from a data file on disk. This method allows the list contents to vary from one run to the next.

Using the Properties Window

The List property holds the list of items for a list box or combo box. To define the List property at design time, select the control and scroll the Properties window to the List property (Figure 7.3). Click on the down arrow to drop down the empty list and type your first list item. Then press Ctrl + Enter to move to the next list item. Continue typing items and pressing Ctrl + Enter until you are finished (Figure 7.4). On the last list item, do not press Ctrl + Enter, or you will have an extra (blank) item on the list. Press Enter or click anywhere off the list to complete the operation.

Figure   7.3

Select the List property of a list box to enter the list items.

Figure   7.4

Type each list item and press Ctrl + Enter.

Using the AddItem Method

To add an item to a list box at run time, use the **AddItem method**. You may choose to add to a list the contents of the text box at the top of a combo box, a variable, a constant, or the property of another control.

The AddItem Method—General Form

```
Object.AddItem Value [, Index]
```

Value is the value to add to the list. If the value is a string literal, enclose it in quotation marks.

The optional *Index* specifies the position within the list to place the new item; the first element in the list has an Index of 0.

When you omit the Index, the new item generally goes at the end of the list. However, you can alter that by setting the control's **Sorted property** to True. Then the new item will be placed alphabetically in the list.

The AddItem Method—Examples

```
lstSchools.AddItem "Harvard"
lstSchools.AddItem "Stanford"
lstSchools.AddItem txtSchools.Text
cboMajors.AddItem cboMajors.Text
cboMajors.AddItem stMajor
```

When the user types a new value in the text box portion of a combo box, that item is not automatically added to the list. If you want to add the newly entered text to the list, use the AddItem method:

```
cboCoffee.AddItem cboCoffee.Text
```

Clearing the List

In addition to adding items during run time, you can also clear all items from a list. Use the **Clear method** to empty a combo box or list box.

The Clear Method—General Form

```
Object.Clear
```

The Clear Method—Examples

```
lstSchools.Clear
cboMajors.Clear
```

The ListIndex Property

When a project is running and the user selects (highlights) an item from the list, the index number of that item is stored in the **ListIndex property** of the list box. Recall that the ListIndex of the first item in the list is 0. If no list item is selected, the ListIndex property is set to negative 1.

You can use the ListIndex property to select an item in the list or deselect all items in code.

Example

```
lstCoffeeTypes.ListIndex = 3     'Select the fourth item in list
lstCoffeeTypes.ListIndex = -1    'Deselect all items in list
```

The ListCount Property

The application uses the **ListCount property** of a list box or combo box to store the number of items in the list. We will use the ListCount property later in this chapter to process each element in the list. ListCount is also handy when you need to display the count at some point in your project.

Remember, ListCount is always one more than the highest ListIndex, since ListIndex begins with 0. For example, if there are 20 items in a list, ListCount is 20 and the highest ListIndex is 19.

Example

```
iTotalItems = lstItem.ListCount
```

The List Property

If you need to display one item from a list, you can refer to one element of the **List property**. The List property of a list box or combo box holds the text of all of the list elements. You specify which element you want by including an index. This technique can be useful if you need to display a list item in a label on another form. Later in this chapter we will use the List property to send the contents of the list box to the printer.

Using the List Property—General Form

```
Object.List(Index) [ = Value]
```

The index of the first list element is 0, so the highest index is ListCount negative 1.

You can retrieve the value of a list element or set an element to a different value.

Using the List Property—Examples

```
lstSchools.List(5) = "University of California"
lblMyMajor.Caption = cboMajors.List(iIndex)
lblSelectedMajor.Caption = cboMajors.List(cboMajors.ListIndex)
```

To refer to the currently selected element of a list, you must combine the List property and the ListIndex property:

```
stSelectedFlavor = lstFlavor.List(lstFlavor.ListIndex)
```

Removing an Item from a List

Earlier you learned how to clear all the elements from a list. However, you might want to remove individual elements from a list. To remove an element from the list, use the **RemoveItem method**.

The RemoveItem Method—General Form

```
Object.RemoveItem Index
```

The Index is required; it specifies which element to remove. The Index of the first list element is 0, and the Index of the last element is ListCount negative 1.

The RemoveItem Method—Examples

```
lstNames.RemoveItem 0            'Remove the first name from the list
cboSchools.RemoveItem iIndex     'Remove the element in position iIndex
cboCoffee.RemoveItem cboCoffee.ListIndex   'Remove the currently selected item
```

List Box and Combo Box Events

Later in the chapter we will perform actions in event procedures for events of list boxes and combo boxes. Some useful events are the Change, GotFocus, and LostFocus. *Note:* Although we haven't used these events up until this point, many other controls have these same events. For example, you can code event procedures for the Change event of text boxes.

The Change Event

As the user types text into the text box portion of a combo box (styles 0 and 1), the Change event occurs. Each keystroke generates another change event. This event will be used later to match the characters typed to the elements in the list. A list box does not have a Change event because it does not have a text box associated with it.

The GotFocus Event

When a control receives the focus, a GotFocus event occurs. As the user tabs from control to control, a GotFocus event fires for each control. Later you will learn to make any existing text appear selected when the user tabs to a text box or the text portion of a combo box.

The LostFocus Event

You can also write code for the LostFocus event of a control. The LostFocus event fires as the control loses the focus. Often LostFocus event procedures are used for validating input data.

Feedback 7.1

Describe the purpose of each of the following methods or properties for a list box control.

1. ListCount
2. ListIndex
3. List
4. AddItem
5. Clear
6. RemoveItem
7. Sorted

Do/Loops

Until now, there has been no way to repeat the same steps in a procedure without calling them a second time. The computer is capable of repeating a group of instructions many times without calling the procedure for each new set of data. The process of repeating a series of instructions is called *looping.* The group of repeated instructions is called a **loop.** An **iteration** is a single execution of the statement(s) in the loop. In this section you will learn about the `Do/Loop`. Later in this chapter you will learn about another type of loop—a `For/Next` loop.

A `Do/Loop` terminates based on a condition that you specify. Execution of a `Do/Loop` continues *while* a condition is True or *until* a condition is True. You can choose to place the condition at the top or the bottom of the loop. Use a `Do/Loop` when the exact number of iterations is unknown.

Align the **Do** and **Loop statements** with each other and indent the lines of code to be repeated in between.

The Do and Loop Statements—General Form

```
Do {While | Until} Condition
  'statements in loop
Loop


or


Do

  'statements in loop
Loop {While | Until} Condition
```

The first form of the `Do/Loop` tests for completion at the top of the loop. With this type of loop, also called a ***pretest***, the statements inside the loop may never be executed if the terminating condition is True the first time it is tested.

Example

```
iTotal = 0
Do Until iTotal = 0
     'statements in loop
Loop
```

Since iTotal is zero the first time the condition is tested, the condition is True and the statements inside the loop will not execute. Control will pass to the statement following the `Loop` statement.

The second form of the `Do/Loop` tests for completion at the bottom of the loop, which means that the statements in the loop will *always* be executed at least once. This form of loop is sometimes called a ***posttest***. Changing the example to a posttest, you can see the difference.

```
iTotal = 0
Do
     'statements in loop
Loop Until iTotal = 0
```

In this case the statements inside the loop will be executed at least once. Assuming the value for iTotal does not change inside the loop, the condition (iTotal = 0) will be True the first time it is tested and control will pass to the first statement following the `Loop` statement. Figure 7.5 shows flowcharts of pretest and posttest loops, using both `While` and `Until`.

Figure   7.5

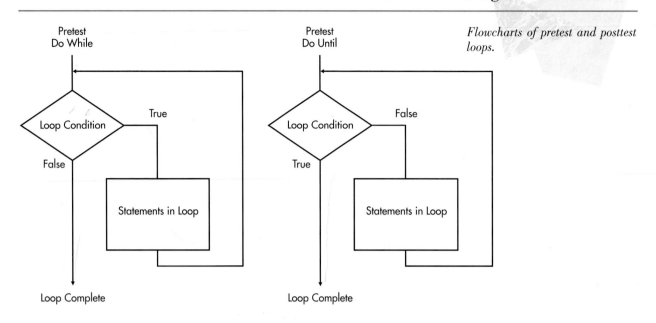

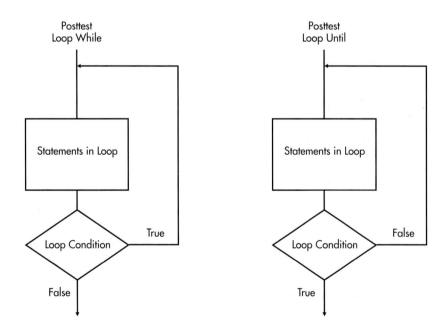

Flowcharts of pretest and posttest loops.

The Do and Loop Statements—Examples

```
Do Until iItemIndex = lstItems.ListCount - 1
      'Statements in loop

Loop

Do While cAmount >= 10 And cAmount <= 20
      'Statements in loop

Loop

Do
      'Statements in loop
Loop Until iTotal > 0
```

The Boolean Data Type Revisited

In Chapter 2 you learned about the Boolean data type, which holds only the values True or False. You will find Boolean variables very useful when setting and testing conditions for a loop. You can set a Boolean variable to True when a specific circumstance occurs, and then write a loop condition to continue until the variable is True.

An example of using a Boolean variable is when you want to search through a list for a specific value. The item may be found or not found, and you want to quit looking when a match is found.

Using a Boolean variable is usually a three-step process. First you must dimension a variable and set its initial value (or use the default VB setting of False). Then, when a particular situation occurs, set the variable to True. A loop condition can then check for True.

```
Dim bItemFound as Boolean
bItemFound = False
Do Until bItemFound        'Checks for True
    ...
```

A Boolean variable is always in one of two states—True or False. Many programmers refer to Boolean variables as *switches* or *flags*. Switches have two states: on or off; flags are considered either up or down.

Using a Do/Loop with a List Box

This small example combines a Boolean variable with a **Do/Loop**. Inside the loop each element of the list is compared to txtNewItem for a match. The loop will terminate when a match is found or when all elements have been tested. Follow through the logic to see what happens when there is a match, when there isn't a match, when the match occurs on the first list element, and when the match occurs on the last list element.

```vb
Private Sub cmdFind_Click()
    'Look for a match between the text box and list elements

    Dim bItemFound As Boolean
    Dim iItemIndex As Integer

    bItemFound = False
    iItemIndex = 0
    Do Until bItemFound Or iItemIndex = lstItems.ListCount
        If txtNewItem.Text = lstItems.List(iItemIndex) Then
            bItemFound = True
        End If
        iItemIndex = iItemIndex + 1
    Loop
    If bItemFound Then
        MsgBox "Item is in the list", vbInformation, "Item match"
    Else
        MsgBox "Item is not is the list", vbInformation, "Item no match"
    End If
End Sub
```

Feedback 7.2

Explain the purpose of each line of the following code:

```vb
bItemFound = False
iItemIndex = 0
Do Until bItemFound Or iItemIndex = lstItems.ListCount
    If txtNewItem.Text = lstItems.List(iItemIndex) Then
        bItemFound = True
    End If
    iItemIndex = iItemIndex + 1
Loop
```

For/Next Loops

When you want to repeat the statements in a loop a specific number of times, the **For/Next loop** is ideal. The For/Next loop uses the **For** and **Next** statements and a counter variable, called the *loop index*. The loop index determines the number of times the statements inside the loop will be executed.

```vb
Dim iLoopIndex as Integer
Dim iMaximum as Integer
iMaximum = lstSchools.ListCount - 1

For iLoopIndex = 0 To iMaximum
    'The statements inside of the loop are indented
    ' and referred to as the body of the loop
Next iLoopIndex
```

When the `For` statement is reached during program execution several things occur. The loop index, iLoopIndex, is established as the loop counter and is initialized to 0. The final value for the loop index is set to the value of iMaximum, which was assigned the value of lstSchools.ListCount − 1 in the previous statement.

Execution is now "controlled by" the `For` statement. After the value of iLoopIndex is set, it is tested to see if iLoopIndex is greater than iMaximum. If not, the statements in the body of the loop are executed. The `Next` statement causes the iLoopIndex to be incremented by one. The control passes back to the `For` statement. Is the value of iLoopIndex greater than iMaximum? If not, the loop is again executed. When the test is made and the loop index is greater than the final value, control passes to the statement immediately following the `Next`.

A counter-controlled loop generally has three elements (see Figure 7.6 for a flowchart of loop logic).

1. Initialize the counter.
2. Increment the counter.
3. Test the counter to determine when it is time to terminate the loop.

Figure 7.6

A flowchart of the logic of a `For/Next` *loop.*

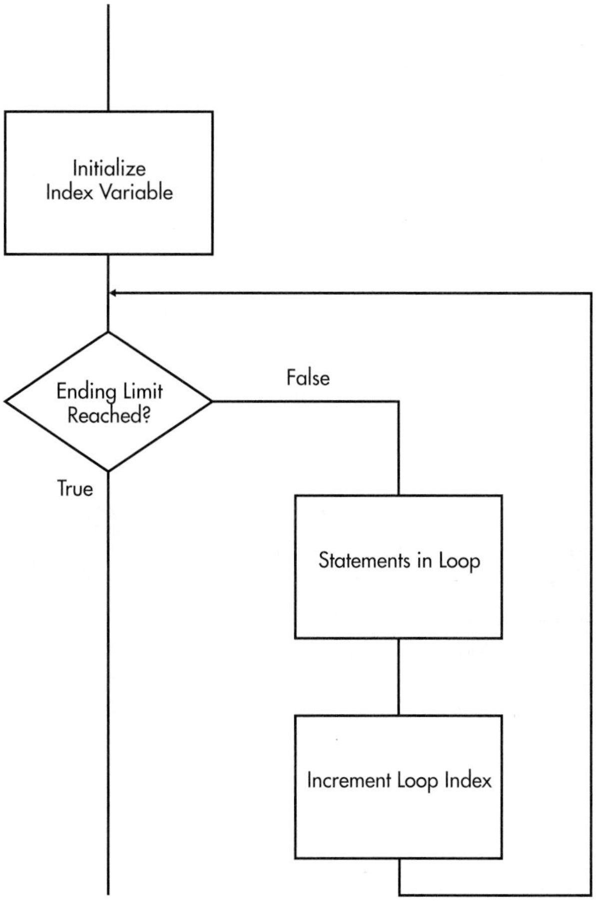

The For and Next Statements—General Form

```
For LoopIndex = InitialValue To TestValue [Step Increment]
    ::
      ::(Body of loop)
    ::
Next [LoopIndex]
```

LoopIndex must be a numeric variable; InitialValue and TestValue may be constants, variables, numeric property values, or numeric expressions. The optional word `Step` may be included, along with the value to be added to the loop index for each iteration of the loop. When the `Step` is omitted, the increment is assumed to be 1.

The For and Next Statements—Examples

```
For iIndex = 2 To 100 Step 2
For iCount = iStart To iEnding Step iIncrement
For iCounter = 0 To cboCoffeeType.ListCount - 1
For iNumber = (iNumberCorrect - 5) To iTOTAL_POSSIBLE
For cRate = .05 To .25 Step .05
For iCountDown = 10 To 0 Step -1
```

Each `For` statement has a corresponding `Next` statement, which must follow the `For`. All statements between the `For` and `Next` are considered to be the body of the loop and will be executed the specified number of times.

The first example `For` statement will count from 2 to 100 by 2. The statements in the body of the loop will be executed 50 times—first with iIndex = 2, next with iIndex = 4, next with iIndex = 6, and so forth.

When the comparison is done, the program checks for *greater than* the test value—not equal to. When iIndex = 100 in the preceding example, the body of the loop will be executed one more time. Then, at the `Next` statement, iIndex will be incremented to 102, the test made, and control will pass to the statement following the `Next`. If you were to display the value of iIndex *after completion* of the loop, its value would be 102.

Negative Increment or Counting Backward

You may use a negative number for the `Step` increment. This has the effect of decreasing the loop index rather than increasing it. When the `Step` is negative, Basic will test for *less than* the test value instead of greater than.

```
'Count Backwards
For iCount = 10 To 1 Step -1

Next iCount
```

Tip

Use a For/Next loop when you know the number of iterations needed for the loop. Use a Do/Loop when the loop should end based on a condition.

Conditions Satisfied before Entry

At times the final value will be reached before entry into the loop. In that case the statements in the body of the loop will not be executed at all.

```
'An unexecutable loop
iFinal = 5
For iIndex = 6 to iFinal
    'The execution will never reach here
Next iIndex
```

Altering the Values of the Loop Control Variables

Once a For loop has been entered, the values for InitialValue, TestValue, and Increment have already been set. Changing the value of these control variables within the loop will have no effect on the number of iterations of the loop. Many texts admonish against changing the values within the loop. However, Visual Basic just ignores you if you try.

```
'Bad Example—Changing the Control Variable
iFinal = 10
iIncrease = 2
For iIndex = 1 to iFinal Step iIncrease
    iFinal = 25
    iIncrease = 5
Next iIndex
```

If you tried this example and displayed the values of iIndex, you would find that the final value will remain 10 and the increment value will be 2.

The value that you *can* change within the loop is the LoopIndex. This practice is considered poor programming.

```
'Poor Programming
For iIndex = 1 To 10 Step 1
    iIndex = iIndex + 5
Next iIndex
```

Endless Loops

Changing the value of a LoopIndex variable is not only considered a poor practice but also may lead to an endless loop. Your code could get into a loop that is impossible to exit. Consider the following example; when will the loop end?

```
'More Poor Programming
For iIndex = 1 To 10 Step 1
    iIndex = 1
Next iIndex
```

Exiting For/Next Loops

In the previous example of an endless loop, you will have to break the program execution manually. You can click on your form's close box, or use the Visual Basic menu bar or toolbar to stop the program. If you can't see the menu bar or toolbar, you can usually move or resize your application's form to bring it into view. If you prefer, press Ctrl + Break to enter break time; you may want to step program execution to see what is causing the problem.

Usually, `For/Next` loops should proceed to normal completion. However, on occasion you may need to terminate a loop before the loop index reaches its final value. Visual Basic provides an `Exit For` statement for this situation. Generally the `Exit For` statement is part of an `If` statement.

The Exit For Statement—General Form

```
Exit For
```

The Exit For Statement—Example

```
For iLoopIndex = 1 to 10
    If txtInput.Text = "" Then   'Nothing was entered into the Input textbox
        MsgBox "You must enter something"
        Exit For
    End If
    ...                          'Statements in loop
Next iLoopIndex
```

Feedback 7.3

1. Identify the statements that are correctly formed and those that have errors. For those with errors, state what is wrong and how to correct it.
   (a) `For cIndex = 3.5 To 6, Step .5`
       `Next cIndex`
   (b) `For iIndex = iBegin To iEnd Step iIncrement`
       `Next iEnd`
   (c) `For 4 = 1 To 10 Step 2`
       `Next For`
   (d) `For iIndex = 100 To 0 Step -25`
       `Next iIndex`
   (e) `For iIndex = 0 To -10 Step -1`
       `Next iIndex`
   (f) `For iIndex = 10 To 1`
       `Next iIndex`

2. How many times will the body of the loop be executed for each of these examples? What will be the value of the loop index *after* normal completion of the loop?
   (a) For iCounter = 2 To 11 Step 3
   (b) For iCounter = 10 To 1 Step —1
   (c) For cCounter = 3 To 6 Step .5
   (d) For iCounter = 5 To 1
   (e) For iCounter = 1 To 3

Using the MsgBox Function

You have been using the MsgBox statement to display messages since Chapter 4. In each case the box displayed only an OK button. You can also use the **MsgBox function** to display a dialog box with more than one button; the function returns a value to indicate which button was pressed.

Consider a message box that asks if you really want to clear a combo box. You need to display Yes and No buttons and then be able to determine which button the user clicked. Figure 7.7 illustrates a message box with Yes and No buttons.

Figure   7 . 7

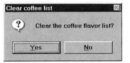

Display a message box with more than one button and check which button was clicked with the MsgBox function.

The MsgBox Function—General Form

```
MsgBox(Prompt [, Buttons] [, Title])
```

The MsgBox Function—Example

```
Dim iResponse As Integer
iResponse = MsgBox("Do you wish to continue?", vbYesNo + vbQuestion, "Title")
If iResponse = vbYes Then        '...Continue processing

If MsgBox(stMsg, vbOKCancel) = vbOK Then
    ClearList
Else
    CancelOperation
End If
```

Function Return Values

The MsgBox function returns a value that can be tested in a condition using the value (numbers 1 through 7) or the associated intrinsic constant.

Return Values

Constant	Value	Button Pressed
vbOk	1	OK
vbCancel	2	Cancel
vbAbort	3	Abort
vbRetry	4	Retry
vbIgnore	5	Ignore
vbYes	6	Yes
vbNo	7	No

Specifying the Buttons and/or Icons to Display

You can specify which buttons to display by using numbers or the Visual Basic intrinsic constants. If you want to choose the buttons and an icon, use a plus sign to add the two values together.

Button and Icon Values

Buttons to Display	Value	Constant
OK	0	vbOKOnly
OK and Cancel	1	vbOKCancel
Abort, Retry, and Ignore	2	vbAbortRetryIgnore
Yes, No, and Cancel	3	vbYesNoCancel
Yes and No	4	vbYesNo
Retry and Cancel	5	vbRetryCancel

Icons to Display	Value	Constant
Critical Message	16	vbCritical
Warning Query	32	vbQuestion
Warning Message	48	vbExclamation
Information Message	64	vbInformation

To display Yes, No, and Cancel buttons along with a question mark icon, use one of these statements:

```
iResponse = MsgBox(stMsg, vbYesNoCancel + vbQuestion, "Good Question")
iResponse = MsgBox(stMsg, 3 + 32, "Good Question")
iResponse = MsgBox(stMsg, 35, "Good Question")
```

MsgBox Example

Earlier you learned to use the `Clear` method to clear the contents of a list box or combo box. In this example we will give the user a chance to confirm whether or not to really clear the list. (Refer to Figure 7.7 for the message box displayed by this procedure.)

```
Private Sub mnuEditClear_Click()
    'Clear the coffee list
    Dim iResponse As Integer

    iResponse = MsgBox("Clear the coffee flavor list?", _
        vbYesNo + vbQuestion, "Clear coffee list")
    If iResponse = vbYes Then
        cboCoffee.Clear
    End If
End Sub
```

Using String Functions

When you need to look at part of a string, rather than the entire string, Visual Basic provides the **Left**, **Right**, and **Mid functions** that return the specified section of a string.

The Left, Right, and Mid Functions—General Form

```
Left(StringExpression, NumberOfCharacters)
Right(StringExpression, NumberOfCharacters)
Mid(StringExpression, StartPosition, [NumberOfCharacters])
```

StringExpression in each of these statements may be a string variable, string literal, or text property. NumberOfCharacters and StartPosition are both numeric and may be variables, literals, or numeric expressions. In the `Mid` function, if you omit the NumberOfCharacters argument, the function returns all characters starting with StartPosition.

The Left, Right, and Mid Functions—Examples

```
Left(txtName.Text , 5)        'Returns first 5 characters
Right(stLongString, 1)        'Returns last 1 character
Mid("Mad Hatter", 5, 3)       'Returns 3 characters beginning with character 5
Mid(stProductID, 4)           'Returns all characters beginning with character 4
```

Examples Using Left, Right, and Mid Functions

```
Dim stExample As String
stExample = "It's a wonderful life"
lblMessage.Caption = Left(stExample, 1)     'Returns "I"
lblMessage.Caption = Left(stExample, 6)     'Returns "It's a"
lblMessage.Caption = Left(stExample, 21)    'Returns "It's a wonderful life"
lblMessage.Caption = Left(stExample, 50)    'Returns "It's a wonderful life"
lblMessage.Caption = Right(stExample, 1)    'Returns "e"
lblMessage.Caption = Right(stExample, 4)    'Returns "life"
lblMessage.Caption = Mid(stExample, 8, 9)   'Returns "wonderful"
lblMessage.Caption = Mid(stExample, 8)      'Returns "wonderful life"

If Left(txtDirection.Text, 1) = "N" Then
    lblDirection.Caption = "North"
End If
```

The Len Function

You can use the **Len function** to determine the length of a string expression. You may need to know how many characters the user has entered or how long a list element is.

The Len Function—General Form

```
Len(StringExpression)
```

The value returned by the Len function is an integer count of the number of characters in the string.

The Len Function—Examples

```
Len("Visual Basic")     'Returns 12
Len(txtEntry.Text)      'Returns the number of characters in the text box
Len(stSelection)        'Returns the number of characters in the string variable

If Len(txtName.Text) = 0 Then
    MsgBox "Enter a name", vbInformation, "Data Missing"
End If
```

You can combine the Len function with two new properties of text boxes and the text portion of a combo box—the SelStart and SelLength properties. The SelStart property sets or returns the position of the first selected character; the SelLength property sets or returns the number of selected characters. You can make the current contents of a text box or the Text property of a combo box appear selected when the user tabs into the control and it receives the focus.

```
Private Sub txtName_GotFocus()
    'Select the current entry

    With txtName
        .SelStart = 0                        'Begin selection at start
        .SelLength = Len(txtName.Text)   'Select the number of characters
    End With
End Sub
```

Selecting Entries in a List Box

When a list box has a very large number of entries, you can help the user by selecting the matching entry as he types in a text box. This method is similar to the way the Help Topics list in Visual Basic works. For example, when you type *p* the list quickly scrolls and displays words beginning with *p*. Then if you next type *r*, the list scrolls down to the words that begin with *pr*, and the first such word is selected. If you type *i* next, the first word beginning with *pri* is selected. This small example implements this feature. See if you can tell what each statement does.

```
Private Sub txtCoffee_Change()
    'Locate first matching occurrence in the list

    Dim iIndex As Integer
    Dim bFound As Boolean

    Do While Not bFound And iIndex < lstCoffee.ListCount
        If UCase(Left(lstCoffee.List(iIndex), Len(txtCoffee.Text))) = _
            UCase(txtCoffee.Text) Then
            lstCoffee.ListIndex = iIndex
            bFound = True
        End If
        iIndex = iIndex + 1
    Loop
End Sub
```

Sending Information to the Printer

So far, any printed output has been done with the PrintForm method. When you print using PrintForm, all output is produced as a graphic, which does not produce attractive text. In addition to printing forms, you will need to create reports or print small bits of information on the printer. You can use VB's **Print method** to print text on a Form, on the Printer object, or in the Debug window.

Visual Basic was designed to run under Windows, which is a highly interactive environment. It is extremely easy to create forms for interactive programs, but not easy at all to print on the printer. Most professional programmers using Visual Basic use a separate utility program to format printer reports. The VB Professional Edition and Enterprise Edition include an add-in utility called Crystal Reports. Newer versions of Crystal Reports and several other printing utilities may be purchased separately.

Printing to the Printer

You can send output to the printer using `Printer.Print` (Object.Method). Visual Basic sets up a Printer object in memory for your output. When your job terminates or it receives an `EndDoc` or `NewPage` method, VB actually sends the contents of the Printer object to the printer.

Formatting Lines

The format of a print line uses punctuation from earlier versions of Basic, the comma and semicolon, as well as a `Tab` function and a `Spc` function. When a line of output contains multiple items to be printed, the items will be separated by commas or semicolons. The list of items may contain literals, variables, or the contents of objects.

When you print on the printer, it is important to consider the font being used. Normally, printing is done with proportional fonts, which means that the amount of space for one character varies with the character. For example, a *w* takes more space than an *i*. You can use a fixed-pitch font, such as Courier, if you want every character to take the same amount of space.

Commas

Consider that the output page has preset tab settings with the line being divided into five columns. Each column is referred to as a **print zone**. Use a comma to advance the output to the next print zone.

The statement

```
Printer.Print ,"R 'n R"
```

prints the "R 'n R" in the second print zone. You can use two commas to advance two print zones:

```
Printer.Print "Name", ,"Phone"
```

The string literal "Name" is printed in print zone 1 and "Phone" is placed in print zone 3. Note that the line prints as though print zone 2 had an empty string literal.

The only way to control the size of a print zone is to change the font size. The width of a print zone is 14 characters, based on the average size of a character for the font being used. That means if you use many narrow characters, such as *i* and *t,* more than 14 characters will fit, but if you are printing many wide characters, such as *w* and *m,* fewer than 14 characters will print in a print zone. Therefore, you may find that some items you print exceed the width of the print zone.

Conceptually, print zones resemble tab stops in a word processor. Each time a comma is encountered, it means "Jump to the next tab stop." Sometimes you may print a string that extends further than you expected (past the beginning of the next print zone). Then the next comma jumps to the following print zone, perhaps causing your columns to align improperly. In the following example the label will be placed in print zone 4.

```
Printer.Print "The average amount of sales for the current month is ", _
              lblSales.Caption
```

When the number of print zones exceeds the number for a single line, the output will automatically wrap to the next line on the printed page.

```
Printer.Print 1, 2, 3, 4, 5, 6
```

will output as

```
1               2               3           4           5
6
```

Semicolons

If you need to separate items without advancing to the next print zone, use a semicolon between the two items. If you leave spaces between items, VB adds a semicolon in the code for you. If the value of txtName.Text is "Mary" the line of code

```
Printer.Print "Name: "; txtName.Text
```

will output as

```
Name: Mary
```

Note that the number of spaces left inside the string literal will print out exactly as indicated. If you do not put spaces inside the quotes, you may well end up with one item printing right next to the previous one. The semicolon does not provide spacing on the output, only a means of listing items to print.

Trailing Commas and Semicolons

If the last character on a line of output is a comma or semicolon, the next `Print` method will continue on the same line without advancing the line.

```
Printer.Print "First this ",
Printer.Print "Then this"
```

will output as

```
First this    Then this
```

The print zone rule is still in effect because the first **Print** method ended with a trailing comma.

```
Printer.Print "First this ";
Printer.Print "Then this"
```

will output as

```
First this Then this
```

Printing Blank Lines

When you want to print a blank line on your printed report, use a **Print** method without any item to print:

```
Printer.Print    'Print a blank line
```

The Tab Function

Creating program output that is pleasing, properly spaced, and correctly aligned can be a difficult task. VB has functions to assist in the formatting process.

You can control the placement of variables and constants on a printed line by using the **Tab function**. In the **Tab** function you specify the column position where you want the output to appear. (*Note:* Basic uses the average character width to determine the column position.) The value of the column position argument must be numeric (fractional values will be rounded up), but it may be a constant, a variable, or a numeric expression (calculation).

The column position is absolute, meaning that the 1st position on the line is **Tab(1)** and the 20th position is **Tab(20)**.

The Tab Function—General Form

```
Tab(Position)
```

The Tab Function—Examples

```
Printer.Print Tab(20); "R 'n R—for Reading 'n Refreshment"
Printer.Print Tab(10); "Name"; Tab(30); "Pay"
Printer.Print Tab(iCOLUMN1); txtName.Text; Tab(iCOLUMN2); cPay
```

If you try to tab to a column that precedes the previous output on the line, the `Tab` will advance to the specified column position on the next line. Do not use a comma following a `Tab` function; after tabbing to the specified position, it will still advance to the next print zone, destroying the effect of your `Tab`.

The Spc Function

Another function that controls horizontal spacing on the line is the `Spc` (space) function. The **Spc function** differs from the `Tab` in that you specify the number of spaces on the line that you want to advance *from the last item printed*.

The Spc Function—General Form

```
Spc(NumberOfCharacters)
```

The Spc Function—Examples

```
Printer.Print Tab(20); "Name"; Spc(5); "Phone"; Spc(5); "Address"
```

Notice that you can combine `Tab` and `Spc` on one print line.

Aligning String and Numeric Data

VB handles spacing for string and numeric data a little differently. String values print with no extra spacing between items. For example, the statement

```
Printer.Print "Sweet"; "Pea"
```

prints as

```
SweetPea
```

Numeric data prints with additional spacing. VB allows one space before each number for a sign. For negative values, a minus sign appears in the position; for positive values, the space remains blank. VB also adds a space following each numeric value. The statement

```
Printer.Print 1; 2; 3; -1; -2; -3
```

outputs this line

```
 1    2    3 -1 -2 -3
```

If you combine string and numeric data you must be aware of the difference in the spacing. This example combines string and numeric data using print zones.

```
Printer.Print  "Item",  "Quantity"
Printer.Print  "Scissors",  10
Printer.Print  "Rocks",  -2
Printer.Print  "Porcupines",  1
```

The output from these statements appears aligned like this:

```
Item       Quantity
Scissors    10
Rocks       -2
Porcupines  1
```

Selecting the Font

Changing the font of printed output is similar to changing the font of a control. The Printer object has a Font property, which refers to the Font object. However, you cannot use the Properties window and *Font* dialog box to change the Font properties; you must change properties in code. When you change the font name, make sure you enter a font name supported by the target printer, spelled correctly. *Hint:* Display the *Font* dialog box for a control and make a note of the available font names. If you aren't sure which fonts are supported by your printer, stick with TrueType fonts (such as Arial and Times New Roman), which should work on any printer properly installed in Windows.

Examples

```
Printer.Font.Name = "Times New Roman"
Printer.Font.Size = 12
```

You need to change the font name and size only once, before the first item you print.

Terminating the Page or the Job

The `NewPage` method sends the current page to the printer and clears the printer object in memory so you can begin a new page. The `EndDoc` method sends the current page to the printer and terminates the printer job. *Note:* When your program terminates, Visual Basic automatically sends an `EndDoc`.

```
Printer.NewPage       'Send page and begin a new page
Printer.EndDoc        'Send page and terminate the print job
```

Use the `NewPage` or `EndDoc` methods after sending the information to the printer.

Example

```
Private Sub Form_Click()
    Printer.Print
    Printer.Print Tab(13); "Monthly Sales Summary"
    Printer.Print
    Printer.Print
    Printer.Print Tab(10); "Sales"; Tab(30); "Returns"
    Printer.Print Tab(10); "============================"
    Printer.Print
    Printer.Print Tab(10); Format(mcSalesTotal, "currency"); _
                  Tab(30); Format(mcReturnsTotal, "currency")
    Printer.EndDoc
End Sub
```

Printing the Contents of a List Box

You can combine the techniques for printing, a loop, and the list box properties to send the contents of a list box to the printer. You know how many iterations to make, using the ListCount property. The List property allows you to print out the actual values from the list.

```
Private Sub mnuFilePrintAll_Click()
    'Print the contents of the coffee flavors
    'combo box on the printer

    Dim iIndex As Integer
    Dim iFinalValue As Integer
    iFinalValue = cboCoffee.ListCount - 1 'List index starts at 0
    For iIndex = 0 To iFinalValue
        Printer.Print cboCoffee.List(iIndex)
    Next iIndex
    Printer.EndDoc
End Sub
```

Aligning Decimal Columns

When the output to the printer includes numeric data, the alignment of the decimal points is important. One solution you may wish to use incorporates the Len function.

To right align numeric output:

STEP 1: Assign the formatted value to a string variable.

STEP 2: Determine the column position for the Tab at the position where you want the formatted value to *end.*

STEP 3: Tab the difference between the Tab position and the length of the formatted string variable.

STEP 4: Print the formatted value.

For example, if you want to right align a column for total pay on a printed report, you can use the following code:

```
Dim stFormattedNumber As String

stFormattedNumber = Format$(cTotalPay, "Currency")
Printer.Print Tab(10); stName ; Tab(50 - Len(stFormattedNumber)); _
          stFormattedNumber
```

The formatted cTotalPay will print right aligned at column 50.

Feedback 7.4

What will print for each of these code segments? Try to determine the results by hand; then enter them into the computer to verify your results.

1. ```
   Printer.Print "Half a loaf ";
   Printer.Print "Is better than none"
   ```
2. `Printer.Print "Half, ", "My Eye"`
3. `Printer.Print "Hawks"; 0, "Doves"; 0`
4. ```
   Printer.Print 1,
   Printer.Print 2,
   Printer.Print 3,
   Printer.Print 4,
   Printer.Print 5,
   Printer.Print 6
   ```
5. `Printer.Print 1, 2, 3, 4, 5, 6`
6. `Printer.Print Tab(10); 3; Tab(20); 5`
7. `Printer.Print Spc(10); 3; Spc(20); 5`

Your Hands-On Programming Example

Create a project for R 'n R—for Reading 'n Refreshment that contains a dropdown combo box of the coffee flavors and a list box of the syrup flavors. Adjust the size of the boxes as needed when you test the project. The controls should have labels above them containing the words *Coffee* and *Syrup*. Enter the initial values for the syrup flavors and coffee flavors in the Properties window. The user will be able to add more coffee flavors to the list at run time.

Coffee Flavors	Syrup Flavors
Espresso Roast	Chocolate
Jamaica Blue Mountain	Irish Cream
Kona Blend	Hazelnut
Chocolate Almond	Orange
Vanilla Nut	

Include one menu item to print all the flavors on the printer and another to print only a selected item from each list. These two menu print commands belong on the *File* menu along with the *Exit* command. Use a separator bar between the *Print*s and the *Exit*.

Include an *Edit* menu with commands to *Add coffee flavor*, *Remove coffee flavor*, *Clear coffee list*, and *Display coffee count*.

Add the About form from Chapter 6 into your project and add a *Help* menu with an *About* command.

After you have completed the project, try using different styles for the combo box and rerun the project. As an added challenge, modify the add coffee flavor routine so that duplicates are not allowed.

Planning the Project

Sketch a form (Figure 7.8), which your users sign off as meeting their needs.

Figure 7.8

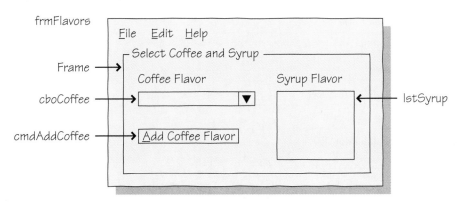

A sketch of the main form for the hands-on project.

Plan the Objects and Properties

Object	Property	Setting
frmFlavors	Name	frmFlavors
	Caption	R 'n R—for Reading 'n Refreshment
Frame1	Name	Frame1
	Caption	Select Coffee and Syrup
Label1	Caption	Coffee Flavor
Label2	Caption	Syrup Flavor
cboCoffee	Name	cboCoffee
	Style	0 - Dropdown combo
	Text	(blank)
	List	Chocolate Almond Espresso Roast Jamaica Blue Mtn. Kona Blend Vanilla Nut
	Sorted	True
lstSyrup	Name	lstSyrup
	Sorted	True
	List	Chocolate Hazelnut Irish Creme Orange
cmdAddCoffee	Name	cmdAddCoffee
	Caption	&Add to Coffees
mnuFile	Name	mnuFile
	Caption	&File
mnuFilePrintSelect	Name	mnuFilePrintSelect
	Caption	Print &Selected Flavors
mnuFilePrintAll	Name	mnuFilePrintAll
	Caption	Print &All Flavors
mnuSep	Name	mnuSep
	Caption	-
mnuEdit	Name	mnuEdit
	Caption	&Edit
mnuEditAdd	Name	mnuEditAdd
	Caption	&Add coffee flavor

(continued)

Object	Property	Setting
mnuEditRemove	Name	mnuEditRemove
	Caption	&Remove coffee flavor
mnuEditClear	Name	mnuEditClear
	Caption	&Clear coffee list
mnuEditCount	Name	mnuEditCount
	Caption	Count coffee &list
mnuFileExit	Name	mnuFileExit
	Caption	E&xit
mnuHelp	Name	mnuHelp
	Caption	&Help
mnuHelpAbout	Name	mnuHelpAbout
	Caption	&About

Plan the Event Procedures

Main Form

Procedure	Actions

cmdAddCoffee	If text box in cboCoffee not empty then
	    Add contents of cboCoffee text box to list
	    Clear the text box in cboCoffee.
	Else
	  Display error message.
	End If
	Set the focus to cboCoffee.

mnuFilePrintSelect	If both coffee and syrup selected
	  Print only selected items.
	Else
	  Display error message.
	End If

mnuFilePrintAll	Print title and headings. Use a loop to send all flavor names to the printer.
mnuFileExit	Terminate the Project.
mnuEditAdd	Call cmdAddCoffee_Click.

mnuEditRemove	If coffee flavor selected then
	  Remove selected item.
	Else
	  Display error message.
	End If

mnuEditClear	Clear the coffee list.
mnuEditCount	Display list count in message box.
mnuHelpAbout	Display the About box.

About Form

Procedure	Action
cmdOK	Hide the About box.

Write the Project

- Follow the sketch in Figure 7.8 to create the form. Figure 7.9 shows the completed form.

Figure 7.9

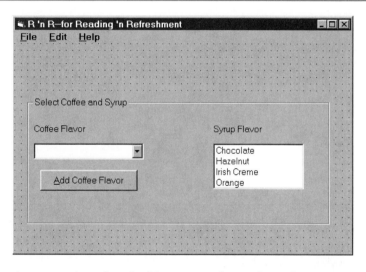

The form for the hands-on project.

- Set the properties of each object as you have planned.

- Write the code. Working from the pseudocode, write each event procedure.

- When you complete the code, use a variety of data to thoroughly test the project.

The Project Coding Solution

Main Form

```
'Module:       frmFlavors
'Programmer:   A. Millspaugh
'Date:         July 1997
'Description:  Print the selected flavor of coffee and syrup
'              or print a list of all of the coffee flavors.
'Folder:       Ch0701


Option Explicit
```

```
Private Sub cmdAddCoffee_Click()
    'Add a new coffee flavor to the coffee list

    If cboCoffee.Text <> "" Then
        With cboCoffee
            .AddItem cboCoffee.Text
            .Text = ""
        End With
    Else
        MsgBox "Enter a coffee name to add", vbExclamation, "Missing data"
    End If
    cboCoffee.SetFocus
End Sub


Private Sub mnuEditAdd_Click()
    'Add a new coffee to list

    cmdAddCoffee_Click
End Sub


Private Sub mnuEditClear_Click()
    'Clear the coffee list

    cboCoffee.Clear
End Sub


Private Sub mnuEditCount_Click()
    'Display a count of the coffee list

    MsgBox "The number of coffee types is " & cboCoffee.ListCount
End Sub


Private Sub mnuEditRemove_Click()
    'Remove the selected coffee from list

    If cboCoffee.ListIndex <> -1 Then
        cboCoffee.RemoveItem cboCoffee.ListIndex
    Else
        MsgBox   "First select the coffee to remove", vbInformation, _
                "No selection made"
    End If
End Sub


Private Sub mnuHelpAbout_Click()
    'Display frmAbout

    frmAbout.Show
End Sub
```

```
Private Sub mnuFileExit_Click()
    'Terminate the project

    End
End Sub
```

```
Private Sub mnuFilePrintAll_Click()
    'Print the contents of the coffee flavors
    'combo box on the printer

    Dim iIndex          As Integer
    Dim iFinalValue     As Integer

    Printer.Print                           'Blank line
    Printer.Print Tab(20); "Coffee Flavors"
    Printer.Print                           'Blank line
    iFinalValue = cboCoffee.ListCount - 1
    'List index starts at 0
    For iIndex = 0 To iFinalValue
        Printer.Print Tab(20); cboCoffee.List(iIndex)
    Next iIndex
    Printer.EndDoc
End Sub
```

```
Private Sub mnuFilePrintSelect_Click()
    'Send the current selection of coffee flavor
    ' and syrup flavor to the printer

    If cboCoffee.ListIndex <> -1 And lstSyrup.ListIndex <> -1 Then
        Printer.Print    'Blank line
        Printer.Print Tab(15); "Coffee Selection"
        Printer.Print    'Blank line
        Printer.Print Tab(10); "Coffee Flavor: "; _
                    cboCoffee.List(cboCoffee.ListIndex)
        Printer.Print    'Blank line
        Printer.Print Tab(10); "Syrup Flavor: "; _
                    lstSyrup.List(lstSyrup.ListIndex)
        Printer.EndDoc
    Else
        MsgBox "Make a selection for coffee and syrup.", vbExclamation, _
            "Missing Data"
    End If
End Sub
```

About Form

```
'Module:        frmAbout
'Programmer:    A. Millspaugh
'Date:          July 1997
'Description:   Display information about the program
'               and the programmer
'Folder:        Ch0701
Option Explicit
```

```
Private Sub cmdOK_Click()
    'Returns to the main form

    frmAbout.Hide
End Sub
```

S u m m a r y

1. List boxes and combo boxes hold lists of values. The three styles of combo boxes are simple combo boxes, dropdown combo boxes, and dropdown lists.
2. The size of a list box or combo box is determined at design time. If all of the items will not fit into the box, VB automatically adds scroll bars.
3. Initial values for the items in a list can be entered in the List property in the Properties window. At run time, items are added to lists using the AddItem method.
4. The `Clear` method may be used to remove the contents of a list box.
5. The ListIndex property can be used to select an item in the list or to determine which item is selected.
6. The ListCount property holds the number of elements in the list.
7. The List property holds all of the elements of the list. The individual elements can be referenced by using an index.
8. The RemoveItem method removes one element from a list.
9. Code can be written for several events of list boxes and combo boxes. Combo boxes have a Change event; both combo boxes and list boxes have GotFocus and LostFocus events.
10. A loop allows a statement or series of statements to be repeated. `Do/Loops` continue to execute the statements in the loop until a condition is met.
11. `Do/Loops` can have the condition test at the top or the bottom of the loop and can use a `While` or `Until` to test the conditon.
12. A `Do/Loop` can be used to locate a selected item in a combo box.
13. A loop index controls `For/Next` loops; the index is initialized to a starting value. After each iteration the loop index is incremented by the `Step` value, which defaults to 1. The loop is terminated when the loop index reaches the ending value.
14. The `Left`, `Right`, and `Mid` functions return a part of a string.
15. The `Len` function returns the number of characters in a string.
16. The `Printer.Print` statement sends lines of text to the printer, rather than printing the graphical form.
17. The `Print` method uses commas, semicolons, and the `Spc` function to control spacing. The `Tab` function can be used to align columns of information.

18. By default, the `Print` method uses proportional fonts, which allow a variable amount of space for a character, depending on the character width. Judging the number of characters in a print zone or the amount of space text will require using proportional fonts is difficult.

19. Aligning columns of numbers is difficult because print zones and the `Tab` function left align values. Numbers can be right aligned with the assistance of the `Len` function.

K e y T e r m s

AddItem method *232*
`Clear` method *233*
combo box control *230*
`Do` and `Loop` statements *236*
`Do/Loop` *239*
dropdown combo box *230*
dropdown list *230*
`For` and `Next` statements *240*
`For/Next` loop *240*
iteration *236*
`Left` function *247*
`Len` function *248*
list box control *230*
List property *234*
ListCount property *234*

ListIndex property *233*
loop index *240*
loop *236*
`Mid` function *247*
`MsgBox` function *245*
posttest *237*
pretest *237*
`Print` method *250*
print zone *250*
`RemoveItem` method *235*
`Right` function *247*
simple combo box *230*
Sorted property *232*
`Spc` function *253*
`Tab` function *252*

R e v i e w Q u e s t i o n s

1. What is a list box? a combo box?
2. Name and describe the three styles of combo boxes.
3. How can you make scroll bars appear on a list box or combo box?
4. Explain the purpose of the ListIndex property and the ListCount property.
5. When and how is information placed inside a list box or a combo box?
6. In what situation would a loop be used in a procedure?
7. Explain the difference between a pretest and a posttest in a `Do/Loop`.
8. Explain the differences between a `Do/Loop` and a `For/Next` loop.
9. What are the steps in processing a `For/Next` loop?
10. Discuss how and when the values of the loop index change throughout the processing of the loop.
11. What is the purpose of `Printer.Print`?
12. How do the `Left`, `Right`, and `Len` functions operate?
13. How do you control the horizontal spacing of printer output?

Programming Exercises

7.1 Create a project for obtaining student information.

Startup form controls are as follows:

- Text boxes for entering the name and units completed.
- Option buttons for Freshman, Sophomore, Junior, and Senior.
- Check box for Dean's List.
- Use a list box for the following majors: Accounting, Business, Computer Information Systems, and Marketing.
- A simple combo for name of high school—initially loaded with Franklin, Highland, West Highland, and Midtown. If the user types in a new school name, it should be added to the list.
- Print command button that will print the data from the form. Send the output to the printer, nicely formatted. (Do not use PrintForm.)
- An OK (for Enter) button that will clear the entries from the form and reset the focus. Set the button's Default property to True.

Menu: The *File* menu will have an option for *Print Schools* and *Exit.* The *Help* menu will have an option for the *About* box.

Note: Print your name at the top of the printer output for the schools.

7.2 R 'n R—for Reading 'n Refreshment needs a project that contains a form for entering book information.

Form Controls:

- Text boxes for author and title.
- Option buttons for type: fiction or nonfiction.
- Dropdown list for Subject that will include: Best-Seller, Fantasy, Religion, Romance, Humor, Science Fiction, Business, Philosophy, Education, Self-Help, and Mystery.
- List box for Shelf Number containing RC-1111, RC-1112, RC-1113, and RC-1114.
- Print command button that will print the data from the form. (Do not use PrintForm.)
- An OK (for Enter) button that will clear the entries from the form and reset the focus. Set the Default property to True.

Menu: The *File* menu will have an option for *Print Subjects* and *Exit.* The *Help* menu will have an option for the *About* box.

Note: Print your name at the top of the printer output for the subjects.

7.3 Create a project to input chartering information about yachts and print a summary report showing the total revenue and average hours per charter.

Startup Form:

The startup form will contain a menu. The *File* menu will contain commands for *New Charter, Print Summary, Print Yacht Types,* and *Exit.* Place separator bars before *Print Summary* and after *Print Yacht Types.* The *Edit* menu should have commands for *Add Yacht Type, Remove Yacht Type,* and *Display Count of Yacht Types.* The *Help* menu will contain an *About* command.

New Charter Form:

- The new charter form will contain text boxes for responsible party and hours chartered.
- A dropdown combo box will contain the type of yacht: Ranger, Wavelength, Catalina, Coronado, Hobie, C & C, Hans Christian, and Excalibur. Any items that are added to the text box during processing must be added to the list.
- Another dropdown list will contain size: 22, 24, 30, 32, 36, 38, 45. (No new sizes can be entered at run time.)
- An OK command button will add to the totals, print a line on the summary report (do not end the page), and return to the startup form. The print line will contain the yacht type, size, responsible party, hours chartered, and total revenue for the hours chartered. The calculations will require price per hour—use the following chart:

Size	Hourly Rate
22	95.00
24	137.00
30	160.00
32	192.00
36	250.00
38	400.00
45	550.00

A Cancel command button will return to the startup form with no calculations.

Set the Default property of the OK button to True; set the Cancel property of the Cancel button to True.

Summary Report: The summary report will print the summary information and send the report to the printer. The summary information will include *Total Revenue* and *Average Hours Chartered.*

7.4 Create a project that contains a list box with the names of the United States and territories. When the user types the first letters of the state into a text box, set the ListIndex property of the list box to display the appropriate name.

Alabama

Alaska

American Samoa

Arizona

Arkansas

California

Colorado

Connecticut

Delaware

District of Columbia

Florida

Georgia

Guam

Hawaii

Idaho

Illinois

Indiana

Iowa

Kansas

Kentucky

Louisiana

Maine

Maryland

Massachusetts

Michigan

Minnesota

Mississippi

Missouri

Montana

Nebraska

Nevada

New Hampshire

New Jersey

New Mexico

(continued)

New York
North Carolina
North Dakota
Ohio
Oklahoma
Oregon
Pennsylvania
Puerto Rico
Rhode Island
South Carolina
South Dakota
Tennessee
Texas
Trust Territories
Utah
Vermont
Virgin Islands
Virginia
Washington
West Virginia
Wisconsin
Wyoming

7.5 Generate mailing labels with an account number for catalog subscriptions. The project will allow the user to enter Last Name, First Name, Street, City, State, and the ZIP Code, and Expiration Date for the subscription. A dropdown list box will contain the names of the catalogs: *Odds and Ends, Solutions, Camping Needs, ToolTime, Spiegel, The Outlet,* and *The Large Size.*

Use validation to make sure there are entries in the Last Name, ZIP code, and Expiration Date fields.

The account number will consist of the first two characters of the last name, the first three digits of the ZIP code, and the expiration date. Display the account number in a label on the form when the user clicks on the *Display Account Number* button or menu option.

The menu or command buttons for the project should have options for Print Label, Display Account Number, Exit, and Clear.

The *Print label* menu command will print the label using the following format:

First Name Last Name Account Number
Street
City, State ZIP Code

7.6 Maintain a list of bagel types for Bradley's Bagels. Use a dropdown combo box to hold the bagel types and use command buttons or menu choices to Add Bagel Type, Remove Bagel Type, Clear Bagel List, Print Bagel List, Display Bagel Type Count, and Exit. Keep the list sorted in alphabetic order.

Do not allow a blank type to be added to the list. Display an error message if the user selects Remove without first selecting a bagel type.

Before clearing the list, display a message box to confirm the operation.

Here are some suggested bagel types. You can make up your own list.

Plain	Poppy seed
Egg	Sesame seed
Rye	Banana nut
Salt	Blueberry

....

CASE STUDIES

Modify your project from Chapter 6 by adding a dropdown combo box to the New Item form. The combo box will contain the names of the catalogs: *Odds and Ends, Solutions, Camping Needs, ToolTime, Spiegel, The Outlet,* and *The Large Size.*

Add a *Print Catalog List* to your menu on the startup form and remove the *Print* that uses a `PrintForm` from the menu.

When the user begins a new order, print the *Bill To* section and the invoice headings on the printer.

VB Mail Order

Print one line for each item when the OK button is pressed on the New Item form; do not use the `EndDoc` method until after the summary information has been printed in the PrintInvoice event.

Note: You may want to disable the *Print Catalog List* menu option while an invoice is in progress. Set `mnuFilePrintCatalogList.Enabled = False` when you begin an invoice, and reset it to True after an invoice is complete.

Bill To: Customer Name
            Customer Street Address
            Customer City, State, Zip
Catalog Name   Description   Quantity   Each Price

Total Price
Tax
Shipping and Handling
Total Due

Create a project for the car wash located at VB Auto Center.

VB Auto Center

The form will contain three list box or combo box controls that do not permit the user to add items at run time. The first list will contain the names of the packages available for detailing a vehicle: Standard, Deluxe, Executive, or Luxury.

The contents of the other two lists will vary depending upon the package selected. Display one list for the interior work and one list for the exterior work. Store the descriptions of the items in string constants.

The list for the interior and exterior must be cleared and new items added each time a selection is made from the package list.

Use a dropdown list to allow the user to select the fragrance. The choices are Hawaiian Mist, Baby Powder, Pine, Country Floral, Pina Colada, and Vanilla.

Include menu commands for *Print*, *Clear*, and *Exit*. The printout will contain the package name, the interior and exterior items being formed, and the fragrance selected. Use a `For/Next` loop when printing the interior and exterior lists.

	Item Description	S	D	E	L
Exterior	Hand Wash	✓	✓	✓	✓
	Hand Wax		✓	✓	✓
	Check Engine Fluids			✓	✓
	Detail Engine Compartment				✓
	Detail Under Carriage				✓
Interior	Fragrance	✓	✓	✓	✓
	Shampoo Carpets		✓	✓	✓
	Shampoo Upholstery				✓
	Interior Protection Coat (dashboard and console)				
	Scotchgard™				✓

Note: S—Standard; D—Deluxe; E—Executive; L—Luxury

8

Arrays

At the completion of this chapter, you will be able to...

1. Set up and use a control array.

2. Code selection logic using a `Select Case` statement.

3. Establish an array of variables and refer to individual elements in the array with variable subscripts.

4. Use the `For Each/Next` to traverse the array.

5. Create user-defined data types for multiple fields of related data.

6. Accumulate totals using arrays.

7. Distinguish between direct access and indirect access of a table.

8. Combine the advantages of list box controls with arrays.

9. Coordinate lists and arrays using the ItemData property.

10. Store data in multidimensional arrays.

Control Arrays

When you plan to include a group of option buttons or check boxes on a form, it often makes sense to create a control array. A ***control array*** is a group of controls that all have the same name. All controls in an array must be the same class. An advantage of using a control array, rather than independent controls, is that the controls share one Click event. In the array's Click event, you can use a Case structure (discussed in the next section) to determine which button or box is selected.

For an example, assume that you are using a group of five option buttons to allow the user to choose a color. After creating the five buttons (Figure 8.1), begin setting the properties by setting the Name property. Name the first option button *optColor*. Then change the Name property of the second option button to *optColor* also (Figure 8.2); a message box will appear (Figure 8.3), asking if you want to create a control array.

Figure 8.1

The five option buttons allow the user to choose the color.

Figure 8.2

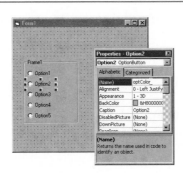

Set the name of the first button to optColor.

Figure 8.3

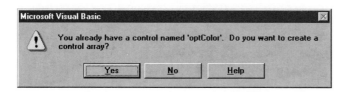

After naming a second control with the same name, this dialog box appears. Select Yes to create a control array.

After you select Yes, the name in the top of the Properties window becomes *optColor(0)* for the first control and *optColor(1)* for the second. The number inside the parentheses is called an **index** and is used to refer to the specific control within the array. All subsequent controls given the same name will automatically have an index attached.

The option buttons in Figure 8.1 are named optColor(0), optColor(1), optColor(2), optColor(3), and optColor(4).

The Case Structure

In Chapter 4 you used the `If` statement for testing conditions and making decisions. Whenever you want to test a single variable or expression for multiple values, the Case structure provides a flexible and powerful solution. Any program decisions that you can code with a Case structure can also be coded with nested `If` statements, but usually the Case structure is simpler and clearer.

The Select Case Statement—General Form

```
Select Case expression
    Case constant list
        [statement(s)]
    [Case constant list
        [statement(s)]]



    .
    .
    .

    [Case Else]
        [statement(s)]
End Select
```

The expression in a Case structure is usually a variable or property you wish to test.

The constant list is the value that you want to match; it may be a numeric or string constant or variable, a range of values, a relational condition, or a combination of these.

There is no limit to the number of statements that can follow a `Case` statement.

The Select Case Statement—Example

```
Select Case iScore
    Case Is >= 100
        lblMessage1.Caption = "Excellent Score"
        lblMessage2.Caption = "Give yourself a pat on the back"
    Case 80 To 99
        lblMessage1.Caption = "Very Good"
        lblMessage2.Caption = "You should be proud"
    Case 60 To 79
        lblMessage1.Caption = "Satisfactory Score"
        lblMessage2.Caption = "You should have a nice warm feeling"
    Case Else
        lblMessage1.Caption = "Your score shows room for improvement"
        lblMessage2.Caption = ""
End Select
```

This example shows a combination of relational operators and constant ranges. Two points that were illustrated must be noted here:

When using a relational operator (e.g., `Is >= 100`) the word `Is` must be used.

To indicate a range of constants, use the word `To` (e.g., `80 To 99`).

The elements used for the constant list may have any of these forms:

```
constant [,constant...]              Case 2, 5, 9
constant To constant                 Case 25 To 50
Is relational-operator constant      Case Is < 10
```

When you want to test for a string value, you must include quotation marks around the literals.

Example

```
Select Case txtTeamName.Text
    Case "Tigers"
            (Code for Tigers)
    Case "Leopards"
            (Code for Leopards)
    Case "Cougars", "Panthers"
            (Code for Cougars and Panthers)
    Case Else
            (Code for any nonmatch)
End Select
```

Note that in the previous example, the capitalization must also match exactly. A better solution would be

```
Select Case Ucase(txtTeamName.Text)
    Case "TIGERS"
            (Code for Tigers)
    Case "LEOPARDS"
            (Code for Leopards)
    Case "COUGERS", "PANTHERS"
            (Code for Cougars and Panthers)
    Case Else
            (Code for any nonmatch)
End Select
```

Although the `Case Else` clause is optional, generally you will want to include it in `Select Case` statements. The statements you code beneath `Case Else` will execute only if none of the other `Case` conditions is matched. This clause will provide checking for any invalid or unforeseen values of the expression being tested. If the `Case Else` clause is omitted and none of the `Case` conditions is True, the program will continue execution at the statement following the `End Select`.

If more than one `Case` value is matched by the expression, only the statements in the first matching `Case` clause will be executed.

Testing Option Buttons with the Case Structure

The Case structure is ideal for testing which option button in a control array is selected. When the user selects one of the option buttons, their common Click event occurs. Notice in the following example that Visual Basic passes Index as an argument to the event procedure. Index holds the number of the selected button (0, 1, 2, 3, or 4). You can use the value of Index in a `Select Case` statement.

Note: The argument inside the parentheses, "Index as Integer," means that Visual Basic is passing a variable called *Index*, with a data type of integer.

Example

```
Private Sub optColor_Click(Index As Integer)
    'Set the color to match the selected option button

    Select Case Index
        Case 0        'First button is selected
            lblMessage.ForeColor = vbBlue
        Case 1        'Second button is selected
            lblMessage.ForeColor = vbBlack
        Case 2        'Third button is selected
            lblMessage.ForeColor = vbRed
        Case 3        'Fourth button is selected
            lblMessage.ForeColor = vbWhite
        Case 4        'Fifth button is selected
            lblMessage.ForeColor = vbYellow
    End Select
End Sub
```

As you know, making changes occur for the Click event of an option button violates one of the standards for Windows programming. The color should actually be changed in the Click event for a command button. However, the option button's Index is not available in the command button's Click event. Therefore, the best practice is to set up a module-level variable to hold the selection. In the Click event for the option button, set the value of the variable; in the Click event for the command button, check the value of the variable.

Example

```
'General Declarations
    Option Explicit
    Dim mlSelectedColor As Long    'The color constants are long integers
```

```
Private Sub cmdDisplay_Click()
    'Change the color of the label

    lblMessage.ForeColor = mlSelectedColor
End Sub
```

```
Private Sub optColor_Click(Index As Integer)
    'Save color selection

    Select Case Index
        Case 0    'Blue button is selected
            mlSelectedColor = vbBlue
        Case 1    'Black button is selected
            mlSelectedColor = vbBlack
        Case 2    'Red button is selected
            mlSelectedColor = vbRed
        Case 3    'White button is selected
            mlSelectedColor = vbWhite
        Case 4    'Yellow button is selected
            mlSelectedColor = vbYellow
    End Select
End Sub
```

Feedback 8.1

1. Convert the following If statement to a Select Case.

```
If iTemp <= 32 Then
    lblComment.Caption = "Freezing"
ElseIf iTemp > 80 Then
    lblComment.Caption = "Hot"
Else
    lblComment.Caption = "Moderate"
End If
```

2. Convert the following to a `Select Case` in the Click event procedure for optCoffee.

```
If optCoffee(0).Value = True Then
    cPrice = 2
ElseIf optCoffee(1).Value = True Then
    cPrice = 2.25
ElseIf optCoffee(2).Value = True Then
    cPrice = 1.75
ElseIf optCoffee(3).Value = True
    cPrice = 2.5
End If
```

3. Add a clause to the previous `Select Case` to display a message box if no option button is selected.

Single-Dimension Arrays

You have just seen how you can set up an array of controls in which several controls have the same name. Now you will find similar advantages to creating and using an array of variables.

A variable array can contain a list of values, similar to a list box or a combo box. In fact, Visual Basic actually stores the List property of a list box or a combo box in an array. You can think of an array as a list box without the box. Any time you need to keep a series of variables for later processing, such as reordering, calculating, or printing, you need to set up an array.

Consider an example that has a form for entering product information, one product at a time. After the user has entered many products, you will need to calculate some statistics and perhaps use the information in different ways. Of course, each time the user enters the data for the next product, the previous contents of the text boxes are replaced. You could assign the previous values to variables, but they also would be replaced for each new product. Another approach might be to create multiple variables, such as stProduct1, stProduct2, stProduct3, and so on. This approach might be reasonable for a few entries, but what happens when you need to store 50 or 500 products?

When you need to store multiple values, use an array. An **array** is a series of individual variables, all referenced by the same name. Sometimes arrays are referred to as **tables** or **subscripted variables**. When you use a control array, the individual controls are referenced as optCoffee(0) or opt-Coffee(1). The same notation is used with variable arrays. Therefore, in an array for storing names, you may have stName(0), stName(1), stName(2), and so on.

Each individual variable is called an **element** of the array. The individual elements are treated the same as any other variable and may be used in any statement, such as an assignment or a `Printer.Print`. The **subscript** (which may also be called an *index*) inside the parentheses is the position of the element within the array. Figure 8.4 illustrates an array of 10 elements with subscripts from 0 to 9.

stName array

(0)	Janet Baker
(1)	George Lee
(2)	Sue Li
(3)	Samuel Hoosier
(4)	Sandra Weeks
(5)	William Macy
(6)	Andy Harrison
(7)	Ken Ford
(8)	Denny Franks
(9)	Shawn James

An array of string variables with 10 elements. Subscripts are 0 through 9.

Subscripts

The real advantage of using an array is not realized until you use variables for subscripts in place of the constants.

```
stName(iIndex) = ""
Printer.Print stName(iIndex)
```

Subscripts may be constants, variables, or numeric expressions. Although the subscripts must be integers, Visual Basic will round any noninteger subscript.

A question has probably occurred to you by now—how many elements are there in the stName array? The answer is that you must specify the number of elements in a Dim statement.

The Dim Statement for Arrays—General Form

```
Dim ArrayName( [LowerSubscript To] UpperSubscript) [As Datatype]
```

The Dim Statement for Arrays—Examples

```
Dim stName(0 to 25) As String
Dim cBalance(10) As Currency
Dim iCollected(iCount) As Integer
Public gstProduct(1 To 100) As String
Dim miValue(-10 To 10) As Integer
```

The `Dim` statement allocates storage for the specified number of elements and initializes each numeric variable to 0. In the case of string arrays, each element is set to an empty string (zero characters). It is not necessary to specify the lower subscript value. If no value is set for the lower subscript, then the lowest subscript is 0.

Arrays can be dimensioned with empty parentheses, such as

```
Dim gstCustomer() As String
```

An array dimensioned in this way is referred to as a *dynamic array,* because the number of elements may change during program execution by using the `Redim` statement. All other arrays are *static arrays.* Each static array may be dimensioned only once in a project. Any attempt to change the size of a static array after its first use causes the following error message: *Array already dimensioned.* This text treats all arrays as static.

More on Subscripts

A subscript must reference a valid element of the array. If a list contains 10 names, it wouldn't make sense to ask: What is the 15th name on the list? or What is the 2½th name on the list? Visual Basic rounds fractional subscripts and gives the error message: *Subscript out of range* for invalid subscripts.

Feedback 8.2

```
Dim stName(20) As String
Const iValue As Integer = 10
```

After execution of the preceding statements, which of the following are valid subscripts?

1. `stName(20)`
2. `stName(iValue)`
3. `stName(iValue * 2)`
4. `stName(iValue * 3)`
5. `stName(0)`
6. `stName(iValue - 20)`
7. `stName(iValue / 3)`
8. `stName(iValue / 5 - 2)`

For Each/Next Statements

When you use an array, you need a way to reference each element in the array. `For/Next` loops, which you learned to use in Chapter 7, work well to traverse the elements in an array. Another handy loop construct is the **For Each** and **Next**. The significant advantage of using the `For Each/Next` is that you don't have to manipulate the subscripts of the array.

The For Each and Next Statements—General Form

```
For Each ElementName In ArrayName
    statement(s) in loop
Next [ElementName]
```

Visual Basic automatically references each element of the array, assigns its value to ElementName, and makes one pass through the loop. If the array has 12 elements, for example, the loop will execute 12 times. The variable used for ElementName must be a variant data type.

In the following examples assume that the arrays stName and iTotal have already been dimensioned and that they hold data.

The For Each and Next Statements—Examples

```
Dim vOneName As Variant
For Each vOneName In stName
    Printer.Print vOneName      'Print one element of the array
Next vOneName

Dim vTotal As Variant
For Each vTotal In iTotal
    vTotal = 0                  'Set one element of the array to zero
Next vTotal
```

The For Each loop will execute if the array has at least one element. All the statements within the loop are executed for the first element. If the array has more elements, the loop continues to execute until all the elements are processed. When the loop finishes, execution of code continues with the line following the Next statement.

Note: You may use an Exit For statement within a loop to exit early, just as in a For/Next loop.

Initializing an Array Using For Each

Although all numeric variables are initially set to 0, it is sometimes necessary to reinitialize variables. To zero out an array, each individual element must be set to 0.

```
For Each vTotal In iTotal
    vTotal = 0   'Set value of each element to 0
Next vTotal
```

User-Defined Data Types

You have been using the Visual Basic data types, such as integer, string, and currency, since Chapter 3. You can also define your own data types by combining multiple fields of data into a single unit. A **user-defined data type** can be used to combine several fields of related information. For example, an Employee data type may contain last name, first name, Social Security number, street, city, state, ZIP code, date of hire, and pay code. A Product data type might contain a description, product number, quantity, and price. The fields can be combined into a user-defined data type using the **Type** and **End Type statements.**

The Type Statement—General Form

```
Type NameOfNewDataType
    List of fields
End Type
```

The Type Statement—Examples

```
Type Employee
    stLastName              As  String
    stFirstName             As  String
    stSocialSecurityNumber  As  String
    stStreet                As  String
    stState                 As  String
    stZipCode               As  String
    dHireDate               As  Date
    iPayCode                As  Integer
End Type

Type Product
    stDescription           As  String
    stProductNumber         As  String
    iQuantity               As  Integer
    cPrice                  As  Currency
End Type

Private Type SalesDetail
    cSales(7)               As  Currency
End Type
```

Once you have created your own data type, you may use it to declare variables just as you use any other data type.

```
Dim Widget As Product
Dim Inventory(1 To 100) As Product
Dim HomeFurnishings As SalesDetail
Dim Housewares As SalesDetail
Dim Office As Employee
Dim Warehouse As Employee
```

Type statements can appear only at the module level in the General Declarations section of a standard code module or a form module. When placed in a standard code module, they are Public by default. If Type statements are placed at the module level of a form, *they must be declared as Private.*

Example of a Type statement in a form module:

```
'General Declarations section
Option Explicit
Private Type Item
    iCount        As Integer
    stDescription As String
End Type
```

Accessing Information with User-Defined Data Types

Each field of data within a user-defined type is referred to as an *element* of the data type. To access the elements use the dot notation similar to that used for objects: Specify Variable.Element.

```
Widget.stDescription
Widget.iQuantity
Widget.cPrice
Inventory(iIndex).stDescription
Inventory(iIndex).iQuantity
HomeFurnishings.cSales(iIndex)
Office.stLastName
Item.iCount
```

Notice the use of indexes in the preceding examples. Each example was taken from the preceding Type and Dim statements. A variable that is not an array, such as Widget, does not need an index. However, for Inventory, which was dimensioned as an array of 100, you must specify not only *which* Inventory item but also the element within the data type. HomeFurnishings is a different situation: The variable was dimensioned as a single variable (not an array). Now look back at the Type statement for SalesDetail on the preceding page; there are eight elements in the data type. Therefore, you must use an index on the element within the data type.

Note: You could even declare an array of a data type that includes an array. This type of array requires an index on the variable name and another index on the element name.

Example

```
Dim Clothing(3) as SalesDetail
```

The following line references one element:

```
Clothing(iClothingIndex).cSales(iSalesIndex)
```

You specify the type name in the dimension, but you do not refer to the type name anywhere else in the program. This syntax is consistent with using the built-in data types such as currency and integer; we don't usually use the type names anywhere beyond the declaration.

Note: The For Each statement cannot be used with an array of user-defined Types. No problem; just use For/Next and keep track of the number of elements used.

Feedback 8.3

(Don't forget, subscripts start at zero unless declared otherwise.)

1. Write a Type statement to hold student data containing last name, first name, student number, number of units completed, and GPA. The new data type should be called StudentInfo.
2. Declare an array of 100 students that will use the user-defined data type for student information.
3. Code the Type statement for a data type called Project containing project name, form name (up to 10), and the folder name.
4. Declare a variable called MyProject with a data type of Project.
5. Declare an array (with 100 elements) called OurProjects with a data type of Project.

Using Array Elements for Accumulators

Array elements are regular variables and perform in the same ways as all variables used so far. You may use the subscripted variables in any way you choose, such as for counters or total accumulators.

To demonstrate the use of array elements as total accumulators, eight totals will be accumulated. For the example, eight scout troops are selling raffle tickets. A separate total must be accumulated for each of the eight groups. Each time a sale is made, the number of tickets must be added to the correct total. The statement

```
Dim iTotal(1 To 8) As Integer
```

declares the eight accumulators.

Adding to the Correct Total

Assume that your user inputs a group number into txtGroup.Text and the number of tickets sold into txtSale.Text. The sales may be input in any order, with multiple sales for each group. Your problem is to add each ticket count to the correct total (1 to 8).

You will use the group number as the subscript to add to the correct total. If the first sale of 10 tickets is for group 4, the 10 must be added to the group 4 total. (Figure 8.5 shows the form and the variables used for this example.)

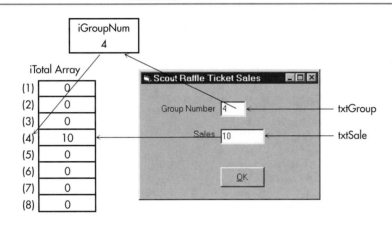

The group number entered in the txtGroup text box is used as a subscript to determine the correct iTotal array element to which to add.

```
iGroupNum = Val(txtGroup.Text)
cSale = Val(txtSale.Text)
iTotal(iGroupNum) = iTotal(iGroupNum) + cSale
```

Of course, there is always the danger that the user will enter an incorrect group number. Since it is undesirable for the user to get the error message *Subscript out of range*, the group number must be validated.

```
iGroupNum = Val(txtGroup.Text)
If iGroupNum >= 1 And iGroupNum <= 8 Then
    cSale = Val(txtSale.Text)
    iTotal(iGroupNum) = iTotal(iGroupNum) + cSale
Else
    MsgBox "Please Enter a Valid Group Number (1-8)", vbExclamation, "Data error"
End If
```

Using the group number as an index to the array is a technique called **direct reference**. The groups are assigned numbers from one to eight, which match the subscripts of the array.

Table Lookup

Things don't always work out so neatly as having sequential group numbers that can be used to access the table directly. Sometimes you will have to do a little work to find (**lookup**) the correct value. Reconsider the eight scout troops and their ticket sales. Now the groups are not numbered 1 to 8, but 101, 103, 110, 115, 121, 123, 130, and 145. The group number and the number of tickets sold are still input and the number of tickets must be added to the correct total. But now you must do one more step—determine to which array element to add the ticket sales.

The first step in the project is to establish a user-defined type with the group numbers and totals and then dimension an array of the new type. Before any processing is done, load the group numbers into the table.

Place the following statements in the General Declarations section of a form module:

```
Private Type GroupInfo
    iNumber As Integer
    iTotal As Integer
End Type
Dim mGroup(1 To 8) As GroupInfo
```

Then initialize the values of the array elements by placing these statements into the Form_Load procedure:

```
mGroup(1).iNumber = 101
mGroup(2).iNumber = 103
mGroup(3).iNumber = 110
```

etc.

During program execution the user still enters the group number and the number of tickets sold into text boxes.

The technique used to find the subscript is called a *table lookup*. In this example the object is to find the element number (1 to 8) of the group number and use that element number as a subscript to the total table. If the user enters the third group number (110), the sale is added to the third total. If the seventh group number (130) is entered, the sale is added to the seventh total, and so on. Hence, you need a way, given the group number in txtGroup.Text, to find the corresponding subscript of the mGroup array.

When Visual Basic executes the statement

```
mGroup(iGroupNum).iTotal = mGroup(iGroupNum).iTotal + cSale
```

the value of iGroupNum must be a number in the range 1 to 8. The task for the lookup operation is to find the number to place in iGroupNum, based on the value of txtGroup.Text. Figure 8.6 shows the variables used for the lookup. Figure 8.7 shows the flowchart of the lookup logic.

Figure 8.6

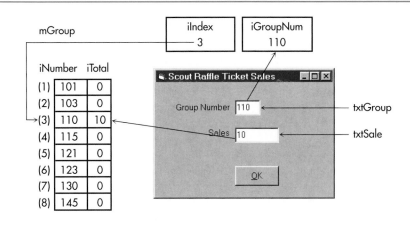

A lookup operation: The group number is looked up in the mGroup array; the correct subscript is found and used to add the sale to the correct iTotal.

Figure 8.7

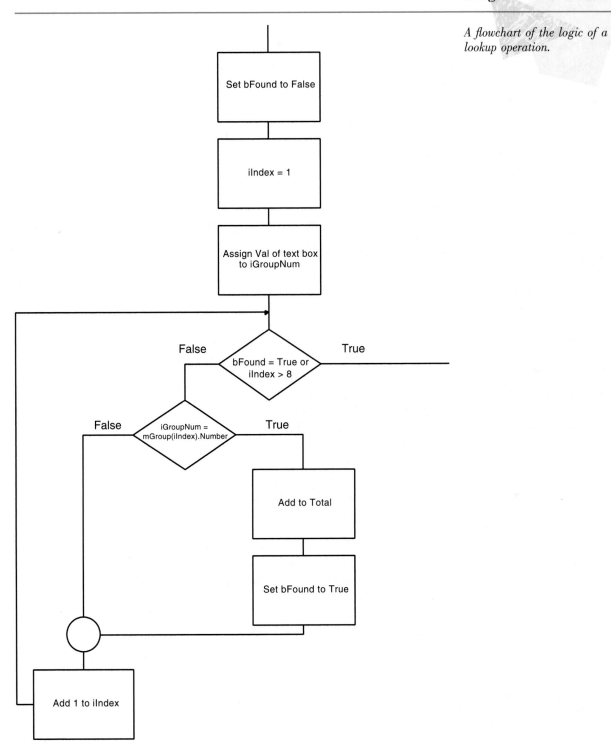

A flowchart of the logic of a lookup operation.

Coding a Table Lookup

For a table lookup, you will find that a Do/Loop works better than For Each. As you compare to each element in the array and eventually find a match, you need to know the subscript of the matching element.

```
Dim iGroupNum As Integer
Dim iIndex    As Integer
Dim cSale     As Currency
Dim bFound    As Boolean

bFound = False
iIndex = 1
iGroupNum = Val(txtGroup.Text)
Do Until bFound Or iIndex > 8
    If iGroupNum = mGroup(iIndex).iNumber Then
        cSale = Val(txtSale.Text)
        mGroup(iIndex).iTotal = mGroup(iIndex).iTotal + cSale
        bFound = True
    End If
    iIndex = iIndex + 1
Loop
```

Once again, you should do some form of validation. If the user enters an invalid group number, you should display a message box. You can check the value of the Boolean variable bFound after completion of the loop to determine whether the loop terminated because of a match or without a match.

```
If bFound = False Then  'No match was found
    MsgBox "Invalid group number—Sale not added to a total", vbInformation, _
        "Data error"
End If
```

The table-lookup technique will work for any table, numeric or string. It isn't necessary to arrange the fields being searched in any particular sequence. The comparison is made to one item in the list, then the next, and the next—until a match is found. In fact, you can save processing time by arranging the table with the most-often-used entries at the top so that fewer comparisons must be made.

Using List Boxes with Arrays

In the previous example of a lookup, the user had to type some information into a text box, which was used to look up the information in an array. A more efficient and friendly solution might be to substitute a list box for the text box. You can store the eight group numbers in a list box and allow the user to select from the list.

The initial List property can contain the values 101, 103, 110, 115, 121, 123, 130, and 145.

You have probably already realized that you can use the ListIndex property to determine the array subscript. Remember that the ListIndex property holds the position or index of the selected item from the list. You could then use this index with one minor change to access the group total. Recall that the ListIndex property always begins with 0. If you plan to coordinate an array and a list, dimension the array with elements beginning with zero. For this example, we'll change the dimension in the General Declarations section to

```
Dim miTotal(0 to 7) As Integer
```

In place of the lookup operation, we can use this code:

```
Dim iGroupNum As Integer
Dim cSale     As Currency

iGroupNum = lstGroup.ListIndex

If iGroupNum >= 0 And iGroupNum <= 7 Then
    cSale = Val(txtSale.Text)
    miTotal(iGroupNum) = miTotal(iGroupNum) + cSale
Else
    MsgBox "You must select a group number from the list", _
        vbInformation, "Data error"
End If
```

The ItemData Property

Visual Basic offers another handy property for list boxes and combo boxes that can be a big help when working with indexes. A problem can arise when you use the ListIndex of the items in the list as an array subscript. What happens if you sort the data in the list? The ListIndex of each list element could be different than it was previously, which means the position in the array would be incorrect. The **ItemData property** can associate a specific number with each item in the list. Each element of the List property can have a corresponding ItemData that does not change when the list is sorted.

You can set initial values for the ItemData property, just as you set initial values for the List property. If you add an item to the list during run time, you can also add a corresponding value to the ItemData property.

The ItemData Property—General Form

```
Object.ItemData(Index) [= number]
```

In this next example, we'll use a combo box for a list of names and a corresponding array holding the phone numbers for each name in the list.

The array of phone numbers will have the same positions as the original list of names. When the data is first entered into the list, the ItemData property must also be assigned. The ListIndex and the ItemData properties match when first entered.

cboName.List	cboName.ItemData	cboName.ListIndex	stPhone()
Jones, Bill	0	0	111-1111
Lee, Brian	1	1	222-2222
Platt, Cece	2	2	333-3333
Adams, Keith	3	3	444-4444
Lopex, Ana	4	4	555-5555

Notice that after the sort the ItemData property stayed with the associated list item. The ListIndex still represents the position within the array.

cboName.List	cboName.ItemData	cboName.ListIndex
Adams, Keith	3	0
Jones, Bill	0	1
Lee, Brian	1	2
Lopex, Ana	4	3
Platt, Cece	2	4

You can use the ItemData property to access the proper array element.

```
Dim iIndex As Integer
iIndex = cboName.ItemData(cboName.ListIndex) 'Save position number of current
                                              selection
If iIndex <> -1 Then                         'If a selection is made
    lblPhone.Caption = stPhone(iIndex)       'Assign corresponding array element to
                                              label
Else
    MsgBox "Please select a name from the list", vbExclamation, "Data error"
End If
```

Using Nonsequential ItemData Values

The values that are placed in the ItemData property do not need to be in sequence. In our earlier scouting example, we could give names to the groups and have those names associated with the group numbers 101, 103, 110, 115, 121, 123, 130, and 145.

lstGroupName.List	lstGroupName.ItemData
Eagles	101
Bats	103
Wolves	110
Tigers	115
Bears	121
Mountain Lions	123
Panthers	130
Cobras	145

The value stored in the ItemData property is a long integer, but it may hold any numeric value you wish. Using ItemData is an easy way to assign such things as a product number to a description.

Adding Items with ItemData to a List

You learned in Chapter 7 to use the AddItem method to add a new item to a list box or combo box. If you want to store an ItemData property for the new list item, you must include an additional step. Assume that the user enters a new group name and number (using the previous scout group example), using txtGroupName and txtGroupNumber. You can use the AddItem method to add the group name. But then you must know the index of the new item in order to add the corresponding ItemData.

If your list is unsorted, the new item is always last—in the highest ListIndex position. (Remember that the highest ListIndex is one less than ListCount.) Therefore, these statements will add the group name and number to corresponding positions in the list:

```
lstGroupName.AddItem txtGroupName.Text
lstGroupName.ItemData(lstGroupName.ListCount - 1) = txtGroupNumber.Text
```

However, if your list is sorted, the AddItem method adds the new item alphabetically in the list. You can determine the index of the new item using the **NewIndex property**, which VB sets to the index of the new item.

```
lstGroupName.AddItem txtGroupName.Text
lstGroupName.ItemData(lstGroupName.NewIndex) = txtGroupNumber.Text
```

Note that you can use the second method (using the NewIndex property) for an unsorted list as well as a sorted list.

Multidimensional Arrays

You may need to use two subscripts to identify tabular data, where data are arranged in rows and columns.

Many applications of two-dimensional tables quickly come to mind—insurance rate tables, tax tables, addition and multiplication tables, postage rates, foods and their nutritive value, population by region, rainfall by state.

To define a two-dimensional array or *table*, the `Dim` statement specifies the number of rows and columns in the array. The **row** is horizontal and the **column** is vertical. The following table has three rows and four columns:

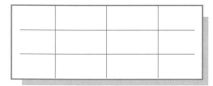

The Dim Statement for Two-Dimensional Arrays— General Form

```
Dim ArrayName([LowerLimit To] UpperLimit, [LowerLimit To] UpperLimit) As Datatype
```

The Dim Statement for Two-Dimensional Arrays— Examples

```
Dim stName(2, 3) As String
Dim stName(0 To 2, 0 To 3) As String
```

Either of these two statements establishes an array of 12 elements, with three rows and four columns. You must always use two subscripts when referring to individual elements of the table. Specify the row with the first subscript and the column with the second subscript.

(0,0)	(0,1)	(0,2)	(0,3)
(1,0)	(1,1)	(1,2)	(1,3)
(2,0)	(2,1)	(2,2)	(2,3)

The elements of the array may be used in the same ways as any other variable—in accumulators, counts, reference fields for lookup; in statements like assignment and printing; and as conditions. Some valid references to the table include

```
stName(1, 2) = "Value"
stName(iRowIndex, iColIndex) = "Value"
lblDisplay.Caption = stName(1, 2)
Printer.Print stName(iRowIndex, iColIndex)
```

Invalid references for the stName table would include any value greater than 2 for the first subscript or greater than 3 for the second subscript.

Initializing Two-Dimensional Arrays

Although numeric array elements are initially set to 0 and string elements are set to empty strings, many situations require that you initialize arrays to 0 or some other value. You can use nested For/Next loops or For Each/Next to set each array element to an initial value.

Nested For/Next Example

The assignment statement in the inner loop will be executed 12 times, once for each element of stName.

```
Dim iRow   As Integer
Dim iCol   As Integer

For iRow = 1 To 3
    For iColumn = 1 To 4
        stName(iRow, iColumn) = ""   'Initialize each element
    Next iColumn
Next iRow
```

For Each/Next Example

You can also perform the initialization with a For Each statement, which initializes all 12 elements.

```
Dim vName As Variant
For Each vName In stName
    vName = ""                      'Initialize each element
Next vName
```

Printing a Two-Dimensional Table

When you want to print the contents of a two-dimensional table, you can also use a For Each/Next loop.

```
Dim vName As Variant
For Each vName In stName
    Printer.Print vName
Next vName
```

If you wish to print an entire row in one line, use a `For/Next` loop and set up the print statements for multiple elements.

```
For iRowIndex = 0 To 2
  Printer.Print stName(iRowIndex, 0); Tab(15); stName(iRowIndex, 1); _
    Tab(30); stName(iRowIndex, 2); Tab(45); stName(iRowIndex, 3)
Next iRowIndex
```

Summing a Two-Dimensional Table

You can find the sum of a table in various ways. You may sum either the columns or the rows of the table; or, as in a cross-foot, you may sum the figures in both directions and double-check the totals.

To sum the array in both directions, each column needs one total field and each row needs one total field. Two one-dimensional arrays will work well for the totals. Figure 8.8 illustrates the variables used in this example.

Figure 8.8

Two one-dimensional arrays hold totals for the two-dimensional array.

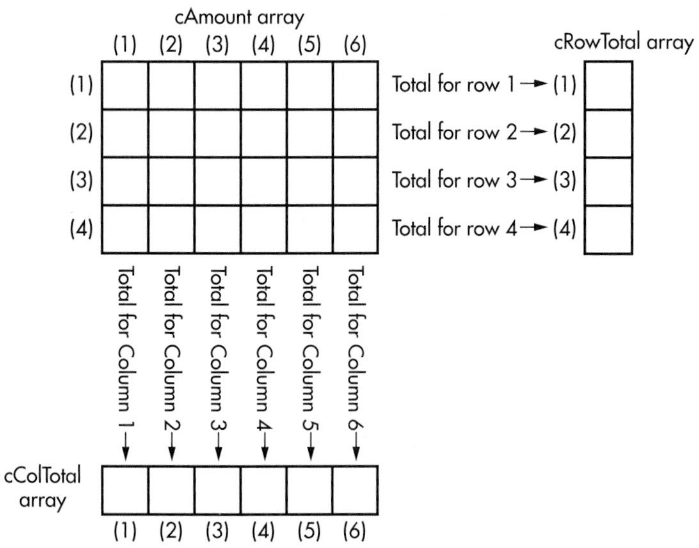

```
Dim cAmount(1 To 4, 1 To 6) As Currency
Dim cRowTotal(1 To 4) As Currency
Dim cColTotal(1 To 6) As Currency
Dim iRowIndex As Integer
Dim iColIndex As Integer

For iRowIndex = 1 To 4
  For iColIndex = 1 To 6
    cRowTotal(iRowIndex) = cRowTotal(iRowIndex) _
      + cAmount(iRowIndex, iColIndex)
    cColTotal(iColIndex) = cColTotal(iColIndex) _
      + cAmount(iRowIndex, iColIndex)
  Next iColIndex
Next iRowIndex
```

Feedback 8.4

Write VB statements to do the following:

1. Dimension a table called cTemperature with five columns and three rows.
2. Set each element in the first row to 0.
3. Set each element in the second row to 75.
4. For each column of the table, add together the elements in rows 1 and 2, placing the sum in row 3.
5. Print the entire table.

Lookup Operation for Two-Dimensional Tables

When you look up items in a two-dimensional table, you can use the same techniques discussed with single-dimensional arrays—direct reference and table lookup. The limitations are the same.

1. To use a direct reference, row and column subscripts must be readily available. For example, you can tally the hours used for each of five machines (identified by machine numbers 1 to 5) and each of four departments (identified by department numbers 1 to 4).

```
iRowIndex = Val(txtMachine.Text)
iColIndex = Val(txtDepartment.Text)
cHours = Val(txtHours.Text)
MachineTotal(iRowIndex, iColIndex) = MachineTotal(iRowIndex, iColIndex) + cHours
```

2. A table lookup is the most common lookup technique.

Many two-dimensional tables used for lookup require additional one-dimensional arrays or lists to aid in the lookup process. For an example, use a shipping rate table (Figure 8.9) to look up the rate to ship a package. The shipping rate depends on the weight of the package and the zone to which it is being shipped. You could design the project with the weight and zones in dropdown list boxes, or you could use a text box and let the user input the data.

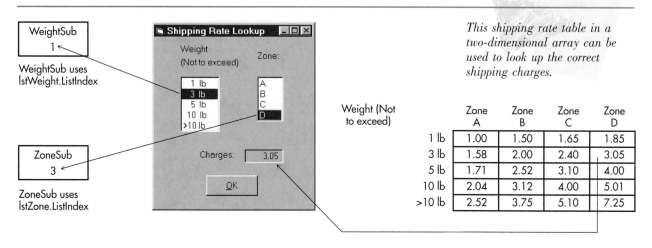

This shipping rate table in a two-dimensional array can be used to look up the correct shipping charges.

Weight (Not to exceed)	Zone A	Zone B	Zone C	Zone D
1 lb	1.00	1.50	1.65	1.85
3 lb	1.58	2.00	2.40	3.05
5 lb	1.71	2.52	3.10	4.00
10 lb	2.04	3.12	4.00	5.01
>10 lb	2.52	3.75	5.10	7.25

Using List Boxes

In this example a list box holds the weight limits, and another list holds the zones. The values for the two lists are set with the List and ItemData properties at design time. The five-by-four rate table is two dimensional, and the values are preloaded. The best way to preload values is to load the values from a data file, which is discussed in Chapter 9. The other alternative is to assign the values in the Form_Load procedure of the startup form.

```
Dim mcRate(0 to 4, 0 to 3) As Currency   'Module-level array for lookup
Dim iWeightSub   As Integer
Dim iZoneSub     As Integer
iWeightSub = lstWeight.ListIndex
iZoneSub = lstZone.ListIndex

If iWeightSub <> -1 And iZoneSub <> -1 Then
    lblShipping.Caption = mcRate(iWeightSub, iZoneSub)
Else
    MsgBox "Please select the weight and zone from the proper lists."
End If
```

Using Text Boxes

If you are using text boxes for data entry rather than list boxes, the input requires more validation. Both the weight and zone entries must be looked up before the correct rate can be determined. The valid zones and weight ranges will be stored in two separate one-dimensional arrays. The first step in the project is to establish and fill the two arrays. The five-by-four rate table is two dimensional, and the values should be preloaded, as in the previous example.

```
Dim mcRate(0 to 4, 0 to 3) As Currency     'Module-level array for lookup
Dim iWeight(0 To 4) As Integer
Dim stZone(0 to 3)   As String
Dim iWeightSub       As Integer
Dim iZoneSub         As Integer
Dim iIndex           As Integer
Dim iWeightInput     As Integer
Dim bWeightFound     As Boolean
Dim bZoneFound       As Boolean
```

```
'Look up the weight to find the iWeightSub

iWeightInput = Val(txtWeight.Text)
bWeightFound = False
iIndex = 0
Do Until bWeightFound or iIndex > 4
    If iWeightInput <= iWeight(iIndex) Then
        iWeightSub = iIndex
        bWeightFound = True
    End If
    iIndex = iIndex + 1
Loop
If Not bWeightFound Then
    iWeightSub = 4
End If

'Look up the zone to find the iColIndex
bZoneFound = False
iIndex = 0
Do Until bZoneFound or iIndex > 3
    If txtZone.Text = stZone(iIndex) Then
        iZoneSub = iIndex
        bZoneFound = True
    End If
    iIndex = iIndex + 1
Loop

'Display the appropriate rate
If (iWeightSub >= 0 And iWeightSub <= 4) And _
        (iZoneSub >= 0 And iZoneSub <= 3) Then
    lblShipping.Caption = mcRate(iWeightSub, iZoneSub)
Else
    MsgBox "Invalid zone or weight entered", vbExclamation, "Invalid data"
End If
```

Your Hands-On Programming Example

Create a project for R 'n R—for Reading 'n Refreshment that determines the price per pound for bulk coffee sales. The coffees are divided into categories: regular, decaf, and special blend. The prices are set by the ¼ pound, ½ pound, and full pound. Use a Find Price command button to search for the appropriate price based on the selections.

	Regular	**Decaf**	**Blend**
¼ pound	2.60	2.90	3.25
½ pound	4.90	5.60	6.10
Full pound	8.75	9.75	11.25

Create a user-defined data type that contains the coffee type, amount, and price. Set up a variable called mTransaction that is an array of 20 elements of your data type. Each time the Find Price button is pressed, add the data to the array.

When the Exit button is pressed, print appropriate headings and the data from the mTransaction array.

Planning the Project

Sketch a form (Figure 8.10), which your users sign off as meeting their needs.

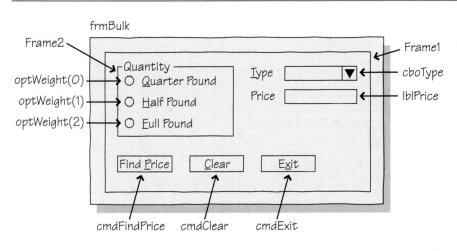

Figure 8.10

A planning sketch of the form for the hands-on programming example.

Plan the Objects and Properties

Object	Property	Setting
frmBulk	Name	frmBulk
	Caption	R 'n R—for Reading 'n Refreshment
Frame1	Caption	(blank)
Frame2	Caption	Quantity
Label1	Caption	Type
Label2	Caption	Price
lblPrice	Name	lblPrice
	Caption	(blank)
cboType	Name	cboType
	List	Regular
		Decaffeinated
		Special Blend
	ItemData	0
		1
		2
	Sorted	True
	Style	2 - Dropdown list
optWeight	Name	optWeight
	Caption	Quarter pound
optWeight	Name	optWeight
	Caption	Half pound
optWeight	Name	optWeight
	Caption	Full pound
cmdFindPrice	Name	cmdFindPrice
	Caption	Find &Price
cmdClear	Name	cmdClear
	Caption	&Clear
cmdExit	Name	cmdExit
	Caption	E&xit

Plan the Event Procedures

You need to plan the actions for the event procedures and the Form_Load event.

Procedure	Actions
Form_Load	Create and load the price table.
cmdFindPrice	Look up the price in the table. Display the price in the label. Store type, quantity, and price in the array.
cmdClear	Erase the price. Set list box indexes to −1.
cmdExit	Print the Transaction array. Terminate the project.

Write the Project

● Follow the sketch in Figure 8.10 to create the form. Figure 8.11 shows the completed form.

Figure 8.11

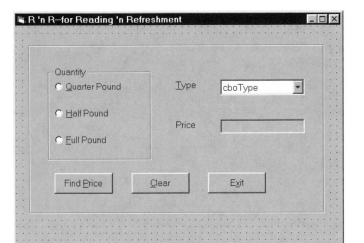

The form for the hands-on programming example.

● Set the properties of each object, according to your plan.

● Write the code. Working from the pseudocode, write each event procedure.

● When you complete the code, use a variety of data to thoroughly test the project.

The Project Coding Solution

```
'Module:        frmBulk
'Programmer:    A. Millspaugh
'Date:          July 1997
'Description:   Look up the price for bulk coffee
'               based on quantity and type.
'Folder:        Ch0801

Option Explicit
Dim mcPrice(0 To 2, 0 To 2) As Currency     'Table to store coffee prices

Private Type CoffeeSale
    stType As String
    stQuantity As String
    cPrice As Currency
End Type

Dim mTransaction(20)        As CoffeeSale           'Store transactions for report
Dim miNumberTransactions    As Integer
Dim mlWeight                As Long
```

```
Private Sub cmdClear_Click()
    'Remove the selection from the lists and
    '    clear the price
    Dim iIndex As Integer

    cboType.ListIndex = -1   'Clear selection
    lblPrice.Caption = ""
    mlWeight = 0
    For iIndex = 0 To 2
        optWeight(iIndex).Value = False
    Next iIndex
End Sub
```

```
Private Sub cmdExit_Click()
    'Print report and terminate the project

    Dim iIndex          As Integer
    Dim stPrintPrice    As String
```

```
    Printer.Print Tab(45); "Sales Report"
    Printer.Print ""
    Printer.Print Tab(15); "Type"; Tab(40); "Quantity"; Tab(60); "Price"
    Printer.Print ""
    For iIndex = 0 To miNumberTransactions - 1
        stPrintPrice = Format$(mTransaction(iIndex).cPrice, "Currency")
        Printer.Print Tab(10); mTransaction(iIndex).stType; _
            Tab(35); mTransaction(iIndex).stQuantity; _
            Tab(65 - Len(stPrintPrice)); stPrintPrice
    Next iIndex
    End
End Sub
```

```
Private Sub cmdFindPrice_Click()
    'Lookup the price using the quantity and type

    Dim iRow    As Integer
    Dim iCol    As Integer
    Dim cPrice  As Currency

    iRow = mlWeight
    If miNumberTransactions <= 20 Then          'Allow only 20 transactions
        If cboType.ListIndex <> -1 Then
            iCol = cboType.ListIndex
            Select Case mlWeight
                Case 0
                    mTransaction(miNumberTransactions).stQuantity = "Quarter Pound"
                Case 1
                    mTransaction(miNumberTransactions).stQuantity = "Half Pound"
                Case 2
                    mTransaction(miNumberTransactions).stQuantity = "Full Pound"
                Case Else
                    'Default to quarter pound
                    mTransaction(miNumberTransactions).stQuantity = "Quarter Pound"
            End Select
            cPrice = mcPrice(iRow, iCol)
            lblPrice.Caption = Format$(cPrice, "Currency")
            mTransaction(miNumberTransactions).stType = cboType.List(iCol)
            mTransaction(miNumberTransactions).cPrice = cPrice
            miNumberTransactions = miNumberTransactions + 1
        Else
            MsgBox "Select a type and quantity", vbExclamation, "Entry Error"
        End If
    End If
End Sub
```

```
Private Sub Form_Load()
    'Load prices into the table

    mcPrice(0, 0) = 2.6
    mcPrice(0, 1) = 2.9
    mcPrice(0, 2) = 3.25
    mcPrice(1, 0) = 4.9
    mcPrice(1, 1) = 5.6
    mcPrice(1, 2) = 6.1
    mcPrice(2, 0) = 8.75
    mcPrice(2, 1) = 9.75
    mcPrice(2, 2) = 11.25
End Sub
```

```
Private Sub optWeight_Click(Index As Integer)
    'Find the selected weight

    mlWeight = Index
End Sub
```

Programming Hints

The Array Function

As you saw in the earlier programming example, initializing an array at run time is somewhat tedious (refer to the Form_Load procedure in the hands-on programming example). Visual Basic provides another method of initializing an array that uses a variant variable. You declare the variable to be an array and assign a list of values to it with the **Array** function.

The Array Function—General Form

```
Variable = Array(list of values)
```

The Array Function—Examples

```
vNames = Array("Ann", "Mary", "Jorge", "Peter")
vCodes = Array(45, 76, 53, 24)
```

The values within the array are accessed with the same subscript notation as a dimensioned array.

```
Dim vMonth As Variant
vMonth = Array("Jan", "Feb", "Mar", "Apr", "May", "Jun", "Jul", "Aug", _
   "Sep", "Oct", "Nov", "Dec")
```

After the previous declaration and assignment, the statement

```
Printer.Print vMonth(4)
```

would print *May*. (As usual, the subscripts start at 0.)

Summary

1. A series of controls with the same name is called a control array. Each individual control is referenced using an index, which is its position number within the array.
2. The controls in a control array share one event procedure.
3. A `Select Case` statement may be used when an expression is being tested for many different values or ranges of values. The statement also includes a `Case Else` for the situation that none of the values specified was a match.
4. A series of variables with the same name is called an array. The individual values are referred to as elements, and each element is accessed by its subscript, which is a position number.
5. A special form of the `For` loop called `For Each` is available for working with arrays. The `For Each` eliminates the need for the programmer to manipulate the subscripts of the array.
6. In addition to the existing data types, programmers may use the `Type` statement to combine fields and create user-defined data types. `Type` statements must appear in the General Declarations section of a module.
7. Arrays can be used like any other variables; they can be used to accumulate a series of totals or store values for a lookup procedure.
8. The information in arrays may be accessed directly by subscript, or a table lookup may be used to determine the correct table position.
9. List box and combo box controls have an ItemData property that can be used to assign a numeric value to each item in the list.
10. Arrays may be multidimensional. A two-dimensional table contains rows and columns and is processed similarly to a one-dimensional array. Access of a multidimensional array frequently requires the use of nested loops.

Key Terms

array *277*

column *292*

control array *272*

direct reference *285*

element *277*

For Each and Next *279*

index *273*

ItemData property *289*

lookup *285*

NewIndex property *291*

row *292*

subscript *277*

subscripted variable *277*

table *277*

Type/End Type statements *281*

user-defined data type *281*

Review Questions

1. Define the following terms:
   (a) array
   (b) element
   (c) subscript
   (d) control array
   (e) subscripted variable
2. Describe the logic of a table lookup.
3. Name some situations in which it is important to perform validation when working with subscripted variables.
4. Why would a list box control need both a ListIndex property and an Item-Data property?
5. Compare a two-dimensional table to an array of a user-defined data type.
6. When initializing values in a two-dimensional table, what statements should be used?

Programming Exercises

8.1 (*Array of user-defined type*) Create a project to analyze an income survey. The statistics for each home include an identification code, the number of members in the household, and the yearly income. A menu will contain *File*, *Reports*, and *Help*. The *File* menu will contain *Enter Data* and *Exit*. As the data are entered, they should be assigned from the text boxes to the elements of a user-defined type.

The reports for the project will be sent to the printer and include the following:
(a) A three-column report displaying the input data.
(b) A listing of the identification number and income for each household that exceeds the average income.
(c) The percentage of households having incomes below the poverty level.

Test Data

Poverty Level: 8000 for a family of one or two, plus 2000 for each additional member.

ID Number	Annual Income	Number of Persons
2497	12500	2
3323	13000	5
4521	18210	4
6789	8000	2
5476	6000	1
4423	16400	3
6587	25000	4
3221	10500	4
5555	15000	2
0085	19700	3
3097	20000	8
4480	23400	5
0265	19700	2
8901	13000	3

Check Figures

Households exceeding average income:
   You should have 7 entries on the list.
Households below poverty level:
   21.43%

8.2 (*Two-dimensional table*) Modify project 8.1 to assign the data to a multidimensional array rather than use an array of user-defined types.

8.3 Create a project to keep track of concert ticket sales by your club. Ticket prices are based on the section of the auditorium in which the seats are located. Your program should calculate the price for each sale, accumulate the total number of tickets sold in each section, display the ticket price schedule, and print a summary of all sales.

   The form will contain a sorted list box of the sections for seating and use an ItemData property to store the ticket price subscript.

Section	Price
Orchestra	40.00
Mezzanine	27.50
General	15.00
Balcony	10.00

Special Consideration: Do not allow the user to receive a subscript-out-of-range error message.

8.4   (*Array of a user-defined type*) Create a project that will allow a user to look up state names and their two-letter abbreviations. The user will have the options to *Look up the Abbreviation* or to *Look up the State Name*. In the event that a match cannot be found for the input, print an appropriate error message.

Use an option button control array and a `Select Case` to determine which text box (state name or abbreviation) should have the focus and which should be disabled.

Data

AL	Alabama
AK	Alaska
AS	American Samoa
AZ	Arizona
AR	Arkansas
CA	California
CO	Colorado
CT	Connecticut
DE	Delaware
DC	District of Columbia
FL	Florida
GA	Georgia
GU	Guam
HI	Hawaii
ID	Idaho
IL	Illinois
IN	Indiana
IA	Iowa
KS	Kansas
KY	Kentucky
LA	Louisiana
ME	Maine
MD	Maryland
MA	Massachusetts
MI	Michigan
MN	Minnesota

(continued)

MS	Mississippi
MO	Missouri
MT	Montana
NE	Nebraska
NV	Nevada
NH	New Hampshire
NJ	New Jersey
NM	New Mexico
NY	New York
NC	North Carolina
ND	North Dakota
OH	Ohio
OK	Oklahoma
OR	Oregon
PA	Pennsylvania
PR	Puerto Rico
RI	Rhode Island
SC	South Carolina
SD	South Dakota
TN	Tennessee
TX	Texas
TT	Trust Territories
UT	Utah
VT	Vermont
VA	Virginia
VI	Virgin Islands
WA	Washington
WV	West Virginia
WI	Wisconsin
WY	Wyoming

8.5 (*Two-dimensional table*) Create a project that looks up the driving distance between two cities. Use two dropdown lists that contain the names of the cities. Label one list *Departure* and the other *Destination*. Use a command button to calculate distance.

   Store the distances in a two-dimensional table.

	Boston	Chicago	Dallas	Las Vegas	Los Angeles	Miami	New Orleans	Toronto	Vancouver	Washington DC
Boston	0	1004	1753	2752	3017	1520	1507	609	3155	448
Chicago	1004	0	921	1780	2048	1397	919	515	2176	709
Dallas	1753	921	0	1230	1399	1343	517	1435	2234	1307
Las Vegas	2752	1780	1230	0	272	2570	1732	2251	1322	2420
Los Angeles	3017	2048	1399	272	0	2716	1858	2523	1278	2646
Miami	1520	1397	1343	2570	2716	0	860	1494	3447	1057
New Orleans	1507	919	517	1732	1858	860	0	1307	2734	1099
Toronto	609	515	1435	2251	2523	1494	1307	0	2820	571
Vancouver	3155	2176	2234	1322	1278	3447	2734	2820	0	2887
Washington DC	448	709	1307	2420	2646	1057	1099	571	2887	0

8.6 *(Two-dimensional table)* Create a project in which the user will complete a 10-question survey. Create a form containing labels with each of the questions and a group of option buttons for each question with the following responses: Always, Usually, Sometimes, Seldom, and Never.

Use a two-dimensional array to accumulate the number of each response for each question.

Have a menu or command option that will print an item analysis on the printer that shows the question number and the count for each response.

Sample of partial output:

Question	Always	Usually	Sometimes	Seldom	Never
1	5	2	10	4	6
2	2	2	10	2	1
3	17	0	10	0	0

CASE STUDIES

VB Mail Order

Create a project that will calculate shipping charges from a two-dimensional table of rates. The rate depends on the weight of the package and the zone to which it will be shipped. The Wt. column specifies the maximum weight for that rate. All weights over 10 pounds use the last row.

Wt.	Zone	A	B	C	D
1		1.00	1.50	1.65	1.85
3		1.58	2.00	2.40	3.05
5		1.71	2.52	3.10	4.00
10		2.04	3.12	4.00	5.01
>10		2.52	3.75	5.10	7.25

VB Auto Center

VB Auto sells its own brand of spark plugs. In order to cross-reference to major brands, it keeps a table of equivalent part numbers. VB Auto wants to computerize the process of looking up part numbers in order to improve its customer service.

The user should be able to enter the part number and brand and look up the corresponding VB Auto part number. You may allow the user to select the brand (Brand A, Brand B, or Brand X) from a list or from option buttons.

You can choose from two alternate approaches for the lookup table. Either store the part numbers in a two-dimensional table or in an array of user defined types. In either case, use the part number and brand entered by the user; look up and display the VB Auto part number.

VB Auto	Brand A	Brand C	Brand X
PR214	MR43T	RBL8	14K22
PR223	R43	RJ6	14K24
PR224	R43N	RN4	14K30
PR246	R46N	RN8	14K32
PR247	R46TS	RBL17Y	14K33
PR248	R46TX	RBL12-6	14K35
PR324	S46	J11	14K38
PR326	SR46E	XEJ8	14K40
PR444	47L	H12	14K44

9

Data Files

At the completion of this chapter, you will be able to . . .

1. Create data files.

2. Read and write records to disk.

3. Determine the appropriate locations for data file–related code.

4. Understand the significance of a `Close` statement.

5. Differentiate between sequential and random files.

6. Trap user errors and handle errors to avoid run-time errors.

7. Incorporate fixed-length strings into user-defined data types.

8. Read and write random files.

9. Perform add, delete, and edit operations on random files.

10. Allow the user to input data using the `InputBox` function.

Data Files

In all of your projects so far, the user has entered information through text boxes. Although this input method is satisfactory for many applications, some situations require large quantities of data or information to be processed week after week.

Many computer applications require data to be saved from one run to the next. Some examples are personal tasks, such as budgeting, mailing lists, and sports-team records, and business applications, such as inventory records, customer files, and master files. This chapter deals with methods to store and access **data files** on disk.

Data Files and Project Files

In computer terminology anything that you store on a diskette or hard disk is given its own unique name and called a **file**. Each of your Visual Basic projects requires multiple files—for the forms, standard code modules, and project information. However, the files you will create now are different; they contain actual data, such as names and addresses, inventory amounts, and account balances.

Data File Terminology

The entire collection of data is called a file. The file is made up of **records**— one record for each entity in the file. Each record can be broken down further into **fields** (also called *data elements*). For example, in an employee file, the data for one employee are one record. In a name and address file, the data for one person are a record.

In the name and address file, each person has a last name field, a first name field, address fields, and a phone number field. Each field in a record pertains to the same person. Figure 9.1 illustrates a name and address file.

F i g u r e   9 . 1

The rows in this data file represent records; the columns represent fields.

Last Name	First Name	Street	City	State	Zip	Phone	Email
Maxwell	Harry	795 W. J Street	Ontario	CA	91764	909-555-1234	
Helm	Jennifer	201 Cortez Way	Pomona	CA	91766	818-555-2222	JHelm@ms.org
Colton	Craig	1632 Granada Place	Pomona	CA	91766	909-555-3333	

A record | A field

The data stored in files is nearly always entered in an organized manner. Records may be stored in account number order, alphabetically by name, by date, or by the sequence in which they are received. One field in the record is the organizing factor for the file (such as account number, name, or date). This field, which is used to determine the order of the file, is called the **record key,** or **key field.**

A key field may be either a string or numeric field. In an employee file, if the records are in order by an employee number, then the employee number is the key field. If the order is based on employee name, then the name is the key field, although key fields are normally unique data items.

File Organizations

The manner in which data are organized, stored, and retrieved is called the *file organization.* Two common file organizations are *sequential* and *random.* In this chapter you will learn to read and write both sequential and random files.

Opening and Closing Data Files

Three steps are necessary to process data files:

1. *Open* the file. Before any data may be placed on the disk or read from the disk, the file must be opened. Generally you will open the file in the Form_Load procedure.
2. *Read* or *write* the data records. You will read or write in a save procedure associated with the data entry form.
3. *Close* the file. You must always close a file when you are finished with it.

The Open Statement—General Form

```
Open "FileName" For {Input | Output | Append | Random} As #FileNumber [Len = RecLength]
```

The elements shown in the braces are the **file mode,** indicating the way in which a file will be accessed. The braces indicate that a choice may be made, but that the entry is required. The first three choices are used for sequential files. The FileNumber may be from 1 to 511. The record length can be up to 32,767 characters.

The Open Statement—Examples

```
Open "A:\DataFile.Dat" For Output As #1
Open "C:\VB5\CH0701\Names" For Input As #2
```

The first example opens a file called *DataFile.Dat* as an output file, calling it file #1. The second example opens a file in the C: drive called *Names* as an input file, calling it file #2.

File Mode	Description
Output	Data are output from the project and written on the disk. New data is written at the beginning of the file, overwriting any existing data.
Input	Data are input into the project from the disk. This mode reads data previously stored on the disk.
Append	Data are output from the project and written on the disk. The new data are added to the end of the file.
Random	Data can be input or output and records may be accessed in any order.

Remember that a data file must always be opened prior to being used. When a data file is opened, the following actions are taken:

1. The directory is checked for the named file. If the file does not exist, a directory entry is created for this file, with the exception of Input mode, which will cause an error message if the file does not exist.
2. For sequential files a **buffer** is established in memory. A buffer is simply an area of main storage. As the program instructs Visual Basic to write data on the disk, the data are actually placed in the buffer. When the buffer is filled, the data are physically written to the disk. The size of the buffer for a random file is the number specified in the `Len` = clause of the `Open` statement.
3. A **file pointer** is created and set to the beginning of the file for all modes except Append, in which it is set to the end of the file. The pointer is always updated to indicate the current location in the file.
4. The file is given a **file number** for future reference. Each file used in a project must be assigned a unique number; however, the numbers need not begin with 1. After a file is closed, the number may be reused for a different file.

The Close Statement—General Form

```
Close [#filenumber...]
```

The Close Statement—Examples

```
Close #1
Close #1, #2
Close
```

The `Close` statement terminates processing of a disk file. When used without a file number, all open files are closed. The `Close` statement performs many housekeeping tasks:

1. Physically writes the last partially filled buffer on the disk (sequential files only). The `Write` statement places data in the buffer, and the data are written to the disk when the buffer is filled. Generally, the buffer will contain data when the project terminates. Those data must be written to the disk.
2. Writes an end-of-file mark (**EOF**) at the end of the file.
3. Releases the buffer.
4. Releases the file number.

Note: Executing an `End` statement will automatically close all open files, but you should not rely on this technique. A good rule is to always explicitly `Close` every file that has been opened in the project.

The FreeFile Function

When you open a file, you must assign a file number to each file. For a small project with one or two data files, most programmers assign #1 and #2. But in a larger project, selecting a file number can be a problem. If your code will be part of a larger project with code from other programmers and other libraries, you must make sure to avoid any conflicting file numbers. To solve this problem, you can allow the system to assign the next available file number. Use the `FreeFile` function to assign the next available file number to your file, and you will never have conflicts.

```
Dim iFileNumber As Integer
iFileNumber = FreeFile 'Get next available file number
Open "FILE.DAT" For Output As #iFileNumber
```

Viewing the Data in a File

When you wish to look at the data in your file, use the Notepad or Wordpad application available in Windows Accessories (or any other text editor). Sequential files appear as text, with commas separating the fields. When viewing random data files, you may notice some strange characters appearing in your file; these represent numeric fields. Numeric data types such as integer, single, and currency are stored in 2 or 4 bytes that can be reread by a project but look cryptic when displayed by a text editor. When you finish viewing your data file, make sure to exit without saving.

Sequential File Organization

Sequential files contain data elements that are stored one after another in sequence. When you read the data from the disk, it must be read in the same sequence in which it was written. In order to read any particular element of data, all preceding elements must first be read.

As data elements are written on disk, string fields are enclosed in quotation marks and the fields are separated by commas. Records are generally terminated by a carriage return character.

A sequential name and address file on the disk might look like this:

"Maxwell", "Harry", "795 W. J. Street", "Ontario", "CA", "91764"<CR>
"Helm", "Jennifer", "201 Cortez Way", "Pomona", "CA", "91766"<CR>
"Colton", "Craig", "1632 Granada Place", "Pomona", "CA", "91766"<EOF>

Writing Data to a Sequential Disk File

Use the **Write # statement** to place data into a sequential data file. Before the Write # statement can be executed, the file must be opened in either Output mode or Append mode. Remember that for Append mode, the file pointer is placed at the end of the file. If there are no records, the beginning of the file *is* the end of the file. In Output mode, the pointer is placed at the beginning of the file. Use Output mode when you wish to create a new file or write over old data.

The list of fields to write may be string expressions, numeric expressions, or both and may be separated by commas or semicolons.

The Write Statement—General Form

```
Write #FileNumber, ListOfFields
```

The Write Statement—Examples

```
Write #1, txtAccount.Text, txtDescription.Text, txtPrice.Text
Write #2, stAccount
Write #iFileNum, miCount; miQuantity; mcTotal
```

The Write # statement outputs data fields to the disk. As the elements are written on disk, commas are written between elements, string data are enclosed in quotation marks, and a carriage return and a line feed are inserted after the last element.

Creating a Sequential Data File

Sequential files are most commonly used to store small quantities of data that will rarely change. A common use of the sequential file is to store the information from a list box from one run to the next. In Chapter 7 your project added, removed, and cleared items from a list. These changes were not saved, so on the next execution of the project, the list reverted to its original contents stored in the List property of the control. The following save procedure writes the contents of a list box to a sequential file:

```
Private Sub mnuFileSave_Click()
    'Save the list box contents to a sequential file
    Dim iIndex   As Integer
    Dim iMaximum As Integer

    Open "Coffee.Dat" For Output As #1
    iMaximum = cboCoffee.ListCount - 1
    For iIndex = 0 To iMaximum
        Write #1, cboCoffee.List(iIndex)
    Next iIndex
    Close
End Sub
```

After execution of this procedure, the Coffee.Dat file on disk will hold the elements from the list box. VB automatically writes a carriage return at the end of each **Write** # statement and an EOF mark (end-of-file) at the end of the file.

Disk file contents

"Chocolate Almond"<CR>"Espresso Roast"<CR>
   "Jamaica Blue Mtn."<CR>"Kona Blend"<CR> "Vanilla Nut"<EOF>

Reading the Data in a Sequential File

When you want to read a sequential file from the disk, you must open it for input. A successful Open sets the file pointer to the beginning of the file. After you have opened the file in Input mode, you can read the records using the **Input** # **statement**. One word of warning: Recall that if you open a file for input and it does not exist, a run-time error occurs and the program terminates. Later in this chapter you will learn to check for errors and avoid the error message.

The Input # Statement—General Form

```
Input #FileNumber, ListOfFields
```

The Input # Statement—Examples

```
Input #1, lblName.Caption, lblStreet.Caption, lblCity.Caption, lblZipCode.Caption
Input #2, stAccount
Input #iFileNum, iSavedCount, iSavedQuantity, cSavedTotal
```

The FileNumber named on the **Input** # **statement** must be the number of a previously opened data file. The fields named should be separated by commas. It doesn't matter what variable names were used when the data were written to the disk. When the data elements are read from the disk, they may be called by the same variable names or by completely different ones.

If you plan to load a list box from the data stored in a sequential file, the Open in the Form_Load must be followed by a loop that adds the data to the list. The loop will terminate when the end-of-file marker is read.

Finding the End of a Data File

When reading data from the disk, you must know when to stop. Recall that closing the file created an EOF mark. You can read until the EOF mark has been reached. (Attempting to read past the EOF mark causes a run-time error.)

The EOF(N) Function—General Form

```
EOF(FileNumber)
```

The EOF(n) function returns True when the EOF mark is read on the last good record. You can test for EOF using an If statement, but a better solution is to use a loop that continues until the condition is True. This example uses a Do/Loop:

```
Do Until EOF(1)                          'Continue processing until EOF condition is True
    Input #1, stCoffeeFlavor             'Read a record from the data file
    cboCoffee.AddItem stCoffeeFlavor     'Assign the variables to the list boxes
Loop
```

Feedback 9.1

1. Write the Visual Basic statements to
   (a) Open a sequential file called Vendor.dat for Output.
   (b) Write the items in the lstVendor list box to the Vendor.dat file.
   (c) Close the Vendor.dat file.
   (d) Open the Vendor.dat file so it can be used to read the records.
   (e) Read the records from the disk file into a list box.
2. What function is used to find the end of the file?

Trapping Program Errors

You have already learned to use If statements to test field values and shield the user from nasty run-time errors. When you start coding for data files, you will find that some problems cannot be avoided but must be anticipated. One such case is opening a data file for input when the file does not exist. It may be that the user has not inserted the proper disk containing the file or has selected an incorrect option.

When a run-time error occurs, Visual Basic generates an error number and checks it against a table of error codes. You can intercept the error number and take action without terminating the project. The statements used in this **error-trapping** process are the **On Error statement** and the Err object.

For you to trap errors, you must:

1. Turn on the error-handling feature using the **On Error statement**.
2. Create error-handling code routines, which are set off from your other code with line labels.
3. Determine how and where the program is to continue after the error is taken care of.

The On Error Statement

You must place an `On Error` statement at the beginning of any procedure where errors might occur, such as before opening a sequential file for input. The following procedure has minimal error trapping. The individual statements and options will be explained in the sections that follow.

```
Private Sub Form_Load()
    'Open the file

    On Error Go To HandleErrors         'Turn on error trapping
    Open "A:\datafile.txt" For Input As #1

Form_Load_Exit:
    Exit Sub

HandleErrors:                            'Error-handling routine
    'Code here to determine cause of error and display message
    Resume
End Sub
```

You may not want to add error-handling statements until you have tested and debugged your project (assuming the possibility that your projects don't always run perfectly the first time you test them). You want your error-handling code to trap user errors, not any programming errors. You may want to include the error-handling statements but remark them out while debugging. An alternative is to set the environment to disable error handlers while you complete your normal debugging. Choose *Options* on the *Tools* menu. On the *General* tab select *Break on All Errors* and then click OK.

Although there are three forms of the `On Error` statement, you will want to use form 1 and form 3 in most of your work. Form 1 turns on error trapping, and form 3 turns it off. Anytime error trapping is turned off, the project is subject to terminating with an `Error` dialog box.

The On Error Statement—General Form 1

```
On Error Go To LineLabel
```

The `On Error Go To` specifies the label of the line where your error-handling code begins. A **line label** is a name (following identifier naming conventions) on a line by itself and followed by a colon. The error-handling code must be in the same procedure as the `On Error` statement.

The On Error Statement—General Form 2

```
On Error Resume Next
```

Using the `Resume Next` option of error handling causes execution to skip the line that generated the error and continue execution with the following line of code.

The On Error Statement—General Form 3

```
On Error Go To 0
```

The `Go To 0` option of the `On Error` turns off error handling. Any error that occurs after this statement executes will cause a run-time error.

The Err Object

The **Err object** holds information about an error that has occurred. You can check the properties of the Err object to determine the error number and a description of the error. The name of the object or application that caused the error is stored in the **Source property**. The **Number property** contains the error number (ranging from 0 to 65,535), which is described in the **Description property**.

You don't need to define or include the Err object. It has global scope and is automatically a part of your project, similar to the Printer object.

If you transfer execution of your project to another procedure or execute a `Resume` statement, the properties of the Err object are cleared. If you will need these values for further processing, make sure to assign them to variables before performing any action that causes them to clear.

The Err.Number Property

The following table includes a partial list of errors. The complete list of errors may be found in VB Help under the heading *Trappable Errors.*

Err. Number	Err. Description
7	Out of memory
9	Subscript out of range
11	Division by zero
13	Type mismatch
52	Bad file name or number
53	File not found
54	Bad file mode
58	File already exists
61	Disk full
67	Too many files
68	Device unavailable
70	Permission denied
71	Disk not ready
75	Path/file access error
76	Path not found
482	Printer error

Raising Error Conditions

You can use the **Raise** method to set the error code, effectively "turning on" an error, or making it occur. This may be necessary when an error that occurs is not among those that you anticipated and coded for; you may want to turn on the error so that the system handles the error and displays a dialog box for the user.

```
Err.Raise Number:=71
Err.Raise Err
```

The full **Raise** method allows several arguments—only the error number is required.

The Raise Method—General Form

```
Object.Raise Number:=NumericValue
Err.Raise Err                    'Raise the previous unhandled error
```

The numeric value that you assign may be a constant, a named constant, or a variable.

The Raise Method—Examples

```
Err.Raise  Number:=76
Err.Raise  Number:=iPATH_NOT_FOUND
```

Coding Error-Handling Routines

The code that you use to handle errors begins with a line label. Assuming that you have used the statement:

```
On Error Go To HandleErrors
```

your error-handling code begins with the line label:

```
HandleErrors:
```

A line label follows the rules for naming identifiers and is followed by a colon. It must appear on a line by itself and will begin in column 1. If you attempt to insert spaces or a tab before the line label, they are deleted by the editor.

```
HandleErrors:
    'Check to make sure the user put a disk in the drive
    Dim stMsg        As String
    Dim iResponse    As Integer
    Const iERR_NODISK As Integer = 71
    stMsg = "Make sure there is a disk in the drive"

    If Err.Number = iERR_NODISK Then            'Check for Err 71
        iResponse = MsgBox(stMsg, vbOKCancel)   'Returns button pressed
        If iResponse = vbOK Then                'OK button pressed
            Resume                              'Try again
        Else
            mnuFileExit_Click                   'Exit the project
        End If
    Else                                        'Any other error
        Err.Raise Err                           'Cancel with error message
    End If
```

The previous example includes a routine that continues execution if the error is solved and also handles the situation for any unsolved errors.

Using Select Case to Check for Errors

You will probably find the **Select Case** statement very handy when you have a series of errors to check.

```
Select Case Err.Number
    Case 53                    'File not found
        'Code to handle File not found error
    Case 71                    'Disk not ready
        'Code to handle Disk not ready error
    Case 76                    'Path not found
        'Code to handle Path not found error
    Case Else                  'All other errors
        Err.Raise Err          'Make the error re-appear
End Select
Resume
```

The Resume Statement

When you have resolved the problem causing an error, your program should continue execution, if possible. This is accomplished with the **Resume statement.** You can choose to continue with the statement that caused the error, with the statement following the one causing the error, or at a specified location in the code.

The Resume Statement—General Form 1

```
Resume
```

If you use the `Resume` statement in the procedure that originally generated the error, execution of the project continues with the line of code that caused the error to occur. If the error-handling routine calls a different procedure that contains a `Resume`, execution continues with the statement that called the second procedure.

The Resume Statement—General Form 2

```
Resume Next
```

Using the `Next` option of `Resume` continues execution with the statement immediately following the line that caused the error (assuming that the `Resume Next` appears in the same procedure as the line of code causing the error). Similar to form 1, if you call another procedure from the error-handling routine, `Resume Next` continues execution at the line following the call.

The Resume Statement—General Form 3

```
Resume LineLabel
```

Execution continues at the line label, which *must be in the same procedure* as the `Resume`.

Tip

Make sure that you cannot reach a Resume statement without an error occurring. This condition causes an error that generates the message *Resume without an Error.*

Handling Errors

Your error-handling routine should do *something* to handle each error:

- If you identify the error type and the user can correct the problem (such as insert the correct diskette in the drive), use `Resume`, which will reexecute the statement that caused the error. If another error occurs, it will return to the error handler.

- If you identify the error type and execution can proceed without the error-causing statement, use `Resume Next`.

- If you prefer to check in-line for a particular type of error (following the `Open`, for example), use `Resume Next`.

- If the error number is unexpected or unidentified, raise the error again so that Visual Basic will handle it. The system error message will display for the user.

- If you want to exit the current procedure and continue project execution, use `Resume LineLabel`. Make sure to code a line label before your `Exit Sub` statement. For an example, see the following section describing the `Exit Sub` statement.

- If you want to end your project execution without displaying the system error message, call your exit procedure code (e.g., mnuFileExit_Click or cmdExit_Click).

- If you want to turn off error trapping, use `On Error Go To 0`. (Any further error will cause a run-time error and display the system error message to the user.)

The Exit Function and Exit Sub Statements

The statements in your procedure execute sequentially. In order to include an error-handling routine that will not execute accidentally (when no error occurs), you must exit the procedure before the line label. Precede the error-handling line label with an **Exit Sub** or **Exit Function statement** (depending on whether the code is in a sub procedure or a function procedure). The `Exit Sub` or `Exit Function` causes execution to exit the procedure immediately.

You can simplify your error-handling code if you adopt the following pattern for any procedure with error trapping:

1. Include an `On Error` statement at the top of any procedure that might require error handling.
2. Code a line label just before the `Exit Sub` statement. Name the line label the same as the procedure name, plus an underscore and Exit. Example: mnuFileSave_Click_Exit.
3. After the `Exit Sub` statement, code your error-handling routine.

```
Private Sub Form_Load()
    'Template for procedure that includes error handling

    On Error Go To HandleErrors         'Turn on error trapping
    Open "A:\Filename.txt" For Input As #1

Form_Load_Exit:
    Exit Sub

HandleErrors:                               'Error-handling routine
    'Code here to determine cause of error and display message

    Select Case Err.Number
        Case n
            'Code to handle error
        Case n
            'Code to handle error
        Case Else
            'Code to handle any other errors
    End Select
    Resume
End Sub
```

Here is an error-handling sub procedure to handle any errors that occur when opening a sequential file for input.

```
Private Sub Form_Load()
    'Load the Coffee list
    Dim stCoffee As String

    On Error GoTo HandleErrors
    Open "Coffee.Dat" For Input As #1
    Do Until EOF(1)
      Input #1, stCoffee
      cboCoffee.AddItem stCoffee
    Loop
    Close #1

Form_Load_Exit:
    Exit Sub

HandleErrors:
    Dim iResponse As Integer
```

```
      Select Case Err.Number
         Case 53, 76                    'File or path not found
               iResponse = MsgBox("Create a new file?", _
                    vbYesNo + vbQuestion, "File not Found")
               If iResponse = vbYes Then
                     Resume Form_Load_Exit
               Else
                     mnuFileExit_Click
               End If
         Case 71                        'Disk not ready
               iResponse = MsgBox("Disk not ready. Retry?", _
                    vbRetryCancel + vbQuestion, "Disk Error")
               If iResponse = vbRetry Then
                     Resume                      'Try again
               Else
                     mnuFileExit_Click           'Exit project
               End If
         Case Else                     'All other errors should cancel execution
               Err.Raise Err
      End Select
      Resume
End Sub
```

Feedback 9.2

What is the purpose of the following statements?

1. `On Error Go To 0`
2. `On Error Go To WhatToDo`
3. `Err.Raise Number:=53`
4. `Resume`
5. `Resume Next`

Sequential File Programming Example

This programming example is based on the hands-on example at the end of Chapter 7, which contains a dropdown combo box with the flavors of coffee (Figure 9.2). The user can add new flavors to the list, remove items from the list, or clear the list. However, in Chapter 7 those changes were not saved from one program run to the next. If you wish to allow the user to update the list of flavors, the data should be stored in a data file. For each program run, the list will be loaded from the data file during the Form_Load procedure of the startup form. If the flavors file does not yet exist, the program skips over loading the combo box to allow the user to add coffee flavors and create the file.

Figure 9.2

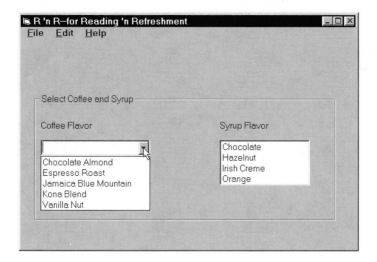

The dropdown combo box from Chapter 7. Users can add new flavors, delete flavors, and clear the list.

The user can choose to save the coffee list into a disk file by selecting a menu choice. Also, when the *Exit* menu choice is selected, if any changes have been made to the list, the project prompts the user to save the file. A Boolean variable is used to determine if any changes have been made since the file was last saved.

Notice that this example is only a partial program, showing the changes made to the hands-on example program from Chapter 7. Only a few procedures are changed.

```
'Module:        frmFlavors
'Programmer:    A. Millspaugh
'Date:          August 1997
'Description:   Print the selected flavor of coffee and syrup
'               or print a list of all of the coffee flavors.
'Folder:        Ch0901

Option Explicit
Dim mbUnsavedChange As Boolean

Private Sub cmdAddCoffee_Click()
    'Add a new coffee flavor to the coffee list

    If cboCoffee.Text <> "" Then
        With cboCoffee
            .AddItem cboCoffee.Text
            .Text = ""
        End With
        mbUnsavedChange = True
    Else
        MsgBox "Enter a coffee name to add", vbExclamation, "Missing data"
    End If
    cboCoffee.SetFocus
End Sub
```

```
Private Sub Form_Load()
    'Load the coffee list
    Dim stCoffee As String

    On Error GoTo HandleErrors
    Open "Coffee.Dat" For Input As #1
    Do Until EOF(1)
      Input #1, stCoffee
      cboCoffee.AddItem stCoffee
    Loop
    Close #1

Form_Load_Exit:
    Exit Sub

HandleErrors:
    Dim iResponse As Integer

    Select Case Err.Number
        Case 53, 76                     'File or path not found
            iResponse = MsgBox("Create a new file?", _
                vbYesNo + vbQuestion, "File not Found")
        If iResponse = vbYes Then
            Resume Form_Load_Exit       'Exit the procedure
        Else
            mnuFileExit_Click           'Exit the project
        End If
        Case 71                         'Disk not ready
            iResponse = MsgBox("Disk not ready. Retry?", _
                vbRetryCancel + vbQuestion, "Disk Error")
        If iResponse = vbRetry Then
            Resume                      'Try again
        Else
            mnuFileExit_Click           'Exit project
        End If
        Case Else               'All other errors should cancel execution
            Err.Raise Err
    End Select
End Sub

Private Sub mnuEditClear_Click()
    'Clear the coffee list
    Dim iResponse As Integer

    iResponse = MsgBox("Clear the coffee flavor list?", _
        vbYesNo + vbQuestion, "Clear coffee list")
    If iResponse = vbYes Then
        cboCoffee.Clear
        mbUnsavedChange = True
    End If
End Sub
```

```
Private Sub mnuEditRemove_Click()
    'Remove the selected coffee from list

    If cboCoffee.ListIndex <> -1 Then
        cboCoffee.RemoveItem cboCoffee.ListIndex
        mbUnsavedChange = True
    Else
        MsgBox "First select the coffee to remove", vbInformation, _
        "No selection made"
    End If
End Sub
```

```
Private Sub mnuFileSave_Click()
    'Save the list box contents to a sequential file
    Dim iIndex   As Integer
    Dim iMaximum As Integer

    Open "Coffee.Dat" For Output As #1
    iMaximum = cboCoffee.ListCount - 1
    For iIndex = 0 To iMaximum
        Write #1, cboCoffee.List(iIndex)
    Next iIndex
    Close #1
    mbUnsavedChange = False
End Sub
```

```
Private Sub mnuFileExit_Click()
    'Terminate the project
    Dim iResponse As Integer

    If mbUnsavedChange = True Then
        iResponse = MsgBox("Coffee list has changed. Save the list?", _
            vbYesNo + vbQuestion, "Coffee List Changed")
        If iResponse = vbYes Then
            mnuFileSave_Click
        End If
    End If
    End
End Sub
```

The previous procedures are a partial program listing that demonstrate loading a combo box from a sequential file. Notice that the error handling in the Form_Load procedure traps for any error on the Open. If there is no error, the combo box is loaded with a Do/Loop.

If error number 53 or 76 occurs (File not found or Path not found), a message box asks the user whether or not to create the file. An answer of No terminates the program, but a Yes continues execution without attempting the read.

The user can enter new flavors during program execution, remove flavors, or clear the list. If any changes are made to the list, the Boolean variable mbUnsavedChange is set to True. When the project exits, if mbUnsaved-Change is True, the user is prompted to save the list.

Random Data Files

The primary difference between sequential files and random files is that you may read and write the data in any order in a **random file**. With sequential files, you must always start at the beginning of the file and proceed in order through the file. Random files offer greater speed as well as the capability for random access.

You can visualize random files as a table in which each entry may be referenced by its relative position. Each entry in a file is one record, which is referred to by its record number. Any record in the file may be read or written without accessing the preceding records. Figure 9.3 illustrates the table concept of random files.

All records in a random file are exactly the same size. The fields within the record are fixed in length and position. That is, if the name takes the first 30 bytes (characters) in one record, every record will allocate the first 30 bytes for the name. This scheme is a departure from sequential files with their variable length fields and records. Before reading or writing a random file, the record structure or layout must be defined. The `Type/End Type` statements set up record structures. The only modification you will need is to use fixed-length strings.

Fixed-Length Strings

String variables may be variable length or fixed length. Until this point, all strings have been variable length. But for random files you will need to specify fixed-length strings. You can define a specific number of characters for elements of user-defined data types and dimension fixed-length single variables and arrays.

If the value you store in a field is less than its specified length, the extra positions are filled with spaces. If you assign a value that is longer than the fixed length, the extra characters are truncated (chopped off) when the value is stored in the fixed-length string.

To specify the string length, add an asterisk (*) followed by the size to the string declaration.

```
Dim  stName            As  String  *  30


Type  FullName
     stLastName        As  String  *  20
     stFirstName       As  String  *  20
End  Type
```

Defining a Record for a Random File

To define a record for a random file, first set up its structure with a **Type** statement. Then dimension a record variable of the data type.

Note: You can code **Type** statements in a standard code module or the General Declarations section of a form module. In a form module you must specify **Private**.

```
Private  Type  MemberStructure
     stLastName        As  String  *  20
     stFirstName       As  String  *  20
     stPhone           As  String  *  12
End  Type
Dim  mMemberRecord     As  MemberStructure
```

Opening a Random File

The **Open** statement for a random file is the same as for sequential files, using a file mode of Random. This mode allows you to input and output to the same file without closing and reopening it.

```
Open  "b:\Data\Names.txt"  For  Random  As  #1  Len  =  52
Open  "A:MEMBERS.DAT"  For  Random  As  #2  Len  =  Len(mMemberRecord)
```

For a random file, the **Len** (length) entry refers to the length of a single record. In the second example, the second **Len** is actually the **Length** function that returns the size in bytes of the item enclosed in parentheses. The item in parentheses is the name used for the record variable you declared.

Reading and Writing a Random File

The input/output statements that you will be using for a random file differ from those used for sequential files. When accessing a random file, the data are handled a record at a time. The statements used are **Get** and **Put**, which include the record position in the file and the name of the variable defined as the record.

You can **Get** and **Put** records in a random file in any order you choose. That is, you may first write record #5, then #1, then #20, or any other order. When record #5 is written in the file, VB skips enough space for four records and writes in the fifth physical location. Record positions 1 to 4 are skipped until such time as records are written in those locations. See the diagram in Figure 9.4.

	Last Name Field	First Name Field	Phone Number Field
(1)			
(2)			
(3)			
(4)			
(5)				← Write record #5
(6)			
(7)			
(8)			
....			

Writing record # 5. The record is written into the fifth location in the file.

The record numbers start at record 1. This rule will probably feel strange to you, since you are used to arrays and lists beginning with an index of 0. If you attempt to Get or Put a record number of zero, you receive a *Bad Record Number* error.

The Get Statement—General Form

```
Get [#]FileNumber, [RecordNumber], RecordName
```

The Get Statement—Examples

```
Get #2, RecNumber, mMemberRecord
Get #1, iRecordNumber, mInventoryRecord(iRecordNumber)
Get #2, iCustomerNumber, gCustomerRecord(iIndex)
Get #3, 4, AccountRecord
Get #1,, mMemberRecord
```

The **Get statement** reads data from a random disk file and places the data into the record-name variable. This variable should be one declared with a user-defined data type. If the variable is an array, the appropriate subscript number must be included.

When you omit the record number, the *next* record (after the last Get or Put that was processed) is read from the file. Either a variable or a constant may be used for the record number. Generally you will want to use a variable to allow selection of any record in the file.

The Put Statement—General Form

```
Put [#]FileNumber, [RecordNumber], RecordName
```

The Put Statement—Examples

```
Put  #2,  RecNumber,  mMemberRecord
Put  #1,  iRecordNumber,  mInventoryRecord(iRecordNumber)
Put  #2,  iCustomerNumber,  gCustomerRecord(iIndex)
Put  #3,  4,  AccountRecord
Put  #1,  ,  mMemberRecord
```

The **Put statement** takes the contents of the specified record and writes it on the disk. The record number determines the relative location within the file for the record. If the record number is omitted, the record will be placed in the *next* location from the last Get or Put. Note that the next location is likely not the end of the file. Be careful not to write over other data by accident. If you wish to add a record to the end of the file, add 1 to the current number of records and Put the record at that position.

Accessing Fields in a Random Record

The Get and Put statements always read or write an entire record. In order to access the individual fields within the record, the elements must be referenced by the record name, a period, and the element name that is defined with the Type statement.

```
Get  #1,  iRecordNumber,  mMemberRecord
lstName.AddItem  mMemberRecord.LastName
```

Finding the End of a Random File

To find the end of a random file, use the **LOF function** (length of file) rather than the EOF function. The LOF function returns the size of the file in bytes. Although EOF can sometimes be used, problems can occur if records are written randomly and any gaps exist in the file.

The FileNumber entry is the file number from a currently open file.

To determine the highest record number in the file, divide the return value of the LOF function by the size of one record (the name dimensioned using the user-defined data type).

The LOF Function—General Form

```
LOF(FileNumber)
```

The LOF Function—Example

```
iNumberRecords  =  LOF(1)  /  Len(mMemberRecord)
```

VISUAL BASIC Data Files

You can use the LOF function to find out how may records are in the file prior to using a For/Next loop that might load the data into a table or list.

```
'Read a random file and store member names into a list box
Dim iNumberRecords As Integer
Dim iIndex As Integer 'Index for the loop

iNumberRecords = LOF(1) / Len(mMemberRecord)
For iIndex = 1 To iNumberRecords
    Get #1, iIndex, mMemberRecord
    lstNames.AddItem mMemberRecord.LastName
Next iIndex
```

When you are adding to the end of the file, you can use a calculation to find the next record number.

```
iRecordNumber = LOF(1) / Len(mMemberRecord) + 1
Put #1, iRecordNumber, mMemberRecord
```

The Seek Function

At times you may need to determine the position of the file pointer within the file. The **Seek function** returns the current location of the pointer. For a sequential file, the current byte number is returned. For a random file, Seek returns the position (record number) of the *next* record in the file.

The Seek Function—General Form

```
Seek(FileNumber)
```

FileNumber is the file number of a currently open file.

The Seek Function—Example

```
iNextRecord = Seek(1)
```

Using a List Box to Store a Key Field

When you Get or Put a record in a random file, you need to know the record number. However, keeping track of record numbers is inconvenient. Who wants to remember record numbers?

A slick visual solution to the record number problem is to display the name or identifying information in a list box. The list box can have its Sorted property set to True, which makes it easy for the user to find the desired record. Each name's corresponding ItemData property can hold the record number. When the user selects a record from the list, you can use the number stored in ItemData to retrieve the correct record. Figure 9.5 illustrates using a list box for record selection.

F i g u r e   9 . 5

	List box List property	ItemData property
User selects this name from list.	Brooks, Barbara	5
	Chen, Diana	3
	Dunning, Daniel	1
	Khan, Brad	6
	Lester, Les	2
	Nguyen, Ahn	4
	Potter, Pete	8
	Stevens, Roger	7

The list box holds customer names in the List property and corresponding record numbers in the ItemData property.

Program reads record 6 from file.

The following code segment concatenates a first and last name, adds to the list box, and then assigns the record number to the ItemData property.

```
Public Sub AddtoList(iIndex As Integer)
    'Add to the list box and the ItemData
    Dim StName As String

    stName = Trim(gEmployee.stLastName) & ", " & gEmployee.stFirstName
    lstEmployee.AddItem stName
    lstEmployee.ItemData(lstEmployee.NewIndex) = iIndex
End Sub
```

When concatenating fixed-length strings the entire string length, including the spaces, is used. You can use a trim function to avoid printing the extra spaces.

Trimming Extra Blanks from Strings

The **Trim**, **LTrim**, and **RTrim functions** remove extra blank characters in a string. When you have fixed-length strings, such as the fields in a random file, the strings are likely padded with extra spaces. The LTrim function removes extra spaces at the left end of the string; RTrim removes extra spaces on the right, and Trim removes extra spaces from both the left and right ends of the string.

The Trim, LTrim, and RTrim Functions—General Form

```
Trim(StringExpression)
LTrim(StringExpression)
RTrim(StringExpression)
```

The Trim, LTrim, and RTrim functions return a string with the extra spaces removed.

The Trim, LTrim, and RTrim Functions—Examples

```
Trim(" Harry  Rabbit ")     'Returns "Harry  Rabbit"
LTrim(" Harry  Rabbit ")     'Returns "Harry  Rabbit "
RTrim(" Harry  Rabbit ")     'Returns " Harry  Rabbit"
```

Navigating through a Random File

When displaying information from a file, you should allow your user to move through the records within the file. Common options for navigation are First, Last, Previous, and Next. The First button or command displays the first record from the file, and Last displays the last record. Previous and Next move one record in the desired direction.

Since we are using a sorted list box to control the sequence of the records, the option for Next takes you to the data for the next item in the list box. This task is easy to accomplish by using the properties of the list box. ListIndex indicates the currently selected record. You can move to the next or previous record by adding or subtracting 1 to/from the ListIndex property. Make sure that the result of the calculation will be a valid record number, not less than one and not exceeding the record count. Figure 9.6 illustrates using the list box for navigation.

Figure 9.6

	ListIndex property	List box List property	ItemData property
	(0)	Brooks, Barbara	5
	(1)	Chen, Diana	3
	(2)	Dunning, Daniel	1
	(3)	Khan, Brad	6
	(4)	Lester, Les	2
	(5)	Nguyen, Ahn	4
	(6)	Potter, Pete	8
	(7)	Stevens, Roger	7

When record 6 displays, the ListIndex property is 3.

The list box ItemData property holds the record number. To move through the file sequentially, use the ListIndex property to determine the next customer and then use the ItemData property to read the correct record.

Add 1 to ListIndex, then read record 2.

Coding the Navigation Buttons

```
Private Sub cmdPrevious_Click()
    'Display the previous record from sorted list

    If frmMain!lstEmployee.ListIndex < 1 Then
        cmdLast_Click          'Go to end of file when at beginning
    Else
        'Subtract one from the list box ListIndex
        frmMain!lstEmployee.ListIndex = frmMain!lstEmployee.ListIndex - 1
        ReadRecord             'Read the new record based on the ItemData property
    End If
End Sub
```

```
Private Sub cmdNext_Click()
    'Display the next record from sorted list

    If frmMain!lstEmployee.ListIndex < frmMain!lstEmployee.ListCount - 1 Then
        'Add one to the list box ListIndex
        frmMain!lstEmployee.ListIndex = frmMain!lstEmployee.ListIndex + 1
        ReadRecord             'Read the new record based on the ItemData property
    Else
        cmdFirst_Click         'Go to beginning of file when at end
    End If
End Sub
```

You can find the first and last record using list box properties. Remember that the ListIndex of the first record is 0. The ListIndex of the last record is one less than the ListCount.

```
Private Sub cmdFirst_Click()
    'Display the first record from sorted list

    frmMain!lstEmployee.ListIndex = 0
    ReadRecord                'Read the new record, based on the ItemData property
End Sub
```

```
Private Sub cmdLast_Click()
    'Display the last record from sorted list

    frmMain!lstEmployee.ListIndex = frmMain!lstEmployee.ListCount - 1
    ReadRecord                'Read the new record, based on the ItemData property
End Sub
```

Navigation during an Add or Delete

If the user is allowed to click on the navigation button when an Add or Delete
operation is in progress, a problem can arise. You can avoid this problem by
disabling the navigation buttons during an Add or Delete. You will need to
enable the buttons during an Update or Browse operation.

```
Private Sub DisableNavigation()
    'Disable the navigation commands

    cmdLast.Enabled = False
    cmdFirst.Enabled = False
    cmdPrevious.Enabled = False
    cmdNext.Enabled = False
End Sub
```

```
Private Sub EnableNavigation()
    'Enable the navigation commands

    cmdLast.Enabled = True
    cmdFirst.Enabled = True
    cmdPrevious.Enabled = True
    cmdNext.Enabled = True
End Sub
```

Locking the Contents of Controls

Another technique for keeping the user out of trouble is to lock text boxes
when you don't want to allow any changes. Although you can set the Enable
property of a text box to False, the contents will display as grayed. A better
approach is often to set its Locked property to True. If you lock text boxes,
make sure to unlock them again when you *do* want to allow changes.

```
txtLastName.Locked = True
txtFirstName.Locked = True
txtStreet.Locked = True
```

Updating a Random File

A file update generally consists of routines to add records, update records, delete records, and browse through records. The procedures for these options might be selected from a command button or a menu command.

Each routine must display the fields from the file, so we will use one form and refer to it as the *data form*. This form will contain text boxes for each of the fields of a record along with the appropriate labels. (Figure 9.7 shows the data form for the random file update in the hands-on programming example.)

F i g u r e   9 . 7

The data entry form for the hands-on programming example.

Adding and Editing Records

When the user wants to add a record, all of the text boxes must be cleared. After the data are entered, the record will be written to the disk file. The record will be written at the end of the file. The list box must be updated and the record number stored in the ItemData property for the list. It is a good idea to set the current ListIndex to the new record.

```
miIndex = LOF(1) / Len(gEmployee) + 1    'Find next available record number
gEmployee.stDeleted = "N"
SaveData                                 'Send text box fields to record variables
WriteRecord                              'Write record variable in file
frmMain.AddtoList (miIndex)              'Add entry to list box on main form
frmMain!lstEmployee.ListIndex = frmMain.lstEmployee.NewIndex   'Set ListIndex
```

An alternative approach would be to search through the records in the file to find the location of a deleted record. You could add a new record in the location of the deleted record. For this example we will add all new records at the end of the file.

Deleting a Record

You can delete a record from a random file in several ways. A common method is to mark a record in some way to indicate that the record is deleted rather than to actually remove it. If you were to actually remove a record, you would also have to move forward all of the remaining records. That would take time and also change the record numbers. (Often the record number is used as a form of identification.)

One technique is to write some special character in a field of the record to indicate that the record has been deleted. A drawback of this method is that the data in the record cannot be recovered later, if you want to add undelete routines.

Another more popular method is to add a special field to the record description. The field, commonly called a *delete flag* or *delete code*, holds one of two values, such as *Y* and *N*; or *A* for *active* and *D* for *deleted*; or True/False values. We will use this approach.

In the following data type, the field stDeleted indicates whether a record is deleted. A *Y* in stDeleted means that the record is deleted. When a record is added, *N* is placed in the field.

```
Type PersonalInfo
     stLastName   As  String * 15
     stFirstName  As  String * 10
     stStreet     As  String * 20
     stCity       As  String * 15
     stState      As  String * 2
     stZip        As  String * 5
     stPhone      As  String * 15
     stEmail      As  String * 25
     stDeleted    As  String * 1
End Type
Public gEmployee As PersonalInfo
```

To mark a record as deleted, store a *Y* in the stDeleted field.

```
gEmployee.stDeleted = "Y"
```

When records are loaded into the list box, only those without the *Y* will be loaded.

```
If gEmployee.stDeleted <> "Y" Then
    AddtoList (iIndex)
End If
```

Keep the List Box Up-to-Date

Whenever a record is deleted from the file, the list box must also be updated. Use a `RemoveItem` method to delete the reference to the deleted record from the list. The next code segment puts together the steps for deletion.

```
'Set the record number to match the list box ItemData property
miIndex = frmMain!lstEmployee.ItemData(frmMain!lstEmployee.ListIndex)
gEmployee.stDeleted = "Y"          'Set the delete field to indicate deleted record
WriteRecord                        'Write the record back into the file
'Remove the current list element from the list box
frmMain!lstEmployee.RemoveItem frmMain!lstEmployee.ListIndex
```

Confirm the Deletion

You may want to verify that the record is really to be deleted. If you do so, make sure to offer a Cancel button.

The Read and Write Procedures

Good programming technique uses a single procedure for reading a file and one for writing to the data file. Write a procedure to write a record and call it from any location that needs a write. Then code a single procedure to read a record and call it as needed. The following code segment writes a record in the file:

```
Private Sub WriteRecord()
    'Write to disk

    Put #1, miIndex, gEmployee
End Sub
```

Notice that for this procedure to work correctly, miIndex must be set to the record number, and gEmployee must have the fields for the record.

The Read procedure is very much the same, but it must find which record to read by checking the selection in the list box. Notice that the ItemData property is used to get the record number, miIndex. After the record is read, the data is displayed.

```
Private Sub ReadRecord()
    'Use ItemData to directly access record in the file

    'Set the record number to the current ItemData
    miIndex = frmMain!lstEmployee.ItemData(frmMain!lstEmployee.ListIndex)
    Get #1, miIndex, gEmployee          'Read the record
    DisplayData                         'Move fields into text boxes to display
End Sub
```

Feedback 9.3

1. Write the `Type` statement called *Inventory*, which contains 30 characters for a description, 5 characters for a part number, a price (currency), and a quantity (integer).
2. Declare a variable called *InventoryRecord* that will use the Inventory data type.
3. Write the statement to open a random file using the disk file Inventory.Dat on the C: drive.
4. Write the statement(s) to find the number of records in the Inventory.Dat file.
5. Write the statement to write one record to the Inventory.Dat file using a record number called *iRecordNumber*.

6. What value is returned by the Seek function if the current record is record # 5?

7. Write the statement to read one record from the Inventory.Dat file.

Your Hands-On Programming Example

The employee file for R 'n R will be maintained using a random file. Create a project with two forms: a main form and a data form.

The main form will have a list box of employee names and command buttons for Add, Delete, Update, and Browse. When the user clicks on one of the command buttons, the data form will display, set for the correct action.

The data form for the file will display the fields in text boxes and provide OK and Cancel buttons for changes to the file. The data form will also include navigation buttons (First, Last, Next, and Previous), which are enabled for the Update and Browse options, but disabled for the Add and Delete options.

The project will use the list box on the main form for navigation. The user selects a record by the employee name, and the correct record is read from the file. The list box ItemData property holds the record number for the random reads. Refer to Figure 9.5 for an illustration of the list box.

Add option

Display the data form with the fields empty. When the user clicks the OK button, save the record in the next-available record position.

Delete option

Display the data form with the selected record displayed. The user can then choose OK to delete the record or to cancel the operation.

Update option

Display the data form with the selected record displayed. The user can then choose OK to save any change or to cancel the operation.

Browse option

Display the data form with the text boxes locked. The user can use the navigation buttons to move through the file, but cannot make any changes.

Planning the Project

Sketch a main form (Figure 9.8*a*) and a data form (Figure 9.8*b*), which your users sign off as meeting their needs.

Figure 9.8

Sketches of the two forms for the hands-on programming example: (a) The main form and (b) the data entry form.

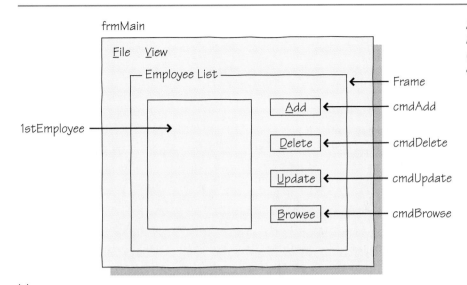

(a)

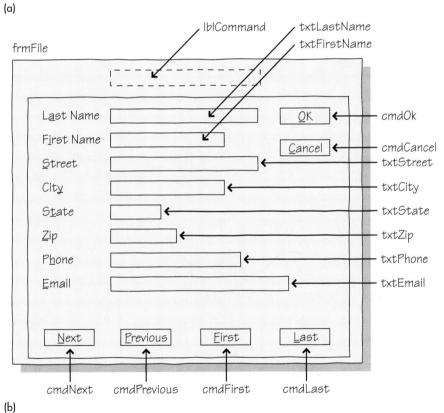

(b)

Plan the Objects and Properties: Main Form

Object	Property	Setting
frmMain	Name	frmMain
	Caption	R 'n R—for Reading 'n Refreshment
Frame1	Name	Frame1
	Caption	Employee List
lstEmployee	Name	lstEmployee
	Sorted	True
cmdAdd	Name	cmdAdd
	Caption	&Add
cmdDelete	Name	cmdDelete
	Caption	&Delete
cmdUpdate	Name	cmdUpdate
	Caption	&Update
cmdBrowse	Name	cmdBrowse
	Caption	&Browse
mnuFile	Name	mnuFile
	Caption	&File
mnuFileExit	Name	mnuFileExit
	Caption	E&xit
mnuView	Name	mnuView
	Caption	&View
mnuViewEmployee	Name	mnuViewEmployee
	Caption	&Employee File

Plan the Event Procedures: Main Form

Procedure	Actions

Form_Load	If file not empty Then
	  Open the file.
	  Load the list box.
	Else
	  Prompt user for new file.
	End If

cmdAdd	Set the Action flag for Add. Display the data form.

(continued)

Procedure	Actions

cmdDelete	If employee selected Then
	   Set the Action flag for Delete.
	   Display the data form.
	Else
	   Display error message.
	End If

cmdUpdate	If employee selected Then
	   Set the Action flag for Update.
	   Display the data form.
	Else
	   Display error message.
	End If

cmdBrowse	Set the Action flag for Browse. Display the data form.
mnuFileExit	Close the file. Terminate the project.
MnuViewEmployee	Set Action flag for Browse. Display the data form.
AddtoList	Concatenate first and last name Add name to list box. Set ItemData to record number.

Plan the Objects and Properties: Data Form

Object	Property	Setting
frmFile	Name	frmFile
	Caption	Employee Information
lblCommand	Name	lblCommand
	Caption	(blank)
Frame1	Caption	Employee List
Label1	Caption	L&ast Name
Label2	Caption	F&irst Name
Label3	Caption	&Street
Label4	Caption	Cit&y
Label5	Caption	S&tate
Label6	Caption	&Zip
Label7	Caption	P&hone
Label8	Caption	&Email
txtLastName	Name	txtLastName
	Text	(blank)

(continued)

Object	Property	Setting
txtFirstName	Name	txtFirstName
	Text	(blank)
txtStreet	Name	txtStreet
	Text	(blank)
txtCity	Name	txtCity
	Text	(blank)
txtState	Name	txtState
	Text	(blank)
txtZip	Name	txtZip
	Text	(blank)
txtPhone	Name	txtPhone
	Text	(blank)
txtEmail	Name	txtEmail
	Text	(blank)
cmdOK	Name	cmdOK
	Caption	&OK
	Default	True
cmdCancel	Name	cmdCancel
	Caption	&Cancel
	Default	True
cmdNext	Name	cmdNext
	Caption	&Next
cmdPrevious	Name	cmdPrevious
	Caption	&Previous
cmdFirst	Name	cmdFirst
	Caption	&First
cmdLast	Name	cmdLast
	Caption	&Last

Plan the Event Procedures: Data Form

Procedure	Actions
Form_Activate	Case Add Set label to Add. Clear text boxes.

(continued)

Procedure	Actions
	Disable navigation buttons.
	Set the focus.
	Case Delete
	Set label to Delete.
	Read a record.
	Disable navigation buttons.
	Lock controls.
	Case Update
	Set label to Update.
	Read a record.
	Enable navigation buttons.
	Unlock controls.
	Case Browse
	Set label to Browse.
	Lock controls.
	Enable navigation buttons.
	cmdFirst_Click.
Write Record	Save to disk.
Read Record	Get record number from ItemData.
	Get record from disk.
	Display data fields.
ClearTextBoxes	Clear the contents of text boxes.
DisableNavigation	Set Enable to False for navigation command buttons.
EnableNavigation	Set Enable to True for navigation command buttons.
DisplayData	Transfer data from record to text boxes.
SaveData	Transfer data from text boxes to record.
LockTheControls	Set Locked to True for the text boxes.
UnlockTheControls	Set Locked to False for the text boxes.
CmdOK	Case Add
	Save record.
	Add to list box.
	Case Delete
	Set Deleted to Y.
	Save record.
	Delete from list box.
	Case Update
	Save record.
	Change list box.
	End Select
	Hide the data form.
cmdCancel	Hide the data form.
cmdNext	If not on last record Then
	Add one to list index.
	Read the record.
	Else
	Go to first record.
	End If

(continued)

Procedure	Actions

cmdPrevious	If on first record Then
	  Go to last record.
	Else
	  Subtract one from list index.
	  Read the record.
	End If

cmdFirst	Set ListIndex to zero. Read the first record.
cmdLast	Set ListIndex to last record. Read the last record.

Write the Project

- Follow the sketches in Figure 9.8 to create the forms. Figure 9.9 shows the completed forms.

Figure   9.9

The two forms for the hands-on programming example: (a) The main form and (b) the data entry form.

(a)

(b)

- Set the properties of each of the objects according to your plan.

- Write the code. Working from the pseudocode, write each event procedure.

- When you complete the code, use a variety of data to thoroughly test the project.

The Project Coding Solution

Standard Code Module

```
'Module        Filetype.bas
'Programmer:   A. Millspaugh
'Date:         Aug 1997
'Description:  Define the record
'Folder:       Ch0902

Option Explicit
Type PersonalInfo
    stLastName    As String * 15
    stFirstName   As String * 10
    stStreet      As String * 20
    stCity        As String * 15
    stState       As String * 2
    stZip         As String * 10
    stPhone       As String * 15
    stEmail       As String * 25
    stDeleted     As String * 1
End Type


Public gEmployee        As PersonalInfo
Public gstFileAction    As String
```

Main Form: frmMain

```
'Form          FrmMain
'Programmer:   A. Millspaugh
'Date:         Aug 1997
'Description:  This project uses a random file to store employee
'              information. It stores employee names in a list box
'              and allows file updating and browsing.
'Folder:       Ch0902

Private Sub cmdAdd_Click()
    'Display a blank form for an add

    gstFileAction = "A"
    frmFile.Show vbModal
End Sub


Private Sub cmdBrowse_Click()
    'Look at the file

    gstFileAction = "B"
    frmFile.Show vbModal
End Sub
```

```
Private Sub cmdDelete_Click()
    'Display and delete the selected item from list

    If lstEmployee.ListIndex <> -1 Then
        gstFileAction = "D"
        frmFile.Show vbModal
    Else
        MsgBox "Select record to Delete", vbOKOnly + vbInformation, "Delete"
    End If
End Sub
```

```
Private Sub cmdUpdate_Click()
    'Display the selected item from list

    If lstEmployee.ListIndex <> -1 Then
        gstFileAction = "U"
        frmFile.Show vbModal
    Else
        MsgBox "Select record to update", _
          vbOKOnly + vbInformation, "Update"
    End If
End Sub
```

```
Private Sub Form_Load()
    'Read the file and store in the sorted list box.
    'Store the random record number into ItemData.

    Dim iIndex    As Integer
    Dim iResponse As Integer

    On Error GoTo HandleErrors
    Open "a:\Employee.Dat" For Random As #1 Len = Len(gEmployee)
    If LOF(1) / Len(gEmployee) > 0 Then    'If file not empty
        For iIndex = 1 To LOF(1) / Len(gEmployee)
            Get #1, iIndex, gEmployee
            If gEmployee.stDeleted <> "Y" Then
                AddtoList (iIndex)
            End If
        Next iIndex
    Else
        iResponse = MsgBox("File is empty. Create new file?", _
            vbYesNo + vbQuestion, "No File")
        If iResponse = vbNo Then
            mnuFileExit_Click    'Exit project
        End If
    End If

Form_Load_Exit:
    Exit Sub
```

```
HandleErrors:
    If Err.Number = 71 Then
        iResponse = MsgBox("No disk. Retry?", _
            vbRetryCancel + vbQuestion, "No Disk in Drive")
        If iResponse = vbRetry Then
            Resume                   'Try again
        Else
            mnuFileExit_Click     'Exit project
        End If
    Else
        On Error GoTo 0          'Turn off error handling
    End If
End Sub
```

```
Private Sub mnuFileExit_Click()
    'Terminate the project

    Close #1
    End
End Sub
```

```
Private Sub mnuViewEmployee_Click()
    'Display the Employee file form

    gstFileAction = "B"          'Browse
    frmFile.Show vbModal
End Sub
```

```
Public Sub AddtoList(iIndex As Integer)
    'Add to the list box and the ItemData
    Dim stName As String

    stName = Trim(gEmployee.stLastName) & ", " & gEmployee.stFirstName
    lstEmployee.AddItem stName
    lstEmployee.ItemData(lstEmployee.NewIndex) = iIndex
End Sub
```

Data Entry Form: frmFile

```
'Form:          frmFile
'Programmer:    A. Millspaugh
'Date:          Aug 1997
'Description:   Obtain and display data for the employee file
'Folder:        Ch0902

Option Explicit
Dim miIndex As Integer
```

```
Private Sub cmdCancel_Click()
    'Return to main form with no action

    frmFile.Hide
End Sub
```

```
Private Sub DisplayData()
    'Transfer from record to text fields

    txtLastName.Text = gEmployee.stLastName
    txtFirstName.Text = gEmployee.stFirstName
    txtStreet.Text = gEmployee.stStreet
    txtCity.Text = gEmployee.stCity
    txtState.Text = gEmployee.stState
    txtZip.Text = gEmployee.stZip
    txtPhone.Text = gEmployee.stPhone
    txtEmail.Text = gEmployee.stEmail
End Sub
```

```
Private Sub SaveData()
    'Transfer from text fields to data record

    gEmployee.stLastName = txtLastName.Text
    gEmployee.stFirstName = txtFirstName.Text
    gEmployee.stStreet = txtStreet.Text
    gEmployee.stCity = txtCity.Text
    gEmployee.stState = txtState.Text
    gEmployee.stZip = txtZip.Text
    gEmployee.stPhone = txtPhone.Text
    gEmployee.stEmail = txtEmail.Text
End Sub
```

```
Private Sub cmdFirst_Click()
    'Display the first record from sorted list

    frmMain!lstEmployee.ListIndex = 0
    ReadRecord
End Sub
```

```
Private Sub cmdLast_Click()
    'Display the last record from sorted list

    frmMain!lstEmployee.ListIndex = frmMain!lstEmployee.ListCount - 1
    ReadRecord
End Sub
```

```
Private Sub cmdNext_Click()
    'Display the next record from sorted list
```

```
        If frmMain!lstEmployee.ListIndex < frmMain!lstEmployee.ListCount - 1 Then
            frmMain!lstEmployee.ListIndex = frmMain!lstEmployee.ListIndex + 1
            ReadRecord
        Else
            cmdFirst_Click
        End If
End Sub
```

```
Private Sub cmdOK_Click()
    'Choose action depending upon the command
    Dim stName As String

    Select Case gstFileAction
    Case "A"
        miIndex = LOF(1) / Len(gEmployee) + 1
        gEmployee.stDeleted = "N"
        SaveData
        WriteRecord
        frmMain.AddtoList (miIndex)
        frmMain!lstEmployee.ListIndex = frmMain!lstEmployee.NewIndex
    Case "D"
        miIndex = frmMain!lstEmployee.ItemData(frmMain!lstEmployee.ListIndex)
        gEmployee.stDeleted = "Y"
        WriteRecord
        frmMain!lstEmployee.RemoveItem frmMain!lstEmployee.ListIndex
    Case "U"
        SaveData
        miIndex = frmMain!lstEmployee.ItemData(frmMain!lstEmployee.ListIndex)
        WriteRecord
        'Change name in list box if needed
        frmMain!lstEmployee.RemoveItem frmMain!lstEmployee.ListIndex
        frmMain.AddtoList (miIndex)
    Case "B"
        UnlockTheControls
    End Select

    'Return to main form
    frmFile.Hide
End Sub
```

```
Private Sub cmdPrevious_Click()
    'Display the previous record from sorted list

    If frmMain!lstEmployee.ListIndex < 1 Then
        cmdLast_Click
    Else
        frmMain!lstEmployee.ListIndex = frmMain!lstEmployee.ListIndex - 1
        ReadRecord
    End If
End Sub
```

```
Private Sub DisableNavigation()
    'Disable the navigation commands

    cmdLast.Enabled = False
    cmdFirst.Enabled = False
    cmdPrevious.Enabled = False
    cmdNext.Enabled = False
End Sub
```

```
Private Sub ReadRecord()
    'Use ItemData to directly access record in the file

    miIndex = frmMain!lstEmployee.ItemData(frmMain!lstEmployee.ListIndex)
    Get #1, miIndex, gEmployee
    DisplayData
End Sub
```

```
Private Sub WriteRecord()
    'Write to disk

    Put #1, miIndex, gEmployee
End Sub
```

```
Private Sub ClearTextBoxes()
    'Clear all of the text boxes

    txtLastName.Text = ""
    txtFirstName.Text = ""
    txtStreet.Text = ""
    txtCity.Text = ""
    txtState.Text = ""
    txtZip.Text = ""
    txtPhone.Text = ""
    txtEmail.Text = ""
End Sub
```

```
Private Sub Form_Activate()
    'Set up the form and set the focus to the name field

    Select Case gstFileAction
        Case "A"
            lblCommand.Caption = "Add a Record"
            ClearTextBoxes
            DisableNavigation
            UnlockTheControls
            txtLastName.SetFocus
        Case "D"
            ReadRecord
            lblCommand.Caption = "Delete this record?"
            DisableNavigation
            LockTheControls
```

```
        Case "U"
            ReadRecord
            lblCommand.Caption = "Update"
            EnableNavigation
            UnlockTheControls
        Case "B"
            lblCommand.Caption = "Browse"
            LockTheControls
            EnableNavigation
            cmdFirst_Click
    End Select
End Sub
```

```
Private Sub LockTheControls()
    'Lock the text boxes so no edits can be made

    txtLastName.Locked = True
    txtFirstName.Locked = True
    txtStreet.Locked = True
    txtCity.Locked = True
    txtState.Locked = True
    txtZip.Locked = True
    txtPhone.Locked = True
    txtEmail.Locked = True
End Sub
```

```
Private Sub UnlockTheControls()
    'Unlock the text boxes

    txtLastName.Locked = False
    txtFirstName.Locked = False
    txtStreet.Locked = False
    txtCity.Locked = False
    txtState.Locked = False
    txtZip.Locked = False
    txtPhone.Locked = False
    txtEmail.Locked = False
End Sub
```

```
Private Sub EnableNavigation()
    'Enable the navigation commands

    cmdLast.Enabled = True
    cmdFirst.Enabled = True
    cmdPrevious.Enabled = True
    cmdNext.Enabled = True
End Sub
```

Programming Hints

The InputBox Function

When you need to request input from the user, you can always use a text box, either on the current form or on a new form. Visual Basic also provides a quick and easy way to pop up a new form that holds a text box, using the `InputBox` function.

The `InputBox` function is similar to `MsgBox`. In the input box you can display a message, called the *prompt*, and allow the user to type input into the text box (Figure 9.10).

Figure   9.10

The InputBox function produces a dialog box with a prompt and a text box for entering program input.

The InputBox Function—General Form

```
VariableName = InputBox("Prompt" [, "Title"] [, Default] [, XPos] [, YPos])
```

The prompt must be enclosed in quotation marks and may include NewLine characters (`vbCrLf`) if you want the prompt to appear on multiple lines. The Title displays in the title bar of the dialog box; if the Title is missing, the project name appears in the title bar. Any value you place in *Default* appears in the text box when it is displayed; otherwise, the text box is empty. (If *Default* is a string, it must be enclosed in quotation marks.) *XPos* and *YPos*, if present, define the measurement in twips for the left edge and top edge of the box.

The InputBox Function—Examples

```
stName = InputBox("Enter your name.")
iQuantity = InputBox("How many do you want?", "Order Quantity")
```

Using the InputBox to Randomly Retrieve a Record

You will find the input box to be a great tool when you need to retrieve a record from a random file. Many applications use the record number as a method of identification, such as customer number or product number. If you request this number, you can read the correct record in the random file directly.

```
Dim iRecordNumber As Integer
iRecordNumber = Val(InputBox("Enter Customer Number"))
If iRecordNumber >= 0 And iRecordNumber <= LOF(1) / Len(Customer) Then
    Get #1, iRecordNumber, Customer
Else
    MsgBox "Invalid Customer Number"
End If
```

Summary

1. A data file is made up of records, which can be further broken down into fields or data elements. The field used for organizing the file is the key field.
2. An `Open` statement is needed to access data files. The `Open` allows modes for Input, Output, Append, and Random. A FileNumber is associated with a file at the time the file is opened.
3. A `Close` statement should be used prior to the termination of a program that uses data files.
4. The `FreeFile` function can be used to find the next available file number.
5. Sequential files use the `Write #` and `Input #` statements for writing and reading records. Each field to be written or read is listed in the statement.
6. The records in a sequential file must be accessed in order, and the file is either input or output, not both. With a random file the records may be accessed in any order and may be read or written without closing the file.
7. The `EOF` function returns True when the end of a file is reached.
8. The `On Error` statement allows the programmer to test for known error situations and handle errors without the application aborting. An example of the type of error that can be found through error trapping is the failure of the user to place a disk in the disk drive.
9. The Err object holds the error number and description of the current error.
10. The `Resume` statement continues execution after an error condition.
11. Random file access uses fixed-length records and requires the string fields to be a specified length. Use the `Type` statement to define the record structure for a random file.
12. The `Get` and `Put` statements read and write records in a random file.
13. A file update program allows the user to make changes to the data file, such as adding a record, changing the contents of a record, and deleting a record.
14. The `LOF` function returns the length of a random file in bytes. You can use the result to calculate the number of records in the file and the record number of the next available record.
15. You can use list box to allow the user to select a record from a random file. The ItemData property of the list box is set to the record number so that random reads can retrieve the correct record.

16. The `Trim`, `LTrim`, and `RTrim` functions remove extra spaces from fixed-length strings.
17. The input box is similar to a message box; it allows the user to enter information that can be returned to the project.

Key Terms

buffer *314*	key field *313*
data element *312*	line label *320*
data file *312*	`LOF` function *333*
Description property *320*	`LTrim` function *336*
EOF *315*	Number property *320*
`EOF` function *315*	`On Error` statement *319*
`Err` object *320*	`Put` statement *333*
error trapping *319*	random file *330*
`Exit Function` statement *324*	record *312*
`Exit Sub` statement *324*	record key *313*
field *312*	`Resume` statement *323*
file *312*	`RTrim` function *336*
file mode *313*	`Seek` function *334*
file number *314*	sequential files *315*
file pointer *314*	Source property *320*
`Get` statement *332*	`Trim` function *336*
`Input #` statement *317*	`Write #` statement *316*

Review Questions

1. What is the difference between a Visual Basic project file and a data file?
2. Explain what occurs when an `Open` statement is executed.
3. List and explain the file modes for data files.
4. What is the significance of a file number?
5. Differentiate between the Output and Append modes.
6. What is the format for the statements to read and write sequential files?
7. When would an `On Error` statement be used?
8. Explain the function and use of the Err object.
9. Differentiate between a random file and a sequential file.
10. What does *updating a data file* mean?
11. Give examples for using the `InputBox` function.
12. What function can be used to determine an available file number?

Programming   Exercises

9.1 (*Sequential file*) Rewrite project 8.4 using a sequential file to store the state names and abbreviations. You will need two projects. The first will allow the typist to enter the state name and the abbreviation in text boxes and store them in a sequential file. The second project will perform the functions specified in 8.4.

9.2 Create a *sequential file* for employee information and call it *employee.dat*. Each record will contain fields for first name, last name, Social Security number, and hourly pay rate.

Write a project to process payroll. The application will load the employee data into an array of user-defined types from the sequential file with an extra field for the pay. The form will contain labels for the information from the array and display one record at a time.

A command button called *FindPay* will use a `For  Next` loop to process the array. First you will display an input box for the number of hours worked, calculate the pay, and add to the totals. Then you will display the labels for the next employee. (Place the pay into the extra field in the array.)

The Exit button will print a report on the printer and terminate the project. (Print the array.)

Processing: Hours over 40 will receive time-and-a-half pay. Accumulate the total number of hours worked, the total number of hours of overtime, and the total amount of pay.

Sample Report

	Ace Industries			
Employee Name	Hours Worked	Hours Overtime	Pay Rate	Amount Earned
Janice Jones	40	0	5.25	210.00
Chris O'Connel	35	0	5.35	187.25
Karen Fisk	45	5	6.00	285.00
Tom Winn	42	2	5.75	247.25
Totals	162	7		929.50

9.3 (*Sequential file*) Modify project 7.6 to store the list box for Bradley's Bagels in a sequential file. Load the list during the Form Load and then close the file. Be sure to use error checking in case the file does not exist.

In the exit procedure, prompt the user to save the bagel list back to the disk.

9.4 (*Random file*) Create a project that stores and updates personal information for a little electronic "Black Book." The fields in the file should include

Last name	Street
First name	City
	State
Birthday	ZIP code
Phone number—home	Phone number—work
Phone number—pager	E-mail address

9.5   Create a *random file* project that stores and updates student information. Use a list box to display the student names, and store record numbers in the ItemData property, similar to the chapter hands-on example project.

The fields include

Name
Major—use a dropdown combo box to list available majors.
Class level—use option buttons for Freshman, Sophomore, Junior, and Senior.
Dean's list—use a check box.

CASE STUDIES

VB Mail Order

Modify the project created in Chapters 6 and 7 to include a sequential file to store catalog names and a random file to store customer information.

The list of catalog names must be stored in a sequential file and loaded into a dropdown combo box during the initial processing. Any catalogs that are added during execution of the program must be written to the disk. (If the file does not yet exist, either write another project to create it or allow the user to create it using the combo box and the Add button.)

When customer information is processed, allow the user to select the customer name from a list box or type in the customer number. The remaining controls for customer information will be changed from text boxes to labels. The information displayed in these labels will be found through a search of the random file. You may use techniques similar to the ones used to search an array, or you may load the file into an array or list box and search it.

You must create the customer random file and provide routines to update the records. Fields include name, street, city, state, and ZIP. The customer number is the record number, which you can use to directly reference a record when the user enters the number.

VB Auto Center

Create a project that maintains a random file for vehicle inventory. The fields contained in each record should be an inventory ID number, manufacturer, model name, year, vehicle ID number, and cost value.

Hint: Refer to the hands-on programming example in this chapter for ideas for the data entry screen, menus, and command buttons.

10

Accessing Database Files

At the completion of this chapter, you will be able to...

1. Use database terminology correctly.

2. Differentiate between the data control and data-bound controls.

3. Create a project to view an existing database table.

4. Set up a lookup table for a database field.

5. Change records, add new records, and delete records in a database table.

6. Write code to help prevent user errors.

Visual Basic and Database Files

You can use Visual Basic to write projects that view and update database files. You can use the data control in the Learning Edition to create database applications with very little coding. However, if you want to use the more advanced features, including creating new databases and modifying the structure of existing database tables, you will need the Professional Edition or Enterprise Edition of Visual Basic. The applications in this text can be done with the Standard Edition or the Learning Edition.

Database Formats Supported by Visual Basic

Visual Basic directly supports database files in several formats. The native format is Microsoft Access, using the Jet database engine. However, by setting just one property, the VB Standard Edition and Learning Edition can access files created with dBASE III, dBASE IV, dBASE 5.0, Excel, FoxPro, Lotus, Paradox, or text files. With the Professional Edition and Open Data-Base Connectivity (ODBC), you can use many other database formats, such as SQL Server, Oracle, and DB2.

Database Terminology

In order to use database files, you must understand the standard terminology of relational databases. Although there are various definitions of standard database terms, we will stick with those used by Access.

An Access **file** (with an .MDB extension) can hold multiple **tables**. Each table can be viewed as a spreadsheet—with **rows** and **columns**. Each row in a table represents the data for one item, person, or transaction and is called a *record*. Each column in a table is used to store a different element of data, such as an account number, a name, address, or numeric amount. The elements represented in columns are called *fields*. You can think of the table in Figure 10.1 as consisting of rows and columns or of records and fields.

Figure 10.1

ISBN	Title	Author	Publisher
0-15-500139-6	Business Programming in C	Millspaugh, A. C.	The Dryden Press
0-446-51652-X	Bridges of Madison County	Waller, Robert James	Warner Books
0-451-16095-9	The Stand	King, Stephen	Signet
0-517-59905-8	How to Talk to Anyone, Anytime, Anywhere	King, Larry	Crown
0-534-26076-4	A Quick Guide to the Internet	Bradley, Julia Case	Integrated Media Group
0-670-85332-1	How to Be Hap-Hap-Happy Like Me	Markoe, Merrill	Viking
0-671-66398-4	Seven Habits of Highly Effective People	Covey, Stephen R.	Fireside
0-697-12897-0	QuickBasic and QBasic Using Modular Structure	Bradley, Julia Case	B & E Tech
0-697-21361-7	Desktop Publishing Using PageMaker 5.0	Bradley, Julia Case	B & E Tech
0-8007-1213-7	Secrets of Closing the Sale	Ziglar, Zig	Revell
1-55615-484-4	Code Complete	McConnell, Steve	Microsoft Press

A database table consists of rows (records) and columns (fields).

Record or row

Field or column

Most tables use a **key field** (or combination of fields) to identify each record. The key field is often a number, such as employee number, account number, identification number, or Social Security number; or it may be a text field, such as last name, or a combination, such as last name and first name.

Any time a database table is open, one record is considered the **current record**. As you move from one record to the next, the current record changes.

Creating Database Files for Use by Visual Basic

Although you cannot create a new database file with the VB Standard Edition or Learning Edition, you have other options. You can use Access to create the database, or you can use the Visual Data Manager add-in application that comes with Visual Basic.

You can run the VB Visual Data Manager by selecting *Visual Data Manager* from the *Add-Ins* menu (Figure 10.2). The VisData application window opens (Figure 10.3); you can create a new file or open and modify an existing database file. The application is quite straightforward; you can use Help if you need instructions.

Figure   10.2

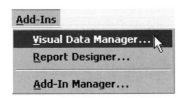

Select Visual Data Manager from the Add-Ins menu to run the VB Visual Data Manager.

Figure   10.3

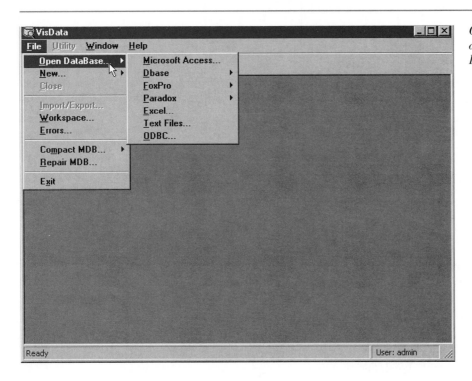

Create a new database or modify an existing one using the Visual Data Manager window.

Using the Data Control

You will find programming with the Visual Basic data control quite easy and powerful. Figure 10.4 shows the toolbox tool for creating a data control, and Figure 10.5 shows a data control on a form.

Figure   10.4

The toolbox tool for the data control.

Figure 10.5

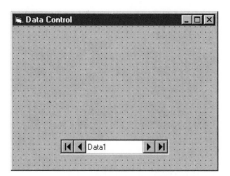

A data control on a form.

The Data Control and Data-Bound Controls

Using a data control is a two-step process. First you place a data control on a form and set the properties to link it to a database file and table. Then you create the controls, such as labels and text boxes, to display the actual data. Each control is bound to a particular field in the table. In this example, the label is called a ***data-bound*** control and will automatically display the contents of the bound field when the project runs. Figure 10.6 shows a form with a data control and two data-bound labels.

Figure 10.6

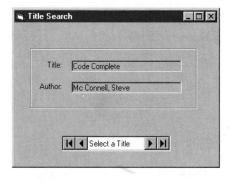

The data control binds the form to a database table. The data-bound labels each display a field from the table.

Microsoft also uses the term *data aware* for controls that can be bound to a database table. You might say that labels are data aware; therefore, you can use a label to create a data-bound control. The standard data-aware controls are labels, text boxes, check boxes, list boxes, combo boxes, images, picture boxes, data-bound list boxes, data-bound combo boxes, and data-bound grids.

A data control generally links one form with one table. If you want to have data-bound controls on a second form, you must place a data control on that form. You may place more than one data control on a single form when you wish to reference more than one table.

Properties of the Data Control

After you place a data control on a form, you must set its properties (Figure 10.7). By default, the Name and Caption are set to Data1. First change the Name property, using "dat" as its three-character prefix. The Caption appears inside the control (refer to Figure 10.6).

Figure 10.7

*Set the properties for a data
control in the Properties window.*

Set the **Connect property** of the data control to the type of database
file (Figure 10.8). Access is the default, but you can choose dBASE III, IV,
or 5.0; Excel 3.0, 4.0, 5.0, or 8.0; FoxPro 2.0, 2.5, 2.6, or 3.0; Lotus WK1,
WK3, or WK4; Paradox 3.*x*, 4.*x*, or 5.*x*; or text.

Figure 10.8

*Set the Connect property to the
type of database you plan to use.*

Then set the **DatabaseName property**. Although you can type the path
and filename into the Settings box, the easy way is to click on the Settings
button and open the *DatabaseName* dialog box (Figure 10.9). After you have
specified the filename, the next step is to select the name of the table from
within the file.

Figure 10.9

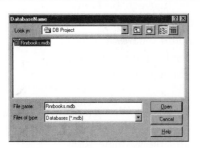

*Select the database file in the
DatabaseName dialog box.*

Set the **RecordSource property**. When you click on the Settings button, a list appears with the names of the tables and queries in the database file (Figure 10.10). *Note:* A query is a named subset of the data in one or more tables and is sometimes referred to as a *view*. You can set the RecordSource of the data control to any table or query named in the database file.

Select the table name for the RecordSource property.

If you don't want the user to be able to change the data in the table, set the ReadOnly property to True. Otherwise, any changes made to the data on the screen are automatically saved in the file.

After setting the properties for the data control, you are ready to set the properties for the data-bound controls.

Properties of Data-Bound Controls

Place the controls that you want to display in the database fields on the form and then change their properties. Use labels for any fields you don't want the user to be able to change; use text boxes if the field content is user updatable. Use check boxes for fields with a True/False or Yes/No value; the check box will display a check mark for True or Yes and remain blank for False or No.

After setting the Name and Text or Caption properties of your text boxes or labels, set the two properties that bind the control to a particular field in a table.

First set the **DataSource property** of the text box or label to point to the data control. Click on the down arrow in the Settings box to drop down the list of data controls on the form (Figure 10.11). Once you have selected the data control, VB knows the name of the file and table. Next you specify the particular field to bind to the control.

Select the name of the data for the data-bound control's DataSource property.

Set the **DataField property** by clicking on the down arrow in the Settings box. The list of fields in the selected table will appear (Figure 10.12). After choosing the field name for one of your data-bound controls, set the DataSource and DataField properties for the rest of your controls.

Figure 10.12

Set the DataField property to the name of the field to bind to the control.

That's all there is to it. Once you have bound the table and fields to the controls on your form, you are ready to run the application. With no code at all, the fields will fill with data when your project begins. You can use the navigation buttons on the data control to move from one record to the next.

Viewing a Database File—Step-by-Step

In this step-by-step tutorial, you will create a simple project to display the data from the Books table for R 'n R—for Reading 'n Refreshment. The only code required is for the Exit procedure.

Design and Create the Form

Figure 10.13 shows the user interface for this project.

Figure 10.13

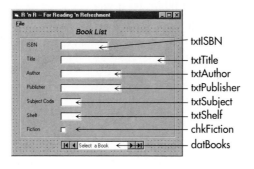

The user interface for the database step-by-step tutorial.

The Form

STEP 1: Create a new form large enough to hold the controls (see Figure 10.13).

The Controls

STEP 1: Click on the data control tool and draw a data control along the bottom of the form.

STEP 2: Create a large frame to hold the labels and text boxes; then delete the frame's Caption property.

STEP 3: Create labels that describe the data and the form title (Book List).

STEP 4: Create the controls to hold the data. Use text boxes for ISBN, Title, Author, Publisher, Subject Code, and Shelf; use a check box for Fiction.

The Menu

STEP 1: Open the Menu Editor window and create a *File* menu with an *Exit* command. Name the menu mnuFile and the command mnuFileExit.

Set the Properties for the Data Control

STEP 1.: Select the data control and display the Properties window.

STEP 2: Change the Name property to datBooks.

STEP 3: Change the Caption property to Select a Book.

STEP 4: Click on the Settings button for the DatabaseName property to display the *DatabaseName* dialog box.

STEP 5: Change the drive and directory as necessary to locate the database file called RnrBooks.mdb. It was supplied on your student diskette and may be installed on the local hard drive or network. (Consult your instructor or lab technician if you can't find it.) Click OK after selecting the filename.

STEP 6: Scroll to the RecordSource property and click the down arrow in the Settings box. The list of tables should appear; click on *Books*.

STEP 7: Change the ReadOnly property to True.

Set the Properties for the Data-Bound Controls

STEP 1: Select the text box to hold the ISBN number; switch to the Properties window.

STEP 2: Set the following properties:

STEP 3: Click on the Settings down arrow for the DataSource property and select datBooks (the name of the data control).

Name	txtISBN
Caption	(blank)

STEP 4: Click on the Settings down arrow for the DataField property; the list of fields in the Books table appears. Click on ISBN.

STEP 5: Set the properties for the rest of the data-bound controls.

Object	Property	Setting
txtTitle	Name	txtTitle
	Text	(blank)
	DataSource	datBooks
	DataField	Title
txtAuthor	Name	txtAuthor
	Text	(blank)
	DataSource	datBooks
	DataField	Author
txtPublisher	Name	txtPublisher
	Text	(blank)
	DataSource	datBooks
	DataField	Publisher
txtSubject	Name	txtSubject
	Text	(blank)
	DataSource	datBooks
	DataField	Subject_Code
txtShelf	Name	txtShelf
	Text	(blank)
	DataSource	datBooks
	DataField	Shelf_Location
chkFiction	Name	chkFiction
	Caption	(blank)
	DataSource	datBooks
	DataField	Fiction

Write the Code

The coding for this project will surprise you. All you need are a few remarks and an Exit procedure.

STEP 1: Select the *Exit* command from the *File* menu to open the mnuFileExit_Click procedure.

STEP 2: Type the following code:

```
'Exit the project

End
```

STEP 3: Switch to the General Declarations section and type the remarks:

```
'Program Name: R 'n R Book List Database
'Programmer:   Your Name
'Date:         Today's date
'Purpose:      Display book information in the
'              R 'n R Book database
'Folder:       Ch1001
```

STEP 4: Save your form and project. You will use them again later in this chapter.

Run the Project

STEP 1: Start the project running. You should see your form on the screen filled with the data for the first record. (Maybe a "Wow" is in order?)

STEP 2: Try the navigation buttons on the data control: Click on the arrows for Move Next, Move Previous, Move First, and Move Last (Figure 10.14).

Figure 10.14

Click on the navigation buttons to display different records.

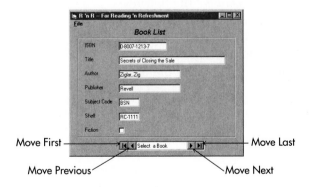

Feedback 10.1

Use this information to fill in the answers to the following questions.

Database name:	Classes.mdb
Table name:	Teachers
Field name:	Name
Data control name:	datClasses
Text box name:	txtTeacher

You want to display the name field in txtTeacher. How should these properties be set?

1. datClasses.DatabaseName
2. datClasses.RecordSource
3. txtTeacher.DataSource
4. txtTeacher.DataField
5. txtTeacher.Text

Navigating the Database in Code

The navigation buttons on the data control can be used to move from record to record, or you can make the data control invisible and provide the navigation in code. You can use the **Recordset object** to manipulate the database.

The Recordset Object

When you set the RecordSource property of a data control to the name of a table or query, you are defining a new object called a *Recordset*. The Recordset object has its own set of properties and methods, which you can use to move from record to record, check for the beginning or end of the file, and search for records to match a condition (covered in Chapter 11).

When you refer to the Recordset object, you must first name the data control:

```
DataControl.Recordset.Property
DataControl.Recordset.Method
```

Using the MoveNext, MovePrevious, MoveFirst, and MoveLast Methods

The `MoveNext`, `MovePrevious`, `MoveFirst`, and `MoveLast` methods provide the same functions as the data control buttons. Each method is applied to the Recordset object created by the data control.

```
datBooks.Recordset.MoveNext      'Move to the next record
datBooks.Recordset.MoveLast      'Move to the last record
datBooks.Recordset.MovePrevious  'Move to the previous record
datBooks.Recordset.MoveFirst     'Move to the first record
```

Checking for BOF and EOF

Two handy properties of the Recordset object are **BOF** (beginning of file) and **EOF** (end of file). The BOF property is automatically set to True when the record pointer is before the first record in the Recordset. This condition happens when the first record is current and the user chooses MovePrevious. The BOF property is also True if the Recordset is empty (contains no records).

The EOF property is similar to BOF; it is True when the record pointer moves beyond the last record in the Recordset and when the Recordset is empty.

When you are doing your own navigation in code, you need to check for BOF and EOF so that run-time errors do not occur. If the user clicks MoveNext when on the last record, what do you want to do? Have the program cancel with a run-time error? display a message? wrap around to the first record? keep the record pointer on the last record? (The last approach matches the action of the navigation buttons on the data control.)

In the examples that follow, we will use the wrap around method. If the user clicks on the MoveNext button from the end of the table, the first record becomes the active record.

```
Private Sub cmdNext_Click()
    'Move to the next record

    datBooks.Recordset.MoveNext
    If datBooks.Recordset.EOF Then
        datBooks.Recordset.MoveFirst
    End If
End Sub
```

Just as with any other object reference in Visual Basic, you can use the With/End With statements to refer to the Recordset object. This style of coding not only simplifies the VB code but also makes a project run a little faster.

```
Private Sub cmdNext_Click()
    'Move to the next record

    With datBooks.Recordset
        .MoveNext
        If .EOF Then
            .MoveFirst
        End If
    End With
End Sub
```

Using List Boxes and Combo Boxes as Data-Bound Controls

Beginning with release 4.0 of Visual Basic, list boxes and combo boxes are data aware. You can see the value of using data-bound lists when you have a list of acceptable values for a field. The user can select an item from the list when updating records or adding new ones.

Setting Up a Lookup Table for a Field

To set up a lookup table of acceptable values for a field, use a combo box. You can bind the combo box to a field in the database *and* specify initial values for the List property. Figure 10.15 shows a combo box as a data-bound control, displaying the Subject field from the database. When the user selects a subject from the dropdown combo box, the field's contents are updated to the new value. (In the following example, we set the ReadOnly property of the database to False so that changes can actually occur.)

Figure 10.15

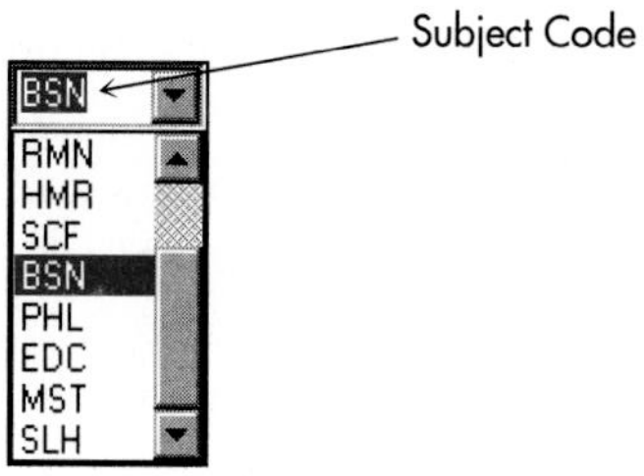

The List property of the combo box shows the acceptable choices for the field. Select an entry from the list to change the contents of the field.

Adding a Lookup Table and Navigation—Step-by-Step

For this step-by-step example, we add navigation buttons and two lookup combo boxes to the previous programming example.

Modify the User Interface

STEP 1: Open the previous program example.
STEP 2: Resize the form and add four command buttons for navigation. (See Figure 10.16.)

Figure 10.16

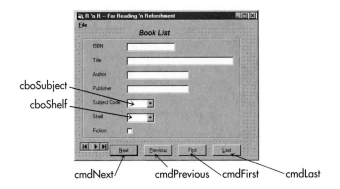

STEP 3: Delete the text box for Subject Code and add a combo box in its place.

STEP 4: Delete the text box for Shelf and add a combo box in its place.

Change the Properties

STEP 1: Set the properties of the four command buttons.

Object	Property	Setting
cmdNext	Name	cmdNext
	Caption	&Next
	Default	True
cmdPrevious	Name	cmdPrevious
	Caption	&Previous
cmdFirst	Name	cmdFirst
	Caption	Fi&rst
cmdLast	Name	cmdLast
	Caption	&Last

STEP 2: Change the Visible property of the data control to False.

STEP 3: Change the ReadOnly property of the data control to False.

STEP 4: Change the Locked property of txtISBN to True. This setting prevents the user from changing the ISBN, which is the key field for the table.

STEP 5: Set the properties of the two combo boxes as described in the following table.

Object	Property	Setting
cboSubject	Name	cboSubject
	Text	(blank)
	DataSource	datBooks
	DataField	Subject_Code
	List	BSS (Ctrl + Enter after each) FNT RLG RMN HMR SCF BSN PHL EDC MST SLH
cboShelf	Name	cboShelf
	Text	(blank)
	DataSource	datBooks
	DataField	Shelf_Location
	List	RC-1111 (Ctrl + Enter after each) RC-1112 RC-1113 RC-1114

Reset the Tab Order for the Controls

STEP 1: Click on the text box for the ISBN (txtISBN) on the form, switch to the Properties window, and change the TabIndex to 0.

STEP 2: Click on the second text box on the form (txtTitle), and the TabIndex property for txtTitle should appear in the Properties window. Change it to 1.

STEP 3: Click on the next text box (txtAuthor) and change its TabIndex property to 2.

STEP 4: Click on the next text box (txtPublisher) and change its TabIndex property to 3.

STEP 5: Click on the combo box for subject (cboSubject) and change its TabIndex property to 4.

STEP 6: Set the TabIndex properties for the rest of the controls.

cboShelf	5
chkFiction	6
cmdNext	7
cmdPrevious	8
cmdFirst	9
cmdLast	10

Write the Code

STEP 1: Change the remarks in the General Declarations section to reflect the changes.

STEP 2: Add coding for each command button. See the following listing for help.

```
'Program Name:  R 'n R Book List Database
'Programmer:    J.C. Bradley
'Date:          August 1997
'Purpose:       Display and update book information in the
'               R 'n R Book database, using buttons for
'               navigation and combo boxes for field lookup
'Folder:        Ch1002

Private Sub cmdFirst_Click()
    'Move to first record

    datBooks.Recordset.MoveFirst
End Sub

Private Sub cmdLast_Click()
    'Move to last record

    datBooks.Recordset.MoveLast
End Sub

Private Sub cmdNext_Click()
    'Move to next record

    With datBooks.Recordset
        .MoveNext
        If .EOF Then
            .MoveFirst
        End If
    End With
End Sub
```

```
Private Sub cmdPrevious_Click()
    'Move to previous record

    With datBooks.Recordset
        .MovePrevious
        If .BOF Then
            .MoveLast
        End If
    End With
End Sub
```

```
Private Sub mnuFileExit_Click()
    'Exit the project

    End
End Sub
```

Testing the Navigation and Lookup Tables

Save the project; then test it. Try each of your navigation buttons. Make sure that you can move forward and backward and that the project properly handles moving before the first record and after the last.

As you move from record to record, notice the contents of the two lookup combo boxes. Try selecting a new subject for a record; then move to the next record. Move back to the changed record, and you will see that the change has been made. *Caution:* All changes you make to the data records are permanently saved when you move to another record or exit the database. You do not have an option to abandon changes; all changes are recorded in the file.

Updating a Database File

As you saw in the previous example, a project that displays data from a database allows updates automatically. If you don't want the user to change the data, you must set the ReadOnly property of the data control to True. You can also keep the user from making changes to the data by displaying fields in labels rather than in text boxes.

The Recordset object has an **Update method**, which you can use to save any changes in the data. Most of the time, updating is automatic, since Visual Basic automatically executes the Update method any time the user clicks one of the navigation buttons or one of the Move methods executes.

Adding Records

When you want to add new records to a database, you have a couple of choices. If you are using the data control's navigation buttons (rather than your own code for navigation), you can allow Visual Basic to do the adds automatically. Set the data control's EOFAction property to 2-AddNew. When the user moves to the end of the table and clicks the arrow for Next Record, an *Add* operation begins. The data in all bound controls are cleared so that new data can be entered. Then, when the user clicks one of the arrow buttons, the `Update` method is automatically executed and the new record is written in the file.

You need a different approach when you use code to accomplish record navigation. Assume that you have a command button or menu choice to add a new record. In the Click event for the command button, use the Recordset's **AddNew method:**

```
datBooks.Recordset.AddNew
```

When this statement executes, all bound controls are cleared so that the user can enter the data for the new record. After the data fields are entered, the new record must be saved in the file. You can explicitly save it with an `Update` method; or, if the user moves to another record, the `Update` method is automatically executed.

```
datBooks.Recordset.Update
```

You may want to use two buttons for adding a new record—an Add button and a Save button. For the Add button, use an `AddNew` method; for the Save button, use the `Update` method.

When adding new records, some conditions can cause errors to occur. For example, if the key field is blank on a new record, a run-time error halts program execution. See "Preventing Errors" later in this chapter for some solutions.

In the sample project for this chapter, the Locked property for txtISBN will have to be set to False. If you are going to allow adds, the user must be able to enter a new key field. (You might also consider setting the Locked property to False during an Add operation and True the rest of the time.)

Deleting Records

The **Delete method** deletes the current record. The user should display the record to delete and click a Delete command button or menu choice. When a record is deleted, the current record is no longer valid. Therefore, a `Delete` method must be followed by a `MoveNext` (or any other `Move`) method.

```
With datBooks.Recordset
    .Delete
    .MoveNext
End With
```

But what if the record being deleted is the last record in the table? Remember that if the navigation buttons are used to navigate, moving beyond EOF just resets the current record to the last record. No problem. However, if you are using event procedures for navigation, you must take care of this situation. If a `MoveNext` causes an EOF condition, then the program should do a `MovePrevious`.

```
Private Sub cmdDelete_Click()
    'Delete the current record

    With datBooks.Recordset
        .Delete          'Delete the current record
        .MoveNext        'Move to the following record
        If .EOF Then     'If last record deleted
            .MovePrevious
        End If
    End With
End Sub
```

Did you find another problem with this code? Stop and look at the preceding delete routine a moment. What will happen if the user deletes the *only* record in the Recordset?

Did you spot the problem? If the user deletes the last and only record in the Recordset, you must check for both EOF and BOF.

```
Private Sub cmdDelete_Click()
    'Delete the current record

    With datBooks.Recordset
        .Delete              'Delete the current record
        .MoveNext            'Move to the following record
        If .EOF Then         'If last record deleted
            .MovePrevious
            If .BOF Then 'If BOF and EOF true, no records remain
                MsgBox "The recordset is empty.", vbInformation, "No records"
                'Take any other desired action for empty recordset
            End If
        End If
    End With
End Sub
```

Preventing Errors

It is considered very poor programming style to allow your users to get run-time errors. Catching errors before they can cancel a program is called **error trapping**. In Chapter 9 you learned to use the On Error statement for error trapping with data files; in Chapter 11 you will learn to use error trapping and validation with the data control.

In the meantime you can do some simple things to prevent user errors, such as disabling command buttons. In Chapter 9 you learned to disable navigation buttons during an Add or a Delete operation. Those techniques can keep a user out of trouble in a database Recordset also.

Protecting an Add Operation

When the user clicks on the Add button, the cmdAdd_Click event will occur:

```
Private Sub cmdAdd_Click()
    'Add a new record

    datBooks.Recordset.AddNew      'Clear out fields for new record
End Sub
```

Once the Add operation starts, you want the user to fill in the text boxes for the new record and click on *Save*. However, if the user clicks on one of the navigation buttons first, any data that she has already entered in the text boxes is saved automatically. How can the user be forced to click on *Save*? How can she be allowed to cancel the operation?

Limiting User Actions

The best way to avoid errors is to avoid any extra options that can cause trouble. Once the Add begins, the user should have two choices only: *Save* or *Cancel*. The navigation buttons and the *Delete* button should be disabled. Figure 10.17 illustrates a data form used for updating; Figure 10.18 shows the same form during an Add operation with only two buttons available.

F i g u r e   1 0 . 1 7

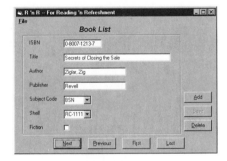

The update form as it appears before the user clicks on Add.

F i g u r e   1 0 . 1 8

The update form as it appears during the Add operation. The Caption on the Add button changes to Cancel.

In the following example, when the user clicks on the Add button, several actions occur:

1. An `AddNew` method clears the bound controls to await entry of new data.
2. The focus is set in the first text box.

3. The navigation buttons and the *Delete* button are disabled.
4. The *Save* button is enabled.
5. The caption of the *Add* button changes to *Cancel*, which gives the user only two choices: *Save* or *Cancel*.

Sharing the Functions of a Command Button

Sometimes the best technique is to have one command button perform different actions, depending on the situation. Notice in Figures 10.17 and 10.18 that the *Save* button becomes the *Cancel* button during an Add operation. Of course, this isn't the only solution: You could create a separate Cancel button and disable it.

To make a command button perform more than one action, you must change its Caption when appropriate. Then in the button's Click event, check the Caption before responding to the event.

A good programming practice is to disable buttons when they shouldn't be used. It is not good practice to make them invisible and suddenly appear.

```
Private Sub cmdAdd_Click()
    'Add a new record or cancel an add

    If cmdAdd.Caption = "&Add" Then
        'Code to handle Add
        cmdAdd.Caption = "&Cancel"   'Change the button's Caption
    Else                             'A Cancel action is selected
        'Code to handle Cancel
        cmdAdd.Caption = "&Add"      'Reset the button's Caption
    End If
End Sub
```

Coding the New Add Procedure

The new cmdAdd_Click event performs two distinct operations: Add or Cancel. A new statement, the **CancelUpdate method**, also appears in the Cancel operation. CancelUpdate does what it sounds like—it cancels the Add and returns to the record that was active before the Add started.

```
Private Sub cmdAdd_Click()
    'Add a new record

    If cmdAdd.Caption = "&Add" Then
        datBooks.Recordset.AddNew      'Clear out fields for new record
        txtISBN.SetFocus
        DisableButtons                 'Disable navigation
        cmdSave.Enabled = True         'Enable the Save button
        cmdAdd.Caption = "&Cancel"     'Allow a Cancel option
    Else                               'A Cancel action is selected
        datBooks.Recordset.CancelUpdate 'Cancel the Add
        EnableButtons                  'Enable navigation
        cmdSave.Enabled = False        'Disable the Save button
        cmdAdd.Caption = "&Add"        'Reset the Add button
    End If
End Sub
```

Procedures to Disable and Enable Buttons

These two new general procedures simplify the disable/enable operations.

```
Private Sub DisableButtons()
    'Disable navigation buttons

    cmdNext.Enabled = False
    cmdPrevious.Enabled = False
    cmdFirst.Enabled = False
    cmdLast.Enabled = False
    cmdDelete.Enabled = False
End Sub

Private Sub EnableButtons()
    'Enable navigation buttons

    cmdNext.Enabled = True
    cmdPrevious.Enabled = True
    cmdFirst.Enabled = True
    cmdLast.Enabled = True
    cmdDelete.Enabled = True
End Sub
```

The Save Procedure

When the user clicks on Save, you must first save the new record by executing the Update method. Then reset the controls to their "normal" state.

```
Private Sub cmdSave_Click()
    'Save the current record

    datBooks.Recordset.Update
    EnableButtons
    cmdSave.Enabled = False
    cmdAdd.Caption = "&Add"
End Sub
```

Your Hands-On Programming Example

This example displays and maintains a database table to keep track of books for R 'n R—for Reading 'n Refreshment. This project puts together all the examples shown in this chapter. If you have completed the second example, you can just add the buttons and coding for Add, Cancel, Save, and Delete and change the Locked property for txtISBN.

Planning the Project

Sketch the modified form (Figure 10.19). Your user checks it over and approves the design.

Figure   10.19

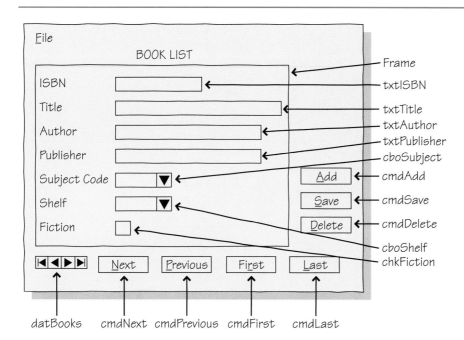

The planning sketch of the data entry form for the hands-on programming example.

Plan the Objects and Properties

Object	Property	Setting
frmBookData	Name	frmBookData
	Caption	R 'n R—for Reading 'n Refreshment
datBooks	Name	datBooks
	Caption	Select a Book
	Connect	Access
	DatabaseName	RNRBOOKS.MDB
	RecordSource	Books
	Read Only	False
	Visible	False
Frame1	Caption	(blank)
Label1	Caption	ISBN

Object	Property	Setting
Label2	Caption	Title
Label3	Caption	Author
Label4	Caption	Subject Code
Label5	Caption	Shelf
Label6	Caption	Fiction
txtISBN	Name	txtISBN
	Text	(blank)
	DataSource	datBooks
	DataField	ISBN
	Locked	False
txtTitle	Name	txtTitle
	Text	(blank)
	DataSource	datBooks
	DataField	Title
txtAuthor	Name	txtAuthor
	Text	(blank)
	DataSource	datBooks
	DataField	Author
txtPublisher	Name	txtPublisher
	Text	(blank)
	DataSource	datBooks
	DataField	Publisher
cboSubject	Name	cboSubject
	Text	(blank)
	DataSource	datBooks
	DataField	Subject_Code
	List	BSS
		FNT
		RLG
		RMN
		HMR
		SCF
		BSN
		PHL
		EDC
		MST
		SLH

(continued)

Object	Property	Setting
cboShelf	Name	cboShelf
	Text	(blank)
	DataField	Shelf_Location
	List	RC-1111
		RC-1112
		RC-1113
		RC-1114
chkFiction	Name	chkFiction
	Caption	(blank)
	DataSource	datBooks
	DataField	Fiction
cmdAdd	Name	cmdAdd
	Caption	&Add
cmdSave	Name	cmdSave
	Caption	&Save
	Enabled	False
cmdDelete	Name	cmdDelete
	Caption	&Delete
cmdNext	Name	cmdNext
	Caption	&Next
	Default	True
cmdPrevious	Name	cmdPrevious
	Caption	&Previous
cmdFirst	Name	cmdFirst
	Caption	Fi&rst
cmdLast	Name	cmdLast
	Caption	&Last
mnuFile	Name	mnuFile
	Caption	&File
mnuFileExit	Name	mnuFileExit
	Caption	E&xit

Plan the Code Procedures

Plan the actions for the event procedures and the general procedures.

Procedure	Actions
mnuFileExit_Click	Terminate the project.

cmdAdd_Click	If button caption = "Add" Then
	  AddNew record.
	  Set the focus in txtISBN.
	  Disable buttons.
	  Enable the Save button.
	  Set Add button caption to "Cancel."
	Else
	  CancelAdd method.
	  Enable buttons.
	  Disable the Save button.
	  Set button caption to "Add."

cmdDelete_Click	Delete record.
	Move to next record.
	If EOF Then
	  Move to the previous record.
	  If BOF Then (no records in recordset)
	   Display message.
	   Disable buttons.
	  End If
	End If

cmdSave_Click	Update record. Enable buttons. Disable the Save button. Set cmdAdd caption to "Add."

cmdNext_Click	Move to next record.
	If EOF Then
	  Move to first record.
	End If

cmdPrevious_Click	Move to previous record
	If BOF Then
	  Move to last record.
	End If

cmdFirst_Click	Move to first record.
cmdLast_Click	Move to last record.

Write the Project

- Follow the sketch in Figure 10.19 to create the form. Figure 10.20 shows the completed form. If you have done the preceding step-by-step examples in this chapter, you can just modify the previous project.

Figure 10.20

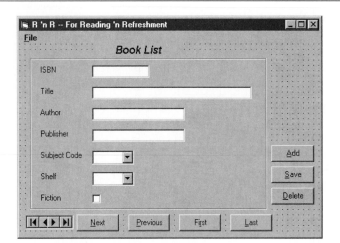

The data entry form for the hands-on programming example.

● Set the properties of each of the objects, as you have planned.

● Write the code. Working from the pseudocode, write each procedure.

● Thoroughly test the project. Make sure to try every option, including canceling an Add and deleting the last record in a table.

The Project Coding Solution

```
'Program Name:    R 'n R Book List Database
'Programmer:      J.C. Bradley
'Date:            August 1997
'Purpose:         Display and update book information in the
'                 R 'n R Book database, using buttons for
'                 navigation and combo boxes for field lookup
'Folder:          Ch1003
```

```
Private Sub cmdAdd_Click()
    'Add a new record

    If cmdAdd.Caption = "&Add" Then
        datBooks.Recordset.AddNew        'Clear out fields for new record
        txtISBN.SetFocus
        DisableButtons                   'Disable navigation
        cmdSave.Enabled = True           'Enable the Save button
        cmdAdd.Caption = "&Cancel"       'Allow a Cancel option
    Else
        datBooks.Recordset.CancelUpdate  'Cancel the Add
        EnableButtons                    'Enable navigation
        cmdSave.Enabled = False          'Disable the Save button
        cmdAdd.Caption = "&Add"          'Reset the Add button
    End If
End Sub
```

```
Private Sub cmdDelete_Click()
    'Delete the current record

    With datBooks.Recordset
        .Delete              'Delete the current record
        .MoveNext            'Move to the following record
        If .EOF Then         'If last record deleted
            .MovePrevious
            If .BOF Then                 'If BOF and EOF true, no records remain
                MsgBox "The recordset is empty.", vbInformation, "No records"
                DisableButtons
            End If
        End If
    End With
End Sub
```

```
Private Sub cmdFirst_Click()
    'Move to first record

    datBooks.Recordset.MoveFirst
End Sub
```

```
Private Sub cmdLast_Click()
    'Move to last record

    datBooks.Recordset.MoveLast
End Sub
```

```
Private Sub cmdNext_Click()
    'Move to next record

    With datBooks.Recordset
        .MoveNext
        If .EOF Then
            .MoveFirst
        End If
    End With
End Sub
```

```
Private Sub cmdPrevious_Click()
    'Move to previous record

    With datBooks.Recordset
        .MovePrevious
        If .BOF Then
            .MoveLast
        End If
    End With
End Sub
```

```
Private Sub cmdSave_Click()
    'Save the current record

    datBooks.Recordset.Update
    EnableButtons
    cmdSave.Enabled = False
    cmdAdd.Caption = "&Add"
End Sub
```

```
Private Sub mnuFileExit_Click()
    'Exit the project

    End
End Sub
```

```
Private Sub DisableButtons()
    'Disable navigation buttons

    cmdNext.Enabled = False
    cmdPrevious.Enabled = False
    cmdFirst.Enabled = False
    cmdLast.Enabled = False
    cmdDelete.Enabled = False
End Sub
```

```
Private Sub EnableButtons()
    'Enable navigation buttons

    cmdNext.Enabled = True
    cmdPrevious.Enabled = True
    cmdFirst.Enabled = True
    cmdLast.Enabled = True
    cmdDelete.Enabled = True
End Sub
```

Programming Hints

1. If you have trouble with your project running correctly, try single-stepping through the execution. Place a breakpoint at the top of a suspect procedure and begin execution. When the program halts at the breakpoint, press F8 (the shortcut for Step) repeatedly and watch the execution. While the project is in break time, you can highlight any expression in code and wait a second; the current value of the expression will display.

2. You can look up all properties, events, and methods for the data control in the Object Browser (Figure 10.21). Select *Object Browser* from the *View* menu, drop down the */Project/Library* list, and choose *VB*; then select *Data*.

Look up the properties and methods for the data control in the Object Browser.

S u m m a r y

1. Microsoft Access is Visual Basic's native format for database files.
2. In database terminology a *file* consists of *tables*, which consist of *rows* or *records*, which consist of *columns* or *fields*. Each record is identified by its *key* field. One record is always the *current* record.
3. A data control placed on a form links to a database file and a particular table within that file. Data-bound controls link to a data control for the table name and to a particular field within the table.
4. Data-aware controls (those that can become data bound) are labels, text boxes, check boxes, list boxes, combo boxes, images, picture boxes, data-bound list boxes, and data-bound grids.
5. Set the Connect, DatabaseName, and RecordSource properties of a data control to link it to a database table.
6. Set the DataSource and DataField properties of data-aware controls to bind them to a field in a database table.
7. The Recordset object defined by the data control has its own properties and methods. Use the `MoveNext`, `MovePrevious`, `MoveFirst`, and `MoveLast` methods to navigate the database. The BOF and EOF properties indicate the beginning or end of file.
8. A combo box can be used as a data-bound control, and its List property can hold the possible choices for the field.
9. Any data that the user changes on the screen is automatically written into the file unless the ReadOnly property is set to True.
10. The `AddNew` method clears the fields on the screen to allow the user to add a new record. After the Add, an `Update` method is needed; however, an `Update` occurs automatically when the user moves to another record.
11. The `Delete` method removes a record from the table. A `Move` must be executed after a `Delete`, because the current record is no longer valid.
12. To protect the user from making errors, you can disable and enable buttons. During an Add operation, the user have only the options to Save or to Cancel. A `CancelUpdate` method cancels an Add operation.

Key Terms

AddNew method   *378*

BOF   *373*

CancelUpdate method   *382*

column   *326*

Connect property   *366*

current record   *363*

DatabaseName property   *366*

data-bound control   *365*

DataField property   *368*

DataSource property   *367*

Delete method   *379*

EOF   *373*

error trapping   *380*

field   *362*

file   *362*

key field   *363*

record   *362*

Recordset object   *372*

RecordSource property   *367*

row   *362*

table   *362*

Update method   *378*

Review Questions

1. Assume you have a database containing the names and phone numbers of your friends. Describe how the terms *file, table, row, column, record, field,* and *key* apply to your database.
2. Explain the difference between a data control and a data-bound control.
3. Which controls can be data bound?
4. Explain how the BOF and EOF properties are set and how they might be used in a project.
5. What properties must be set for a combo box in order for it to be bound to a field in a database and display a dropdown list of the choices for that field?
6. What steps are needed to add a new record to a database?
7. What steps are needed to delete a record from a database?
8. What steps are needed to change the data in a database record?
9. How can you check for the user deleting the only record in a Recordset?

Programming Exercises

10.1 The Rnrbooks.mdb database file holds two tables: the Books table used in this chapter and the Subjects table. The Subjects table has only two fields: the Subject Code (the key) and the Subject Name. Write a project that will display the Subjects table. Include command buttons for record navigation, make the data control invisible, and set the table to ReadOnly.

10.2 Write a project to maintain the Subjects table described in project 10.1. Use the (visible) data control for record navigation. Set the EOFAction property of the data control to 2-AddNew. Include command buttons for Add, Delete, and Exit.

10.3 Write a project to maintain the Subjects table described in project 10.1. Use menu choices rather than command buttons for the following program functions:

Menus

File	Record	Help
Exit	Next	About
	Previous	
	First	
	Last	

Add New
Delete Current

Give each menu command a keyboard shortcut (in the Menu Editor) if you wish, to make selecting a command quicker.

Include two command buttons on the form—a Save button and a Cancel button, which are both disabled most of the time. When the user chooses Add New, make the Save and Cancel buttons enabled. If the user clicks on Save, update the record; a click on Cancel cancels the Add operation. After either a Save or Cancel, make both buttons disabled again.

Make the Save button the default button. Set the Cancel property to True on the Cancel button.

Disable the menu options for navigation, Add, and Delete when an Add is in progress.

10.4 Write a project to display the Publishers table from the Biblio.mdb database that comes with Visual Basic. (Biblio.mdb should be stored in the VB directory.) Include command buttons for record navigation and hide the data control. Do not allow the user to change the data.

Hint: Copy the Biblio.mdb file to the directory where your project will be stored before setting the properties for the data control.

Fields in the Publishers table

PubID (Publisher Identification—key field)

Name

Company Name

Address

City

State

ZIP

Telephone

Fax

Note: The Biblio.mdb database included with VB4 was 288 KB, small enough to easily fit on a diskette. The version included with VB5 is 3.5 MB—too large for a diskette. The older version is included on your Student Diskette. The two versions of the file have the same structure; the size difference is due to the large number of records added to the newer version.

10.5 Write a project to maintain the Publishers table described in project 10.4. Allow Adds and Deletes to the database. On an Add, disable the navigation and Delete buttons so that the only options are Save or Cancel.

Hint: Copy the Biblio.mdb file to the directory where your project will be stored before setting the properties for the data control. See the note in Exercise 10.4 about the file size.

CASE STUDIES

VB Mail Order

VB Mail Order Assignment 1—Display Only

Create a project to display the VB Mail Order Customer table from the Vbmail.mdb database on your student diskette. Set the database ReadOnly property to True so that the user cannot change the data.

Make the data control invisible; instead, include command buttons for Next, Previous, First, and Last.

VB Mail Order Assignment 2—Display and Update

Create a project to display and maintain the customer table. See project 10.3 for a list of the menu choices.

Allow adds and deletions to the database through menu selections. During an Add, allow the user to Save or to Cancel only.

Fields

| Customer ID |
| LastName |
| FirstName |
| Address |
| City |
| State |
| ZipCode |

VB Auto Center

VB Auto Center Assignment 1—Display Only

Create a project to display the VB Auto Center Vehicle table from the Vbauto.mdb database on your student diskette. Set the database ReadOnly property to True so that the user cannot change the data.

Make the data control invisible; instead, include command buttons for Next, Previous, First, and Last.

VB Auto Center Assignment 2—Display and Update

Create a project to display and maintain the Auto Center Vehicle table. See project 10.3 for a list of the menu choices.

Allow adds and deletions to the database through menu selections. During an Add, allow the user to Save or to Cancel only.

Fields

| InventoryID |
| Manufacturer |
| ModelName |
| Year |
| VehicleID |
| CostValue |

11

Advanced Data Handling—Grids, Validation, Selection, and SQL

At the completion of this chapter, you will be able to...

1. Write a database application using the DB Grid control.

2. Improve database validation techniques with error-trapping techniques.

3. Find records that meet a specific criterion using both the `Find` and the `Seek` methods.

4. Differentiate among tables, dynasets, and snapshot recordsets.

5. Reorder table type recordsets using indexes.

6. Create a new dynaset using Structured Query Language (SQL).

Displaying Data in Grids

In Chapter 10 you learned to display database tables in bound controls, such as labels, text boxes, check boxes, and list boxes. Another good way to display data is in **grids**, which present tables in rows and columns similar to a spreadsheet.

Visual Basic comes with two grid controls: the DBGrid and the MSFlex-Grid. In addition, many companies sell powerful grid controls that you can include in your project. In the following example, you will create a simple application using Microsoft's DBGrid control.

A Grid Control—Step-by-Step

This step-by-step tutorial shows you how to create an application that displays the Books table for R 'n R. Although the application is quite simple, it does allow the user to add, change, and delete data records. You also learn how to display the record number and record count. Figure 11.1 shows the completed form.

Figure   11.1

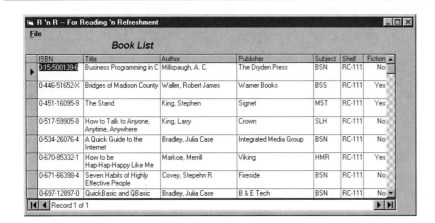

The completed form using the grid control.

Create The Form and Controls

STEP 1: Begin a new project and widen the form. You may want to close the Project Explorer and Form Layout windows and float the Properties window to allow room to work on the wide form (Figure 11.2).

Figure   11.2

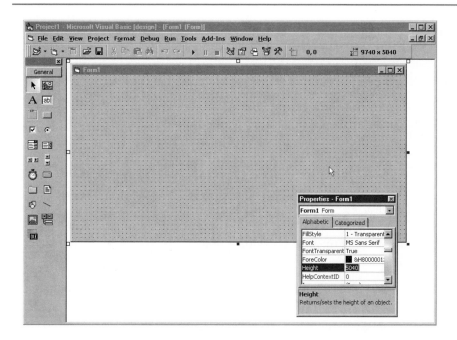

Modify the screen layout to work on a wide form.

STEP 2: Add a data control along the bottom of the form. Set the control's Name property to *datBooks* and its DatabaseName property to *Rnr-Books.mdb*. (This file should be on your student diskette.) Set the RecordSource property to *Books* and verify that the RecordsetType is *1 - Dynaset*.

STEP 3: Select *Project/Components* to display the *Components* dialog box. Then locate *Microsoft Data Bound Grid Control,* select it, and close the dialog box. You should see the new tool in the toolbox (Figure 11.3).

Figure   11.3

Add the DB Grid control to your toolbox.

STEP 4: Click on the DBGrid tool and draw a large grid on the form (Figure 11.4). Then, using the Properties window, change the control's Name property to *dbgBooks* and its DataSource property to *datBooks*.

Figure   11.4

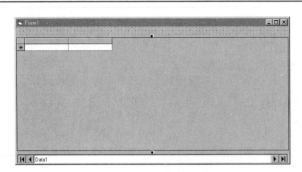

STEP 5: Create the menu bar. It should have a *File* menu with only an *Exit* command.

STEP 6: Create the large label at the top of the form with the form's title: *Book List*. Change the font and size to something you like.

Set the Properties of the Form

STEP 1: Set the form's Name property to *frmBookGrid* and its Caption property to *R 'n R—For Reading and Refreshment*.

Set the Properties of the Grid

STEP 1: Point to the grid control and right-click to display the shortcut menu. Select *Retrieve Fields* and watch as the grid changes to display all the fields from the Books table. One column is set up for each field, with the field name at the top of the column as a caption.

We are going to set more properties to improve the display of the table, but at this point the application will work. We'll make a quick test before setting the rest of the properties.

STEP 2: Start the project running. You should see the grid fill with data. Scroll to the right and view all the fields. You can also scroll down to see more records.

Next we will resize the columns, change captions for some columns, fix the display format of the Yes/No field (Fiction), and make the long titles and names wrap to a second line.

STEP 3: Stop program execution, point to the grid control, and right-click to display the shortcut menu. Select *Properties* (Figure 11.5), and the custom *Property Pages* dialog box appears (Figure 11.6). Although you can change the properties in the regular Properties window, the process is much easier from this custom dialog box.

Figure 11.5

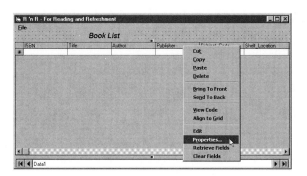

Right-click on the grid control to display the shortcut menu; select Properties.

Figure 11.6

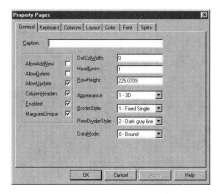

Modify the properties of the grid control using the custom Property Pages dialog box.

STEP 4: On the *General* tab select *AllowAddNew* and *AllowDelete*. Change the *Row Height* entry to *450* (approximately double the default entry).

STEP 5: Change to the *Columns* tab and make these changes:

> Column4 (Subject_Code)
>   *Caption*:   Subject
> Column5 (Shelf_Location)
>   *Caption*:   Shelf
> Column6 (Fiction)
>   *Number Format*:   Yes/No

STEP 6: Click *Apply* to apply the changes without closing the *Property Pages* dialog box.

STEP 7: Change to the *Layout* tab and make the following changes. You may want to click *Apply* after each change.

Column0 (ISBN)
  Locked: Checked
  Width: *1200* (measurements in twips)
Column1 (Title)
  WrapText: Checked
  Width: *2000*
Column2 (Author)
  WrapText: Checked
  Width: *2000*
Column3 (Publisher)
  WrapText: Checked
  Width: *2000*
Column4 (Subject_Code)
  Width: *700*
Column5 (Shelf_Location)
  Width: *700*

STEP 8: Click OK to close the custom *Property Pages* dialog box.
STEP 9: Resize the form and data control as you wish.

Write the Exit Procedure

STEP 1: Code the mnuFileExit_Click procedure with an **End** statement.

You could run the project now and have a functioning database grid. However, we are going to add one more feature to the project and make the record number appear in the data control.

Displaying the Record Number and Record Count

Often it is useful to display the record number and record count when viewing database records. You can use the **RecordCount** and **AbsolutePosition** **properties** of the data control's recordset to display both, for example: *Record 10 of 45.*

The RecordCount and AbsolutePosition Properties

The RecordCount property holds the number of records in a recordset; the AbsolutePosition holds the position of the current record in the recordset. However, AbsolutePosition is zero based; that is, the first record has an AbsolutePosition of zero. Therefore you must add one to the property to produce the record number.

Example

```
iCurrentRecord = datBooks.Recordset.AbsolutePosition + 1
```

If the recordset is at BOF or EOF, the AbsolutePosition property has a value of 0. *Note:* You cannot use the AbsolutePosition property as a record number because the position number changes as records are added and deleted.

To display the record number and count in the caption of the data control, you can create a sub procedure and use this code:

Tip

Quickly switch back and forth between the Code window and the Form window using keyboard shortcuts. F7 takes you to the Code window; Shift + F7 switches to the Form window.

```
Private Sub SetRecordNumber()
    'Display the record number
    Dim iRecordCount    As Integer
    Dim iCurrentRecord  As Integer

    iRecordCount = datBooks.Recordset.RecordCount
    iCurrentRecord = datBooks.Recordset.AbsolutePosition + 1
    If datBooks.Recordset.EOF Then
        datBooks.Caption = "EOF"
    Else
      datBooks.Caption = "Record " & iCurrentRecord & " of " & iRecordCount
    End If
End Sub
```

Note: This technique for displaying the record number works only for a dynaset or snapshot type recordset, not for a table recordset. See *Recordsets* later in this chapter.

Opening the Database

When you run a project with a data control, the database file is opened automatically. The actual file open occurs *after* the Form_Load event finishes. If you want to do any initialization steps for the database file, you can explicitly open the file in the Form_Load event procedure. Use the data control's **Refresh method** to open the database.

The Refresh Method—General Form

```
datControlName.Refresh
```

The Refresh Method—Example

```
datBooks.Refresh
```

The Refresh method opens or reopens the database specified by the data control.

You can use the Form_Load event procedure to open the database and call the SetRecordNumber sub procedure illustrated earlier. When the database is first opened, the recordset's RecordCount property does not yet know the total number of records. Use a MoveLast method, which updates the RecordCount; then use a MoveFirst to return to the beginning of the recordset.

```
Private Sub Form_Load()
    'Open the database and display the record count

    With datBooks
        .Refresh                'Open the database
        .Recordset.MoveLast     'Get the record count
        .Recordset.MoveFirst
    End With
    SetRecordNumber
End Sub
```

The Reposition Event

The previous code displays the record number and count when the database is first opened. To display the record number as the user moves from record to record, use the data control's **Reposition event**. The Reposition event occurs each time a new record becomes current; it also occurs at BOF and EOF.

```
Private Sub datBooks_Reposition()
    'Display the record number

    SetRecordNumber
End Sub
```

Putting it Together

Now that you have seen the code for explicitly opening the database and displaying the record number, add the steps to your DB Grid project. Code the Form_Load and datBook_Reposition event procedures and the SetRecordNumber sub procedure.

The Code for the DB Grid Example

```
'Program Name:   R 'n R Book List Grid
'Programmer:     J.C. Bradley
'Date:           December 1997
'Purpose:        Display and update book information in the
'                R 'n R Book database using a grid control.
'Folder:         Ch1101

Option Explicit
```
```
Private Sub datBooks_Reposition()
    'Display the record number

    SetRecordNumber
End Sub
```

```
Private Sub Form_Load()
    'Open the database and display the record count

    With datBooks
        .Refresh                'Open the database
        .Recordset.MoveLast     'Get the record count
        .Recordset.MoveFirst
    End With
    SetRecordNumber
End Sub
```

```
Private Sub mnuFileExit_Click()
    'Exit the project

    End
End Sub
```

```
Private Sub SetRecordNumber()
    'Display the record number
    Dim iRecordCount        As Integer
    Dim iCurrentRecord      As Integer

    iRecordCount = datBooks.Recordset.RecordCount
    iCurrentRecord = datBooks.Recordset.AbsolutePosition + 1
    If datBooks.Recordset.EOF Then
        datBooks.Caption = "EOF"
    Else
        datBooks.Caption = "Record " & iCurrentRecord & " of " & iRecordCount
    End If
End Sub
```

Validation and Error Trapping

When a computer program aborts and displays a cryptic system error message, who is to blame? the user? the programmer? the computer? Programmers sometimes tend to blame "stupid" users who just don't know what they are doing, but an amazing fact is that *really* good programmers seem to have "smarter" users who use programs correctly and make fewer errors. To become a good programmer, you must anticipate all possible actions of users (who don't have the benefit of your excellent logic abilities). Any action that it is possible for your program to take will be tried by some user. If your form has a button or command that shouldn't be pressed in some situations, be assured that one of your users will press it.

In Chapters 9 and 10 you learned to disable and enable command buttons to shield the user. In this section you will learn to use the database Validation event to check for some user errors, trap database errors using the On Error statement, and give your user a chance to recover after some errors, such as a missing or misplaced data file.

The programming examples in this section build on the hands-on project in Chapter 10. We will add data validation and error-trapping routines and incorporate other techniques to try to keep the user from making errors.

Locking Text Boxes

In prevous projects you disabled controls that you didn't want the user to select. In the case of text boxes, you can also lock them, which prevents any changes without making the control appear disabled. Set a text box's **Locked property** to True to lock it and to False to unlock it.

In the R 'n R Book List example, we don't want the user to change the ISBN, since that is the key field. However, we don't want to use a label for the ISBN, since we need to be able to type in an ISBN during an Add operation. Therefore, we will keep txtISBN locked most of the time and unlock it when an Add is in progress.

In the procedure to begin an Add (cmdAdd_Click), include this statement:

```
txtISBN.Locked = False
```

Because the only two actions that the user can take after beginning an Add are Save and Cancel, you should include the following statement in both routines:

```
txtISBN.Locked = True
```

Validating Data in the Validate Event

When you want to make sure that a required field has an entry or that a field has valid data, the Validate event is a good location to check. If the field is not valid, you can display an error message and cancel the operation.

The data control's Validate event occurs just before a new record becomes current (with a Move) or when an Update, AddNew, Delete, or Close occurs. You can do some checking before allowing the operation to complete.

The Validate Event—General Form

```
Private Sub DataControl_Validate(Action As Integer, Save As Integer)
```

The Validate Event—Example

```
Private Sub datBooks_Validate(Action As Integer, Save As Integer)
```

The values for the Action and Save arguments are passed to the sub procedure. You can check and/or modify their values inside the procedure. Both Action and Save are passed as integer values; you can use the actual numbers or the Visual Basic constants.

Action: The setting of the Action argument indicates the operation that occurred to cause the Validate event. You can change the value of Action. For example, change Action to 0 (vbDataActionCancel) to cancel the operation when the Sub terminates.

Constant	Integer Setting	Action That Caused Validate Event
vbDataActionCancel	0	Cancel when Sub exits
vbDataActionMoveFirst	1	MoveFirst
vbDataActionMovePrevious	2	MovePrevious
vbDataActionMoveNext	3	MoveNext
vbDataActionMoveLast	4	MoveLast
vbDataActionAddNew	5	AddNew
vbDataActionUpdate	6	Update
vbDataActionDelete	7	Delete
vbDataActionFind	8	Find
vbDataActionBookMark	9	Bookmark set
vbDataActionClose	10	Close
vbDataActionUnload	11	Form is being unloaded

Save: The value of the Save argument is set to True if any data have changed in a bound control on the form, meaning that the changed data should be saved in the file. You can set the value of Save to False if you don't want any changes to be saved.

Allowable Operations

There are some things you can do inside the Validate event procedure and some things you cannot. You *can* tell it to complete or cancel the operation and to save or not save any changes. But you *cannot* execute any other database methods during the Validate event. For example, you may determine that you need to do a Move or an AddNew. Rather than place the method in the Validate event (which causes an error), set a module-level Boolean variable to indicate the condition and check that variable after the current operation finishes. In the Validate procedure that follows, the variable mbValidationError is set to False at the top of the procedure and set to True if a validation error occurs. A little later in the chapter you will see that the cmdSave_Click procedure checks the value of mbValidationError.

Example Validate Event Procedure

The following example adds validation to the R 'n R database project from Chapter 10. In this example we want to make sure that the user enters 13 characters for the ISBN, since any other length is invalid. If an Add is in progress (the action is Update) and the length of txtISBN.Text is not exactly 13, an error condition occurs. We display a message box, reset the focus and select the text, set the Boolean variable mbValidationError to True, set the procedure's Action argument to cancel the operation, and set the Save argument to not save any changed data. *Note:* The variable mbValidationError must be dimensioned in the General Declarations Section.

```
Private Sub datBooks_Validate(Action As Integer, Save As Integer)
    'This sub is entered for every action in the database.
    'Validate the data for an Add operation
    Dim stMessage As String

    mbValidationError = False              'Set flag for no errors
    If Action = vbDataActionUpdate Then    'A new add is being saved
        With txtISBN
            If Len(.Text) <> 13 Then       'All ISBNs must be 13 characters
                stMessage = "Invalid ISBN"
                MsgBox stMessage, vbExclamation, "Data Entry Error"
                .SetFocus
                .SelStart = 0
                .SelLength = Len(.Text)
                mbValidationError = True
                Action = vbDataActionCancel
                Save = False
            End If
        End With
    End If
End Sub
```

Using the LostFocus Event

Another good time to check the contents of a control is in the control's **LostFocus event** procedure. This event occurs if the control has the focus and then loses it, usually when the user tabs to a new field or clicks on a button. In the previous example the check for a valid ISBN could be coded in the LostFocus event rather than in the Validate event.

```
Private Sub txtISBN_LostFocus()
    'Check the validity of the control during an Add
    'Note: the control is locked at all times except during an Add

    With txtISBN
        If Len(.Text) <> 13 Then       'All ISBNs must be 13 characters
            stMessage = "Invalid ISBN"
            MsgBox stMessage, vbExclamation, "Data Entry Error"
        End If
    End With
End Sub
```

You may notice that this example does not reset the focus in the text box after the error, as was done in the Validate event example. Before you code validation in the LostFocus event, you need to consider all possible actions that the user can take. The LostFocus event occurs when the user tabs out of the field *or* selects any other control. If the user clicks the Cancel button or chooses *File/Exit*, this procedure executes. If you reset the focus to the text box when the data are not valid, you may trap the user, requiring him or her to make a valid entry before canceling or exiting.

Trap Errors with On Error

Error trapping with `On Error` is very important when working with database files. You need to include the `On Error` in every procedure that accesses the database, such as the Add, Delete, Update, and all Moves. In each case trap for any errors you think are likely. For many routines you can just code an `On Error Resume Next`, which ignores the error and continues execution.

```
Private Sub cmdFirst_Click()
    'Move to first record

    On Error Resume Next
    datBooks.Recordset.MoveFirst
End Sub
```

Handling Error Conditions that Cancel an Operation

If an error occurs that will cancel an operation, such as a Delete or Add operation, the user should be notified. You can display a message and continue with program execution.

```
Private Sub cmdDelete_Click()
    'Delete the current record

    On Error GoTo HandleDeleteError
    With datBooks.Recordset
        .Delete                          'Delete the current record
        .MoveNext                        'Move to the following record
        If .EOF Then                     'If last record deleted
            .MovePrevious
            If .BOF Then                 'If BOF and EOF true, no records remain
                MsgBox "The recordset is empty.", vbInformation, "No records"
                DisableButtons
            End If
        End If
    End With

cmdDelete_Click_Exit:
    Exit Sub
```

```
HandleDeleteError:
    Dim stMessage As String
    stMessage = "Cannot complete operation." & vbCrLf & vbCrLf _
            & Err.Description
    MsgBox stMessage, vbExclamation, "Database Error"
    On Error GoTo 0                        'Turn off error trapping
End Sub
```

Handling Errors after an Add Operation

When the user clicks *Save* after an Add operation, several errors are possible. A duplicate key will cause an error, as will a missing key field.

You must decide what action you want to take when the user has entered a complete new record and the ISBN duplicates one already in the file. Do you want to clear the data? Do you want to display a message and abort the operation? In this example we will allow the user to change the ISBN and continue with the Add if desired. To make this happen, you must save the contents of the controls on the screen, execute an `AddNew` method, and replace the contents of the controls. We will place this code in a separate sub procedure.

Note: You can find the complete list of error codes in the Help topic *Trappable Errors.*

```
Private Sub cmdSave_Click()
    'Save the current record

    On Error GoTo HandleSaveErrors
    datBooks.Recordset.Update
    If Not mbValidationError Then      'Passed the validation
        txtISBN.Locked = True          'Reset all
        EnableButtons
        cmdSave.Enabled = False
        cmdAdd.Caption = "&Add"
    End If

cmdSave_Click_Exit:
    Exit Sub

HandleSaveErrors:
    Dim stMessage As String
    Select Case Err.Number
        Case 3022                 'Duplicate key field
            stMessage = "Duplicate ISBN--Record not saved."
            MsgBox stMessage, vbExclamation, "Database Error"
            SetUpAddRecord        'Allow user to change ISBN and complete add
            On Error GoTo 0       'Turn off error trapping to allow completion
        Case 3058, 3315           'No entry in key field
            stMessage = "ISBN must be completed before save."
            MsgBox stMessage, vbExclamation, "Database Error"
            SetUpAddRecord        'Give another chance to complete record
            On Error GoTo 0       'Turn off error trapping to allow completion
```

```
        Case Else
            stMessage = "Record could not be saved." & vbCRLF _
                    & Err.Description
            MsgBox stMessage, vbExclamation, "Database Error"
            datBooks.Recordset.CancelUpdate
            Resume Next
    End Select
End Sub
```

```
Private Sub SetUpAddRecord()
    'Set up a new Add to allow the user another try
    Dim savISBN As String, savTitle As String, savAuthor As String
    Dim savPublisher As String, savSubject As String
    Dim savLocation As String, savFiction As Variant

    On Error Resume Next

    'Save the contents of the form controls
    savISBN = txtISBN.Text
    savTitle = txtTitle.Text
    savAuthor = txtAuthor.Text
    savPublisher = txtPublisher.Text
    savSubject = cboSubject.Text
    savLocation = cboLocation.Text
    savFiction = chkFiction.Value

    'Start a new Add
    datBooks.Recordset.AddNew

    'Place saved data back in form controls
    With txtISBN
        .Text = savISBN
        .SelStart = 0
        .SelLength = Len(.Text)
        .SetFocus
    End With
    txtTitle.Text = savTitle
    txtAuthor.Text = savAuthor
    txtPublisher.Text = savPublisher
    cboSubject.Text = savSubject
    cboLocation.Text = savLocation
    chkFiction.Value = savFiction
End Sub
```

Trapping File Open Errors

When your application begins, VB opens the database file that you specified in the data control's DatabaseName property. If the file or path cannot be found, a fatal error occurs.

Trapping for an open error is a little tricky because the database open does not occur in any of your event procedures. By default, the open executes after Form_Load finishes but before the Form_Paint event. The easiest way to trap for an error on the open is to explicitly open the database yourself in the Form_Load event. That way, you can include error trapping.

In this example we will open the database in the Form_Load event. If the database file isn't found, the GetNewDatabaseName function is called. In the GetNewDatabaseName function, we will display the *Open* common dialog box so the user can locate the file. If any other error occurs, the MsgBox displays the system error for the current error (Err.Description) and exits the project by calling the mnuFileExit_Click procedure.

```
Private Sub Form_Load()
    'Open the database

    On Error GoTo HandleFormLoadError
    datBooks.Refresh                       'Open the database

Form_Load_Exit:
    Exit Sub

HandleFormLoadError:
    Dim stNewDatabaseName     As String
    Select Case Err.Number
        Case 3004, 3024, 3044              'Database, file, or path not found
            stNewDatabaseName = GetNewDatabaseName
            If stNewDatabaseName = "" Then 'User canceled operation
                mnuFileExit_Click
            Else
                datBooks.DatabaseName = stNewDatabaseName
                Resume                     'Reopen the database
            End If
        Case Else
            MsgBox Err.Description, vbOKOnly + vbExclamation, "Unexpected Error"
            mnuFileExit_Click              'Exit the project
    End Select
End Sub
```

In the GetNewDatabaseName function, notice the in-line error checking for the common dialog box. If the user clicks the Cancel button on the *Open* dialog box, error number 32755 occurs. The On Error Resume Next instructs Visual Basic to continue processing after the statement causing the error (the dlgOpen.ShowOpen statement). The next statement after ShowOpen should check the Err object to determine if the Cancel key was pressed.

```
Private Function GetNewDatabaseName() As String
    'Allow user to browse for the database
    Dim iResponse As Integer
    Dim stMsg     As String

    stMsg = "Database file not found." & vbCrLf & vbCrLf & _
            "Do you want to locate the file?"
    iResponse = MsgBox(stMsg, vbYesNo + vbQuestion, "File or Path not Found")
    If iResponse = vbNo Then
        GetNewDatabaseName = ""          'Set return filename to empty string
    Else                                 'Allow browse for file name
        With dlgOpen
            .filename = datBooks.DatabaseName
            .Filter = "Database files (*.mdb)|*.mdb|All files (*.*)|*.*"
            On Error Resume Next                'Trap for the Cancel button
            .ShowOpen                           'Display Open dialog box
            If Err.Number = cdlCancel Then      'Cancel button pressed
                GetNewDatabaseName = ""         'Set return filename to empty string
            Else
                GetNewDatabaseName = .Filename  'Set return filename to selected file
            End If
        End With
    End If
End Function
```

Notice the actions taken after the user selects a new filename. The DatabaseName property of the data control is set to the Filename property of the common dialog control. However, that isn't enough to make the database open with the new filename—it must be opened with a Refresh method. Back in the Form_Load error handler, after getting the new filename, the Resume statement sends execution back to the statement that caused the original error.

Feedback 11.1

1. Write the statement(s) to display the record number in a label.
2. Write the statement(s) to instruct VB to ignore any error and just keep processing.
3. What statement(s) would appear in a data control's Validate event to prevent saving any changed data for all operations except an Update?
4. Write the statement(s) to check for an empty string in txtName (a data-bound control) in the txtName_LostFocus event procedure. If no data exists, display a message box.
5. Write an error-handling routine that executes a Resume Next for error numbers 3022, 3058, and 3109. For all other errors, display a message and exit the program.
6. Explain what will display for this statement:

```
MsgBox "Error " & Err.Number & ": " & Err.Description
```

Programming Example Showing Validation Techniques

This example starts with the hands-on programming example from Chapter 10 and adds numerous validation routines that combine many of the techniques discussed in the previous sections. Figure 11.7 shows the form for this project.

Figure 11.7

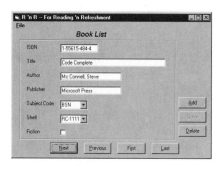

The form for the database validation example.

```
'Program Name:   R 'n R Book List Database
'Programmer:     J.C. Bradley
'Date:           September 1997
'Purpose:        Display and update book information in the
'                R 'n R Book database, using buttons for
'                navigation and combo boxes for field lookup
'Folder:         Ch1102

Option Explicit
Dim mbValidationError    As Boolean
```

```
Private Sub cmdAdd_Click()
    'Add a new record

    On Error GoTo HandleAddErrors
    If cmdAdd.Caption = "&Add" Then
        datBooks.Recordset.AddNew          'Clear out fields for new record
        txtISBN.Locked = False
        txtISBN.SetFocus
        DisableButtons                     'Disable navigation
        cmdSave.Enabled = True             'Enable the Save button
        cmdAdd.Caption = "&Cancel"         'Allow a Cancel option
    Else
        datBooks.Recordset.CancelUpdate    'Cancel the Add
        txtISBN.Locked = True
        EnableButtons                      'Enable navigation
        cmdSave.Enabled = False            'Disable the Save button
        cmdAdd.Caption = "&Add"            'Reset the Add button
    End If
```

```
cmdAdd_Click_Exit:
    Exit Sub

HandleAddErrors:
    Dim stMessage As String
    stMessage = "Cannot complete operation." & vbCrLf & vbCrLf _
            & Err.Description
    MsgBox stMessage, vbExclamation, "Database Error"
    On Error GoTo 0                 'Turn off error trapping
End Sub
```

```
Private Sub cmdDelete_Click()
    'Delete the current record

    On Error GoTo HandleDeleteError
    With datBooks.Recordset
        .Delete                 'Delete the current record
        .MoveNext               'Move to the following record
        If .EOF Then            'If last record deleted
            .MovePrevious
            If .BOF Then        'If BOF and EOF true, no records remain
                MsgBox "The recordset is empty.", vbInformation, "No records"
                DisableButtons
            End If
        End If
    End With

cmdDelete_Click_Exit:
    Exit Sub

HandleDeleteError:
    Dim stMessage As String
    stMessage = "Cannot complete operation." & vbCrLf & vbCrLf _
            & Err.Description
    MsgBox stMessage, vbExclamation, "Database Error"
     On Error GoTo 0                 'Turn off error trapping
End Sub
```

```
Private Sub cmdFirst_Click()
    'Move to first record

    On Error Resume Next
    datBooks.Recordset.MoveFirst
End Sub
```

```
Private Sub cmdLast_Click()
    'Move to last record

    On Error Resume Next
    datBooks.Recordset.MoveLast
End Sub
```

```vb
Private Sub cmdNext_Click()
    'Move to next record

    On Error Resume Next
    With datBooks.Recordset
        .MoveNext
        If .EOF Then
            .MoveFirst
        End If
    End With
End Sub
```

```vb
Private Sub cmdPrevious_Click()
    'Move to previous record

    On Error Resume Next
    With datBooks.Recordset
        .MovePrevious
        If .BOF Then
            .MoveLast
        End If
    End With
End Sub
```

```vb
Private Sub cmdSave_Click()
    'Save the current record

    On Error GoTo HandleSaveErrors
    datBooks.Recordset.Update
    If Not mbValidationError Then        'Passed the validation
        txtISBN.Locked = True            'Reset all
        EnableButtons
        cmdSave.Enabled = False
        cmdAdd.Caption = "&Add"
    End If

cmdSave_Click_Exit:
    Exit Sub

HandleSaveErrors:
    Dim stMessage As String
    Select Case Err.Number
    Case 3022                            'Duplicate key field
        stMessage = "Duplicate ISBN--Record not saved."
        MsgBox stMessage, vbExclamation, "Database Error"
        SetUpAddRecord                   'Allow user to change ISBN and complete Add
        On Error GoTo 0                  'Turn off error trapping to allow completion
```

```
      Case 3058, 3315              'No entry in key field
          stMessage = "ISBN must be completed before save."
          MsgBox stMessage, vbExclamation, "Database Error"
          SetUpAddRecord              'Give another chance to complete record
          On Error GoTo 0             'Turn off error trapping to allow completion
      Case Else
          stMessage = "Record could not be saved." & vbCrLf _
                      & Err.Description
          MsgBox stMessage, vbExclamation, "Database Error"
          datBooks.Recordset.CancelUpdate
          Resume Next
      End Select
End Sub
```

```
Private Sub datBooks_Validate(Action As Integer, Save As Integer)
    'This sub is entered for every action in the database.
    'Validate the data for an Add operation
    Dim stMessage As String

    mbValidationError = False           'Set flag for no errors
    If Action = vbDataActionUpdate Then    'A new Add is being saved
        With txtISBN
            If Len(.Text) <> 13 Then        'All ISBNs must be 13 characters
                stMessage = "Invalid ISBN"
                MsgBox stMessage, vbExclamation, "Data Entry Error"
                .SetFocus
                .SelStart = 0
                .SelLength = Len(.Text)
                mbValidationError = True
                Action = vbDataActionCancel
                Save = False
            End If
        End With
    End If
End Sub
```

```
Private Sub Form_Load()
    'Open the database

    On Error GoTo HandleFormLoadError
    datBooks.Refresh                        'Open the database

Form_Load_Exit:
    Exit Sub

HandleFormLoadError:
    Dim stNewDatabaseName    As String
```

```vb
    Select Case Err.Number
        Case 3004, 3024, 3044                'Database, file, or path not found
            stNewDatabaseName = GetNewDatabaseName
            If stNewDatabaseName = "" Then 'User canceled operation
                mnuFileExit_Click
            Else
                datBooks.DatabaseName = stNewDatabaseName
                Resume                       'Reopen the database
            End If
        Case Else
            MsgBox Err.Description, vbOKOnly + vbExclamation, "Unexpected Error"
            mnuFileExit_Click                'Exit the project
    End Select
End Sub
```

```vb
Private Sub mnuFileExit_Click()
    'Exit the project

    End
End Sub
```

```vb
Private Sub DisableButtons()
    'Disable navigation buttons

    cmdNext.Enabled = False
    cmdPrevious.Enabled = False
    cmdFirst.Enabled = False
    cmdLast.Enabled = False
    cmdDelete.Enabled = False
End Sub
```

```vb
Private Sub EnableButtons()
    'Enable navigation buttons

    cmdNext.Enabled = True
    cmdPrevious.Enabled = True
    cmdFirst.Enabled = True
    cmdLast.Enabled = True
    cmdDelete.Enabled = True
End Sub
```

```
Private Function GetNewDatabaseName() As String
    'Allow user to browse for the database
    Dim iResponse As Integer
    Dim stMsg     As String

    stMsg = "Database file not found." & vbCrLf & vbCrLf & _
            "Do you want to locate the file?"
    iResponse = MsgBox(stMsg, vbYesNo + vbQuestion, "File or Path not Found")
    If iResponse = vbNo Then
        GetNewDatabaseName = ""              'Set return filename to empty string
    Else                                     'Allow browse for file name
        With dlgOpen
            .filename = datBooks.DatabaseName
            .Filter = "Database files (*.mdb)|*.mdb|All files (*.*)|*.*"
            On Error Resume Next             'Trap for the Cancel button
            .ShowOpen                        'Display Open dialog box
            If Err.Number = cdlCancel Then   'Cancel button pressed
                GetNewDatabaseName = ""      'Set return filename to empty string
            Else
                GetNewDatabaseName = .filename 'Set return filename to selected file
            End If
        End With
    End If
End Function
```

```
Private Sub SetUpAddRecord()
    'Set up a new Add to allow the user another try
    Dim savISBN As String, savTitle As String, savAuthor As String
    Dim savPublisher As String, savSubject As String
    Dim savLocation As String, savFiction As Variant

    On Error Resume Next

    'Save the contents of the form controls
    savISBN = txtISBN.Text
    savTitle = txtTitle.Text
    savAuthor = txtAuthor.Text
    savPublisher = txtPublisher.Text
    savSubject = cboSubject.Text
    savLocation = cboLocation.Text
    savFiction = chkFiction.Value

    'Start a new Add
    datBooks.Recordset.AddNew
```

```
        'Place saved data back in form controls
        With txtISBN
            .Text = savISBN
            .SelStart = 0
            .SelLength = Len(.Text)
            .SetFocus
        End With
        txtTitle.Text = savTitle
        txtAuthor.Text = savAuthor
        txtPublisher.Text = savPublisher
        cboSubject.Text = savSubject
        cboLocation.Text = savLocation
        chkFiction.Value = savFiction
End Sub
```

Recordsets

Visual Basic supports three kinds of **recordsets**:

1. A **table recordset** represents a single table as it exists in a database file. Table recordsets are usually updateable, unless the file is locked or it is opened for ReadOnly.

2. A **dynaset** is a temporary set of data taken from one or more tables in the underlying file. A dynaset may be a query that was defined in an Access database, a single table, a subset of a table, or the result of joining multiple tables. Like a table, a dynaset is updateable if the file is not locked or opened for ReadOnly. The data in a dynaset are "live"—that is, any changes made to the data as your project is executing will appear in your recordset. *Note:* Some dynasets created from joining tables are nonupdateable; see "The SQL Select Statement—Examples" later in this chapter.

3. A **snapshot** recordset, like a dynaset, may be taken from one or more tables. The differences are that a snapshot is not updateable and also not live. You can think of a snapshot recordset like a photograph—a picture of reality at a given point in time.

The data control has a **RecordsetType property**, which you can set at design time or run time (Figure 11.8). The default type is dynaset. Table recordsets are faster than dynasets, but dynasets are more flexible, as you will see in the section "Creating a New Dynaset" later in this chapter. If you are planning to print a report, a snapshot is most efficient.

Figure 11.8

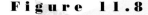

Set the RecordsetType property at design time or run time.

Searching for a Specific Record—Dynasets and Snapshots

You can search for a particular value in any field in a dynaset or snapshot. For example, you could request a certain name, account number, phone number, book title, author—any field stored in the database and bound to one of your controls. Use the **FindFirst**, **FindLast**, **FindNext**, and **FindPrevious** **methods** to locate any data.

The FindFirst, FindLast, FindNext, and FindPrevious Methods—General Form

```
datControl.Recordset.{FindFirst | FindLast | FindNext | FindPrevious} Criteria
```

The criteria specify the field name from the database and the contents for which you are searching. When we cover SQL statements later in this chapter, you will see that the criteria in a Find is like a Where clause in SQL, but without the word *Where*.

The Find methods may be used on a dynaset or a snapshot recordset, but not on a table recordset. (For tables, the Seek method is used. Seek is covered later in this chapter.)

The FindFirst, FindLast, FindNext, and FindPrevious Methods—Example

```
datBooks.Recordset.FindFirst "ISBN = '123-456-789-X'"
datMembers.Recordset.FindNext "FirstName = 'Dennis'"
datMembers.Recordset.FindFirst "FirstName = '" & txtName.Text & "'"
datMembers.Recordset.FindFirst "Amount > 100"
datMembers.Recordset.FindNext "Amount > " & txtAmount.Text
```

For a string search criterion, the string must be enclosed in single quotes, as in the first two examples. In the third example, the confusing mix of quotes produces the correct search string. If txtName.Text holds the name "Theresa", then the search string is FirstName = 'Theresa'.

When searching in a numeric field, do not enclose the numeric value in single quotes. The fourth example above includes a numeric constant, and the fifth example searches for the value entered in a text box. Assuming that the text box holds the number "123", the search string will be Amount > 123.

If you are searching a field which has any spaces in its name, the field name must be enclosed in square brackets:

```
datEmployees.Recordset.FindFirst "[Pay Rate] > 30000"
```

The FindNext and FindPrevious operations always begin with the current record and move in the direction indicated. FindFirst begins at the beginning of the file, and FindLast begins its search at the end of the file.

For the comparison operator, you may use =, >, <, <=, >=, <>, Like, Between, and In. To use the Like operator, use an asterisk as a wildcard character to match any character(s) in that position.

Examples

```
"PayRate <= 50000"
"LastName Like 'Br*'"          'Find all last names beginning with "Br"
"Amount Between 50 And 100"
"LastName Not Like 'A*'"       'All last names not beginning with "A"
"LastName In('Adams', 'Baker', 'Charles')   'All matching last names
```

The NoMatch Property

After you attempt to Find a record, always test the **NoMatch property** of the data control. When you begin a Find, NoMatch is set to False. If no record is found to meet your criteria, NoMatch is set to True. If a match is found, the record becomes current and is displayed in the data-bound controls. If no match is found, the current record number is unpredictable. A good way to take care of a no-match situation is to use a bookmark.

Bookmarks

You can set a bookmark on any record in a dynaset and use the bookmark later to return to that record. Set a variable equal to the recordset's **Book-Mark property** to save it for future reference. Any time you set the Book-Mark property to the variable name, the bookmarked record becomes the current record. *Note:* Use variant datatype for a variable to hold a bookmark.

```
'Make sure RecordsetType is set to Dynaset for this to work
Dim vBookMark      As Variant

vBookMark = datBooks.Recordset.BookMark          'Save record number _
                                                  in bookmark variable
datBooks.RecordSet.FindFirst "Title Like 'How*'"
If datBooks.RecordSet.NoMatch = True Then
    MsgBox "No record was found.", vbInformation, "No Match"
    datBooks.Recordset.BookMark = vBookMark 'Return to bookmarked _
                                             record
End If
```

Seeking with Table Indexes—Table Recordsets

The fastest way to search for a particular record is to use the **Seek method**, which can be used only with a Table recordset type. The Seek method uses indexes for the search, which is much faster than checking every record in the table as you do in a Find.

In order to do a Seek, the field (or fields) on which you search must be defined with an index. With the Learning Edition of Visual Basic and the data control, you can use only those indexes already defined in the database; with the Professional or Enterprise Edition, you can create your own indexes at run time using DAO (data access objects). *Note:* DAO is beyond the scope of this text.

The Seek Method—General Form

```
datControl.Recordset.Seek ComparisonOperator, FieldValue
```

The comparison operator must be enclosed in quotation marks and can be any one of these: "=", ">=",">","<=","<". The FieldValue is the actual value for which to search. String literals must be enclosed in quotation marks; numeric values must not be so enclosed.

The Seek Method—Examples

```
datBooks.Recordset.Seek "=", "0-671-66398-4"
datBills.Recordset.Seek ">=", 1 'Find first record greater than or _
                            equal to 1 in the first position of the key
datCustomers.Recordset.Seek ">=", stSearchString
```

Before you can Seek, you *must* first set the recordset's **Index property** to the name of an index in your table. In an Access table, the index on the primary key is called *PrimaryKey.* If other indexes are also defined in the table, usually the index name is the same as the field name.

Notice in the following program example that you can also use the Book-Mark and NoMatch properties with the Seek method.

```
Private Sub cmdSearch_Click()
    'Search for a book, based on its ISBN (the primary key)
    'Make sure RecordsetType is set to Table for this to work
    Dim vBookMark      As Variant
    Dim stISBN         As String

    vBookMark = datBooks.Recordset.Bookmark
    stISBN = InputBox("Enter ISBN", "Find a Book")
    datBooks.Recordset.Index = "PrimaryKey"      'Set the index
    datBooks.Recordset.Seek ">=", stISBN          'Seek the record
    If datBooks.Recordset.NoMatch Then
        MsgBox "No match found", vbExclamation, "Find a book"
        datBooks.Recordset.Bookmark = vBookMark
    End If
End Sub
```

Reordering a Table Recordset

You saw in the preceding section that you can select an index field for a table recordset. Changing the current index effectively changes the order in which records are displayed. Although the physical order of the records does not change, as you navigate through a table the records appear in order by the index.

In the following example, the table may be displayed in ISBN order (the primary key), in Title order (a secondary index defined in the table), or in Entry order, which is the order in which the records were added to the table.

For this continuing Books table example for R 'n R, an *Organize* menu is added to the form (Figure 11.9). The user can choose to display the records in order by ISBN, by Title, or in Entry order.

The Organize menu offers choices to display the Books table in three orders. Change the recordset's Index property to change the order.

```
Private Sub mnuOrgISBN_Click()
    'Set the index for ISBN Order

    On Error GoTo HandleErrors
    datBooks.Recordset.Index = "PrimaryKey"
    Exit Sub

HandleErrors:
    MsgBox "That index does not exist", vbExclamation, "Index Error"
    On Error GoTo 0
End Sub
```

```
Private Sub mnuOrgTitle_Click()
    'Set the index for Title Order

    On Error GoTo HandleErrors
    datBooks.Recordset.Index = "Title"
    Exit Sub

HandleErrors:
    MsgBox "That index does not exist", vbExclamation, "Index Error"
    On Error GoTo 0
End Sub
```

```
Private Sub mnuOrgEntry_Click()
    'Set the index for Data-entry Order

    On Error GoTo HandleErrors
    datBooks.Recordset.Index = ""
    Exit Sub
```

```
HandleErrors:
    MsgBox "That index does not exist", vbExclamation, "Index Error"
    On Error GoTo 0
End Sub
```

Feedback 11.2

1. What type(s) of recordset is always read-only? What type(s) may be updateable *or* read-only?
2. In what type(s) of recordset is the data "live;" that is, any changes will be automatically saved in the file?
3. In what type(s) of recordset can the `FindFirst`, `FindLast`, `FindNext`, and `FindPrevious` methods be used?
4. In what type(s) of recordset can the `Seek` method be used?
5. In what type(s) of recordset can you set the Index property to a different index?
6. Write the code statement using `FindFirst` to find the first record with a name beginning with "K" in a CustomerName field. Make up any needed control or variable names.
7. Write the code statement using `Seek` to find the first record with a name beginning with "K" in a CustomerName field. Make up any needed control or variable names; the table has an index defined for the Customer-Name field.

Working with Database Fields

In the sections that follow, we will be referencing individual fields from a recordset by name, reading the contents of fields, loading field values into a list box, and selecting records using criteria.

Referring to Database Fields

At times you may want to refer to a single field in the current recordset. Use either of these formats to refer to a field:

```
datControl.Recordset!FieldName
```

or

```
datControl.Recordset("FieldName")
```

If the field name in the table is more than one word, you must enclose the name in quotes or square brackets:

```
datBiblio.Recordset![Year Published]
```

or

```
datBiblio.Recordset("Year Published")
```

or

```
datBiblio.Recordset!"Year Published"
```

Loading Database Fields into a List Box

In the earlier examples for Find and Seek, the user entered the search value into an input box. Two better approaches might be to offer a list of possible values or use a combo box that gives the user the opportunity to select *or* enter a new value. To fill a list with values from a recordset, use a Do/Loop. You can place the loop in the Form_Activate procedure or in the Form_Load procedure. Note that by default files are opened between the Load and Activate events. If you prefer to fill the list in the Form_Load procedure, use a Refresh method to open the file first. When you decide whether to fill the list in the Form_Load or Form_Activate procedure, remember that Form_Load occurs once, the first time you show a form. Form_Activate occurs each time you show the form. If the data might have changed since the form was last displayed, use the Form_Activate procedure.

```
Private Sub Form_Load()
    'Fill the Author list

    With datBooks
        .Refresh                 'Open database

        Do Until .Recordset.EOF 'Fill the list
            If .Recordset!Author <> "" Then
                cboAuthor.AddItem .Recordset!Author
            End If
            .Recordset.MoveNext
        Loop
    End With
End Sub
```

Creating a New Dynaset

Recall that a dynaset is a temporary set of data from a database. It may be a complete table, a subset of only certain fields of a table, or only the records that match a given criterion. A dynaset may also be the result of joining the data from multiple tables. As an example of a joined dynaset, consider an application to produce invoices in which a customer number must be joined with name and address information and product codes must be joined with product description and pricing information.

Using SQL

Visual Basic uses Structured Query Language (SQL) to create new dynasets. **SQL** (pronounced either "sequel" or "S, Q, L") is an industry-standard language for accessing relational databases. Entire books and courses are devoted to using SQL. In this brief introduction, we will use SQL to select fields and records from a table and to join the fields from two tables. For more information, see Visual Basic's *Help* or one of the many books available, such as *The Practical SQL Handbook* by Bowman, Emerson, and Darnovsky.

Setting a New RecordSource

Creating a new dynaset is a two-step process. You must set the data control's RecordSource property to an SQL query and then reopen the recordset using the `Refresh` method.

In the following example the Author and Title fields are taken from the Books table, and the Subject is taken from the Subjects table. The Subject Code is used to match the records from the two tables.

```
Dim stSQL              As String

stSQL = "Select Author, Title, Subject From Books, Subjects " & _
          "Where Books.Subject_Code = Subjects.SubjectCode"
datBooks.Recordsource = stSQL          'Set new RecordSource
datBooks.Refresh                       'Open the recordset
```

Format of SQL Select Statements

SQL `Select` statements create a new recordset, based on the criteria you specify. `Select` statements can get quite complicated and can be used to join multiple tables or to group and sort the records. These examples will use some of the basic capabilities of SQL statements. (*Note:* Not all options of the `Select` statement are included here.)

The SQL Select Statement—General Form

```
Select [Distinct] FieldList From TableNames
  Where SearchConditions
  Group By FieldList
  Having GroupCriteria
  Order By FieldList
```

For the FieldList, you can list the field names or use an asterisk to indicate all fields from the named table(s). Multiple-word field names must be enclosed in square brackets.

The optional Distinct drops out duplicates so that no two records are alike.

The SQL Select Statement—Examples

```
Select * From Books

Select * From Books, Subjects
  Where Books.Subject_Code = Subjects.SubjectCode
  Order By Title
```

Note that the second example joins the Books and Subject tables so that the actual name of the subject, not just the Subject Code, can be displayed. This easy method for joining tables creates a recordset that is nonupdateable. To make a joined recordset updateable, you must use the Join clause of the SQL Select statement, which is not covered here.

Tip

For help writing SQL queries, see the Programming Hints at the end of this chapter.

Comparing Database Fields to Visual Basic Fields

The syntax for specifying a field name in an SQL Where clause depends on whether the field is in the table or is a Visual Basic variable or property. The following examples compare a table name to a variable and to a property:

```
'Compare to a string field
stSQL = "Select * From Books " & _
        "Where Subject = '" & stSubject & "'"
datBooks.Recordsource = stSQL
datBooks.Refresh

'Compare to a property
stSQL = "Select * From Books " & _
        "Where Title Like '" & txtSearchTitle.Text & "*'"
```

If you are joining multiple tables, specify field names preceded by the table name:

```
stSQL = "Select * From Books, Subjects " & _
        "Where Books.Title Like '" & txtSearchTitle.Text & "*'" & _
        "And Books.Subject_Code = Subjects.SubjectCode"
```

Check for an Empty Recordset

When you open a recordset, especially one in which the user is searching for particular values, it's quite possible for the recordset to be empty—that is, no records matched the criteria. If a recordset is empty, both BOF and EOF are True after the `Refresh` method.

```
stSQL = "Select * From Books " & _
        "Where Subject = '" & stSubject & "'"
datBooks.Recordsource = stSQL
datBooks.Refresh
If datBooks.Recordset.BOF and datBooks.Recordset.EOF Then
    MsgBox "No records match " & stSubject, vbExclamation, "No Match"
End If
```

Feedback 11.3

Use these two tables to answer the following questions. Assume that the form contains a data control called datInfo.

Table Names:

Fields:

Customers	Cities
Name	ZIPCode
Address	City
ZIP	State
Phone	

1. Write the Visual Basic statements to open a recordset with just the Name and Phone fields from the Customers table.
2. Write the statements to open a recordset of all fields in the Cities table.
3. Write the statements to create a recordset combining all of the fields from the two tables. Include a Where clause to join the two tables on the ZIP code.
4. Write the statements to create a recordset combining the Name, Address, City, State, and ZIP.
5. Modify the code for the previous question to make sure there are no duplicate records.
6. Write the code to check for an empty recordset. Display a message box if the recordset is empty.

Your Hands-On Programming Example

Extra Credit next week

In this project for R 'n R you will create a project that allows the user to select books by author or by subject. The main form displays the complete information about a book (including the complete Subject Name, not just the Code). A *Select* menu allows the user to choose *Select Records* or *All Records*. Be sure to include a check mark next to the currently selected option.

A second form holds dropdown combo boxes filled with the author names and subjects. The user can select either or both (or partial names), and the first form will reappear with only the requested books.

Hints: To have data-bound controls on two forms, both forms must have data controls. A data-bound control must be bound to a data control on the same form. In code you can refer to controls on other forms using the exclamation point:

```
frmBookData!datBooks.RecordSource = ...
```

Planning the Project

Sketch the main form (Figure 11.10) and the selection form (Figure 11.11).
Your users check over the designs, and you are ready to proceed.

Figure   11.10

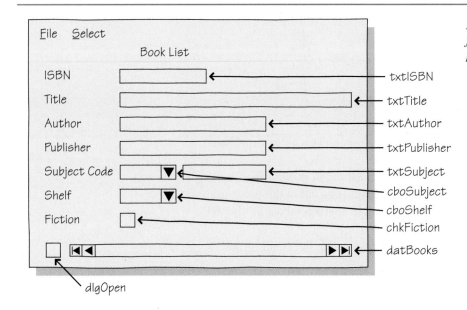

*A planning sketch for the main
form for the hands-on
programming example.*

Figure   11.11

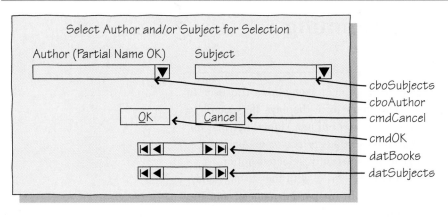

*A planning sketch for the
selection form for the hands-on
programming example.*

Plan the Objects and Properties: Main Form

Object	Property	Setting
frmBookData	Name	frmBookData
	Caption	R 'n R—for Reading 'n Refreshment
datBooks	Name	datBooks
	Connect	Access
	DatabaseName	RnRBooks.mdb
	RecordsetType	Dynaset
	RecordSource	Books
	Visible	True
Label1	Caption	ISBN
Label2	Caption	Title
Label3	Caption	Author
Label4	Caption	Publisher
Label5	Caption	Subject Code
Label6	Caption	Shelf
Label7	Caption	Fiction
txtISBN	Name	txtISBN
	Text	(blank)
	DataSource	datBooks
	DataField	ISBN
txtTitle	Name	txtTitle
	Text	(blank)
	DataSource	datBooks
	DataField	Title
txtAuthor	Name	txtAuthor
	Text	(blank)
	DataSource	datBooks
	DataField	Author
txtPublisher	Name	txtPublisher
	Text	(blank)
	DataSource	datBooks
	DataField	Publisher
cboSubject	Name	cboSubject
	Text	(blank)

(continued)

Object	Property	Setting
cboSubject (*cont'd*)	DataSource	datBooks
	DataField	Subject_Code
	List	ART
		BSS
		FNT
		RLG
		RMN
		HMR
		SCF
		BSN
		PHL
		EDC
		MST
		SLH
txtSubject	Name	txtSubject
	Text	(blank)
	DataSource	datBooks
	DataField	Subject (Not shown in list, must type it in.)
cboShelf	Name	cboShelf
	Text	(blank)
	DataSource	datBooks
	DataField	Shelf_Location
	List	RC-1111
		RC-1112
		RC-1113
		RC-1114
chkFiction	Name	chkFiction
	Caption	(blank)
	DataSource	datBooks
	DataField	Fiction
dlgOpen	Name	dlgOpen
	DialogTitle	"Open Database File"
	CancelError	True
mnuFile	Name	mnuFile
	Caption	&File
mnuFileExit	Name	mnuFileExit
	Caption	E&xit

(continued)

Object	Property	Setting
mnuSelect	Name	mnuSelect
	Caption	&Select
mnuSelectRecords	Name	mnuSelectedRecords
	Caption	&Selected Records
mnuSelectAll	Name	mnuSelectAll
	Caption	Show &All Records
	Checked	True

Plan the Objects and Properties: Selection Form

Object	Property	Setting
frmSelect	Name	frmSelect
	Caption	Select Books
Label1	Caption	Select Author and/or Subject for Selection
Label2	Caption	Author (Partial Name OK)
Label3	Caption	Subject
datBooks	Name	datBooks
	Connect	Access
	DatabaseName	RnRbooks.mdb
	RecordsetType	Dynaset
	RecordSource	Books
	Visible	False
datSubjects	Name	datSubjects
	Connect	Access
	DatabaseName	RnRBooks.mdb
	RecordsetType	Dynaset
	RecordSource	Subjects
	Visible	False
cboAuthor	Name	cboAuthor

(continued)

Object	Property	Setting
cboAuthor (*cont'd*)	Style	0 - Dropdown Combo
	DataSource	datBooks
	DataField	Author
	Sorted	True
cboSubject	Name	cboSubject
	Style	0 - Dropdown Combo
	DataSource	datSubjects
	DataField	Subject
	Sorted	True
cmdCancel	Name	cmdCancel
	Caption	&Cancel
	Cancel	True
cmdOK	Name	cmdOK
	Caption	&OK
	Default	True

Plan the Event Procedures: Main Form

Object	Procedure	Actions
frmBookData	Form_Load	Call DisplayAllRecords.

mnuSelectRecords	Click	Display selection form as modal.
		 If selection made Then
		   Check Selection menu command.
		   Uncheck All menu command.
		 If empty recordset Then
		   Display error message.
		   Call DisplayAllRecords.

mnuSelectAll	Click	Call DisplayAllRecords.
mnuFileExit	Click	End.

(General)	DisplayAllRecords	Set RecordSource to SQL string.
		 Refresh.
		 Check All menu command.
		 Uncheck Selected menu command.
		 Error handler:
		   Case File not Found
		     Call GetNewDatabaseName.
		   Case Else
		     Display error message.
		     Call mnuFileExit_Click.

(continued)

Object	Procedure	Actions
	GetNewDatabaseName	Display MsgBox "Locate File?"

		If response is No Then
		  Set return filename to empty string.
		Else
		  Display Open dialog box.
		  If Cancel pressed
		    Set return filename to empty string.
		  Else
		      Set return filename to selected file.

Plan the Event Procedures: Selection Form

Object	Procedure	Actions
frmSelect	Form_Activate	Clear cboAuthor.
		Set SQL string and open database.

		Do until EOF
		  If Author not empty Then
		    Add Author to cboAuthor.
		  End If
		  Move to next record.
		Loop

		Clear cboSubject.
		Open database.
		Do until EOF
		Add Subject to cboSubject.
		Loop
cmdCancel	Click	Set gbSelectionMade to False.
		Hide the select form.
cmdOK	Click	If Selection made from cboAuthor Then Set bSelectAuthor = True.
		If Selection made from cboSubject Then Set bSelectSubject = True.
		If both Author and Subject selected Then Set up SQL string. ElseIf only Author selected Then Set up SQL string. ElseIf only Subject selected Then Set up SQL string.
		If any selection was made Then Set Recordsource and open the database.
		Hide the form.
cmdCancel	Click	Set gbSelectionMade = False.
		Hide the form.

Write the Project

After completing the planning steps, it's time to create the forms, following the sketches in Figures 11.10 and 11.11. Figures 11.12 and 11.13 show the completed forms.

Figure 11.12

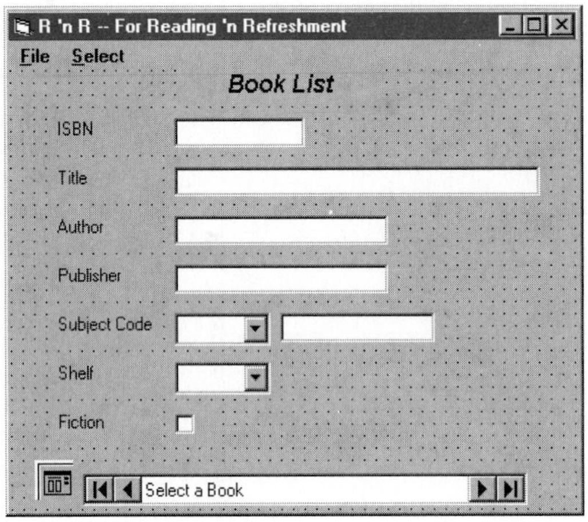

The main form for the hands-on programming example.

Figure 11.13

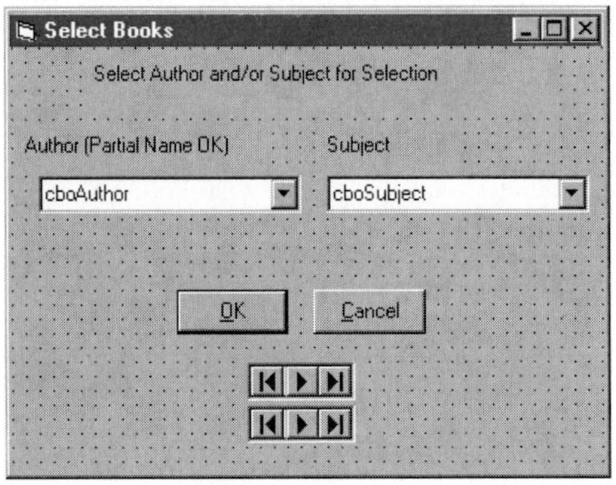

The selection form for the hands-on programming example.

- Set the properties of each of the objects, according to your plan.

- Write the code. Working from the pseudocode, write each event procedure.

- Thoroughly test the project. Make sure to set the data control to a nonexistant filename to test your file open routine. Test all varieties of selection, as well as canceling the selection form.

The Project Coding Solution

The Main Form

```
'Project:          R 'n R Book List Selection
'Programmer:       J.C. Bradley
'Date:             December 1997
'Purpose:          Display book information in the R 'n R Book database.
'                  Combine fields from two tables on the main form.
'                  Allow user to enter criteria and create new recordsets.
'Folder:           Ch1104


Option Explicit
```

```
Private Sub Form_Load()
    'Set the Recordsource for the data control

    DisplayAllRecords
End Sub
```

```
Private Sub mnuFileExit_Click()
    'Exit the project

    End
End Sub
```

```
Private Sub mnuSelectRecords_Click()
    'Display Selection form and setup Recordset
    Dim stSQL             As String

    frmSelect.Show vbModal                'Display the form as modal
    If gbSelectionMade = True Then        'Successful selection
        mnuSelectRecords.Checked = True
        mnuSelectAll.Checked = False
    End If
    If datBooks.Recordset.BOF And datBooks.Recordset.EOF Then
        MsgBox "No records match your criteria", vbExclamation, _
        "No Matching Records"
        DisplayAllRecords
    End If
End Sub
```

```
Private Sub mnuSelectAll_Click()
    'Display all records in table

    DisplayAllRecords
End Sub
```

```vb
Private Sub DisplayAllRecords()
    'Display all records in table
    Dim stSQL               As String
    Dim stMsg               As String
    Dim iResponse           As Integer

    On Error GoTo HandleErrors
    stSQL = "Select * From Books, Subjects " & _
            "Where Books.Subject_Code = Subjects.SubjectCode"
    datBooks.RecordSource = stSQL
    datBooks.Refresh
    mnuSelectAll.Checked = True
    mnuSelectRecords.Checked = False

DisplayAllRecordsExit:
    Exit Sub

HandleErrors:
    Select Case Err.Number
        Case 3004, 3024, 3044               'Database, file, or path not found
            gstNewDatabaseName = GetNewDatabaseName
            If gstNewDatabaseName = "" Then   'User canceled operation
                mnuFileExit_Click
            Else
                datBooks.DatabaseName = gstNewDatabaseName
                Resume                      'Reopen the database
            End If
        Case Else
            MsgBox Err.Description, vbOKOnly + vbExclamation, "Unexpected Error"
            mnuFileExit_Click               'Exit the project
    End Select
End Sub
```

```vb
Private Function GetNewDatabaseName() As String
    'Allow user to browse for the database
    Dim iResponse           As Integer
    Dim stMsg               As String

    stMsg = "Database file not found." & vbCrLf & vbCrLf & _
            "Do you want to locate the file?"
    iResponse = MsgBox(stMsg, vbYesNo + vbQuestion, "File or Path not Found")
```

```
        If  iResponse = vbNo Then
            GetNewDatabaseName = ""              'Set return filename to empty string
        Else                                     'Allow browse for file name
            With dlgOpen
                .filename = datBooks.DatabaseName
                .Filter = "Database files (*.mdb)|*.mdb|All files (*.*)|*.*"
                On Error Resume Next    'Trap for the Cancel button
                .ShowOpen               'Display Open dialog box
                If Err.Number = cdlCancel Then   'Cancel button pressed
                    GetNewDatabaseName = "" 'Set return filename to empty string
                Else
                    GetNewDatabaseName = .filename 'Set return filename to selected file
                End If
            End With
        End If
End Function
```

The Selection Form

```
'Module:        Select.frm
'Programmer:    J.C. Bradley
'Date:          December 1997
'Purpose:       Form to allow selection of records in
'               the R 'n R Books database using SQL queries.
'Folder:        Ch1104
Option Explicit
```

```
Private Sub cmdCancel_Click()
    'Exit the form

    gbSelectionMade = False                      'No selection made
    Me.Hide
End Sub
```

```
Private Sub cmdOK_Click()
    'Setup new Recordset based on selections

    Dim stSQL           As String
    Dim bSelectAuthor   As Boolean
    Dim bSelectSubject  As Boolean

    If cboAuthor.Text <> "" Then            'New author selected
        bSelectAuthor = True
    End If
    If cboSubject.Text <> "" Then           'New subject selected
        bSelectSubject = True
    End If
    gbSelectionMade = False                      'No selection made yet
```

```
    If bSelectAuthor And bSelectSubject Then        'Both selected
        stSQL = "Select * from Books, Subjects " & _
                "Where Books.Author Like '" & cboAuthor.Text & "*' " & _
                "And Subjects.Subject like '" & cboSubject.Text & "*' " & _
                "And Subjects.SubjectCode = Books.Subject_Code"
        gbSelectionMade = True                        'Successful selection
    ElseIf bSelectAuthor Then                         'Author only selected
        stSQL = "Select * from Books, Subjects " & _
                "Where Books.Author Like '" & cboAuthor.Text & "*' " & _
                "And Subjects.SubjectCode = Books.Subject_Code"
        gbSelectionMade = True                        'Successful selection
    ElseIf bSelectSubject Then                        'Subject only selected
        stSQL = "Select * from Books, Subjects " & _
                "Where Subjects.Subject Like '" & cboSubject.Text & "*' " & _
                "And Subjects.SubjectCode = Books.Subject_Code"
        gbSelectionMade = True                        'Successful selection
    End If
    If gbSelectionMade = True Then                    'Successful selection
        frmBookData!datBooks.RecordSource = stSQL
        frmBookData!datBooks.Refresh                  'Reopen main database
    End If
    Me.Hide                                           'Exit this form
End Sub
```

```
Private Sub Form_Activate()
    'Fill (or Refill) the lists

    Dim stSQL As String

    'Fill Author list
    cboAuthor.Clear                                  'Clear out prior contents
    stSQL = "Select Distinct Author From Books "
    With datBooks
        .RecordSource = stSQL
        .Refresh                                     'Reopen table for authors
        Do Until .Recordset.EOF                      'Fill the list
            If .Recordset!Author <> "" Then
                cboAuthor.AddItem .Recordset!Author
            End If
            .Recordset.MoveNext
        Loop
    End With

    'Fill Subject list
    cboSubject.Clear                                 'Clear out prior contents
    With datSubjects
        .Refresh                                     'Reopen table for subjects
        Do Until .Recordset.EOF                      'Fill the list
            cboSubject.AddItem .Recordset!Subject
            .Recordset.MoveNext
        Loop
    End With
End Sub
```

```
Private Sub Form_Load()
    'Get new database filename if changed

    If gstNewDatabaseName <> "" Then              'New file selected
        datBooks.DatabaseName = gstNewDatabaseName
        datSubjects.DatabaseName = gstNewDatabaseName
    End If
End Sub
```

The Standard Code Module

```
'Module:      Books.Bas
'Programmer:  J.C. Bradley
'Date:        December 1997
'Purpose:     Declare global variables for Book database.
'Folder:   Ch1104
Option Explicit


Public gbSelectionMade      As Boolean
Public gstNewDatabaseName   As String
```

Programming Hints

Trapping Database Errors

It's important to place an `On Error` statement in any procedure that does database access. You can write one error-handling sub procedure and include it in a standard code module to be used by all forms in your project. You might consider writing one fairly robust error-handling code module and adding it to all your database projects.

You must pass the error number to the error-handling procedure. Also consider passing a variable that indicates whether a `Resume`, `Resume Next`, `On Error Go To 0`, or program cancellation is needed.

You will still need considerable coding in your database to handle subs. You might consider setting up a template for the error handling and copying it into all routines that do database access. Then you can modify the action you take in each sub, depending on the situation.

Here is a suggested starting place for error handling:

```
Private Sub DatabaseAccess()
    On Error GoTo HandleErrors
    'Do database processing here

DatabaseAccessExit:
    Exit Sub
```

```
HandleErrors:
    Dim ErrorNumber   As Integer
    Dim ErrorOutcome  As Integer
    ErrorNumber = Err.Number
    HandleAllErrors ErrorNumber, ErrorOutcome   'Call Handler
    Select Case ErrorOutcome
        Case Outcome_Resume
            Resume
        Case OutcomeResumeNext
            Resume Next
        Case OutcomeGoTo0
            On Error GoTo 0
        Case OutcomeCancel
            mnuFileExit_Click
    End Select
End Sub
```

```
'Module:        Error handler standard code module
Public Const OUTCOME_RESUME = 0
Public Const OUTCOME_RESUMENEXT = 1
Public Const OUTCOME_GOTO0 = 2
Public Const OUTCOME_CANCEL = 3

Sub HandleAllErrors(ErrorNumber, ErrorOutcome)
    Select Case ErrorNumber
        Case 3004, 3024  'File not found
            ErrorOutcome = OUTCOME_CANCEL
        Case 3021        'No current record
            ErrorOutcome = OUTCOME_RESUMENEXT
    '...
End Sub
```

Advanced Database Processing

If you plan to do serious database application development, you will want to purchase the VB Professional Edition or Enterprise Edition. With these versions you can define and use Data Access Objects; create a new database; modify the structure of a database, including adding and deleting fields; create a new index; and use open database connectivity (ODBC) to connect to external databases.

Get Help Coding SQL Statements

You can get some help writing SQL queries. If you have Microsoft Access installed on your computer, you can open the database in Access and create a query that displays the data you want. Then click the SQL button in Query Design and view the SQL statement. You can copy and paste the statement into Visual Basic (where it will require a little modification). You can also give the Access Query a name, save the file, and then use the query name for the RecordSource property of the data control.

The VisData Add-In to VB can also help you write and test SQL statements. Open VisData, open your database, and write your SQL queries in the SQL window. When you have a query that works correctly, copy and paste it into your VB code.

Summary

1. The DB Grid control can be used to display and/or update database recordsets. The grid displays records in rows and columns, resembling a spreadsheet.
2. Use the data control's `Refresh` method to open or reopen the database.
3. The data control's RecordCount property holds the number of records in a recordset; the AbsolutePosition property holds the record number of the current record. AbsolutePosition is zero based.
4. The data control's Reposition event occurs each time a new record becomes current. Use the event procedure to perform any checking on the individual record.
5. The Locked property of a text box can be set to prevent any changes to the contents.
6. Use the data control's Validate event to check for errors. You can use the Action argument to cancel the operation and the Save argument to prevent changed data from being written into the file.
7. A good location to validate the contents of a text box is the control's Lost-Focus event.
8. Most procedures that perform database access need error trapping with an `On Error` statement.
9. When the user clicks Save after an Add operation, you must trap for a duplicate or missing key field.
10. The three types of recordsets are tables, dynasets, and snapshots. Tables and dynasets are live and can be updated; snapshots represent an unchangeable picture of the data at one point in time.
11. The `FindFirst`, `FindLast`, `FindNext`, and `FindPrevious` methods may be used to search for any value in any field of a dynaset or snapshot recordset. The NoMatch property is set to True if a match is not made.
12. Use the recordset's Bookmark property to store or set the current record number.
13. To search for a particular record in a table recordset, set the recordset's Index property to an existing index name and Seek for a matching value in the key field.
14. Display a table recordset in a different order by changing the Index property to an existing index name.
15. Visual Basic uses SQL to create new recordsets. Set the data control's RecordSource property to an SQL query and execute a `Refresh` method.
16. You can write a generalized error-handling procedure in a standard code module, add it to each project that performs database access, and call the procedure when needed.

Key Terms

AbsolutePosition property *400*

BookMark property *420*

dynaset *418*

FindFirst method *419*

FindLast method *419*

FindNext method *419*

FindPrevious method *419*

grid *396*

Index property *421*

Locked property *404*

LostFocus event *406*

NoMatch property *420*

RecordCount property *400*

recordset *418*

RecordsetType property *418*

Refresh method *401*

Reposition event *402*

Seek method *420*

snapshot *418*

SQL *425*

table recordset *418*

Review Questions

1. When would it be a good idea use a grid control?
2. When does the Validate event occur? What are the Action and Save arguments passed by the Validate procedure?
3. Explain the differences among tables, dynasets, and snapshots.
4. For which type(s) of recordsets is a Find valid (FindFirst, FindNext, FindLast, or FindPrevious)? What types of data can be searched for with a Find?
5. For which type(s) of recordsets is a Seek valid? Which fields in a recordset can be searched with a Seek?
6. What is SQL and how is it used in Visual Basic?

Programming Exercises

11.1 *Grid*: Write a project that will display the Publishers table in a grid. Use the Biblio.mdb sample database that comes with Visual Basic. Make sure that the grid cells are large enough to display all the data, and display the record number and record count in the caption of the data control.

   The Biblio.mdb database should be in the VB folder, the folder where Visual Basic is installed on your system.

   Note: The Biblio.mdb database included with VB4 was 288 KB, small enough to easily fit on a diskette. The version included with VB5 is 3.5 MB—too large for a diskette. The older version is included on your Student Diskette. The two versions of the file have the same structure; the size difference is due to the large number of records added to the newer version.

11.2 *Validation*: Modify project 10.2 or 10.3, which maintain the Subjects table in the R 'n R database. Validation required: Do not allow the user to change the Subject Code (the primary key) except during an Add. If the database isn't found on the open, display an error message and the *Open File* dialog box so the user can select another file. Make sure that no error can cause a run-time error. Do not allow a duplicate key field or deletion of the last record to cancel the project.

If you are modifying Exercise 10.2, add a Cancel button to allow the user to back out of an Add operation.

11.3 *Validation and Find*: Modify project 10.5, which maintains the Publishers table in the Biblio.mdb sample database. Include validation: Do not allow any run-time errors; the primary key field (PubID) cannot be changed except during an Add. Do not allow a duplicate key field or deletion of the last record to cancel the project.

Include menu choices or command buttons to search for a name or a company name using a Find.

Note: See the note in Exercise 11.1 about the size of the file.

11.4 *Reorder by Index:* Write a project that will display a table in order by one of three fields. Use the Titles table in the Biblio.mdb sample database, which comes with Visual Basic. Allow the user to select Title Order, ISBN Order, or Publisher's ID Order.

Display the following fields from the Titles table:

Title	(indexed)
Year Published	
ISBN	(PrimaryKey)
PubID	(indexed)

Note: See the note in Exercise 11.1 about the size of the file.

11.5 *SQL Dynaset*: This project displays fields from the Titles table and the Publishers table in the Biblio.mdb database. The layout of the Publishers table (shown in project 10.4) has a primary key of PubID; the Titles table (described in project 11.4) includes a PubID field, which can be used to join the two tables.

The form should contain these fields:

Titles table: Title, ISBN, Year Published
Publishers table: PubID, Company Name, City
Note: See the note in Exercise 11.1 about the size of the file.

11.6 *SQL Dynaset; Selection from List:* Modify project 11.5 to allow the user to select a subset of the data by Publisher. Include a second form holding a list of publishers. (Do not allow a publisher to be listed more than once.) When the user selects a publisher name from the list, return to the first form to display all records from that publisher.

Include menu choices to select by publisher or display all records. The currently selected option should be checked.

Note: See the note in Exercise 11.1 about the size of the file.

CASE STUDIES

VB Mail Order

Grid

Display the Product table of VB-Mail.mdb in a grid. Include the record number and record count either in the caption of the data control or in a label. Make sure the grid cells are large enough to display all the data.

Allow the user to make Adds and Deletions to the table.

Validation: Table type recordset

Modify the VB Mail Order database project from Chapter 10. The new menu will add choices to seek for a customer by last name or by customer ID. An *Organize* menu will allow the user to display the information in order by LastName or CustomerID.

Do not allow the user to change the CustomerID field (the primary key) except during an Add operation. If the database isn't found on the open, display an error message and the *Open File* dialog box so the user can select another file. Make sure that no error can cause a run-time error.

Include a Cancel button to allow the user to back out of an Add operation.

Note: This exercise uses indexes. The recordset must be table type.

SQL Dynaset

In this project for VB Mail Order, you will create an application that allows the user to select products by catalog name or by description from VBMail.mdb. The main form displays the product number, description, price, weight, and catalog name.

A *Select* menu allows the user to choose *Select Records* or *All Records*. Be sure to include a check mark next to the currently selected option.

A second form holds dropdown combo boxes filled with the catalog names and product descriptions (display only one list entry for each description—no duplicates). The user can select either or both (or partial names), and the first form will reappear with only the requested products.

Tables

Product	Catalog
ProductNumber (indexed) (compound primary key)	Number (primary key)
Catalog Number (indexed) (compound primary key)	Name (indexed)
Description	Phone
Price	
Weight	

Hints: To have data-bound controls on two forms, both must have data controls. A data-bound control must be bound to a data control on the same form. In code you can refer to controls on other forms by using the exclamation point.

Grid

Display the Vehicle table of VBAuto.mdb in a grid. Include the record number and record count either in the caption of the data control or in a label. Make sure the grid cells are large enough to display all the data.

Allow the user to make Adds and Deletions to the table.

Validation; Table type recordset

Modify the VB Auto database project from Chapter 10. The new menu will add choices to seek for a vehicle by inventory ID or by manufacturer. An *Organize* menu will allow the user to display the information in order by Manufacturer or InventoryID. *Note:* You must use a table type recordset.

Do not allow the user to change the InventoryID field (the primary key) except during an Add. If the database isn't found on the open, display an error message and the *Open File* dialog box so the user can select another file. Make sure that no error can cause a run-time error.

Include a Cancel button to allow the user to back out of an Add operation.

SQL Dynaset

Note: This project is a modification of the Chapter 10 assignment; it may not be combined with the previous validation exercises, since the recordset will not be updateable.

In this project for VB Auto Center, you will create a project that allows the user to select products by CustomerName or by InventoryIDNumber. The main

VB Auto Center

form displays the InventoryIDNumber, Manufacturer, ModelName, Year, VehicleIDNumber, CostValue, and the CustomerName. A *Select* menu allows the user to choose *Select Records* or *All Records*. Be sure to include a check mark next to the currently selected option.

A second form holds dropdown combo boxes filled with the customer names (display only one list entry for each description—no duplicates) and inventory ID numbers. The user can select either or both, and the first form will reappear with only the requested products.

Tables

Vehicle
InventoryID (indexed) (primary key)
Manufacturer
Model
Year
CostValue
VehicleID

Customer
Number (primary key)
Name (indexed)
InventoryIDNumber

Hints: To have data-bound controls on two forms, both must have data controls. A data-bound control must be bound to a data control on the same form. In code you can refer to controls on other forms by using the exclamation point.

12

Drag-and-Drop

At the completion of this chapter, you will be able to...

1. Explain the difference between the source and target in a drag-and-drop operation.

2. Code a program that incorporates drag-and-drop.

One of the handy visual tools of Windows is the drag-and-drop operation. In this chapter you will learn how to incorporate drag-and-drop into your programs.

Drag-and-Drop Terminology

Before you are ready to code a drag-and-drop operation, you need to know some terminology. Also, you need to understand the properties that must be set and the difference between a DragOver event and a DragDrop event.

The Source and the Target

In a drag-and-drop operation, an object is moved from one location to another. The object being moved (dragged) is called the **source**; the location to which it is moved is called the **target**. Figure 12.1 shows a form with a source image and a target image. In the example imgPaper is the source and img-Trash is the target.

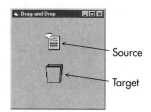

The Source object is dragged to the Target.

Source Object Properties

To make a source object movable, set its **DragMode property** to 1-Automatic. You will also want to set the **DragIcon property** to display an icon; otherwise, when you drag the object, you see only an outline.

DragOver and DragDrop Events

As an object is dragged across a form, events are occurring. The events are for the target objects, not the source. For example, as you drag an image across a form, the form's **DragOver event** occurs. If you drag the image across a control, such as a command button, the command button's DragOver event occurs. As long as you keep the mouse button down and keep moving, DragOver events occur for the form and every control over which you move. When you release the mouse button with the image over a control, the control's **DragDrop event** occurs; of course, if you release the mouse button over the form, the *form's* DragDrop event occurs.

Therefore, for any drag-and-drop operation, multiple DragOver events may occur. Only one DragDrop event occurs—when the operation is complete. All the events occur to the target objects, not to the source object.

Note: You can also code for events that occur for the source object, such as the Click event and the MouseDown, MouseUp, and MouseMove events. This brief introduction focuses on the events for the target objects.

A Step-by-Step Example

In this example you will develop a small application that allows the user to drag the airplane icon into the hangar (use your imagination for the hanger). Notice that Figure 12.2 contains two airplane icons—the source (imgPlane) and another inside the target (imgPlaneParked). The second image has its Visible property set to False, so it won't be seen until the plane is inside the hangar.

This example uses a picturebox control. For further information about pictureboxes, see Chapter 13.

Figure 12.2

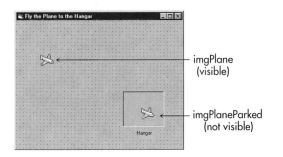

The form for the airplane step-by-step example.

Create the User Interface

STEP 1: Begin a new project and place the picturebox and the two image controls (for the two airplanes) on the form. Make sure to create the second airplane image *inside* the picturebox, which is its container. (If you try to drag the image on top of the picturebox, it will disappear behind the control because of the way the graphic controls are layered on the form. You can either draw the image inside the picturebox or cut-and-paste it inside; dragging does not place the image inside the picturebox.)

STEP 2: Create the label under the picturebox (the one captioned Hangar).

Set the Properties

STEP 1: Set the properties for the form.

Property	Value
Name	frmPlane
Caption	Fly the Plane to the Hangar

STEP 2: Set the properties for the first airplane image.

Property	Value
Name	imgPlane
Stretch	True
Picture	Vb\Graphics\Icons\Industry\Plane.ico
DragIcon	Vb\Graphics\Icons\Industry\Plane.ico
DragMode	1 - Automatic

STEP 3: Set the properties for the second airplane image.

Property	Value
Name	imgPlaneParked
Stretch	True
Picture	Vb\Graphics\Icons\Industry\Plane.ico
Visible	False

STEP 4: Set the Name property of the picturebox to picHangar.
STEP 5: Set the Caption property of the label to Hangar.

Write the Code

STEP 1: Try a test run of the program before you write any code. Click the Run button and try dragging the plane image.

> You should see an icon as you drag, but the original image still appears (Figure 12.3). The next step will be to make the source image invisible as you begin to drag the image over the form.

Figure 12.3

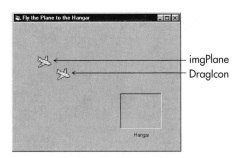

The icon moves as you drag it, but the original image is still visible.

STEP 2: Click the Stop button to halt program operation.

Code the Drag Operation

STEP 3: In the Code window, click on *Form* for the object and sanserif-*DragOver* for the procedure.

STEP 4: Code the following remark and line of code in the Form_DragOver event.

```
'Make the plane invisible

imgPlane.Visible = False
```

STEP 5: Run the program again. When you begin dragging the plane image, the original should disappear, so that it looks like you are actually dragging the image (Figure 12.4). Try dropping it anywhere. (Disappears, doesn't it?) Now it's time to take care of the drop operation.

Figure 12.4

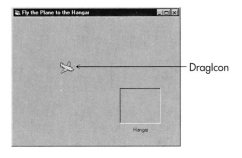

For a proper drag, the original image should disappear.

Click on the Stop button to halt program operation.

Code the Drop Operation

A DragDrop event may occur for the intended target (the picturebox), but perhaps the user misses (how?) or has a change of heart. If a DragDrop event occurs for the form or for any control other than the intended target, the drop is in error and the original image must become visible again.

STEP 6: Code the DragDrop event for the picturebox (picHangar).

```
Private Sub picHangar_DragDrop(Source As Control, X As Single, Y As Single)
    'Good Drop

    imgPlaneParked.Visible = True
End Sub
```

STEP 7: Code the DragDrop event for the form.

```
Private Sub Form_DragDrop(Source As Control, X As Single, Y As Single)
    'Bad Drop

    imgPlane.Visible = True
End Sub
```

STEP 8: Code a DragDrop event for the label control. If the user drops the plane on the label, it's another bad drop.

```
Private Sub Label1_DragDrop(Source As Control, X As Single, Y As Single)
    'Bad Drop

    imgPlane.Visible = True
End Sub
```

Run the Project

STEP 1: Start the project running. Try dragging and dropping the plane on the hangar (Figure 12.5). Then stop the project; restart and try dropping on the form. Stop, restart, and try dropping on the label. For each bad drop, the plane should reappear in its original location.

If you have problems, check the event procedure names. You must code the DragDrop event for the picturebox, the form, and the label.

F i g u r e   1 2 . 5

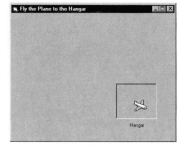

A good drag-and-drop with the airplane in the hangar.

Wouldn't it be helpful to have command buttons to exit the project and to reset the image to its original location?

Add Command Buttons

STEP 1: Add two command buttons to the form (Figure 12.6) and set their properties.

Figure 12.6

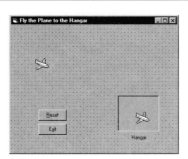

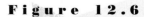

Add a Reset and an Exit command button to the form.

Object	Property	Value
cmdReset	Name	cmdReset
	Caption	&Reset
cmdExit	Name	cmdExit
	Caption	E&xit

STEP 2: Code the cmdReset_Click event.

```
Private Sub cmdReset_Click()
    'Reset to original condition

    imgPlaneParked.Visible = False
    imgPlane.Visible = True
End Sub
```

STEP 3: Code the cmdExit_Click event.

```
Private Sub cmdExit_Click()
    'Exit the project

    End
End Sub
```

You *could* test the project to see what happens when you drop the plane on a command button now, but the plane would disappear from the screen (from radar?). A better practice is to code the DragDrop event for the two command buttons first.

STEP 4: Copy and paste the statements from the Form_DragDrop event procedure into the cmdReset_DragDrop event procedure.

```
Private Sub cmdReset_DragDrop(Source As Control, X As Single, Y As Single)
    'Bad Drop

    imgPlane.Visible = True
End Sub
```

STEP 5: Paste another copy into the DragDrop event for the cmdExit button.

```
Private Sub cmdExit_DragDrop(Source As Control, X As Single, Y As Single)
    'Bad Drop

    imgPlane.Visible = True
End Sub
```

Run the Completed Project

STEP 1: Try each option. Drag the plane and drop it anywhere on the form. Drag it to its hangar and try the Reset button. Then test your Exit button.

Dragging and Dropping Multiple Objects

In the previous example only one object was enabled for drag-and-drop. Recall that the source object becomes invisible in the form's DragOver event procedure. What if the form has more than one possible source object (as in Figure 12.7)? Which object should become invisible? Fortunately, there's an easy answer. Notice the first line of the DragOver event procedure:

```
Private Sub cmdExit_DragOver(Source As Control, X As Single, Y As Single)
```

F i g u r e   1 2 . 7

All four toy icons on this form can be dragged to the target (a toybox).

The Source argument holds the name of the control that caused the DragOver event to occur. You can use the name *Source* to reference the source control in code.

```
Source.Visible = False
```

Passing the Source Argument

There may be times when you want to call another procedure from a DragOver or a DragDrop event procedure. Recall from the previous example that if a source object is dropped on any control other than the target, it is considered a "bad drop." In a bad drop, the source control must be made visible again. Rather than place identical code in the DragDrop event for all other controls on the form, consider writing one BadDrop sub procedure and calling it wherever necessary. The Source argument that is passed to the DragDrop event procedure can be passed along to the BadDrop sub procedure.

```
Private Sub cmdExit_DragDrop(Source As Control, X As Single, Y As Single)
    'Bad drop

    BadDrop Source           'Call the BadDrop procedure and pass along Source
End Sub
```

```
Private Sub cmdReset_DragDrop(Source As Control, X As Single, Y As Single)
    'Bad drop

    BadDrop Source           'Call the BadDrop procedure and pass along Source
End Sub
```

```
Private Sub BadDrop(Source)
    'Make source control visible

    Source.Visible = True
End Sub
```

Note: In this example the BadDrop sub procedure has only one line of code, so it could be argued that it is efficient to place that line in each Drag-Drop event. In many situations, such as the chapter hands-on programming example, there are several things to do for a bad drop. In that case it is best to create a separate general sub procedure.

Changing the Icon of the Target Image

In the airplane step-by-step example, a successful drag-and-drop operation caused a second image to become visible. Another approach is to change the icon of the target image. Continuing with the toybox example (Figure 12.7), when a successful drop is made, the icon of the target changes. Notice in the following code how the Picture property of the target is changed to match the Picture property of the source.

```
Private Sub imgTarget_DragDrop(Source As Control, X As Single, Y As Single)
    'Got a hit

    imgTarget.Picture = Source.Picture
End Sub
```

Setting the DragIcon Property of Source Controls

In most cases you want the DragIcon of a source control to be the same as its Picture property. You can set both properties to the same filename in the Properties window, as you did in the earlier step-by-step example. But a better approach is to set only the Picture property at design time. Then in the Form_Load event set the control's DragIcon property to its Picture property. That way the file is loaded from disk only once.

```
imgPlane.DragIcon = imgPlane.Picture
```

If you have multiple images that can be dragged, consider making them a control array. In the toybox example, the four images are named imgToy(0), imgToy(1), imgToy(2), and imgToy(3). A loop in the Form_Load event procedure will set the DragIcon property for all images. (Note that the number of lines of code remains the same for 15 or 20 or 4 toy images.)

```
Private Sub Form_Load()
    'Setup DragIcon properties
    Dim iCounter

    For iCounter = 0 To 3
        imgToy(iCounter).DragIcon = imgToy(iCounter).Picture
    Next iCounter
End Sub
```

Blanking Out an Image

If you want to remove an icon from an image, you have two choices. You can either use the LoadPicture function with a blank filename or set the image's Picture property to another (blank) image. The second approach is the more efficient but requires you to place an extra image, with no Picture property, on the form.

Method 1

```
imgTarget.Picture = LoadPicture("")
```

Method 2

```
imgTarget.Picture = imgBlank.Picture
```

Feedback 12.1

1. Name two properties of the source object that should be changed for drag-and-drop operations.

2. To what object does the DragDrop event belong?

3. What object does the Source argument of the DragOver event contain?

The Toybox Program

Here are the entire program specifications for the toybox example shown in Figure 12.7. Try entering and running it.

Object	Property	Setting
frmToys	Name	frmToys
	Caption	Put Away the Toys
imgToy(0)	Name	imgToy(0)
	DragMode	1 - Automatic
	Picture	Vb\Graphics\Icons\Industry\Bicycle.ico
imgToy(1)	Name	imgToy(1)
	DragMode	1 - Automatic
	Picture	Vb\Graphics\Icons\Industry\Cars.ico
imgToy(2)	Name	imgToy(2)
	DragMode	1 - Automatic
	Picture	Vb\Graphics\Icons\Industry\Plane.ico
imgToy(3)	Name	imgToy(3)
	DragMode	1 - Automatic
	Picture	Vb\Graphics\Icons\Industry\Rocket.ico
imgTarget	Name	imgTarget
	BorderStyle	1 - Fixed Single
	Stretch	True
imgBlank	Name	imgBlank
cmdReset	Name	cmdReset
	Caption	&Reset
cmdExit	Name	cmdExit
	Caption	E&xit

The Procedures

Object	Procedure	Actions
frmToys	Load	Set DragIcon to Picture property for all four images.
	DragOver	Set source control invisible.
	DragDrop	Call BadDrop procedure.
imgTarget	DragDrop	Set Picture property to picture of source.
cmdExit	Click	Exit the project.
	DragDrop	Call BadDrop procedure.
cmdReset	Click	Set Visible = True for all four images. Set Picture property of target to blank.
	DragDrop	Call BadDrop procedure.
General	BadDrop	Set Visible = True for source image.

The Project Coding Solution

```
'Program:      Toybox Drag-and-Drop Example
'Programmer:   J.C. Bradley
'Date:         December 1997
'Purpose:      Drag-and-drop multiple objects.
'Folder:       Ch1202
Option Explicit
```

```
Private Sub cmdExit_Click()
    'Exit the project

    End
End Sub
```

```
Private Sub cmdExit_DragDrop(Source As Control, X As Single, Y As Single)
    'Bad drop

    BadDrop Source
End Sub
```

```
Private Sub cmdReset_Click()
    'Replace images
    Dim iCounter As Integer

    For iCounter = 0 To 3
        imgToy(iCounter).Visible = True
    Next iCounter
    imgTarget.Picture = imgBlank.Picture
End Sub
```

```
Private Sub cmdReset_DragDrop(Source As Control, X As Single, Y As Single)
    'Bad drop

    BadDrop Source
End Sub


Private Sub Form_DragDrop(Source As Control, X As Single, Y As Single)
    'Bad drop

    BadDrop Source
End Sub


Private Sub Form_DragOver(Source As Control, X As Single, _
        Y As Single, State As Integer)
    'Make the source control invisible

    Source.Visible = False
End Sub


Private Sub Form_Load()
    'Setup DragIcon properties
    Dim iCounter

    For iCounter = 0 To 3
        imgToy(iCounter).DragIcon = imgToy(iCounter).Picture
    Next iCounter
End Sub


Private Sub BadDrop(Source)
    'Make source control visible

    Source.Visible = True
End Sub


Private Sub imgTarget_DragDrop(Source As Control, X As Single, Y As Single)
    'Got a hit

    imgTarget.Picture = Source.Picture
End Sub
```

Your Hands-On Programming Example

This drag-and-drop example combines many of the techniques from the chapter. In addition, you must change target icons more than once. Figure 12.8 shows a sketch of the form; Figures 12.9, 12.10, and 12.11 show the form during run time.

Figure 12.8

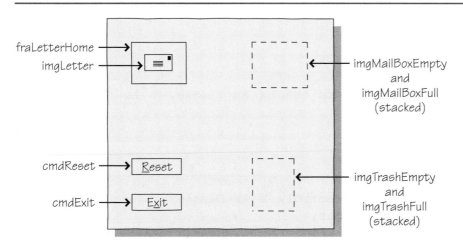

fraLetterHome

imgLetter

imgMailBoxEmpty
and
imgMailBoxFull
(stacked)

cmdReset

cmdExit

imgTrashEmpty
and
imgTrashFull
(stacked)

The planning sketch for the hands-on programming example.

Figure 12.9

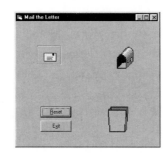

The form as it appears when the project begins execution.

Figure 12.10

When the letter is placed in the mailbox, the flag goes up.

Figure 12.11

When the letter is placed in the trash can, the trash is visible.

When the letter is dropped on the mailbox, the icon changes to a mail-box with the flag up and a letter inside. The letter can be dragged from the mailbox and dropped in the trash can or back in its original frame. When the letter is dropped in the trash can, the icon changes to a trash can with visible trash inside. The letter can also be dragged out of the trash can and dropped either on the mailbox or on the letter's original frame.

Since you want to drag a letter from the mailbox or the trash can, the DragIcon property of each must be set to the same icon as the letter image. (You want to drag a picture of a letter, not a picture of a trash can.)

The two icons for the mailbox are stored in two image controls—one visible and one invisible. Manipulating the two images gets a little tricky, but remember what you learned about multiple controls: You can select multiple controls by dragging a selection box around them or Ctrl-click on them, or you can set similar properties on multiple selected controls in the Properties window (such as their Top, Left, and Width properties). You can also select one control and choose *Send to Back* or *Bring to Front* on the *Edit* menu.

The two image controls for the trash cans are developed in the same way as the mailboxes.

Planning the Project

Sketch the form, which is shown in Figure 12.8.

Plan the Objects and Properties

Object	Property	Setting
frmMail	Name	frmMail
	Caption	Mail the Letter
fraLetterHome	Name	fraLetterHome
	Caption	(blank)
imgLetter	Name	imgLetter
	DragMode	1 - Automatic
	Stretch	True
	Icon	Vb\Graphics\Icons\Mail\Mail02a.ico
imgMailBoxEmpty	Name	imgMailBoxEmpty
	Stretch	True
	Picture	Vb\Graphics\Icons\Mail\mail16a.ico
imgMailBoxFull	Name	imgMailBoxFull
	Stretch	True
	Picture	Vb\Graphics\Icons\Mail\mail16b.ico
	DragMode	1 - Automatic
	Visible	False

(continued)

Object	Property	Setting
imgTrashEmpty	Name	imgTrashEmpty
	Stretch	True
	Picture	Vb\Graphics\Icons\Computer\Trash04b.ico
imgTrashFull	Name	imgTrashFull
	Stretch	True
	Picture	Vb\Graphics\Icons\Computer\Trash04a.ico
	DragMode	1 - Automatic
	Visible	False
cmdReset	Name	cmdReset
	Caption	&Reset
cmdExit	Name	cmdExit
	Caption	E&xit

Plan the Event Procedures

Plan the actions for the event procedures.

Object	Procedure	Actions
frmMail	Load	Set DragIcon of imgLetter, imgMailboxFull, and imgTrashFull to imgLetter.Picture.
	DragOver	Case imgLetter Set Visible = False for imgLetter. Case imgTrashFull Set Visible = False for imgTrashFull. Set Visible = True for imgTrashEmpty. Case imgMailBoxFull Set Visible = False for imgMailBoxFull. Set Visible = True for imgMailBoxEmpty.
	DragDrop	Call BadDrop procedure.
imgMailBoxEmpty	DragDrop	Set Visible = False for imgMailBoxEmpty. Set Visible = True for imgMailBoxFull.
imgTrashEmpty	DragDrop	Set Visible = False for imgTrashEmpty. Set Visible = True for imgTrashFull.
fraLetterHome	DragDrop	Set Visible = True for imgLetter.
cmdExit	Click	Exit the project.
	DragDrop	Call BadDrop procedure.
cmdReset	Click	Set Visible = True for imgLetter, imgMailBoxEmpty, and imgTrashEmpty. Set Visible = False for imgMailBoxFull and imgTrashFull
	DragDrop	Call BadDrop procedure.

(continued)

Object	Procedure	Actions
General sub procedure	BadDrop	Case imgLetter Set Visible = True for imgLetter. Case imgTrashFull Set Visible = True for imgTrashFull. Set Visible = False for imgTrashEmpty. Case imgMailBoxFull Set Visible = True for imgMailBoxFull. Set Visible = False for imgTrashEmpty.

Write the Project

Follow the sketch in Figure 12.8 to create the form. Figures 12.9, 12.10, and 12.11 show the completed form at different stages of run time.

Set the properties of each object according to your plan.

The next step is to write the code. Working from the pseudocode, write each event procedure.

When you complete the code, thoroughly test the project by dragging the letter to each target and resetting from each position.

The Project Coding Solution

```
'Program:      Drag-and-Drop  Hands-On  Example
'Programmer:   J.C.  Bradley
'Date:         December  1997
'Purpose:      Mail  or  trash  a  letter  using  drag-and-drop.
'Folder:       Ch1203
Option Explicit
```

```
Private Sub cmdExit_Click()
    'Exit the project

    End
End Sub
```

```
Private Sub cmdExit_DragDrop(Source As Control, X As Single, Y As Single)
    'Bad drop

    BadDrop Source
End Sub
```

```vb
Private Sub cmdReset_Click()
    'Initialize setup

    imgLetter.Visible = True
    imgMailBoxEmpty.Visible = True
    imgMailboxFull.Visible = False
    imgTrashEmpty.Visible = True
    imgTrashFull.Visible = False
End Sub
```

```vb
Private Sub cmdReset_DragDrop(Source As Control, X As Single, Y As Single)
    'Bad drop

    BadDrop Source
End Sub
```

```vb
Private Sub Form_DragDrop(Source As Control, X As Single, Y As Single)
    'Bad drop

    BadDrop Source
End Sub
```

```vb
Private Sub Form_DragOver(Source As Control, X As Single, _
        Y As Single, State As Integer)
    'Check source of DragOver and determine action

    Select Case Source
        Case imgLetter
            imgLetter.Visible = False
        Case imgTrashFull
            imgTrashFull.Visible = False
            imgTrashEmpty.Visible = True
        Case imgMailboxFull
            imgMailboxFull.Visible = False
            imgMailBoxEmpty.Visible = True
    End Select
End Sub
```

```vb
Private Sub Form_Load()
    'Set DragIcon to Letter

    imgLetter.DragIcon = imgLetter.Picture
    imgMailboxFull.DragIcon = imgLetter.Picture
    imgTrashFull.DragIcon = imgLetter.Picture
End Sub
```

```vb
Private Sub fraLetterHome_DragDrop(Source As Control, X As Single, _
        Y As Single)
    'Good drop

    imgLetter.Visible = True
End Sub
```

```
Private Sub imgMailBoxEmpty_DragDrop(Source As Control, X As Single, _
        Y As Single)
    'Good drop

    imgMailBoxEmpty.Visible = False
    imgMailboxFull.Visible = True
End Sub
```

```
Private Sub imgTrashEmpty_DragDrop(Source As Control, X As Single, _
        Y As Single)
    'Good drop

    imgTrashEmpty.Visible = False
    imgTrashFull.Visible = True
End Sub
```

```
Private Sub BadDrop(Source As Control)
    'Reset source after a bad drop

    Select Case Source
        Case imgLetter
            imgLetter.Visible = True
        Case imgTrashFull
            imgTrashFull.Visible = True
            imgTrashEmpty.Visible = False
        Case imgMailboxFull
            imgMailboxFull.Visible = True
            imgMailBoxEmpty.Visible = False
    End Select
End Sub
```

Programming Hints

Manual Drag-and-Drop

Sometimes you don't want to set the DragMode property of controls to True, because then normal mouse clicks and keystrokes are not recognized for that control. You can use the **Drag method** to drag-and-drop in code. For example, you can begin a Drag operation in the MouseDown event for a control (a text box in this example).

```
Private Sub txtEntry_MouseDown(Button As Integer, Shift As Integer, _
        X As Single, Y As Single)
    txtEntry.Drag
End Sub
```

This action begins a drag operation that behaves just like the automatic dragging in the chapter examples.

S u m m a r y

1. In a drag-and-drop operation, the control being dragged is the source and the destination is the target.
2. Set the source control's DragMode property and DragIcon property.
3. The DragOver event and DragDrop event belong to the target control. DragOver occurs as the source control is moving over the target; DragDrop occurs when the mouse button is released over the target.
4. The system passes the name of the source control to the DragOver and DragDrop event procedures.

K e y   T e r m s

`Drag` method *465*
DragDrop event *448*
DragIcon property *448*
DragMode property *448*

DragOver event *448*
source *448*
target *448*

R e v i e w   Q u e s t i o n s

1. Explain the differences between the source and target in a drag-and-drop operation.
2. What properties must be set for the source control in order to do drag-and-drop?
3. An image of a car is dragged across the form and dropped on an image of a garage. Describe the events that occur (and the objects to which they belong) as the operation takes place.
4. In a form's DragOver event, it is necessary to make the source control invisible. How can you determine which control is the source control?

P r o g r a m m i n g   E x e r c i s e s

12.1 Write a drag-and-drop program to play a game of darts. Use the icon files Vb\Graphics\Icons\Misc\Bullseye.ico and Vb\Graphics\Icons\Point10.ico. Place an invisible dart in the center of the target and make it visible when the target is hit. Also, keep track of the number of hits and display a running count.

　　　The Reset button should reset the dart to its starting location.

12.2 Create a project for a card suit guessing game. The user will drag the images to the boxes along the lower edge of the form. When the correct image is placed in a box, make the image remain there. When all four images are in the correct location, display a message box congratulating the user. The Reset button should replace the suit images at the top of the form and clear out the lower boxes. (*Hint:* For the boxes, use image controls with a border.) Consider using control arrays.

The four images are in the Vb\Graphics\Icons\Misc folder and are called Misc34.ico, Misc35.ico, Misc36.ico, and Misc37.ico.

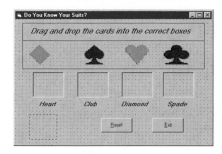

12.3 Create a project that keeps track of the food for the company picnic. The user will enter each person's name into the text box and then drag it to the correct list. Use drag-and-drop to move the names to the lists. (*Hint:* Use AddItem in the DragDrop event procedure.)

Do not allow a blank name to be added to a list; keep the three lists in alphabetic order; clear out the text box and set the focus after adding a name to one of the lists.

12.4 Modify project 12.3 to include a menu bar. Include a *Print* command with a submenu to select the item (Salads, Main Courses, or Desserts). Allow the user to print any of the lists, one at a time.

12.5 Create your own drag-and-drop application using graphic files available to you (or create your own using a draw or paint program). You can use files with the extensions .ico, .wmf, .bmp, .dib, .gif, .jpg, .emf, and .cur.

CASE STUDIES

VB Mail Order

Create a form that allows the user to select express delivery or freight through the use of drag-and-drop. Include a label that will display the words *Express Delivery—overnight* or *Freight—10 working days* after the user drops the appropriate icon in the mailbox.

For this project the empty mailbox (Mail16a.ico) is the empty target. The source will be Mail05b.ico for freight and Mail03.ico for express. When the selected type of delivery reaches the target, change the empty mailbox to have the flag up (Mail16b.ico).

VB Auto Center

Create a game project using drag-and-drop for the VB Auto Center.

The form will contain the following images:

Vb\Graphics\Icons\Traffic\Trffc16.ico in the upper-left corner.

Vb\Graphics\Icons\Misc\Face01.ico in the upper-right corner (visible to begin).

Arranged horizontally across the center of the screen:

Vb\Graphics\Icons\Industry\Wrench.ico
Vb\Graphics\Icons\Industry\Gaspump.ico
Vb\Graphics\Icons\Elements\Water.ico

At the bottom of the screen:

Vb\Graphics\Icons\Misc\House.ico at the lower-left corner.

Vb\Graphics\Icons\Misc\Face03.ico at the lower-right corner (invisible to begin).

The car may be dragged to the icons only in the proper order before it goes home. The correct order: wrench for service, gas pump, and then water for the car wash. When the drops have been made in the proper order and the vehicle gets home, the top face becomes invisible and the lower face becomes visible.

13

Graphics

At the completion of this chapter, you will be able to . . .

1. Understand the measurements in the graphics coordinate system.

2. Display and change colors using the RGB and QBColor functions.

3. Create graphics using graphics methods.

4. Understand the graphics-layering principles.

5. Load and change pictures at run time.

6. Create simple animation.

7. Use the timer control.

8. Use scroll bars to move and resize an image.

In past chapters you learned how to incorporate graphics using the shape, image, and line controls. In this chapter you will learn how to enhance the use of the controls and to use the graphics methods. New controls include the picturebox, the timer, and scroll bar controls.

The Graphics Environment

The measurement system you use in a project is known as the *scale*. You can set the scale to twips, points, pixels, inches, or centimeters, or you can create your own scale.

The default scale is twips. A **twip** is a twentieth of a point. Since a **point** is a printer's measurement of 1/72nd of an inch, a twip is 1/1440th of an inch; in other words, an inch has 1,440 twips.

The term **pixel** is an abbreviation of *picture element,* a dot that makes up a picture. You are probably most familiar with pixels in the determination of the resolution of a monitor. A display of 1280 by 1024 is a reference to the number of pixels horizontally and vertically.

You can change the scale with the ScaleMode property. The examples in this chapter are based on twips.

The Coordinate System

Graphics are measured from a starting point of 0,0 for the *x* and *y* coordinates beginning in the upper-left corner. The *x* is the horizontal position, and *y* is the vertical measurement. The starting point depends on where the graphic is being placed. If the graphic is going directly on a form, the 0,0 coordinates are the upper-left corner of the form. You can also place graphics in containers, such as pictureboxes. In this case the picturebox has its own 0,0 **coordinate system** to be used as the starting point for measuring the location of items within the control (Figure 13.1).

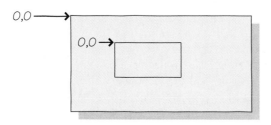

The coordinates for graphics begin with 0,0 in the upper-left corner of a form or container.

You can change the starting point of the coordinate system, the scale, or both. You control these with the ScaleLeft, ScaleTop, ScaleWidth, and ScaleHeight properties. For more information on changing these properties refer to the Help files in Visual Basic.

Picturebox Controls

The **picturebox control** is very similar to the image control, but a picturebox does not contain a Stretch property. However, it does have many other properties for graphics including those relating to the scale. Pictureboxes use more system resources than images use. For that reason, the recommended practice is to use an image control unless you need the added capabilities of a picturebox.

Figure 13.2 shows the toolbox tool for creating a picturebox, and Figure 13.3 shows a picturebox on a form. The three-character prefix for a picturebox name is "pic". Use the chart on the inside back cover of the text to compare the properties that apply to the image and to the picturebox.

Figure 13.2

The picturebox tool from the toolbox.

Figure 13.3

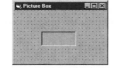

A picturebox control on a form.

Colors

You can specify colors for your graphics in a number of ways. The graphic controls have properties for ForeColor, BackColor, and FillColor. The VB graphics methods use the RGB color functions or the intrinsic color constants (such as vbRed and vbBlue).

The RGB Function

The **RGB function** specifies the quantities of red, green, and blue for the largest variety of colors. The value for each color ranges from 0 to 255, with 0 being the least intense. The color arguments are in the same order as their letters in the function name—red, green, and then blue. You can use the function to assign a color to a property or specify the color in a graphics method. Table 13.1 shows the RGB values for a few colors.

Color	Red Value	Green Value	Blue Value
Black	0	0	0
Blue	0	0	255
Green	0	255	0
Cyan	0	255	255
Red	255	0	0
Magenta	255	0	255
Yellow	255	255	0
White	255	255	255

The RGB values for some standard colors.

The RGB Function—General Form

```
RGB(RedValue, GreenValue, BlueValue)
```

The RGB Function—Examples

```
lblWarning.BackColor = RGB(255, 0, 0)          'Red
txtName.Forecolor = RGB(255, 0, 255)           'Blue and red make magenta
Line (0, 0) - (1000, 1000), RGB(100, 100, 100) 'A gray line
```

The Visual Basic Intrinsic Color Constants

You can use the VB color constants introduced in Chapter 2 to specify colors for properties and for drawing graphics using the graphic methods. The color constants:

vbBlack
vbBlue
vbGreen
vbCyan
vbRed
vbMagenta
vbYellow
vbWhite

The QBColor Function

For compatibility with older versions of Basic, VB allows you to use color numbers that range from 0 to 15. To use these color numbers you must use the **QBColor function**, which converts the color numbers to their RGB equivalent.

Example

```
frmMyForm.BackColor = QBColor(1)          'Blue
```

Table 13.2 shows the sixteen color numbers that you can use with the QBColor function.

Number	Color
0	Black
1	Blue
2	Green
3	Cyan
4	Red
5	Magenta
6	Yellow
7	White
8	Gray
9	Light Blue
10	Light Green
11	Light Cyan
12	Light Red
13	Light Magenta
14	Light Yellow
15	Bright White

The QBColor numbers, included in VB for compatibility with older versions of Basic.

The Graphics Methods

You can use the graphics methods to draw in a Form object, a Picturebox object, or the Printer object. The object you choose to use is considered the **container** for your graphics. If you omit the name of the object, it defaults to the form.

Using the graphics methods, such as Cls, Pset, Line, and Circle to draw graphics differs from using the graphics controls. Controls, such as shapes, lines, and images, appear on the form as it is loaded. If the form is resized or covered by another window and redisplayed, the graphics controls reappear. But the graphics you draw with code display when the code is executed. They do not redraw automatically. Therefore, if you want your graphics to redisplay each time the form is redisplayed, place the statements in the Paint event for the form or picturebox. You may also place graphics methods in a user event such as a command button's Click event.

The Cls Method

The **Cls method** clears the specified object. You could use Cls to clear an existing picture and change the background color of the form or picturebox. Remember that if the object is omitted on any of the graphics methods, the default is the form.

The CLS Method—General Form

```
[Object].Cls
```

The CLS Method—Examples

```
Cls              'Clear the background of the form
picLogo.Cls      'Clear a picture box
```

The PSet Method

The **PSet method** places a single point on the object in the location specified by the *x* and *y* coordinates. You may also specify the color for the point.

The PSet Method—General Form

```
[Object].PSet (x, y)[, Color]
```

The PSet Method—Examples

```
picLogo.PSet (100,100)
PSet (1000,1000), vbCyan
```

When the color is omitted, the ForeColor property setting of the object is used. The *x* and *y* coordinates may also be variables.

The **Rnd function** returns "random" numbers between 0 and the upper limit specified. Try the following code from the Ch1301 programming example, which demonstrates the use of the Rnd function. Figure 13.4 shows the screen generated by this code.

Figure 13.4

```
'Program:        PSet
'Programmer:     A. Millspaugh
'Date:           December 1997
'Description:    Place colored dots randomly on the
'                form.
'Folder:         Ch1301
Option Explicit
```

```
Private Sub cmdExit_Click()
    'Terminate the Project

    End
End Sub
```

```
Private Sub Form_Paint()
    'Place random dots in random colors on form

    Dim iIndex As Integer
    Dim iColor As Integer
    Dim X, Y

    For iIndex = 1 To 1000
        X = Rnd * ScaleWidth
        Y = Rnd * ScaleHeight
        iColor = Rnd * 15
        PSet (X, Y), QBColor(iColor)
    Next iIndex
End Sub
```

The **DrawWidth property** determines the size of the point. Change the DrawWidth of the form in the Ch1301 PSet program to 5. Next try changing the form WindowState to Maximized and experiment with the ScaleHeight and ScaleWidth properties.

You can try this again, placing the dots within an object using Object.Width and Object.Height to control the upper limit.

If you wish to erase a point, place a new point on top of the old one using the BackColor property as the color.

The Line Method

Since a line is used to connect two points, the **Line method** needs two sets of coordinates specified for the line. If the first coordinate is not specified, the line is drawn from the last graphics point created on the screen.

The Line Method—General Form

```
[Object].Line [(x1, y1)]-(x2, y2)[, [Color][, B [ F ] ] ]
```

The Line Method—Examples

```
Printer.Line (5, 0)-(5,1000)
picLogo.Line - (500,100), QBColor(2)
picLogo.Line - (500,300), vbBlue
Line (iXStart, iYStart)-(iXEnd, iYEnd), iLineColor
```

Let's write a program to draw an *X* in a picturebox called picX. (See Figure 13.5.)

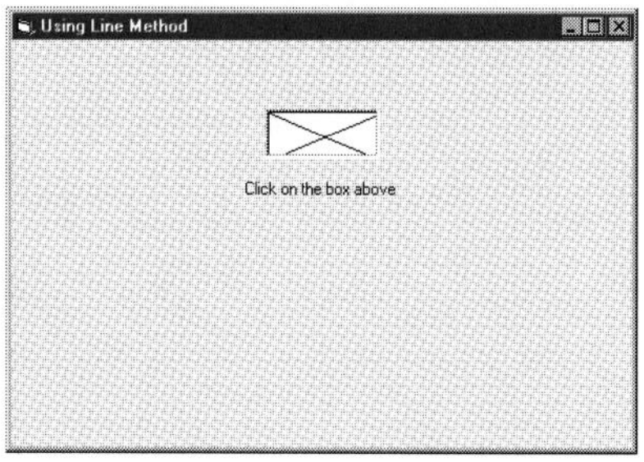

The screen for project Ch1302.

```
'Program:      Line
'Programmer:   A. Millspaugh
'Date:         December 1997
'Description:  Draw lines in a picture box.
'Folder:       Ch1302
Option Explicit
```

```
Private Sub picX_Click()
    'Create an X in the picture box

    picX.Line (0, 0)-(picX.Width, picX.Height)
    picX.Line (0, picX.Height)-(picX.Width, 0)
End Sub
```

Rectangles

You can also use the `Line` method to create boxes by adding the *B* parameter. The *B* stands for *box*. You can fill a box without specifying a color; the box will use the FillColor property. However, make sure to include the commas to indicate that the color argument is missing.

```
Line ( 0, 0)-(500, 500), ,B
```

The box may be filled with a solid color or a pattern, depending on the setting of the FillStyle property.

FillStyle	Name	Pattern
0	Solid	Uses the FillColor to fill the box.
1	Transparent (default)	No fill regardless of the FillColor setting.
2	Horizontal lines	
3	Vertical lines	
4	Upward diagonal lines	
5	Downward diagonal lines	
6	Crosshatch	
7	Diagonal crosshatch	

The *F* option listed in the general form of the `Line` method may be used to *fill* the box instead of using the FillStyle and the FillColor properties. You cannot use the *F* option without the *B*.

The Circle Method

You can draw rounded shapes using the **Circle method**. These shapes include circles, ovals, arcs, and pie-shaped wedges. To draw a circle, specify the coordinates of the center and the radius of the circle. You may also specify the color or let it default to the ForeColor.

```
picFace.Circle (160,100), 60
```

You can choose whether or not the circle is filled by setting the FillStyle property.

```
FillStyle = 0
Circle (1000,1000),500          'A filled circle
FillStyle = 1
Circle (2000,1000),500          'Outline of a circle
```

The full form of the `Circle` method includes an argument for start angle and end angle that will determine arcs and wedges. The aspect ratio argument is used to make ellipses (ovals).

The Circle Method—General Form

```
[Object].Circle (x, y), Radius [, Color [, StartAngle, EndAngle [, AspectRatio] ] ]
```

Arcs of a Circle

To draw parts of a circle, you can specify the beginning and ending points of the arc. The endpoints for the arc are determined by a measurement in radians, counterclockwise from 0 to 2 PI. The angle reference is illustrated below:

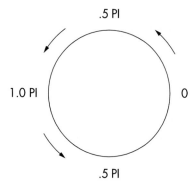

The statements

```
Const PI = 3.14159
Circle (500, 500), 500, , 0, PI
```

draw the top half of a circle, beginning at the right side (angle 0) and proceeding over the top to the left side (angle PI).

The following program uses circles and arcs to draw a happy face. Place the code in the form's Paint event. (See Figure 13.6.)

Figure 13.6

The screen for project Ch1303.

```
'Program:      Circle
'Programmer:   A. Millspaugh
'Date:         December 1997
'Description:  Draw a happy face.
'Folder:       Ch1303
Option Explicit

Private Sub Form_Paint()
    'Draw a happy face on the form
    Const PI = 3.14159

    FillStyle = 1
    Circle (1600, 1000), 600                'Outline of the face
    Circle (1600, 1000), 400, , PI * 1.2, PI * 1.8   'Smile
    FillStyle = 0
    Circle (1400, 900), 50, vbBlue          'Left eye
    Circle (1800, 900), 50, vbBlue          'Right eye
End Sub

Private Sub mnuFileExit_Click()
    'Terminate the project

    End
End Sub
```

Segments of a Pie

You can draw an arc with its endpoints connected to the center of the circle, creating a slice of pie. If you specify an endpoint as a negative number, a radius is drawn from the endpoint to the center point. *Note:* The minus sign preceding the endpoint specifies the radius; it does not indicate a negative angle.

```
Circle (50, 100), 30, , -PI / 2, -PI
```

will produce

Ellipses

By setting the AspectRatio parameter of the `Circle` method, you can draw ellipses and elliptical arcs. The aspect ratio refers to the comparative length of a radius drawn on the horizontal to a radius drawn vertically. When this parameter is omitted, the aspect ratio is assumed to be one and the figure drawn is a circle. When the aspect ratio is less than one, the elliptical figure will be wider than it is tall. When the aspect ratio is greater than one, the ellipse will display taller than it is wide. (Notice the commas in the statements that indicate omitted parameters.)

```
Circle (1000,1000),1000, , , , .5      'Wide ellipse
Circle (3000,1000),1000, , , , 1.5     'Tall ellipse
```

Give the preceding lines of code a try.

The Step Keyword

Each graphics method discussed here can also use the **Step method**, which changes the coordinates from an absolute position to a relative position. Coordinates are normally measured from the starting point of the object (**absolute position**) on which they are drawn. By adding the `Step`, coordinates begin from the last point that was drawn, hence the starting point is a **relative position**.

A variation of the `PSet` method is the `PSet Step` statement that indicates that the x and y coordinates specified are relative to the last point drawn. The statement

```
PSet Step (100,100)
```

draws a point 100 twips to the right and 100 twips down from the last point specified in a graphics method. If there are no previous graphics methods, the offset is from the 0, 0 coordinate.

With the `Line` method you can give the second set of coordinates as an offset from the first.

```
Line -Step(1000, 1000)
```

Try the following lines of code:

```
PSet Step(100, 100)
Line -Step(1000, 1000)
Line -Step(2000, 0)
```

Feedback 13.1

1. Write the statement to draw a vertical line down the center of a form that has the following settings: ScaleWidth 6720, ScaleHeight 4230.
2. Write the statements to draw a "Pacman."

Layering

When displaying information on an object, different types of items are placed on different layers. The complete set of layers produces the output that we can see. (See Figure 13.7.)

Figure 13.7

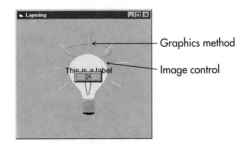

Most controls appear on the top layer, graphics controls appear on the middle layer, and graphics created with graphics methods appear on the bottom layer.

Layer	Contents
Front	Command buttons, check boxes, and other nongraphic controls.
Middle	Labels; graphics controls.
Back	Shapes created with graphics methods.

The items in the back layer are covered by items in the middle layer, which are then covered by controls in the front layer. Usually this arrangement is what you want, allowing your graphics to form a background for the controls. However, these default layers may act differently depending on the settings of the AutoRedraw and ClipControls properties, which contain Boolean values, and on whether the graphics methods are located in the Paint event or elsewhere.

If you set the **AutoRedraw property** to True, you will get **persistent graphics**, which save an image in memory so that it can be redisplayed. Although Windows takes care of windows and controls when objects are moved or resized, it is up to you to control the redraw for graphics. Although it sounds easy to just set AutoRedraw to True, there is a trade-off in performance because the process requires a large amount of memory. The default setting of AutoRedraw is False for forms and True for pictureboxes. It is to your advantage to place graphic images in pictureboxes rather than on forms because less memory is required.

One technique is to leave AutoRedraw set to False and call the Paint event procedure when needed.

The **clipping region** determines which portions of the screen will be painted. A form, frame, or picturebox has a **ClipControls property**. Setting ClipControls to False can also speed up the repainting process but may cause items to be mixed in the layering.

Use these guidelines for redrawing graphics:

1. When AutoRedraw is set to False, place graphics methods in the Paint event of the form or container.
2. Setting AutoRedraw to True will always provide normal layering but will slow the performance because too much memory is required. (Setting ClipControls to False may speed up the form display.)

You can also adjust the stacking order of items within a layer using the **ZOrder method**. This method can be used for forms or controls. Refer to Help for more information on the ZOrder method.

More Properties for Your Graphics Controls

You have used icons for the Picture property of an image control. Pictures in the form of bitmaps, icons, or metafiles may be added to a project during design time or at run time. You can create your own pictures in a Paint or Draw program and then copy and paste them using the Clipboard. Pictures may be placed in an image control, a picturebox control, or a form.

Controlling Pictures at Design Time

All three controls that can contain a picture have a Picture property. If you set the Picture property of a form, the graphic displays behind the controls. An advantage of using the image control rather than the picturebox control is that an image has a Stretch property that can be used to adjust the size of the picture when set to True.

Another way to insert a picture in a control is by using the Clipboard. First copy a picture from clip art or one that you created into the Clipboard. Then switch to Visual Basic and the *Paste* command on the *Edit* menu will be available to transfer the picture from the Clipboard onto the control.

To remove a picture, double-click the setting in the Picture property and press the Delete key.

Controlling Pictures at Run Time

You may also want to add or change a picture at run time. You can do so by having images or pictures that have their original Visible property set to False or by using the **LoadPicture function**.

If you store a picture in an invisible control, you can change the Visible setting to True; or you may decide to copy it to another control.

```
picLogo.Visible  =  True
imgLogo.Picture  =  picLogo.Picture
```

The LoadPicture function can be used in code to retrieve a file during run time. The problem with this method is that the path must be known. When you are running an application on multiple systems the path names may be different.

```
picLogo.Picture  =  LoadPicture("C:\VB\LOGO.BMP")
```

To remove a picture from the display, either hide it or use the LoadPicture function with empty quotes.

```
imgLogo.Visible  =  False
picLogo.Picture  =  LoadPicture("")
```

Moving a Picture

You can move picture controls by changing the values of the Left and Top properties. Another choice is the **Move method**. Since line controls do not have Top and Left properties, you must use the Move method to move them. The Move method produces a smoother appearing move than changing the Top and Left properties of controls.

The Move Method—General Form

```
[Object].Move Left [, Top[, Width[, Height]]]
```

Only the new setting for the Left property is required, but the Top, Width, and Height may also be changed. If no object is specified, the move applies to the current form.

The Move Method—Examples

```
Move 100                          'Changes the Left property of the current form
imgLogo.Move 100, 200
imgLogo.Move imgMove.Left + 50    'Moves relative to current position
```

Notice that a move can be relative to the current location by performing calculations in the Move method.

Simple Animation

Animation can be created by toggling between two pictures, moving a picture, or rotating through a series of pictures. You can also create graphics with the various graphics methods.

Many of the icons in the icon library have similar sizes but opposite states such as a closed file cabinet and an open file cabinet; a mail box with the flag up and with the flag down; a closed envelope and an open envelope; or a traffic light in red, yellow, or green. In Chapter 2 you used the two light bulbs: LightOn and LightOff.

The sample program demonstrates changing between two phone icons (a phone and a phone being held). The two icons are phone12.ico and phone13.ico in the Vb\Graphics\Icons\Comm folder. Two images, imgWithHand and imgNoHand, are set to invisible (Visible = False) and then assigned to imgPhone at run time. (See Figure 13.8.)

Figure 13.8

The screen for project Ch1304.

```
'Program:      Phones
'Programmer:   A. Millspaugh
'Date:         December 1997
'Description:  Change a picture of a phone to
'              show someone holding it.
'Folder:       Ch1304
Option Explicit
```

```
Private Sub cmdChange_Click()
    'Change the phones

    imgPhone.Picture = imgWithHand.Picture
End Sub
```

```
Private Sub cmdExit_Click()
    'Terminate the project

    End
End Sub
```

```
Private Sub cmdStart_Click()
    'Display the phone

    imgPhone.Picture = imgNoHand.Picture
End Sub
```

Several interesting procedures are supplied in a sample project called Blanker that comes with Visual Basic. The path for Blanker is usually Program Files\DevStudio\VB\Samples\PGuide\Blanker.

Try creating a picturebox, name it picAnimate, place one line control inside (called Line1), and use the following code for a command button:

```
Dim X, Y
For Y = 1 to 25
    picAnimate.Cls
    line1.X1 = Int(PicAnimate.Width * Rnd)
    line1.Y1 = Int(PicAnimate.Height * Rnd)
    line1.X2 = Int(PicAnimate.Width * Rnd)
    line1.Y2 = Int(PicAnimate.Height * Rnd)
    For X = 1 To 5000
    Next X              'Keep on screen awhile
Next Y
```

A nicer way to control the delay in the previous example is to use the timer control.

The Timer Control

You can build in a delay with a set interval using the **timer control** and its Timer event. You can place the control anywhere on the form; it is invisible at run time. The tool for the timer control is represented by the little stopwatch in the toolbox (Figure 13.9). The three-character prefix for naming a timer is "tmr".

Figure 13.9

The tool for the timer control.

When you have a timer control on a form, it "fires" each time an interval elapses. You can place any desired code in the Timer event procedure; the code will execute each time the event occurs. You choose the interval for the timer by setting its **Interval property**, which can have a value of 0 to 65,535. This value specifies the number of milliseconds between the calls to the Timer event. One second is equivalent to 1,000 milliseconds. Therefore, for a three-second delay, set the timer's Interval property to 3,000. You can set the value at run time or at design time.

You can keep the Timer event from occurring by setting its **Enabled property** to False. The default value is True.

Your Hands-On Programming Example

In this project you will use a timer control to create simple animation. Place an airplane icon in an image control, move it across the screen, and also make it appear larger as it goes.

First, sketch a plan of the form (Figure 13.10).

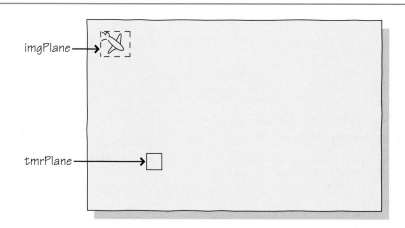

A planning sketch for the hands-on programming example.

Plan the Objects and Properties

Object	Property	Setting
frmPlane	Name	frmPlane
	Caption	Fly the Plane
tmrPlane	Name	tmrPlane
	Interval	50
imgPlane	Name	imgPlane
	Icon	Vb\Graphics\Icons\Industry\Plane.ico

Plan the Event Proecedures

Plan the actions for the event procedure.

Procedure	Actions
tmrPlane_Timer	Move the plane. Adjust the size.

Write the Project

● Follow the sketch in Figure 13.10 to create the form. Figure 13.11 shows the completed form.

Figure 13.11

The form for the hands-on programming example.

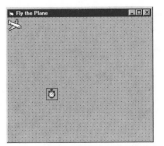

● Set the properties of each object according to your plan.

● Write the code. Working from the pseudocode, write each event procedure.

● Thoroughly test the project.

The Programming Coding Solution

```
'Program:      Plane
'Programmer:   A. Millspaugh
'Date:         December 1997
'Description:  Move a plane with the timer.
'Folder:       Ch1305
Option Explicit
```

```
Private Sub TmrPlane_Timer()
    'Fly the Plane

    imgPlane.Move imgPlane.Left + 10, _
                  imgPlane.Top + 10, _
                  imgPlane.Width + 2, _
                  imgPlane.Height + 2
End Sub
```

More Graphics Techniques

Custom Coordinate Systems

You can specify a custom scale for your graphics by changing the coordinate system. Perhaps you would like the upper-left corner to start at 0,0 and the lower-right corner to be 100,100. Then all of your coordinates for graphics will be between 0 and 100. This change can be accomplished with the **Scale** method.

The Scale Method—General Form

```
[Object].Scale (x1 , y1) - (x2, y2)
```

The Scale Method—Example

```
picLogo.Scale (0, 0) - (100, 100)
```

The handy result of this statement is that you could then use ratios. The midpoint would be (50, 50).

The **Scale** method performs the same function as individually altering the settings in ScaleLeft, ScaleTop, ScaleWidth, and ScaleHeight.

PaintPicture Method

Another graphics method that you have available is the **PaintPicture** method, which can be used to place a graphic file on a form, the printer object, or in a picturebox.

This method is faster than moving picture controls around and can be used to copy graphics, such as when tiling a picture on the screen. By making the destination width a negative number, the graphic file can be flipped horizontally.

The PaintPicture Method—General Form

```
[Object].PaintPicture Picture, x1, y1[, DestinationWidth,_
DestinationHeight]
```

The PaintPicture Method—Example

```
PaintPicture picLogo.Picture, 100, 100
```

The following program creates a tiled image on the form (Figure 13.12).

Figure 13.12

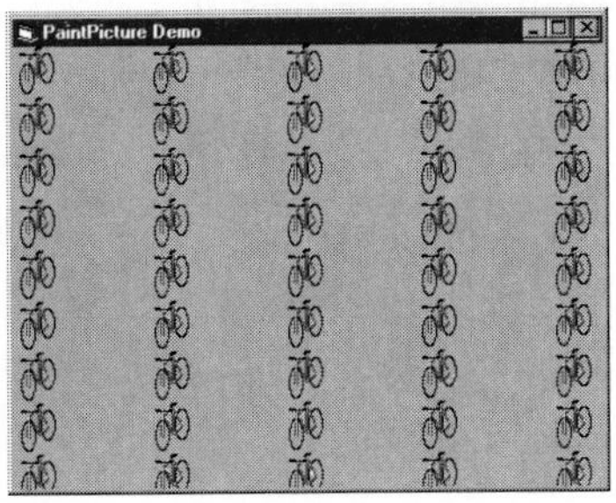

The form for example Ch1306.

```
'Program:      Tile
'Programmer:   A. Millspaugh
'Date:         December 1997
'Description:  Create a tiled background on a form.
'Folder:       Ch1306
Option Explicit

Private Sub Form_Paint()
    'Tile the background of the form
    Dim iIndex1 As Integer
    Dim iIndex2 As Integer

    For iIndex1 = 0 To 10
        For iIndex2 = 0 To 10
            frmTile.PaintPicture picTile.picture, _
                iIndex2 * picTile.Width, _
                iIndex1 * picTile.Height
        Next iIndex2
    Next iIndex1
End Sub
```

The Scroll Bar Controls

You can add **horizontal scroll bars** and **vertical scroll bars** to your form (Figure 13.13). These **scroll bar controls** are similar to the scroll bars in Windows that can be used to scroll through a document or window. Often scroll bars are used to control sound level, color, size, and other values that can be changed in small amounts or large increments.

Figure 13.13

Horizontal scroll bars and vertical scroll bars can be used to select a value over a given range.

Properties for scroll bars are somewhat different than the controls we have worked with previously. Because the scroll bars represent a range of values, they have the following properties: **Min** for the minimum value, **Max** for the maximum value, **SmallChange** for the distance to move when the user clicks on the scroll arrows, and **LargeChange** for the distance to move when the user clicks on the gray area of the scroll bar (Figure 13.14).

Figure 13.14

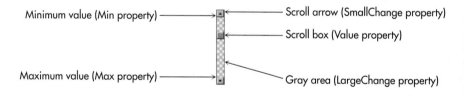

Clicking on the scroll arrow changes the Value property by SmallChange amount; clicking on the gray area of the scroll bar changes the Value property by LargeChange amount.

The Value property indicates the current position of the scroll box and its corresponding value within the scroll bar. When the user clicks the up arrow of a vertical scroll bar, the Value property decreases by the amount of SmallChange (if the Min value has not been reached). Clicking the down arrow causes the Value property to increase by the amount of SmallChange.

When naming scroll bars, use a prefix of "hsb" for horizontal scroll bars and "vsb" for vertical scroll bars. Figure 13.15 shows the horizontal scroll bar tool and vertical scroll bar tool from the toolbox.

Horizontal scroll bar ⟶   ⟵ Vertical scroll bar

The toolbox tools for horizontal scroll bars and vertical scroll bars.

Scroll Bar Events

The events that occur for scroll bars differ from the ones used for other controls. Although a user might click on the scroll bar, there is no Click event; rather there are two events: a Change event and a Scroll event.

When the user clicks on a scroll arrow or the gray area of the scroll bar, a **Change event** occurs. If the user drags the scroll box instead, a **Scroll event** occurs. In fact, multiple scroll events occur, as long as the user continues to drag the scroll box. As soon as the user releases the mouse button, the Scroll events cease and a Change event occurs. When you write code for a scroll bar, usually you will want to code both a Change event procedure and a Scroll event procedure.

A Fun Programming Example

You can try the scroll bars and the shape controls with this little exercise. Open a new project and create a rectangle on the form using a shape control. Make a note of the shape's Location properties—Left, Top, Width, and Height. Then create an image inside the rectangle with its Picture property set to an icon of a car.

A horizontal scroll bar will make the image move sideways in the rectangle, and the vertical scroll bar will make it move up and down. Make sure that you set the Max and Min properties of the scroll bar to reflect the screen location of the rectangle. The SmallChange and LargeChange also need to be set.

Design and Create the Form

Figure 13.16 shows the form for this scroll bar example.

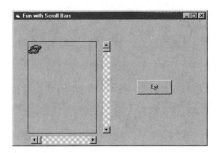

The form for the scroll bar programming example.

Set the Properties

Control	Property	Setting
Form1	Caption	Fun with Scroll Bars
	Name	frmScroll
shpRectangle	Name	shpRectangle
	Shape	0 - Rectangle
	Height	3135
	Left	480
	Top	720
	Width	2415
imgCar	Name	imgCar
	Picture	Vb\Graphics\Icons\Industry\Cars.ico
	Height	480
	Width	480
hsbMoveCar	Name	hsbMoveCar
	Min	480
	Max	1935 (rectangle width - image width)
	LargeChange	50
	SmallChange	10
vsbMoveCar	Name	vsbMoveCar
	Min	720 (top of rectangle)
	Max	3135 (rectangle height)
	LargeChange	50
	SmallChange	10
cmdExit	Name	cmdExit
	Caption	E&xit

Write the Code

Procedure	Actions
cmdExit_Click	Terminate the project.
vsbMoveCar_Change	Assign the scroll bar Value to the Top property of the image.
vsbMoveCar_Scroll	Assign the scroll bar Value to the Top property of the image.
hsbMoveCar_Change	Assign the scroll bar Value to the Left property of the image.
hsbMoveCar_Scroll	Assign the scroll bar Value to the Left property of the image.

The Project Coding Solution

```
'Program:      Scroll
'Programmer:   A. Millspaugh
'Date:         December 1997
'Description:  Use scroll bars to move an image
'              horizontally and vertically within the
'              limits of a rectangle.
'Folder:       Ch1307
Option Explicit

Private Sub cmdExit_Click()
    'Terminate the project

    End
End Sub

Private Sub hsbMoveCar_Change()
    'Controls the side to side movement
    'Used for arrow clicks

    imgCar.Left = hsbMoveCar.Value
End Sub

Private Sub hsbMoveCar_Scroll()
    'Controls the side to side movement
    'Used for scroll box movement

    imgCar.Left = hsbMoveCar.Value
End Sub

Private Sub vsbMoveCar_Change()
    'Positions the up and down movement
    'Used when arrow is clicked

    imgCar.Top = vsbMoveCar.Value
End Sub

Private Sub vsbMoveCar_Scroll()
    'Positions the up and down movement
    'Used when the scroll box is moved

    imgCar.Top = vsbMoveCar.Value
End Sub
```

S u m m a r y

1. Graphics may be measured in twips, points, pixels, inches, or centimeters. The measurement is known as the scale.
2. The coordinate system normally begins with 0,0 at the upper-left corner of the container object.
3. Colors are available using the RGB function, the intrinsic color constants, and the QBColor function.
4. The graphics methods include PSet, Line, and Circle. You can use the Line method to create a rectangular shape. The Circle method may be used for ellipses, arcs, and wedges.
5. Graphics and controls are created in three layers that produce a single display. The AutoRedraw and ClipControls properties affect the order of the layering.
6. Pictures can be loaded, moved, and resized at run time.
7. Animation effects can be created by using similar pictures and by controlling the location and visibility of controls.
8. The timer control can enable a Timer event that occurs at specified intervals.
9. Scroll bar controls are available for both horizontal and vertical control. Properties include Min, Max, SmallChange, and LargeChange. Scroll and Change events are used to control the action.

K e y   T e r m s

Review Questions

1. How big is a twip?
2. To which controls do the graphics methods apply?
3. What happens when no object is specified for a graphics method such as PSet or Cls?
4. Name three methods available for graphics.
5. How is a pie-shaped wedge created?
6. What is the advantage to setting the AutoRedraw to True? to False?
7. What function is used to load a picture at run time?
8. How is a picture removed at run time?
9. What steps are necessary to change an image that contains a turned-off light bulb to a turned-on light bulb?
10. What is the purpose of the timer control?

Programming Exercises

13.1 Create a project that contains a picturebox and two buttons labeled *Smile* and *Frown.* The Smile button will display a happy face in the picturebox; Frown will display a sad face. Use graphics methods to draw the two faces.

13.2 Use graphics methods to create the background of a form. Draw a picture of a house, including a front door, a window, and a chimney.

13.3 Use an image control with a .bmp file from Windows. Set the Stretch property to True. Use a scroll bar to change the size of the image.

13.4 Use graphics from a clip art collection to create a project that has a command button for each month of the year. Have an appropriate image display in a picturebox for each month.

13.5 Use the bicycle icon from Visual Basic and a timer control to move the bicycle around the screen. Add a Start button and a Stop button. The Stop button will position the bicycle back to its original position. (The bicycle icon is stored as Vb\Graphics\Icons\Industry\Bicycle.ico.)

CASE STUDIES

VB Mail Order

Create a logo for VB Mail Order using graphics methods. Place the logo in the startup form for the project from Chapter 6. Add appropriate images and graphics to enhance each form. The graphics may come from .bmp files, clip art, or your own creation from Paintbrush.

VB Auto Center

Have the startup screen initially fill with random dots in random colors. Draw an Auto Center advertisement using graphics methods that will appear on the screen. Have various appropriate images (icons) appear in different locations, remain momentarily, and then disappear.

14

Advanced Topics in Visual Basic

At the completion of this chapter, you will be able to...

1. Use ActiveX controls to extend the functionality of your projects.

2. Create a link from a Visual Basic project to a Web site.

3. Include procedures from dynamic link libraries (DLLs) in your projects.

4. Realize the potential for programming using the Windows API.

5. Use an OLE container control for linking or embedding objects.

6. Recognize the relationship between Visual Basic and VBA.

7. Understand the concepts of an object and a class.

8. Create a report using Crystal Reports.

In addition to the large variety of controls, statements, and functions that are a part of the language, as a Visual Basic programmer you have the opportunity to reach many other sources for your application needs. Controls have been referred to as *objects*. Objects go far beyond the controls that are a part of Visual Basic. Think of **objects** as programming components. You can create your own objects or incorporate those available from word processors, spreadsheets, graphics programs, and the multitude of software available.

Programs that run under Windows have access to other applications' objects through ActiveX controls, the object linking and embedding (OLE) container control, and through dynamic link libraries (DLLs). This chapter introduces these topics as well as some components designed specifically for use with Visual Basic.

ActiveX

The term **ActiveX** was originally used to refer to controls that could be used with the Internet. Since then the term has been expanded to refer to executable files, controls (COM, or Component Object Model, objects), and DLLs that are used by multiple applications. These controls were called *OLE controls* for a period of time, but the term OLE currently refers only to the process of object linking and embedding. The terminology has been changing rapidly and likely will change somewhat in the next few years as the use of the Internet expands.

Using ActiveX Controls

You have used many controls built into Visual Basic, plus some others, such as the grid and the common dialog box, that had to be added to the Visual Basic environment. In general, Microsoft refers to any controls as *ActiveX controls*. These controls may be part of Visual Basic or created by other companies, or you may create your own. The controls that are part of Visual Basic are called *intrinsic controls*; those that must be added later are called *components*. Many ActiveX controls are available in the Professional and Enterprise Editions of Visual Basic, as well as from other software developers.

A large selection of ActiveX controls is available to solve many problems. You can purchase controls to display various types of gauges and indicators, display data in grids, send and receive faxes, display video, scan bar codes, display calendars and appointments, and perform many other functions. Many ActiveX controls are available as shareware, and a few are freeware. Many can be downloaded from various Web sites.

The files for ActiveX controls have extensions of .OCX or .VBX. (Any controls developed for Visual Basic 4.0 or later should be .OCX files.)

Tip

To include objects that are available from other applications, use the *References* dialog box, which you can select from the *Project* menu.

When you select the *Components* command from the *Project* menu, you see a list of the controls available on the system (Figure 14.1). As you select a component name from the list, a line at the bottom of the dialog box shows the name and location of the selected control file. In most cases the file extension will be .OCX.

F i g u r e   1 4 . 1

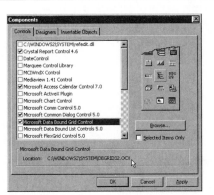

Available ActiveX controls appear in the **Components** *dialog box.*

The Tabbed Dialog Control

One of the handy extra controls that comes with Visual Basic is the Microsoft Tabbed Dialog Control 5.0. The tabbed dialog is a convenient way for placing a large amount of related material in one dialog box. You can find many examples of tabbed dialogs in Visual Basic, such as the *Components* dialog box that has three tabs: *Controls, Designers,* and *Insertable Objects.* Figure 14.2 shows a dialog box with a **Tabbed Dialog control**.

F i g u r e   1 4 . 2

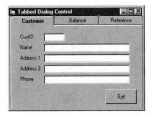

The tabs in this form were created with the Tabbed Dialog control.

To add a Tabbed Dialog control to your project, you must first add the control to your toolbox. Select *Microsoft Tabbed Dialog Control 5.0* from the *Components* dialog box (Figure 14.3). Figure 14.4 shows the Tabbed Dialog tool in the toolbox and a control on a form.

Figure 14.3

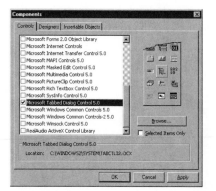

Select the Tabbed Dialog control from the Components *dialog box.*

Figure 14.4

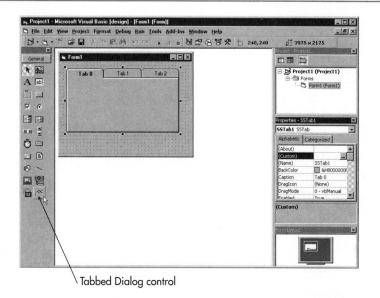

Tabbed Dialog control

The tool for the Tabbed Dialog control as it appear in the toolbox and a control on a form.

The Tabbed Dialog control has many properties and methods that you can set or check at run time or at design time. The default name of the tab is SSTab1. Use the prefix "tab" when naming your control.

The easiest way to initially set up the control is to use the custom *Property Pages* dialog box (Figure 14.5). To display this dialog box, either click on the builder button for *Custom* in the control's Properties window (Figure 14.6) or right-click the control and select *Properties* from the shortcut menu (Figure 14.7). In this dialog box you can specify the number of tabs, tabs per row, and the tab caption of each tab. *Note:* The first tab is tab 0, the next is tab 1, and so forth.

Figure 14.5

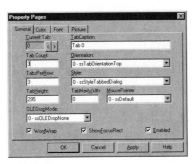

Set the properties for the Tabbed Dialog control in its custom Property Pages dialog box.

Figure 14.6

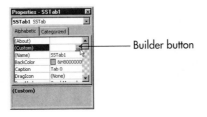

Builder button

One way to display the Property Pages dialog box is to click on the builder button for the Custom entry in the Property window.

Figure 14.7

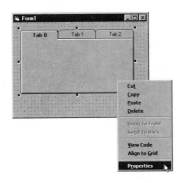

You can display the Property Pages dialog box by right-clicking on the control to display the shortcut menu and selecting Properties.

You can also set up the Tabbed Dialog control using the Properties window. To set the tab captions, click on each tab to select it and then change the caption in the Properties window.

Placing Controls on the Tab Sheets of a Tabbed Control

When you place controls such as text boxes and labels on top of a tabbed dialog control, usually you want the controls to appear only on the one tab page. Select the desired control's toolbox tool and manually draw the new control on top of the tabbed dialog control (do not double-click to place the control). If you double-click on a control in the toolbox, you are actually placing the control on the form and the control will appear on every tab. (This process is similar to the way you place controls inside frame controls; the Tabbed Dialog control is a container for the controls that "belong to" it.) If you *do* want a control to appear on all tabs, such as an Exit button, then place the control by double-clicking.

The Tabbed Dialog control for R 'n R has a *Coffee* tab with a list box and another tab containing a combo box. See Figures 14.8 and 14.9.

Figure   14.8

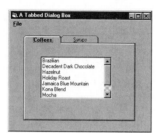

The form for R 'n R has a Tabbed Dialog control with two tabs.

Figure   14.9

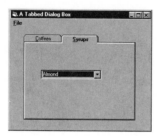

The second tab on the form for R 'n R holds a different list from the first tab.

Browsing the Web from a Visual Basic Project

Another ActiveX control available on the *Components* dialog box is the **Web browser control** (Figure 14.10). To add this control to your toolbox, place a check on the Microsoft Internet Controls in the *Components* selection of the *Project* menu. You can now link your Visual Basic application to the Internet.

New to UB 5!

Figure 14.10

Add a Web browser control to a project by selecting Microsoft Internet Controls in the Components dialog box.

When you add this control to your project, a new window is created (Figure 14.11). Web pages will appear in this window on your form. The default name is WebBrowser1. When naming your control use the prefix "web".

Figure 14.11

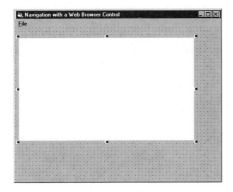

A Web browser control on a form. Web pages will appear in the window created by the control.

One of the methods of the control is `Navigate` that allows you to specify a specific Web site URL. Place the link as a string following the call to the method. The following code will bring up the Microsoft home page if there is a current connection to the Internet:

```
webBrowser.Navigate "Microsoft.com"
```

The computer system must be connected through an Internet provider for this control to work. If no browser is open, the project will attempt to open Internet Explorer. The program will work using Netscape Navigator; open the browser before executing your Visual Basic project.

Creating Your Own ActiveX Controls

In VB5 it is easy to create your own controls. In the *New Project* dialog box, you can choose to begin a new project for an ActiveX control, an ActiveX EXE, or an ActiveX DLL.

An ActiveX Control Project Using the Calendar Control

We will create a new ActiveX control that contains a Microsoft calendar control, a text box, and a command button. The user will enter a date in the text box and click the command button, and the corresponding date will appear on the calendar. Figure 14.12 shows the custom control; the following steps explain how to create it.

Figure 14.12

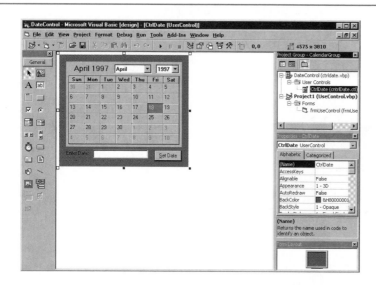

This form and controls make up a new custom control created with VB.

STEP 1: Open a new project selecting the ActiveX control option (Figure 14.13).

Figure 14.13

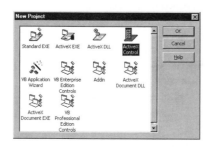

Select New Project from the File menu and select ActiveX Control to create a new control.

STEP 2: Use the *Components* dialog box to add *Microsoft Access Calendar Control 7.0* to your project and form (Figure 14.14).

Figure 14.14

Select Microsoft Access Calendar Control 7.0 in the Components dialog box to add the control to your toolbox.

STEP 3: Design the interface and the code as you would for any other project (Figure 14.15).

Figure 14.15

Set up the form and controls for the new custom control.

STEP 4: Select *Make .OCX* from the *File* menu to compile the code. Name your new control calDate.ocx; the control will automatically be placed in the *Components* dialog box.

STEP 5: Close the window for the control project before adding your new control to a regular VB project.

The Code for the ActiveX Control

The following program code converts the contents of the text box to a date data type. Date functions extract the year, month, and day from the date data type. Setting the properties of the calendar control (calDate) makes the date appear in the calendar.

```
'Project:        Calendar Activex
'Programmer:     A. Millspaugh
'Date:           August 1997
'Description:    Create an ActiveX control
'                that displays the date entered
'                in a text box.
'Folder:         Ch1403
```

```
Private Sub cmdDate_Click()
    'Use the date in the text box
    ' to set the calendar
    Dim dDate As Date

    If IsDate(txtDate.Text) Then
        dDate = txtDate.Text            'Convert the text box to a date data type
        calDate.Year = Year(dDate)      'Find the year and assign to calendar year
        calDate.Month = Month(dDate)    'Find the month and assign to calendar month
        calDate.Day = Day(dDate)        'Find the day and assign to calendar day
        calDate.Refresh                 'Display the Calendar again
    Else
        MsgBox "Not a valid date", vbOKOnly, "Date Check"
    End If
End Sub
```

Using Your New ActiveX Control

The steps for using the new control in a project are the same for using any other control. If your new control does not appear in the toolbox, open the *Components* dialog box; you will find its name there. Select the new control name, and the control will appear in your toolbox. Then add your new control to a form and test the control.

Dynamic Link Libraries

Libraries store commonly used procedures. As a project executes, it can call procedures from libraries. This is especially useful for procedures used by multiple projects; only one copy of the library is kept in memory and its procedures can be called by more than one project. Windows uses **dynamic link libraries (DLLs)** to store collections of procedures. The DLL file is then linked to your project when it runs. *Note:* Look at the list of library selections in the Visual Basic *References* dialog box from the *Project* menu. The line near the bottom of the dialog box shows the path including the .DLL extension (Figure 14.16). Use the Windows Explorer to look in the Windows and Windows\System folders; you will see many library files with the .DLL extension.

Figure 14.16

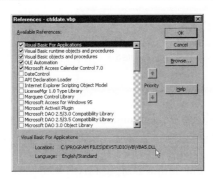

Select a DLL file from the ***References*** *dialog box. The DLL file names appear at the lower edge of the form.*

Windows applications routinely use DLLs. A project can call a function from the library and pass arguments if needed. The function is maintained separately from the programs that call it. Therefore, changes are made to the internal workings of a function in a dynamic link library without having to recode all the projects that call the function.

One extremely useful feature of Visual Basic is that a project can call and use library procedures used by the Windows system. Consequently, functions available in Windows but not available in Visual Basic can still be used. The DLLs that Windows applications use for such tasks as moving and resizing windows are referred to as the Windows application programming interface (**API**). Visual Basic uses many API DLLs to create the Visual Basic environment.

Most of the Windows DLL code is written in the C language and requires some use of C syntax. Don't worry if you don't know C. You don't have to write any C statements; you only have to pass arguments to the library procedures.

Two steps are required for using a DLL. Any time you call a procedure that is in a library, you must include a **Declare statement**. Declare statements tell Visual Basic the name of the procedure and the library where it can be found, along with the arguments the procedure needs. Once you have included the `Declare`, you can call the procedure as you would one of your own. You can call both sub procedures and function procedures from DLLs; the `Declare` statement specifies the type of procedure. (Recall that a function returns a value.)

The Declare Statement

`Declare` statements appear at the module level. You can include them in the General Declarations section of a form module or in a standard code module. Calls to the library procedures may appear in any module.

The Declare Statement—General Form

```
Declare Sub Name Lib LibName$ [Alias AliasName$] _
    ([ArgumentList]) [As Datatype]
Declare Function Name Lib LibName$ [Alias AliasName$] _
    ([ArgumentList]) [As Datatype]
```

The Name parameter refers to the name of the procedure. If the name of the procedure is the same as a reserved word in Visual Basic or one of your existing procedures, you will need to use an alias to give the procedure a new name within your project. The word *Lib* precedes the name of the DLL library file. The argument list specifies the arguments expected by the procedure.

In the first of the following examples, the function procedure is called *sndPlaySound* from the MMSystem library.

The Declare Statement—Examples

```
Declare Function sndPlaySound Lib "winmm" Alias "sndPlaySoundA" _
    (ByVal lpszSoundName As String, ByVal uFlags As Long) As Long

Declare Function GetWindowsDirectory Lib "kernel32" Alias GetWindowsDirectoryA" _
    (ByVal lpBuffer As String, ByVal nSize As Long) As Long
```

The arguments may have a datatype specified and can be passed ByVal or ByRef.

Passing Arguments ByVal and ByRef

Arguments may be passed to a called procedure by value or by reference. When passed **ByVal**, only a copy of the original value is passed; the called procedure cannot alter the original value. When items are passed **ByRef**, the memory address of the original value is passed to the procedure, allowing the procedure to change the original value. You will pass ByVal or ByRef based upon the requirements of the specific DLL. If no specification is made, the default is ByRef.

When you are calling Windows API procedures, always declare a string argument ByVal. Visual Basic and C do not store strings in the same way. A Visual Basic string holds the length of the string at the beginning; strings in C are variable in length and terminated by a NULL character. C does not actually have a string data type, but treats strings as an array of characters.

String arguments and array arguments are treated differently than other (nonarray) arguments. You should declare them as passing ByVal, but what is actually passed is the address of the first element of the array.

Calling a DLL Procedure

You can call a DLL procedure from within any procedure in the scope of the `Declare` statement. The call will look the same as calls to procedures that you have written. The passed arguments may be either variables or constants.

The following procedure uses the `sndPlaySound` function to play a sound wave file (.WAV extension). This shareware wave file sounds like the Laurel and Hardy "Look at the fine mess you've gotten us into now" routine. Although this example plays the sound when a command button is clicked, you might consider playing it in a validation routine when the user makes a mistake.

```
Private Sub cmdsound_Click()
    'Play a sound file
    Dim iTalk As Integer

    Const SYNC = 1
    iTalk = sndPlaySound(ByVal CStr("d:\sharwar\l&h.wav"), SYNC)
End Sub
```

The first parameter converts the path and filename string to a "C string" by using the `CStr` function. The second argument being passed is an integer constant. Compare these arguments with the `Declare` used for this DLL procedure. (*Note:* The path indicated must be valid for your system. This shareware file is included on your Student Diskette.)

```
Declare Function sndPlaySound Lib "winmm" Alias "sndPlaySoundA" _
  (ByVal lpszSoundName As String, ByVal uFlags As Long) As Long
```

The `sndPlaySound` function is very useful for including sounds in a multimedia type of program. You might consider scanning in your own pictures, recording a voice description, and playing back the sound file when the appropriate selection is made from a menu or command button.

Finding the Reference Information for DLLs

You are not expected to learn the names and arguments for DLL procedures. You will find small code samples in magazines, in articles that present tips, or in question-and-answer features. If you ask a "How do I do . . ." question online, the answer you receive may include a few lines of code that include a `Declare` and a call to the procedure.

Visual Basic comes with a reference database for the procedures in the Windows API. You can use the API Viewer VB Add-In to look up the names of library files, procedures, constants, and the format of the `Declare` for each call. In order to use the Add-In, it must be selected when you install VB on your system. Then select *Add-Ins/Add-In Manager* and select *VB API Viewer* from the dialog box to add the API Viewer to the *Add-Ins* menu. Open the viewer and open its text file. The text file should be located in the folder Program Files\DevStudio\VB\Winapi. After you locate the desired `Declare` and `Const` statements, you can copy and paste them into your project.

Accessing System Information with a DLL

Your project may need to know the specific hardware or software on the computer system running the program. Windows maintains this information, and you can access it with a DLL. The following program will determine the current version of Windows and the video configuration.

Figure 14.17 shows the form for this program example.

Figure 14.17

The form for the system information example program using a Windows API DLL.

```
'Project:       Ch1404.bas - Standard code module
'Programmer:    A. Millspaugh
'Date:          December 1997
'Description:   Declares the DLL procedures to find the
'               Windows and system folders.
'Folder:        Ch1404

    'Declare the DLL procedures
    Declare Function GetWindowsDirectory _
      Lib "kernel32" Alias "GetWindowsDirectoryA" _
      (ByVal lpBuffer As String, ByVal nSize As Long) _
      As Long
    Declare Function GetSystemDirectory Lib _
      "kernel32" Alias "GetSystemDirectoryA" _
      (ByVal lpBuffer As String, ByVal nSize As Long) _
      As Long
```

```
'Project:       Ch1404 frmSysInfo
'Programmer:    A. Millspaugh
'Date:          December 1997
'Description:   Uses DLL procedures to find the Windows
'               and system folders.
'Folder:        Ch1404
Option Explicit
```

```
Private Sub Form_Load()
    'Call the DLL procedures and assign return
    '  values to labels
    Dim stWinPath As String
    Dim vTemp
```

```
    'Create a string of 145 null characters
    stWinPath = String(145, Chr(0))
    'Fill the string with the path name
    vTemp = GetWindowsDirectory(stWinPath, 145)
    'Take the left characters up to the null
    lblWindowsDir.Caption = Left(stWinPath, InStr(stWinPath, Chr(0)) - 1)

    stWinPath = String(145, Chr(0))
    vTemp = GetSystemDirectory(stWinPath, 145)
    lblSystemDir.Caption = Left(stWinPath, InStr(stWinPath, Chr(0)) - 1)
End Sub
```

```
Private Sub mnuFileExit_Click()
    'Terminate the project

    End
End Sub
```

Placing Tabs for Columns in a List Box

Visual Basic list boxes and combo boxes do not have tab settings. At times you may want to fill a list with two or more columns. This example uses a Windows DLL to set tab stops in a list box. The project opens the Publishers table from the Visual Basic Biblio.mdb database and fills a list box with the data in three columns (Figure 14.18).

Figure 14.18

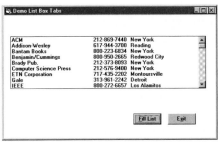

The columns in the list box created by using a Windows DLL to set tab stops.

```
'Project:      Demo Tabs
'Programmer:   J.C. Bradley
'Date:         August 1997
'Description:  Use a DLL to place tab stops in a list box.
'Folder:       Ch1405
Option Explicit
```

```
Private Declare Function SendMessage Lib "user32" Alias "SendMessageA" _
    (ByVal hwnd As Long, ByVal wMsg As Long, ByVal wParam As Long, _
    lParam As Any) As Long
Const LB_SETTABSTOPS = &H192
```

```
Private Sub cmdExit_Click()
    'Exit the project

    End
End Sub
```

```
Private Sub cmdFill_Click()
    'Fill the list box

    SetTabs lstData                   'Call procedure, passing name of list box
    Do Until datBiblio.Recordset.EOF
        '                             'Chr$(9) is a Tab character
        lstData.AddItem datBiblio.Recordset!Name & Chr$(9) & _
            datBiblio.Recordset!Telephone & Chr$(9) & _
            datBiblio.Recordset!City
        datBiblio.Recordset.MoveNext
    Loop
End Sub
```

```
Private Sub SetTabs(Lst As ListBox)
    'Set the tab stops in a listbox

    ReDim iTabs(0 To 1) As Integer      'Two tab stops needed
    Dim lRtn            As Long         'DLL function returns a Long variable
    iTabs(0) = 110                      'Twips measurement for 1st tab stop
    iTabs(1) = 160                      'Twips measurement for 2nd tab stop
    lRtn = SendMessage(Lst.hwnd, LB_SETTABSTOPS, 2, iTabs(0))    'Set the stops
End Sub
```

Object Linking and Embedding

OLE enables you to link or embed objects from other applications into your project, either at run time or at design time. You can access objects from other types of applications without writing the code. Think how much time it would take to program a spreadsheet application. Why should you spend that time when excellent spreadsheets are available? OLE is the means by which each programmer can avoid "reinventing the wheel." The types of objects available to use in a project depend on the applications that are installed on your computer system or network.

Object Linking

Linking causes your program to access an object that is actually maintained by the application that creates it. A reference to the linked object is kept in your code, but the actual object is kept in the other application. This means that any application that has linking ability can access the linked object and change it. When your application runs, you can access the current state of the object.

An example of a linked object could be a spreadsheet showing the current status and costs for a project. The spreadsheet object could be included in a Visual Basic project, in a word processing document, as well as displayed from the spreadsheet application. The data in the linked spreadsheet can also be updated from each of the applications. Because each application is using the same object, any changes made to the spreadsheet would be available to all applications linked to it.

Object Embedding

Embedding places the object into your project. Hence, the object is maintainable only from within your project and cannot be accessed by other projects. Another result of embedding is that the Visual Basic project file becomes significantly larger because of the embedded code.

Consider a project that includes a spreadsheet object created in Excel. You can choose to create a new spreadsheet file or to include an existing spreadsheet. The steps to accomplish the two tasks are similar. First, create a new control on a form using the OLE tool from the toolbox (Figure 14.19); the *Insert Object* dialog box (Figure 14.20) appears automatically. Notice the option button for *Create New* or *Create from File.* Try clicking on the buttons and viewing the changes to the dialog box (Figure 14.21). If you want to create a new item within your project, you must make a selection from the *Object Type* list box.

Figure 14.19

Use the OLE tool from the toolbox to link or embed an OLE object in a project.

Figure 14.20

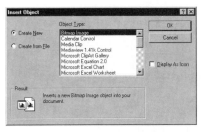

The Insert Object *dialog box with its initial settings for creating a new object.*

Figure 14.21

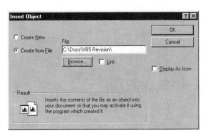

The Insert Object *dialog box as it appears for* Create from File.

The following example places an existing spreadsheet for R 'n R on a form as an embedded object. Figure 14.22 shows the form for this example. The steps are as follows:

Figure   14.22

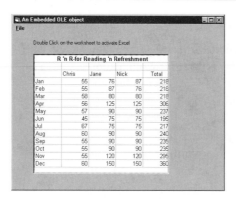

The form for the OLE example project showing an embedded Excel spreadsheet object.

STEP 1: Create a control on your form using the OLE tool from the toolbox; the *Insert Object* dialog box will display (refer to Figure 14.20).
STEP 2: Select the option button for *Create from File*.
STEP 3: Type the filename RNR.XLS in the File text box (or use the Browse button to locate the file in the Ch1406 folder).
STEP 4: Make sure that the Link check box is not selected so that the object will be embedded.

The project Ch1406 displays the interface shown in Figure 14.22 when the program is running.

Creating OLE Objects at Run Time

You can embed and link objects while a project is executing by using the properties and methods of the OLE control. You can create a link to an existing object by setting the control's SourceDoc property and using the `Create Link` method. If you are linking to a datafile and want a specific range of the file, you can set the control's SourceItem property.

To embed an object, set the SourceDoc property and use the `Create Embed` method.

You can also allow the user to select the type of object to be linked or embedded as the project is running. Use the `InsertObjDlg` or the `Paste-SpecialDlg` method. These methods display the *Object* dialog box or the *Paste Special* dialog box, respectively.

Visual Basic for Applications

Each Microsoft Office application, such as Excel, Word, PowerPoint, and Access, includes **Visual Basic for Applications (VBA)** for writing procedures. Most of the Visual Basic features that you have learned carry over to programming in VBA. Take a look at the Code window (Figure 14.23), the Visual Basic toolbar (Figure 14.24), and the Controls Toolbox toolbar (Figure 14.25) in Excel 97. You will find many items that look familiar.

Figure   14.23

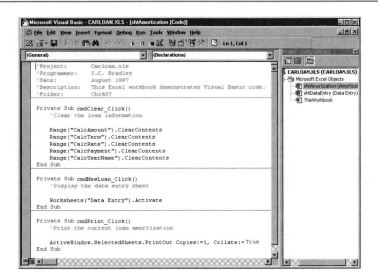

The Visual Basic Code window in Excel 97.

Figure   14.24

The Excel 97 Visual Basic toolbar.

Figure   14.25

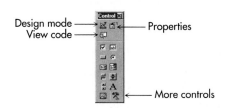

The Excel 97 Control Toolbox toolbar.

Recording an Excel Macro

If you have Excel 97 installed on your computer, you may be interested in trying the activities in this section. Start by recording an Excel macro: Select *Tools/Macros/Record New Macro*, and a dialog box will ask for the name of your macro. Give it the name *Demo;* a little Stop button appears in a toolbar. Then try typing something into your worksheet, such as your name and the date. Then click the Stop button.

Display the Visual Basic toolbar (*View/Toolbars*) and click on the Visual Basic Editor button (Figure 14.26). Then double-click on Module1 in the Project Explorer window. Your procedure (recorded macro) should appear in the Code window (Figure 14.27).

F i g u r e   1 4 . 2 6

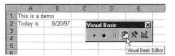

Click on the Visual Basic Editor button to display the Code window.

F i g u r e   1 4 . 2 7

Double-click on Module1 and your new macro appears in the Visual Basic Code window.

Select Module 1

Investigate the environment—the windows, the menus, and the toolbars. This environment is the same Visual Basic environment you are accustomed to. Now look at the code. The Visual Basic notation for remarks includes the name *Demo* that you called your macro. Notice the procedure begins with `Sub` and ends with `End  Sub`. The statements inside the procedure reflect the steps you took while the macro was recording.

The structure of VBA is the same as the structure for Visual Basic. However, a spreadsheet has different objects, properties, events, and methods than Visual Basic has.

You can add objects with which you are familiar. Return to the Worksheet window by clicking on its Taskbar button. Then display the Control Toolbox toolbar (*View/Toolbars*). Create a command button. The tools are the same but you must click the tool and then draw it; the double-click method does not work in VBA.

After you create a new button, change to the design mode of Excel by clicking on the Design mode button on the Visual Basic toolbar. You can toggle between design mode and regular mode with the Design mode button. When you are in design mode, you can display the Properties window, change properties of controls, and write code.

A Sample Excel Visual Basic Application

Your student disk has a file called Carloan.xls for calculating loan payments and printing loan amortizations. It contains two sheets: a worksheet that resembles a dialog box for data entry (Figure 14.28a) and a second worksheet for the loan amortization (Figure 14.28b). The data entry worksheet has three command buttons: Calculate Payment, Display Amortization, and Clear. The loan amortization worksheet has buttons for Print, Clear, and New Loan. You can load the workbook file, run the application, and examine the Visual Basic procedures.

Note: Because there are no validation routines, you must enter all fields. The form is designed to print out the first three years of the loan.

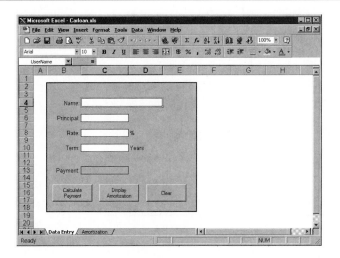

This Excel spreadsheet demonstrates using Visual Basic for Applications in Excel. This demo workbook has two worksheets: (a) The Data Entry sheet and (b) the Amortization sheet.

The Code for the Data Entry Worksheet

```
'Project:       Carloan.xls - Data Entry Sheet
'Programmer:    J.C. Bradley
'Date:          August 1997
'Description:   This Excel workbook file demonstrates using
'               Visual Basic in Excel 97.
'Folder:        Ch1407
Option Explicit
```

```
Private Sub cmdCalculateLoan_Click()
    'Calculate the payment

    Range("CalculatedPayment").Value = "=-PMT(YearlyRate/1200,_
        TermInYears*12, Principal)"
End Sub
```

```
Private Sub cmdClear_Click()
    'Clear the sheet

    Range("UserName").ClearContents
    Range("Principal").ClearContents
    Range("YearlyRate").ClearContents
    Range("TermInYears").ClearContents
    Range("CalculatedPayment").ClearContents
    Range("UserName").Select
End Sub
```

```
Private Sub cmdDisplay_Click()
    'Display Amortization worksheet

    cmdCalculateLoan_Click
    With Worksheets("Amortization")
        .Range("CalcAmount") = Range("Principal")
        .Range("CalcRate").Value = Range("YearlyRate") / 100
        .Range("CalcTerm").Value = Range("TermInYears")
        .Range("Payment").Value = Range("CalculatedPayment")
        .Range("CalcUserName").Value = Range("UserName")
        .Activate
    End With
End Sub
```

```
Private Sub Worksheet_Activate()
    'Set up the worksheet

    Range("UserName").Select
End Sub
```

The Code for the Loan Amortization Worksheet

```
'Project:      Carloan.xls - Loan Amortization Sheet
'Programmer:   J.C. Bradley
'Date:         August 1997
'Description:  This Excel workbook demonstrates Visual Basic code.
'Folder:       Ch1407
Option Explicit
```

```
Private Sub cmdClear_Click()
    'Clear the loan information

    Range("CalcAmount").ClearContents
    Range("CalcTerm").ClearContents
    Range("CalcRate").ClearContents
    Range("CalcPayment").ClearContents
    Range("CalcUserName").ClearContents
End Sub
```

```
Private Sub cmdNewLoan_Click()
    'Display the data entry sheet

    Worksheets("Data Entry").Activate
End Sub
```

```
Private Sub cmdPrint_Click()
    'Print the current loan amortization

    ActiveWindow.SelectedSheets.PrintOut Copies:=1, Collate:=True
End Sub
```

Help with Visual Basic in Excel

Another area that can help you learn more about VBA is Excel's *Help* menu. Under *Help/Contents* and *Index/Contents* select the topic *Microsoft Excel Visual Basic Reference* and expand the topics list. The Visual Basic section of *Help* gives a new index of topics that relate specifically to VB.

In addition to the Help screens, you can also try some demo programs that come with Excel.

Creating Your Own Objects

Beyond the many built-in choices you have for objects to include in your projects, Visual Basic allows you to create your own new object types by creating a **class module**. Just like other object types, your class may have both properties and methods. Remember: Properties are characteristics, and methods are actions that can be performed by a class of object.

Defining a class does not place an object in your form; it merely defines how an object of that type would act. To create a new object you specify the class type. For example, *command button* is a class but *cmdExit* is an actual occurrence or **instance** of the class; the instance is the object. Just as you may have multiple command buttons in a project, you may have many objects of a new class type.

Defining a Class

To create a new class, use the *Add Class Module* from the *Project* menu. You will see a code window similar to the code window for a standard code module. Any public variables that you declare will become the properties of the new class. The subs and functions are the methods.

```
Public cPrice         As  Currency
Public iQuantity      As  Integer
Public stDescription  As String
```

```
Public Function cInventoryValue() As  Currency
    'Calculate the value of the inventory

    cInventoryValue = iQuantity * cPrice
End Function
```

This new class has the following properties: cPrice, iQuantity, and stDescription. The class has only one method: cInventoryValue.

Creating a New Object Using a New Class

Creating a class module only defines a new class; it does not create any objects. This process is similar to defining a new data type; you must then dimension variables of the new type. To create an object using your new class, you must create an instance of the class using the New keyword and specifying the class. This step is referred to as **instantiating** an object.

Dimensioning Objects Using the New Keyword—General Form

```
Dim Public|Private VariableName As New ClassName
```

Dimensioning Objects Using the New Keyword—Examples

```
Dim Emp As New Employee
Private MyInventory As New Inventory
Public NewForm As New frmMain
```

The **New keyword** is used to create a new instance of an object class. The object class can be a class that you create or standard Visual Basic objects such as forms.

Reusable Objects

An advantage of object-oriented code is the ability to reuse objects. When you create a new class by writing a class module, you can then use that class in multiple projects. Every object defined has its own set of properties, just like each control in your project has its own set of properties that act independently. For example, you may use two image objects: imgOne and imgTwo. Each has its own Visible property, which may have a different setting than the other.

You might want to create your own class to provide database access. You could include methods for adding and deleting data members. If you work frequently with sales, you might create an invoice class. The invoice class would likely have properties such as description, quantity, and cost. The methods would probably include finding the current value of the inventory.

Sample Project—Defining and Using a New Class

In this project we will create a new class called Inventory. Then, in a form module, we will dimension and use a new instance of the Inventory class.

Sample Code for Creating the Inventory Class

```
'Module        Class Module
'Programmer:   A. Millspaugh
'Date:         December 1997
'Description:  Declare properties and methods
'              for the inventory class.
'Folder:       Ch1408


Public cPrice       As Currency
Public iQuantity    As Integer
Public stDescription As String
```
```
Public Function cInventoryValue() As Currency
    'Calculate the value of the inventory

    cInventoryValue = iQuantity * cPrice
End Function
```

This example contains three properties defined as Public—cPrice, iQuantity, and stDescription. The method is cInventoryValue. Since the properties and methods are declared as public, they can be accessed from other modules. Private members of the class can be accessed only by procedures within the class module.

Defining and Using an Object of the Inventory Class

The code in this new form module creates an instance of the Inventory class defined in the preceding code. The properties and method are used in the mnuFileCalc_Click event.

```
'Project:      Calculate Inventory
'Programmer:   A. Millspaugh
'Date:         December 1997
'Description:  Calculate inventory amount using the Inventory class.
'              Instantiate the Inventory class as a new object.
'Folder:       Ch1408

Option Explicit
Private MyInventory As New Inventory

Private Sub mnuFileCalc_Click()
    'Calculate the inventory value

    MyInventory.cPrice = txtPrice.Text
    MyInventory.iQuantity = txtQuantity.Text
    MyInventory.stDescription = txtDescription.Text
    lblInventoryValue.Caption = MyInventory.cInventoryValue()
End Sub

Private Sub mnuFileExit_Click()
    'Terminate the project

    End
End Sub
```

Crystal Reports

When you need to create a printed report based on a database, you can use the **Crystal Reports** add-in, available with the Professional and Enterprise Editions of VB. With Crystal Reports you design a report using the **Report Designer**. The report design is saved as a separate file on disk. Then you place a Crystal Reports ActiveX control on your form. You specify the name of the report file as one of the properties of the control. When your project runs, you can set the Action property of the Crystal Reports control, which sends the report to the printer or a Print Preview window on the screen.

To design your Crystal Report, you can run the Report Designer either as a stand-alone application or from within Visual Basic. To run Crystal Reports outside VB, run Crw32.exe in the Report folder beneath the VB folder. From within Visual Basic you will use the *Add-Ins* menu. The following step-by-step tutorial uses Crystal Reports from the VB *Add-Ins* menu.

Designing the Report

You will begin the report design from within VB. It isn't important whether or not you have a project open while you design the report.

STEP 1: Open the *Add-Ins* menu and select *Report Designer*. A new window opens for Crystal Reports Pro (Figure 14.29).

> *Note:* If you see a registration form, click Done.

Figure 14.29

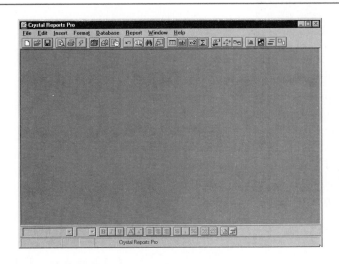

Create and modify reports using the Crystal Reports Pro window.

STEP 2: Select *File/New*, and the *Create New Report* dialog box appears (Figure 14.30). Click on the large button labeled Standard.

Figure 14.30

Choose your report type in the Create New Report dialog box.

The Create Report Expert wizard appears (Figure 14.31). You will use this wizard to select the database file and design the report. Notice that the wizard contains a tabbed dialog with numbered tabs for *Tables*, *Fields*, *Sort*, *Total*, *Select*, and *Style*.

Figure 14.31

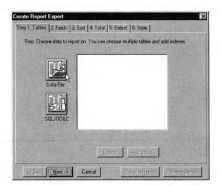

The Create Report Expert wizard can step you through creating a new report.

STEP 3: On the *Tables* tab click on the large Data File button. Specify the name and path of the RnrBooks.mdb database you will be using. After clicking on the Add button, click Done. A *Links* tab will appear.

STEP 4: Click on the Next command button.

STEP 5: On the *Fields* tab select the desired fields from the *Database Fields* list on the left and click the Add button to add the fields to the Report Fields list on the right (Figure 14.32). Select Author, Title, and Publisher, adding each to the report. Your completed list should look like Figure 14.32.

Figure 14.32

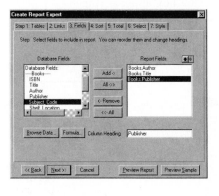

Select from the available fields to choose the fields to display on your report. The fields listed in **Report Fields** *will appear on the report.*

STEP 6: Click on the *Style* tab and type in your title. (Make up any title you wish. It's a good idea to include your name in the title if you are using a shared lab.)

You may want to investigate the other tabs now. As soon as you perform the next step, the wizard will disappear. After that point you must make any further changes in design view.

STEP 7: Click on the Preview Sample button to view the report.

You can click on the *Design* tab to see the design created by the wizard and/or modify it.

STEP 8: Choose *File/Save As*. Change to the folder that holds (or will hold) the Visual Basic project to display the report and name your report file *Rnr*. Crystal Reports will automatically add an extension of .RPT.

STEP 9: Select *File/Exit* to exit Crystal Reports and return to VB.

The report is saved as a file with an .RPT extension. It may now be printed or displayed from within a project.

Adding the Report to a Project

You can add a saved report to any VB project. You may have an application that displays and/or maintains a database, and you want to add report printing capability. You might also have a list of several reports from which the user can select.

To add the report, you add a Crystal Report control to your form. Just as with a Common Dialog control, the Crystal Report control appears on the form at design time, but not during run time. The control contains a variety of properties to control printing to the screen or to the printer and to connect to a specific .RPT file. Use "rpt" for the naming prefix of report controls.

In your VB code, you will set the Action property of the Crystal Report control to 1 to output the specified report. By default, the report goes to the printer, but you can specify the destination by first setting the control's Destination property. For the destination, you can use either the numeric literals or intrinsic constants:

Destination	Literal	Constant
Screen	0	crptToWindow
Printer	1	crptToPrinter

The following code sends a report to the screen for print preview:

```
rptRNR.Destination = crptToWindow
rptRNR.Action = 1
```

The following code sends a report to the printer:

```
rptRNR.Destination = crptToPrinter
rptRNR.Action = 1
```

Add Your Report to a Project

Follow these steps to add the previously created Rnr.RPT to a Visual Basic project:

STEP 1: Open a project (a new project or an existing project).

STEP 2: Open the *Components* dialog box and add *Crystal Report 4.6* to your toolbox. Add this control to your project (Figure 14.33).

Tip

You can display the *Components* dialog box by right-clicking on the toolbox.

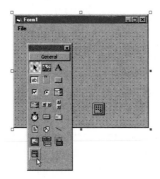

STEP 3: Change the Name property of the new control to rptRnR.

STEP 4: Display the custom *Property Pages* dialog box from either the shortcut menu or the *(Custom)* entry in the Properties window.

STEP 5: On the *General* tab specify the path and filename of the .RPT file you created earlier. (You can click on the Build button to browse for the file.) Close the dialog box.

STEP 6: Create a menu bar with a *File* menu and commands for *Preview Report*, *Print Report*, and *Exit*. Code the mnuFileExit event procedure with an **End** statement.

STEP 7: Write the code to send the report to the screen and the printer. Referring to the code examples that appear before this section, set the Destination and Action properties for each option.

STEP 8: Test the project.

The Coding Solution

```
'Project:      Crystal Reports
'Programmer:   A. Millspaugh
'Date:         July 1997
'Description:  Use the Crystal Report control
'              to display or print a database report
'              created with Crystal Reports.
'Folder:       Ch1409

Private Sub mnuFileExit_Click()
    'Terminate the project

    End
End Sub

Private Sub mnuFilePreview_Click()
    'Send the report to the screen

    rptRnR.Destination = crptToWindow
    rptRnR.Action = 1
End Sub
```

```
Private Sub mnuFilePrint_Click()
    'Send the report to the printer

    rptRnR.Destination = crptToPrinter
    rptRnR.Action = 1
End Sub
```

S u m m a r y

1. ActiveX refers to controls and procedures that can be used by different applications. You can access objects other than the ones in the toolbox by selecting options from the *Components* or *Resources* dialog boxes from the commands on the *Project* menu.
2. The Visual Basic editor enables you to create new controls and to make the .OCX files that are registered in the *Components* dialog box.
3. Dynamic link libraries are procedures in library files, outside of Visual Basic, that can be linked and called when a project is running.
4. DLLs used by Windows are referred to as the Windows application programming interface (API).
5. DLL procedures may pass arguments by value (pass a copy of the value) or by reference (pass the address of the value).
6. Objects created by other applications can be linked to a Visual Basic project using the OLE container control. The object can appear on a Visual Basic form and be manipulated by the user of the Visual Basic project. Linked objects are actually maintained by the application that created them.
7. OLE embedded objects are similar to linked objects except that the files relating to the objects are stored with the Visual Basic project, which greatly increases the size of the project.
8. Visual Basic for Applications is the standard language used for generating procedures (macros) in other Microsoft application packages, such as Word, Excel, and Access.
9. A Visual Basic programmer can create new classes and use them to create new objects.
10. The Crystal Reports Report Designer add-in provides an easy method for designing reports for a database that can be printed from a VB project.

Key Terms

ActiveX   *498*
API   *507*
ByRef   *508*
ByVal   *508*
class module   *519*
Crystal Reports   *522*
`Declare` statement   *507*
dynamic link libraries (DLL)   *506*
embedding   *513*
instance   *520*

instantiating   *520*
linking   *512*
`New` keyword   *521*
object   *498*
OLE   *512*
Report Designer   *522*
Tabbed Dialog control   *499*
Visual Basic for Applications
      (VBA)   *514*
Web browser control   *502*

Review Questions

1. What is an ActiveX control? Give an example.
2. What is a DLL?
3. What does *API* mean?
4. What are the purposes of a `Declare` statement?
5. Differentiate between ByVal and ByRef. When is each used?
6. Explain the difference between linking and embedding an object into a Visual Basic project.
7. What determines the list of objects that can be used with OLE in a particular system?
8. What does the term *object* mean?
9. What are the sources of objects?
10. How can a new type of object be created?

Programming Exercises

14.1 Add an OLE control to a form and select *Create New File*. Look over the list of OLE objects available on your system. Try linking and embedding an object and compare the file size of your projects.

14.2 Examine the .WAV files in your Windows directories. Write a project that prompts the user to guess a number. Have the project generate a random number from 1 to 100. Allow the user to enter a number. Display a message that indicates whether the response is too high or too low. If the user gives the correct answer, use the Tada.wav file to generate a sound.

14.3 If you have access to a multimedia system with a microphone, record a short message to a .WAV file. Write a project that plays back the sound file—a description of an item being displayed, for example.

14.4 Create a new class that calculates the commission to pay on a vehicle sale. The properties will include cost price and selling price. Create a method that calculates the commission as 40 percent of the profit. The profit is the selling price—the cost price. Test the class in a form that includes the vehicle information for the sale, the cost price, the selling price, and the commission.

CASE STUDIES

VB Mail Order

Create an ActiveX control to perform the actions VB Mail from Chapter 1. The class should display the name and telephone number for the contact person of the selected department.

Include command buttons for the Customer Relations, Marketing, Order Processing, and Shipping departments. When the user clicks on the button for a department, display the name and telephone number for the contact person in two labels. Also include identifying labels with Captions *Department Contact* and *Telephone Number*.

Test your control in a form that includes buttons to print the form and to exit.

Test Data

Department	Department Contact	Telephone Number
Customer Relations	Tricia Mills	500-1111
Marketing	Michelle Rigner	500-2222
Order Processing	Kenna DeVoss	500-3333
Shipping	Eric Andrews	500-4444

VB Auto Center

Create a new ActiveX control that includes a list box and a label. Selecting the department name from the list box should display the appropriate special in a label.

Create a form module that incorporates the new control.

Test Data

List Box	Special to Display in Label
Auto Sales	Family wagon, immaculate condition $12,995
Service Center	Lube, oil, filter $25.99
Detail Shop	Complete detail $79.95 for most cars
Employment Opportunities	Sales position: Contact Mr. Mann 551-2134 x475

A

Answers to Feedback Questions

Feedback 2.1

Property	Setting
Name	imgBig
Stretch	True
Appearance	1 - 3D
BorderStyle	1 - Fixed Single
Visible	True

Feedback 2.2

1. `txtCompany.Text = ""`
   `txtCompany.SetFocus`
2. `lblCustomer.Caption = ""`
   `txtOrder.SetFocus`
3. (a) Check box is checked.
   (b) Option button is not selected.
   (c) Image is not visible.
   (d) The appearance is set to three dimensional; border style is fixed.
   (e) Assigns the value in txtCity.Text to lblCity.Caption.

Feedback 3.1

1. Does not indicate the data type with a prefix.
2. Cannot contain special characters such as #.
3. No blank spaces are allowed within an identifier.
4. The periods separate items such as object and property and should not be used in a variable identifier.
5. Cannot contain special characters such as $.
6. *Sub* is a reserved word in Visual Basic.
7. Valid name. Is it meaningful? That would depend upon the situation.
8. *Caption* is a property name and, as such, is a reserved word.
9. If the *c* is being used as a prefix for currency, the *O* should be capitalized to conform to the naming conventions.
10. A prefix should be used to specify the data type.
11. Valid.
12. Valid.

Feedback 3.2

Note: Answers may vary; make sure the prefix indicates the data type.

1. (a) sHoursWorked
   (b) stEmployeeName
   (c) stDepartmentNumber
2. (a) iQuantity
   (b) stDescription
   (c) stPartNumber
   (d) cCost
   (e) cSellingPrice

Feedback 3.3

Note: Answers may vary, make sure the prefix indicates the data type.

1. Dim mcTotal As Currency, declared at module level.
2. Const mcSALES_TAX_RATE As Currency = .07, declared at module level.
3. Dim miParticipantCount As Integer, declared at module level.

Feedback 3.4

1. 18
2. 1
3. 6
4. 5
5. 22
6. 4 to the power of 5; then multiply by 2 (2048).
7. 22
8. 38

Feedback 3.5

1. lblAveragePay.Caption = Format$(mcAveragePay, "Currency")
   $123.46
2. lblPercentCorrect.Caption = Format$(sCorrect, "Percent")
   76.00%
3. lblTotal.Caption = Format$(mcTotalCollected, "Standard")

Feedback 3.6

1. 1.35
2. 01.35
3. 1.3
4. $1
5. $1.3

Feedback 4.1

1. True
2. True
3. True
4. False
5. False
6. True
7. True
8. False
9. True
10. True

Feedback 4.2

1. The frogs option button on; the toads off.
2. It's the toads and the polliwogs.
3. It's false.
4.
```
If txtApples.Text > txtOranges.Text Then
     lblMost.Caption = "Apples"
Else
     lblMost.Caption = "Oranges"
End If
```
5.
```
If cBalance > 0 Then
    optFunds.Value = True
    cBalance = 0
    iCounter = iCounter + 1

Else
    optFunds.Value = False
End If
```

Feedback 5.1

1. Function procedure; a value is returned.
2.
```
Private Function iCalculateAverage (iValue1 As Integer, _
    iValue2 As Integer, iValue3 As Integer) As Integer
```

3. `iCalculateAverage = (iValue1 + iValue2 + iValue3) / 3`
4. The answer is assigned to a field with the name of the function.

Feedback 6.1

1. `Const miFAT_CALORIES As Integer = 9   'module level`
2. `Public gstNameHighest As String        'standard code module`
3. `Const gstCOMPANY_NAME As String = "Babs Bowling Service"`
   `    'standard code module`
4. `Public gcTotalAmount As Currency       'standard code module`
5. `Public giPersonCount As Integer        'standard code module`
6. `Dim cTotal As Currency          'local to procedure`
7. (a) Module-level integer variable.
   (b) Standard code module currency variable.
   (c) Local currency variable.
   (d) Local currency constant.
   (e) Standard code module string constant.
   (f) Local string variable.
   (g) Module-level string variable.
   (h) Standard code module string variable.

Feedback 7.1

1. Tracks the physical number of elements in the list.
2. Stores the position of the currently selected item; has a value of -1 if nothing is selected.
3. String value of an item in the list.
4. Adds an item during run time.
5. Removes all items from the list.
6. Removes the selected or specified item from the list.
7. Displays the list in alphabetic order.

Feedback 7.2

```
bItemFound = False   'Set initial value of found flag to False
iItemIndex = 0                       'Initialize counter for index
'Loop until the item is found or the end of list is reached
Do Until bItemFound Or iItemIndex = lstItems.ListCount
    'Test if the text box entry matches item in list
    If txtNewItem.Text = lstItems.List(iItemIndex) Then
        bItemFound = True         'Set the found flag to True
    End If
    iItemIndex = iItemIndex + 1   'Increment counter for index
Loop
```

Feedback 7.3

1. **(a)** There should not be a comma after the ending value.
   (b) The Next statement must contain the control variable that follows the For, iIndex in this case.
   (c) The item following the word For must be a variable and must be the same as the one on the Next statement.
   (d) Valid.
   (e) Valid.
   (f) Will never execute; should have a negative Step argument.
2. **(a)** Will execute four times with an ending value in iCounter of 14.
   (b) Will execute 10 times with an ending value in iCounter of 0.
   (c) Will execute seven times with an ending value of 6.5.
   (d) Will not execute.
   (e) Will execute three times; iCounter will have an ending value of 4.

Feedback 7.4

1. `Half a loaf is better than none`
2. `Half,        My Eye`
3. `Hawks0       Doves0`
4. `1            2          3          4          5          6`
5. `1            2          3          4          5          6`
6. `             3          5`
7. `             3                      5`

Feedback 8.1

1.
```
Select Case iTemp

        Case Is > 80
            lblComment.Caption = "It's Hot"

        Case Is > 32
            lblComment.Caption = "It's Freezing"

        Case Else
            lblComment.Caption = "It's Freezing"

End Select
```

2. 'General Declarations
   Dim mcCoffeePrice As Currency

```
    Private Sub optCoffee_Click(Index As Integer)
        'Find the price
        Select Case iIndex
            Case 0
                mcCoffeePrice = 2
            Case 1
                mcCoffeePrice = 2.25
            Case 2
                mcCoffeePrice = 1.75
            Case 3
                mcCoffeePrice = 2.5
        End Select
    End Sub
```

3. Use a Case Else:
```
    Case Else
        MsgBox "You must select an option from the Coffee Selections"
```

Feedback 8.2

1. Valid.
2. Valid.
3. Valid.
4. Invalid, beyond the range.
5. Valid.
6. Invalid, negative number.
7. Yields a decimal number, but Basic will use the integer portion.
8. Valid.

Feedback 8.3

1. ```
   Type StudentInfo
           stLastName        As  String
           stFirstName       As  String
           stStudentNumber   As  String
           cUnits            As  Currency
           cGPA              As  Currency

   End Type
   ```
2. `Dim Students(100) As StudentInfo`
3. ```
   Type Project
           stName            As  String
           stForm(10)        As  String
           stSubdirectory    As  String
   End Type
   ```
4. `Dim MyProject As Project`
5. `Dim OurProjects(100) As Project`

Feedback 8.4

```
1. Dim cTemperature(1 to 3, 1 to 5) As Currency
2. For iColumn = 1 To 5
        cTemperature(1, iColumn) = 0
   Next iColumn
3. For iColumn = 1 To 5
          cTemperature(2, iColumn) = 75
   Next iColumn
4. For iColumn = 1 To 5
          cTemperature(3, iColumn) = cTemperature(1, _
               iColumn) + cTemperature(2, iColumn)
   Next Column
5. For Each vTemp in cTemperature
        Printer.Print vTemp
   Next vTemp
```

Feedback 9.1

```
1. (a) Open "Vendor.Dat" For Output As #1
   (b) For iIndex = 0 to lstVendor.ListCount - 1
          Write #1, lstVendor.List(iIndex)
        Next iIndex
   (c) Close #1
   (d) Open "Vendor.Dat" For Input As #1
   (e) Do Until EOF(1)
          Input #1, stVendor
          lstVendor.AddItem stVendor
        Loop
2. EOF()
```

Feedback 9.2

1. Turns off error trapping.
2. Branches execution to the line labeled `WhatToDo` when an error occurs.
3. Sets the error code to 53 and triggers the error condition so that the system will handle it.
4. Continues execution with the statement that caused the error.
5. Continues execution with the statement following the one that caused the error.

Feedback 9.3

```
1. Type  Inventory
            stDescription    As  String * 30
            stPartNumber     As  String * 5
            cPrice           As  Currency
            iQuantity        As  Integer
   End  Type
2. Dim mInventoryRecord As  Inventory
3. Open  "C:\Inventory.Dat"  For  Random  As  #1  Len  =
       Len(mInventoryRecord)
4. iNumberRecords = LOF(1)  /  Len(mInventoryRecord)
5. Put #1,  iRecordNumber,  mInventoryRecord
```
6. 6, the position number of the next record.
```
7. Get #1,  iRecordNumber,  mInventoryRecord
```

Feedback 10.1

datClasses.DatabaseName	CLASSES.MDB
datClasses.RecordSource	Teachers
txtTeacher.DataSource	datClasses
txtTeacher.DataField	Name
txtTeacher.Text	Not important—will display name from table

Feedback 11.1

```
1. iRecordNumber = datControl.Recordset.AbsolutePosition + 1
   If datControl.Recordset.EOF then
       lblRecordNumber.Caption = "EOF"
   Else
       lblRecordNumber.Caption = iRecordNumber
   End If
2. On Error Resume Next
3. If Action <> vbDataActionUpdate then
       Save = False
   End If
4. If txtName.Text = "" Then
       MsgBox "Name required", vbExclamation, "Data Missing"
   End If
```

5. ```
HandleErrors:
    Select Case Err.Number
        Case 3022, 3058, 3109
            Resume Next
        Case Else
            MsgBox "Fatal error: " & Err.Description, vbCritical, _
                "Error Condition"
            mnuFileExit_Click
    End Select
```

6. A message box will apear with the error number and the error description.

# Feedback 11.2

1. Snapshots are always read-only. Tables and dynasets are usually updateable but may be set to read-only.
2. Tables and dynasets hold live data.
3. The Find methods can be used with dynasets and snapshots.
4. The Seek method can be used only for tables.
5. The Index property can be set only for tables.
6. ```
datCustomer.Recordset.FindFirst "CustomerName Like 'K*'"
```
7. ```
datCustomer.Recordset.Index = "CustomerName"
datCustomer.Recordset.Seek ">=", "K"
```

# Feedback 11.3

1. ```
stSQL = "Select Name, Phone From Customers "
datInfo.RecordSource = stSQL
datInfo.Refresh
```
2. ```
stSQL = "Select * From Cities"
datInfo.RecordSource = stSQL
datInfo.Refresh
```
3. ```
stSQL = "Select * From Customers, Cities " & _
        "Where Customers.Zip = Cities.ZipCode"
datInfo.RecordSource = stSQL
datInfo.Refresh
```
4. ```
stSQL = "Select Name, Address, City, State, ZIP " & _
        "From Customers, Cities " & _
        "Where Customers.Zip = Cities.ZipCode"
datInfo.RecordSource = stSQL
datInfo.Refresh
```
5. ```
stSQL = "Select Distinct Name, Address, City, State, ZIP " & _
        "From Customers, Cities " & _
        "Where Customers.Zip = Cities.ZipCode"
datInfo.RecordSource = stSQL
datInfo.Refresh
```
6. ```
If datInfo.RecordSet.BOF And datInfo.RecordSet.EOF Then
    MsgBox "No Records to Display"
End If
```
```

Feedback 12.1

1. The DragMode property and the DragIcon property.
2. The target.
3. The name *Source* can be used to refer to the source control (the control being dragged over the target).

Feedback 13.1

1. `Line (3360, 0) - (3360, 4230)`
2. `Const PI = 3.14159`
   `Circle (1600, 1000), 600, , -PI * 0.2, -PI * 1.8`

B

Functions for Working with Dates and Financial Calculations

Visual Basic includes a wealth of functions that you can use in your projects. The preceding chapters cover only a few of the available functions. Some of the string functions are covered in Chapter 7. Other functions that are covered include `MsgBox`, `Val`, `Ucase/Lcase`, and `Format`.

This appendix introduces some additional functions for handling dates and for performing financial calculations.

Date Functions

Visual Basic has several functions specifically for dealing with dates. The date functions can retrieve the system date, break down a date into component parts, test whether the contents of a field are compatible with the date data type, and convert other data types to a date.

Accessing the System Date

You can retrieve the system date from your computer with the `Date` function, which returns the current date, or the `Now` function which returns both the date and the time. These can be very handy in "time stamping" data or for inclusion in a report heading.

The Date and Now Functions—General Form

```
Now

Date
```

The Date and Now Functions—Examples

```
LblDate.Caption = Date          'Assign the system date to a label

Printer.Print Now
```

Date Variables

The date data type may hold values of many forms that represent a date. Examples could be May 22, 1998 or 5/22/98 or 5-22-1998. When a value is assigned to a date variable, it must be enclosed in # signs.

```
Dim dMyDate as Date
dMyDate = #3-1-97#
```

You can use the `Format$` function to format dates and times. To find the formats available search help for *Named Date/Time Formats*.

Converting Values to a Date Format

In order to store values in a date data type, you may need to convert the value of the data to a date type. You can accomplish this task with the `CDate` (convert to date) function.

The CDate Function—General Form

```
CDate(Variable or Property)
```

The CDate Function—Example

```
dMyDate = CDate(txtDate.Text)
```

When you want to compare two date fields from different sources, you can use the `CDate` function to assure that you are comparing compatible formats. This condition may occur when comparing a date from a database or file with the contents of a text box or date variable.

The DatePart Function

Another handy date function is the `DatePart` function, which can tell you if a date is a weekday, what day of the week, what month, and so on. The part of the date that you extract is determined by a part type (interval) according to the following chart:

Part Type/Interval	Part of Date
yyyy	Year
q	Quarter
m	Month
y	Day of year
d	Day
w	Weekday
ww	Week
h	Hour
n	Minute
s	Second

The DatePart Function—General Form

```
DatePart("PartType", Date)
```

The DatePart Function—Example

```
MsgBox "The Month is " & DatePart("m", dMyDate)
```

Notice in the example that the *m* for the part type is enclosed in quotes.

Finding the Difference Between Dates

You can use the `DateDiff` function to calculate with dates. The `DateDiff` function uses the same intervals as the DatePart function shown above. The `DateDiff` function uses two dates as arguments.

The DateDiff Function—General Form

```
DateDiff("Interval", Date1,Date2)
```

DateDiff Function—Example

```
MsgBox "It has been " & DateDiff("m", dMyDate, Now) & "months"
```

You could use this function to calculate the number of days prior to an event or how many days a payment is overdue.

Summary of Date Functions

Function	Purpose
CDate	Converts text data to date data type.
Date	Retrieves system date.
DateDiff	Finds the difference between two dates.
DatePart	Allows part of date to be accessed.
IsDate	Tests whether data can be converted to date data type.
Now	Retrieves system date and time.

Financial Functions

Visual Basic provides functions for many types of financial and accounting calculations, such as payment amount, depreciation, future value, and present value. When you use these functions, you eliminate the need to know and code the actual formulas yourself. Each financial function returns a value that you can assign to a variable, or to a property of a control.

Category	Purpose	Function
Depreciation	Double-declining balance.	DDB
	Straight line.	SLN
	Sum-of-the-years digits.	SYD
Payments	Payment.	Pmt
	Interest payment.	IPmt
	Principal payment.	PPmt
Return	Internal rate of return.	IRR
	Rate of return when payments and receipts are at different rates.	MIRR
Rate	Interest rate.	Rate
Future value	Future value of an annuity.	FV
Present value	Present value.	PV
	Present value when values are not constant.	NPV
Number of periods	Number of payments.	NPer

You must supply each function with the necessary values, called the *arguments.* You specify the name of the function, followed by parentheses that enclose the arguments.

The Visual Basic editor helps you type the arguments of functions. When you type the parentheses, the arguments will be specified in order. The one to be entered next is in bold. The order of the arguments is important because the function uses the values in the actual formula based on their position in the argument list. For example, the following Pmt function has three arguments: the interest rate, number of periods, and amount of loan. If you supply the values in a different order, the Pmt function will calculate with the wrong numbers.

The PMT Function

You can use the Pmt function to find the amount of each payment on a loan, if the interest rate, the number of periods, and the amount borrowed are known.

The Pmt Function—General Form

```
Pmt(interest rate per period, number of periods, amount of loan)
```

The interest rate must be specified as a decimal and adjusted to the interest rate per period. For example, if the loan is made with an annual rate of 10 percent and monthly payments, the interest rate must be converted to the monthly rate. Convert the annual rate to the monthly rate by dividing by the number of months in a year (.10/12).

The number of periods for the loan is the total number of payments. If you want to know the monthly payment for a five-year loan, you must convert the number of years to the number of months. Multiply the number of years by 12 months per year (12 * 5).

The Pmt Function—Example

```
cMonthlyRate = Val(txtRate.Text)  * 12
cMonths  = Val(txtYears.Text)/12
cAmount = Val(txtAmount.text)
lblMonthlyPayment.Caption = Pmt(cMonthlyRate,  cMonths,  cAmount)
```

Notice in the example that the fields used in the payment function are from text boxes that the user can enter, and the answer is displayed in a label. It would also be wise to use the `Format` function with these data.

The Rate Function

You can use the `Rate` function to determine the interest rate per period when the number of periods, the payment per period, and the original amount of the loan are known.

The Rate Function—General Form

```
Rate(number of periods,  payment per period,  loan  amount)
```

The Rate Function—Example

```
cMonths = Val(txtYears.Text)  * 12

cPayment = Val(txtPayment.Text)

cAmount = Val(txtAmount.Text)

msPeriodicRate = Rate(cMonths,  cPayment,  cAmount)
msAnnualRate = msPeriodicRate  * 12
```

Functions to Calculate Depreciation

If you need to calculate the depreciation of an asset in a business, Visual Basic provides three functions: the double-declining-balance method, the straight-line method, and the sum-of-the-years-digits method.

The DDB function calculates the depreciation for a specific period within the life of the asset, using the double-declining-balance method formula. Once again, you do not need to know what the formula is but only in what order to enter the arguments. Incidentally, the *salvage value* is the value of the item when it is worn out.

The DDB (Double-Declining Balance) Function— General Form

```
DDB(original cost, salvage value, life of the asset, period)
```

The DDB Function—Example

```
cCost = Val(txtCost.Text)

cSalvage = Val(txtSalvage.Text)

cYears = Val(txtYears.Text)

cPeriod = Val(txtPeriod.Text)

lblDepreciation.Caption = DDB(cCost, cSalvage, cYears, cPeriod)
```

The other financial functions work in a similar manner. You can use the *Help* menu to find the argument list, an explanation, and an example.

Numeric Functions

Visual Basic includes functions for many mathematical operations.

Function	Returns
Abs(*x*)	The absolute value of *x*. $\|x\| = x$ if $x >= 0$ $\|x\| = -x$ if $x < 0$
Atn(*x*)	The angle in radians whose tangent is *x*.
Cint(*x*)	The integer closest to *x* (rounded).
Cos(*x*)	The cosine of *x* where *x* is in radians.
Exp(*x*)	The value of e raised to the power of *x*.
Fix(*x*)	The integer portion of *x* (truncated).
Int(*x*)	The largest integer $<= x$.
Log(*x*)	The natural logarithm of *x*, where $x > 0$.
Rnd	A random number in the range 0–1 (exclusive).
Sgn(*x*)	The sign of *x*. -1 if $x < 0$ 0 if $x = 0$ 1 if $x > 0$
Sin(*x*)	The sine of *x* where *x* is in radians.
Sqr(*x*)	The square root of *x* where *x* must be $>= 0$.
Tan(*x*)	The tangent of *x* where *x* is in radians.

Functions for Working With Strings

Visual Basic provides many string functions for working with text. Although several of the functions are covered in this text, many more are available.

Function	Returns
Asc(*StringExpression*)	The number corresponding to the ASCII code for the first character of String.
Chr(*NumericCode*)	A string character that corresponds to the ASCII code in the range 0–255. Reverse of the `Asc` function.
Instr([*StartingPosition,*] *StringExpression, SubString*)	A numeric value that is the position within the string where the substring begins; returns 0 if the substring is not found.
LCase(*StringExpression*)	The string converted to lowercase.
Left(*StringExpression, NumberOfCharacters*)	The left-most characters of the string for the indicated number of characters.
Len(*StringExpression*)	A numeric count of the number of characters in the string.
Mid(*StringExpression, StartingPosition* [,*NumberOfCharacters*])	A substring taken from the string, beginning at StartingPosition for the specified length.
Right(*StringExpression, NumberOfCharacters*)	The right-most characters of the string for the indicated number of characters.
Space(*NumerOfCharacters*)	A string of blank spaces for the specified number of characters.
Str(*NumericExpression*)	The string value of the numeric expression; used to convert numeric values to strings. Reverse of the `Val` function.
String(*NumerOfCharacters, StringExpression*)	A string of the named character(s) for a length of the specified number of characters.
UCase(*StringExpression*)	The string converted to uppercase.
Val(*StringExpression*)	The numeric value of the string expression; used to convert strings to numeric values. Reverse of the `Str` function.

C

Tips and Shortcuts for Mastering the VB Environment

Set Up the Screen for Editing Convenience

As you work with the VB environment, you will find many ways to save time. Here are some tips and shortcuts that you can use to become more proficient using the environment to design, code, and run your projects.

Close Extra Windows

Arrange your screen for best advantage. While you are entering and editing code in the Code window, you don't need the toolbox, the Project Explorer window, the Properties window, or the Form Layout window. Click each window's close button; you can quickly and easily open each window again when you need it.

Display Windows Quickly

An easy way to display windows is to use the VB standard toolbar.

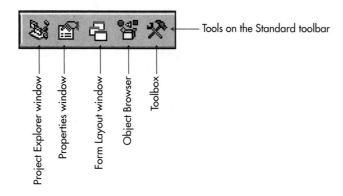

Tools on the Standard toolbar

Project Explorer window   Properties window   Form Layout window   Object Browser   Toolbox

Display Windows Using Keyboard Shortcuts

Project Explorer window	Ctrl + R
Properties window	F4

Jump between the Form Window and Code Window

Form window	Shift + F7
Code window	F7
Jump back and forth	Ctrl + Tab

Dock and Float Windows for Your Convenience

All the toolbars and windows in the VB environment can be docked or floating. Windows toolbars can always be docked or floating; you can set the VB windows to be dockable or not on the *Docking* tab of the *Options* dialog box.

Moving Toolbars

You can drag a toolbar by pointing to a gray area of the toolbar (not on a button), press the mouse button, and drag to a new location. If you drop the toolbar somewhere in the middle of the screen, it will display as an independent window; the toolbar is *floating*. A docked toolbar is attached along one of the edges of the screen. You can dock a toolbar at the top; under the menu bar (the default); or along the bottom, the left, or the right edges of the screen.

Docking the VB Windows

Docking the VB Project Explorer, Properties, and Form Layout windows can be a challenge. Each can be docked independently along any edge of the screen. The windows can also be docked together, which is the default and the way the windows appear in most figures in this text. To dock the three windows along the right edge of the screen, first dock the Project Explorer window. Then drag the Properties window to the lower edge of the Project Explorer window and drop. Sometimes you need more than one try to dock a window correctly. You can watch the window's outline change shape to indicate its floating or docking position. Then drag the Form Layout window to the bottom of the Properties window and drop it. Again, you may need more than one try to dock the window in the right location.

After you dock the three windows, you can resize them by dragging on their borders.

Display the Edit Toolbar

You can save yourself time by displaying and using the Edit toolbar while you are editing code. Choose *View/Toolbars* to select the Edit toolbar. Or you can right-click on any toolbar to pop up a list of the available toolbars and turn any toolbar on or off.

Here is the recommended screen setup to use while entering and editing code in the Code window:

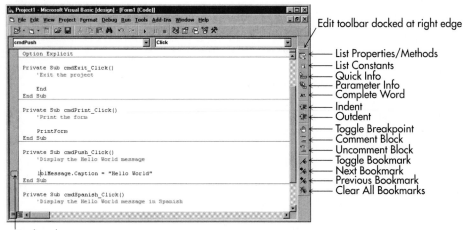

Bookmark set

Block Comment: Use this command when you want to convert some code to comments, especially while you are testing and debugging projects. You can remove some lines from execution, to test the effect, without actually removing them. Select the lines and click the Block Comment button; each line will have an apostrophe appended at the left end.

Undo Block Comment: This command undoes the Block Comment command. Select some comment lines and click the Undo Block Comment button; the apostrophes at the beginning of the lines will be deleted.

Toggle Bookmark: This button sets and clears individual bookmarks. Bookmarks are useful when you are jumping around in the Code window. Set a bookmark on any line by clicking in the line and clicking the Toggle Bookmark button; you will see a mark in the margin area to the left of the marked line. You may want to set bookmarks in several procedures where you are editing or testing code.

Next Bookmark and *Previous Bookmark:* Use these buttons to quickly jump to the previous or next bookmark in the code.

Clear All Bookmarks: You can clear individual bookmarks with the Toggle Bookmark button or clear all bookmarks using this button.

Indent and *Outdent:* You can use these buttons to indent or outdent single lines or blocks of code. The buttons work the same way as the Tab and Shift + Tab keys.

The buttons for List Properties/Methods, List Constants, Quick Info, and Parameter Info can be helpful. By default, these options are turned on, and the lists automatically appear as you are typing code. You might prefer to keep the automatic features turned off and click the buttons when you actually want the lists to appear.

Try clicking the Complete Word button as you are typing the name of an object or a variable. If you have typed enough for the editor to identify the word, it will automatically fill in the rest.

Set Up Options for Your Convenience

The VB environment is customizable, and you may find that you prefer changing some of the options. Choose *Tools/Options* to display the *Options* dialog box. *Note:* If you are working in a shared lab, check with the instructor or lab technician before changing any options.

Editor Tab: For optimum editing, you will want to make sure that *Drag-and-Drop Text Editing*, *Default to Full Module View*, and *Procedure Separator* are selected.

General Tab: In the *Form Grid Settings* frame you can set up the way you want the grid to appear as you work on forms. You can turn the grid off or on, or modify the spacing of the grid dots.

Use Shortcuts When Editing Code

While you are editing code, save yourself time by using keyboard shortcuts.

Task	Shortcut
Delete the current line (insertion point anywhere in line).	Ctrl + Y
Delete from insertion point left to beginning of word.	Ctrl + Backspace
Delete from insertion point right to end of word.	Ctrl + Delete
Complete the word.	Ctrl + Spacebar
Jump to a procedure (insertion point on procedure name). Use this shortcut while working on the general sub procedures and functions that you write. For example, when writing a call to a function, you want to check the coding in the function. Point to the procedure name in the `Call` and press Shift + F2. After you finish looking at the function, press Ctrl + Shift + F2 to return to the original position (the `Call`).	Shift + F2
Jump back to original position after a jump.	Ctrl + Shift + F2
Jump to the top of the current module.	Ctrl + Home
Jump to the bottom of the current module.	Ctrl + End
Indent a block of code.	Highlight lines and use Edit toolbar button or Tab key.
Outdent (Un-indent) a block of code.	Highlight lines and use Edit toolbar button or Shift + Tab.

Split the Edit Window

You can view more than one procedure at a time by splitting the Code window. Point to the Split bar at the top of the vertical scroll bar and drag the bar down to the desired location. To remove the split, you can either drag the split bar back to the top or double-click the split bar.

Use Drag-and-Drop Editing

You can use drag-and-drop to move or copy text to another location in the Code window, to the Code window for another project, to the Immediate window, or to the Watch window.

To move code, select the text, point to the selection, and drag it to a new location. You can copy text (rather than move it) by holding down the Ctrl key as you drag.

Use Shortcuts in the Form Window

You can save time while creating the user interface in the Form window by using shortcuts.

Create Multiple Controls of the Same Type

When you want to create several controls of the same class, you must select the toolbox tool each time you draw a new control. That is, unless you use this method: When you select the toolbox tool for the first control, hold down the Ctrl key as you click. After you create your first new control, the tool will stay selected so that you can create as many more controls of that class as you wish.

When you are finished, press Esc to deselect the tool or click on another toolbox tool.

Display the Form Editor Toolbar

You can display the Form Editor toolbar to save yourself time when working with multiple controls. Turn toolbars on and off from the *View/Toolbars* menu command or by right-clicking any toolbar.

Send to Front
Send to Back
Align Left
(Drop down a list for other alignment options)
Center Horizontal
(Drop down a list for other centering options)
Make Width Same Size
(Drop down a list for other sizing options)
Lock Controls Toggle

Nudge Controls into Place

Sometimes it is difficult to place controls exactly where you want them. Of course, you can use the alignment options on the *Format* menu or the Form Editor toolbar. You can also nudge controls in any direction by holding down the Ctrl key and pressing one of the arrow keys. *Nudging* moves a control one grid dot in the desired direction. If the grid is turned off, the control(s) moves by one pixel.

For example: Ctrl + Right Arrow moves a selected control one grid dot to the right.

Use Shortcuts to Execute a Project

You can use keyboard shortcuts to start and stop project execution.

Task	Shortcut
Run the current project (from Design time).	F5
Continue execution (from Break time).	F5
Restart execution from the beginning (from Break time).	Shift + F5
Stop execution.	Ctrl + Break
Begin execution, single-stepping through code.	F8

Use the Object Browser

The VB Object Browser can be a valuable source of information. You can use the Object Browser to examine objects, properties, methods, and events for VB objects; objects from other applications; and ActiveX controls. You can view a list of the objects, properties, procedures, and variable declarations in your project and jump to a section of your code.

Finding Lists of Constants

You can find listings of the VB constants using the Object Browser. The constants are grouped by function. Select *<All Libraries>* in the *Project/Library* box and then scroll the Classes list and click on the desired group; the constants will appear in the Members list. Or you can type something in the Search Text box and click the Search button.

This example shows the VB color constants:

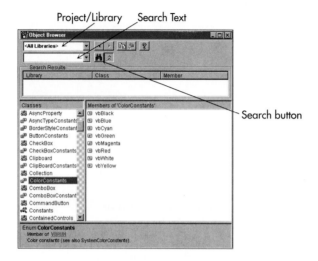

Learning About Objects

The Object Browser can show you all properties, methods, and events for an object. You can choose any of the VB objects; objects from other applications, such as Excel or Project; or an ActiveX control. Before you can display information about an object, it must be selected in the References list (*References* dialog box from the *Project* menu). *Note:* You can display the *References* dialog box directly from the Object Browser if you right-click to display the shortcut menu.

This example shows the listing for a vertical scroll bar control in the VB library.

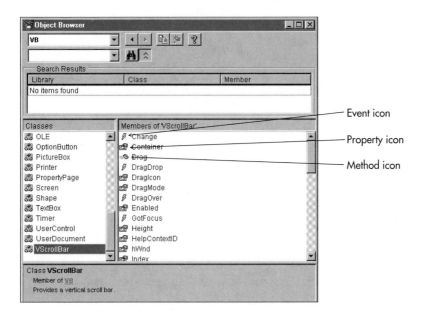

Jumping in Your Code

As soon as you develop a project with several modules, jumping to different sections of your code becomes more difficult. You can use the Object Browser for reference to recall the name you have given to any procedure, variable, or constant or to quickly jump to any position in your code.

Select your project name in the *Project/Library* box and the Classes list will show the modules in your project. The Members list displays all objects, properties, and coded procedures (the methods). To jump to any procedure listing, double-click on the desired name.

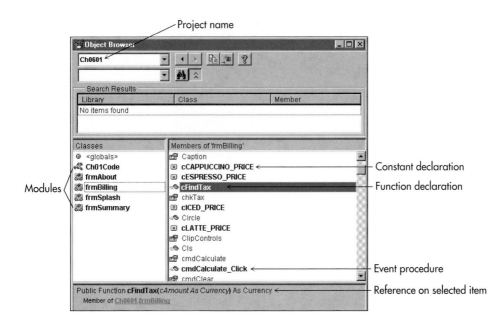

Glossary

About box   A dialog box that contains information about a program.

absolute position   Measurement from the starting point of a graphic object.

access key   Key to press to activate a control rather than using the mouse. Also called keyboard shortcut.

ActiveX   A custom control, program, or DLL that can be added to a project.

API   Application program interface; a collection of DLLs used for Windows programming.

argument   A value being passed to or from a procedure.

array   A series of items, such as a control array or a variable array.

ASCII code   The code used to represent characters on a microcomputer (American Standard Code for Information Interchange).

assignment statement   Assigns a value to a variable or property of an object.

.BAS file   File used to store standard code modules.

BOF   Beginning of file, used for the Recordset object of the data control.

Boolean   A data type that evaluates to True or False.

break time   Temporary break in execution of a program used for debugging.

breakpoint   Indicated point in project code where execution should break; used for debugging.

buffer   Temporary storage area used for reading and writing data files. On a write, data are placed in the buffer until it is filled and then written to disk.

ByRef   Declares that an argument passed to a procedure should be passed as the address of the data so that both calling and called procedures have access to the same memory location. Default type of argument used in DLLs.

ByVal   Declares that an argument passed to a procedure should be passed as a copy of the data. The calling and called procedures do not have access to each other's variables.

cell   Intersection of a row and a column; used for the grid control.

check box   A control used to indicate a value that may be True or False. In any group of check boxes, any number may be selected.

checked   Selected. A menu command preceded by a check mark or a check box containing an X.

class   A prototype or blueprint for an object indicating the properties and methods.

class module   Code used to define a new class of object.

clipping region   Graphics area that defines the area to be redrawn.

code   Programming statements in the Basic language.

Code window   The Visual Basic window in which code is displayed and written.

color constant   Predefined constants for specifying colors, such as vbRed and vbBlue.

column   A vertical section of a grid control.

combo box control   A control that is a combination of a list box and a text box.

command button   A control used to activate a procedure.

common dialog boxes   A set of Windows dialog boxes available to Visual Basic programmers for Open, Save, Fonts, Print, and Color.

compile error   A syntax error (usually spelling or punctuation) found by the compiler before execution begins; causes Visual Basic to enter break time.

compound condition   Multiple conditions combined with the use of the logical operators, And or Or.

concatenation   Joining string (text) fields. The ampersand (&) is used to concatenate text.

condition   An expression that will evaluate True or False. May be a comparison of two values (variables, properties, constants) using relational operators.

constant   A value that cannot be changed during program execution.

context-sensitive Help   Use of the F1 function key to directly access the Help topic related to the code containing the cursor.

control   An object used on a graphical interface, such as an option button, text box, command button, or label.

control array   A group of controls sharing the same name and event procedures.

coordinate system   A measurement system used for creating graphics.

Crystal Reports   A VB add-in that can be used to design and print reports for database files.

current record   The position of the pointer in a database table or data file.

custom controls   Additional controls that may be added to the toolbox for inclusion in a project. Also called *ActiveX* controls.

data element   Unit within a user-defined data type or a data record. Also called a *field*.

data file   Disk file that holds values for data records.

data tip   A small label that displays the current value of a variable, property, or expression. Available only at break time by placing the pointer over the desired value.

data type   Specifies the type of value to be stored in a variable or constant. May be used to indicate

the return type for a function. Examples of data types are integer, currency, and string.

debug window   A window that appears when a project is executed. It contains information about the status of the project and can be used to display or change program values.

debugging   Finding and eliminating computer program errors.

declaration   Nonexecutable code that sets up variables and constants, declares data types, and allocates memory. Can be used to set up arrays and specify the data type returned by a function. Example declaration statements are `Dim`, `Const`, `Static`, `Public`, and `Private`.

design time   The status of the Visual Basic environment while a project is being developed, as opposed to run time or break time.

direct reference   Accessing an element of an array by a subscript when the value of the subscript is known.

DLL   Dynamic link library; a file with an extension of .DLL, used to hold procedures.

dropdown combo box   A combo box control with a down-pointing arrow that allows the user to pull down the list. Allows efficient use of space on a form.

dropdown list   A list box with a down-pointing arrow allowing the user to pull down the list. Allows efficient use of space on a form.

dynaset   Temporary set of data taken from one or more tables in the underlying database file.

element   Single item within a table, array, list, or grid.

embed   An OLE action causing an object from a different application to be contained within a VB application. An embedded object cannot be modified from other applications.

empty string   A string with a length of zero characters.

enabled   A command button or menu command that is available to the user; indicated by a black Caption rather than a gray Caption.

EOF   End of file; a condition that evaluates True when reading sequential files or accessing a database using a Recordset object of the data control.

Err object   A special predefined Visual Basic object that stores the error number and its description when a run-time error occurs.

error trapping   Coding to control the action when an error occurs.

event   An action that may be taken by the user, such as a click, drag, key press, or scroll. Events can also be triggered by an internal action, such as repainting the form or validating a database action.

event-driven programming   Applications designed to respond to actions taken by the user.

event procedure   A procedure written to respond to an action taken by the user.

field   A group of related characters used to represent one characteristic or attribute of an entity in a data file or database.

file mode   Specification for the manner that data can be accessed from a disk file, including Input, Output, Append, Random, and Binary.

file number Buffer number used to read and write records in a data file.

file pointer Used to keep track of the current position when reading or writing a data file.

flag A variable, usually of Boolean type, used to indicate status, such as True or False, On or Off, Found or NotFound. Also called a *switch*.

focus The currently selected control, indicated by an I-beam, selected text, highlighted Caption, or a dotted border. The control with the focus is ready to receive user input.

form An object that acts as a container for the controls in a graphical interface.

form file A file with an .FRM extension; contains the code and control information for a single form.

form module The code related to a single form.

Form window The window in which the form is displayed at design time; can be displayed by pressing the Show Form button in the Project window.

format A specification for the way information will be displayed, including dollar signs, percent signs, and number of decimal positions.

format string A string of characters used to specify a custom-designed format.

frame A control used as a container to group other controls.

function A procedure that returns a value when it is called.

general declarations section The portion of a code module used to declare variables that will be available throughout that module.

global The scope of a variable, constant, or procedure that makes it available in all modules of a project.

graphical user interface (GUI) Program application containing icons, buttons, and menu bars.

grid control A control that has rows and columns and displays data in cells.

handle A small square on a selected control at design time; used to resize a control.

identifier A programmer-supplied name for a variable, constant, procedure, or control.

image A control that can contain a picture; has a stretch property to adjust the size of the contained graphic.

index A variable or a property that stores the position number of the elements in a series; used for list box controls, control arrays, variable arrays, and database records.

instant watch A debugging feature that allows you to quickly see the current value of a variable or expression.

intrinsic constants Constants supplied with a language or application such as vbBlue.

intrinsic controls Basic controls provided in the toolbox.

iteration A single pass through the body of a loop.

key field The field (or fields) on which a data file is organized; used to search for a record.

label A control that displays text as a Caption; cannot be altered by the user.

line-continuation character A space and underscore; used in program code to indicate that a Basic statement continues on the next line.

link An OLE relationship that places an object in your project but allows other applications to access and modify the object. A linked OLE object is not stored inside your project and is maintained by the creating application.

list box control A control that holds a list of values; the user cannot add new values at run time.

literal A string expression enclosed in quotation marks.

local The scope of a variable or constant that limits its visibility to the current procedure.

logic error An error in a project that does not halt execution but causes erroneous results in the output.

logical operator The operators And, Or, and Not; used to construct compound conditions and to reverse the truth of a condition.

lookup An operation that searches a table or an array to find a value when the subscript is not directly known.

loop A control structure providing for the repetition of statements.

loop index A counter variable used in a For/Next loop.

menu A list of choices; the available commands displayed in a menu bar.

message box A dialog box displaying a message to the user. The MsgBox function returns a value indicating the user's response.

method Predefined actions (procedures) provided with objects.

modal A form that requires the user to respond before transferring to any other form in the project.

modeless A form that does not prevent the user from accessing any other form before responding.

module A collection of procedures; may be a form module, a standard code module, or a class module. Each file in a project is a separate module.

navigation Stepping through the records of a database file: next record, previous record, first record, or last record.

nested A statement completely contained within another statement, such as a loop within a loop or a decision within a decision.

object An occurrence of a class type that has properties and methods. A specific instance of a control type or form.

object-oriented programming (OOP) An approach to programming that uses objects and their properties. Each type of object behaves in a certain way. Applications are built by combining objects and coding the actions to be taken when events occur. Visual Basic has many (but not all) of the characteristics of an object-oriented language.

OLE Object linking and embedding; a process used to share objects among applications.

option button A control used to indicate a value that may be True or False (selected or not selected). In any group of option buttons, only one button may be selected.

order of precedence Hierarchy of mathematical operations; the order in which operations are performed.

persistent graphics Graphics that are saved in memory and can be redisplayed.

picturebox A control used as a container; may hold graphics, pictures, text, or other controls.

pixel Picture element; a single dot on the screen; a unit of measurement for displaying graphics.

point A printer's measure used to define the size of a font; 1/72 of an inch.

posttest A loop that has its test condition after the body of the loop; the statements within the loop will always be executed at least once.

pretest A loop that has its test condition at the top; the statements inside the loop may never be executed.

print zone Preset column width used with the Printer object.

private Specifies local scope in a declaration. A procedure declared as private can be called only from another procedure in that module. A private variable is available only in the module in which it is declared.

procedure A unit of code; may be a sub procedure or a function procedure.

Professional Edition A version of Visual Basic that includes more controls than the Standard Edition and allows more robust database programming.

project file A file with a .VBP extension; used to store the information displayed in the Project window.

Project window A window that displays a list of the forms and standard code modules used for a project.

Properties window A window that shows the properties for each object in a form.

property Characteristic or attribute of an object; value may be set at design time or run time depending on the specific property.

public Specifies scope as global. A procedure declared as public can be called from other modules; a public variable is available in other modules in the project.

random file A data file that may be read or written in any order; has fixed-length records.

record A group of related fields; relates to data files and database tables.

recordset The current group of records associated with a data control; may be a table recordset, a dynaset, or a snapshot.

relational operator Comparison operators, including <, >, and =.

relative position In graphics, the position in relation to the last point drawn.

remark A Basic statement used for documentation; not interpreted by the compiler; also called a *comment*.

row A horizontal section of a grid control.

run time While a project is executing.

run-time error An error that occurs as a program executes; causes execution to break.

scope The extent of visibility of a variable or constant. The scope may be global, module level, or local.

search argument The value to be matched in a lookup operation.

separator bar A horizontal line used to separate groups of menu commands.

simple combo box A control that combines a text box and a list box, with no dropdown capability.

single step A debugging feature that executes the project code one line at a time and displays each line.

snapshot A temporary set of data from a database file that is not updateable or "live."

source The object being dragged in a drag-and-drop operation.

SQL Structured Query Language; an industry-standard database language available in Visual Basic.

standard code module A file with a .BAS extension used to declare global variables and constants; can contain procedures that will be called from multiple forms.

startup form The first form to appear when a project begins execution; a project must have a startup form.

statement A line of Visual Basic code.

static A setting for local variables that retains the value for multiple calls to the procedure.

string literal A constant enclosed in quotation marks.

sub procedure A procedure that takes actions but does not return a value.

subscript The position of an element within an array.

subscripted variable An element of an array.

switch See *flag*.

tabbed dialog A control that adds tabs that resemble folder tabs. Used to increase the usable portion of a window and to organize functions.

table A two-dimensional array.

table recordset A recordset defined using a single table in a database file.

text box A control for data entry; its value can be entered and changed by the user. Also called an *edit box*.

third-party control A custom control produced by a company other than Microsoft.

timer control A control that can be made to fire an event at a specified interval; can be used to perform actions repeatedly.

toolbar The group of buttons beneath the menu bar; used as shortcuts for menu commands.

toolbox A window that holds buttons used to create controls on a form.

twip A unit of measure for the display screen; 1/20 of a point or 1/1440 of an inch.

user-defined data type Grouping of data elements to create a new data type that can be used in declaration statements.

user interface The display and commands seen by a user; how the user interacts with an application. In Windows, the graphical display of an application containing controls and menus.

validation Verification of the values entered by the user. Validation may include checking for a range of values, checking for specific values, or verifying the data type.

variable A memory location referred to by a name. The value of a variable can change during execution of an application.

Visual Basic environment The Visual Basic elements used for program development at design time; includes the menu bar, toolbar, toolbox, Form window, Property window, Project window, and Menu editor.

Visual Basic for Applications (VBA) A version of Visual Basic that is included in many Microsoft application programs, such as Excel and PowerPoint.

watch A debugging tool that allows the programmer to view the value of a variable or expression as the project executes.

Web browser A control that has methods to navigate the Internet.

ZOrder method Changes the stacking order of graphical elements.

Index

OBJECTS/PROPERTIES

Object	Control?	Naming prefix	Align	Alignment	Appearance	AutoRedraw	AutoSize	BackColor	Bold	BorderColor	BorderStyle	BorderWidth	Caption	CellSelected	Clip	ClipControls	ColAlignment/Col/Cols	Color	Columns	Connect	ColWidth	ControlBox	CurrentX/CurrentY	DataBase/DatabaseName	DataField/DataSource	Default/Cancel	DragIcon/DragMode	DrawStyle/DrawWidth	Enabled	FillColor/FillStyle	FixedCols/FixedRows	Flags	Font
CheckBox	x	chk		x				x					x												x		x		x				x
ComboBox	x	cbo			x			x																	x		x		x				x
CommandButton	x	cmd			x			x					x													x	x		x				x
CommonDialog	x	dlg																x														x	
Data	x	dat	x		x			x					x							x				x			x		x				x
Err																																	
Font									x																								
Form		frm			x	x		x			x		x			x						x	x					x	x	x			x
Frame	x	fra			x			x			x		x			x													x				x
Grid	x	grd			x			x			x				x		x				x								x	x	x		
HScrollBar	x	hsb																									x		x				
Image	x	img			x						x														x		x		x				
Label	x	lbl		x	x		x	x			x		x												x		x		x				x
Line	x	lin								x	x	x																					
ListBox	x	lst						x											x						x		x		x				x
OLE	x	ole			x			x			x																x		x				
OptionButton	x	opt		x	x			x					x																x				x
PictureBox	x	pic	x		x	x	x	x			x					x							x		x		x	x	x	x			x
Printer																							x					x	x				x
Shape	x	shp						x		x	x	x																		x			
TextBox	x	txt		x	x			x																			x		x				x
Timer	x	tmr																											x				
VScrollBar	x	vsb																									x		x				

OBJECTS/PROPERTIES (continued)

Object	ForeColor	Height	Icon	Image	ItemData	LargeChange	Left	LinkItem	LinkMode/LinkTopic	List/ListCount/ListIndex	MaxButton/MinButton	MultiLine	Name	Number	Picture	Row/Rows	ScaleHeight/Left/Mode/Top	ScrollBars	SelCount	Selected	SelEnd(Start)Row/Col	Shape	SmallChange	SourceItem	Stretch	TabIndex	TabStop	Text	Top	Value	Visible	Width	WindowState
CheckBox	x	x					x						x		x						x					x	x		x	x	x	x	
ComboBox	x	x			x		x			x			x													x	x	x	x		x	x	
CommandButton		x					x						x		x											x	x		x	x	x	x	
CommonDialog													x																				
Data	x	x					x						x																x		x	x	
Err														x																			
Font													x																				
Form	x	x	x	x			x		x		x		x		x		x												x		x	x	x
Frame	x	x					x						x																x		x	x	
Grid	x	x					x						x			x	x				x								x		x	x	
HScrollBar		x				x	x						x										x			x	x		x	x	x	x	
Image		x					x						x		x										x				x		x	x	
Label	x	x					x	x	x				x													x			x		x	x	
Line													x																		x		
ListBox	x	x			x		x			x			x						x	x						x	x		x		x	x	
OLE		x					x						x		x									x		x	x		x		x	x	
OptionButton	x	x					x						x		x											x	x		x	x	x	x	
PictureBox	x	x		x			x	x	x				x		x		x									x			x		x	x	
Printer	x	x															x															x	
Shape		x					x						x									x							x		x	x	
TextBox	x	x					x	x	x			x	x					x			x					x	x	x	x		x	x	
Timer													x																				
VScrollBar		x				x	x						x										x			x	x		x	x	x	x	